W9-DFT-551

Duffy's War

CHICAGO PUBLIC LIBRARY
BEVERLY BRANCH
1962 W. 95th STREET
CHICAGO, IL 60643

Also by Stephen L. Harris

*Duty, Honor, Privilege: New York City's Silk Stocking
Regiment and the Breaking of the Hindenburg Line*

*Harlem's Hell Fighters: The African-American
369th Infantry in World War I*

100 Golden Olympians

Duffy's War

Fr. Francis Duffy, Wild Bill Donovan,
and the Irish Fighting 69th in World War I

STEPHEN L. HARRIS

Potomac Books, Inc.
Washington, D.C.

CHICAGO PUBLIC LIBRARY
BEVERLY BRANCH
1962 W. 95th STREET
CHICAGO, IL 60643

First paperback edition 2008.
Copyright © 2006 by Potomac Books, Inc.

Published in the United States by Potomac Books, Inc. All rights reserved. No part of this book may be reproduced in any manner whatsoever without written permission from the publisher, except in the case of brief quotations embodied in critical articles and reviews.

Library of Congress Cataloging-in-Publication Data

Harris, Stephen L.
  Duffy's war : Fr. Francis Duffy, Wild Bill Donovan, and the Irish fighting 69th in World War I / Stephen L. Harris.— 1st ed.
    p. cm.
  Includes bibliographical references and index.
  ISBN 978-1-57488-651-1 (hardcover : alk. paper)
  1. New York (State). National Guard. Infantry Regiment, 69th—History. 2. World War, 1914–1918—Campaigns—France. 3. World War, 1914–1918—Participation, Irish American. 4. Duffy, Francis Patrick, 1871–1932. 5. Donovan, William J. (William Joseph), 1883–1959. 6. World War, 1914–1918—Personal narratives, American. 7. Irish American soldiers—New York (N.Y.)—Biography. 8. Chaplains, Military—New York (N.Y.)—Biography. I. Title.
  D570.85.N4H37 2006
  940.4'12747—dc22

                                                      2006004222

ISBN 978-1-57488-652-8 (paperback : alk. paper)

Printed in the United States of America on acid-free paper that meets the American National Standards Institute Z39-48 Standard.

Typeset by Lapiz.

Potomac Books, Inc.
22841 Quicksilver Drive
Dulles, Virginia 20166

First Edition

10 9 8 7 6 5 4 3 2 1

For Andrew Lamar.
Thanks Dad for your love of history, your wonderful stories.

For Lyle Andrea, the one and only "Twinkle."
A tough year and a tougher life.

"I suppose you hear all sorts of wild rumors about the regiment, for the Irish imagination is a fertile field, and I have been told that even before we were in any kind of a scrap there were three or four rumors of dead and wounded, but you must not listen to any such tales."
—*Maj. Jim McKenna to his father*

"The people I like best here are the wild Irish."
—*Sgt. Joyce Kilmer*

Contents

CONTENTS

Illustrations

Maps

Photographs

Preface

Duffy's War completes my trilogy of New York City's National Guard regiments in World War I, a project begun more than ten years ago. I opened the trilogy with *Duty, Honor, Privilege*, the story of the old Seventh Regiment, the bluebloods from Manhattan's silk stocking district. I followed up that book with *Harlem's Hell Fighters*, about the African-American soldiers who had to fight on two fronts: at home against prejudice and in France against the German army. *Duffy's War* follows the Irish Americans of the Sixty-ninth Regiment and their chaplain, Father Francis Duffy, from the deserts of Texas in 1916 to the hills overlooking the French city of Sedan in early November 1918.

While reading the letters, diaries, and memoirs of the soldiers for *Duffy's War* I was struck by two things. The first was the romantic view of war and the almost blind patriotism of most of the doughboys, their utter faith in their country—a trait that for better or for worse is missing in today's cynical world—and in what they believed was a righteous cause to drive the Germans out of France. The second thing was the way many of them seemed to laugh in the face of danger, taunting the enemy in their letters and diaries and boasting to their families at home of their valor on the battlefield. Yet not all the soldiers were so cocksure. Many of them mourned the loss of their comrades in arms and described vividly the horror of war—the roar of artillery, chewed up ground littered with body parts and the smell of rotting flesh.

As I quote from these soldiers I have kept their original grammar and spelling, remembering that oftentimes they jotted down their thoughts while on the march or in the stillness after a battle or in the quiet of a hospital bed. Interestingly, the soldier with the oddest spelling was Maj. George Patton, who, of course, earned great fame as a general in World War II. The doughboys called their German enemies different names, often disparaging ones, from "Boche" to "Bologna Benders," from "Dutchmen" to "Heinies," and from "Huns" to "Squareheads"; I have let those epithets stand. I kept French place names the way they were written, even in official documents. Also, there are two spellings for Plattsburgh, New York—one with and one without the "h" at the end.

To get these letters I scoured every New York City newspaper from 1916 through 1919 as well as many suburban newspapers and dozens of newspapers in upstate cities and towns and undated articles pasted in tattered scrapbooks. But the bulk of the letters, and diaries and memoirs, come from the families of the soldiers themselves. One of them, Grosvenor Merle-Smith, the grandson of Capt. Van Santvoord Merle-Smith, wondered how I had tracked down so many families. How I found him is one example.

I started with a complete roster of the Sixty-ninth before it embarked for France—3,600 names and addresses. My wife, Sue, and I ran down as many obituaries of them as we possibly could. Many obituaries contained clues—a college, a surviving son. In Grosvenor's case, I learned that his family had all gone to Princeton. From Princeton I obtained his grandfather's alumni file and in it were wonderful letters. I went on-line and discovered only a handful of Merle-Smiths in the country, and surprisingly one of them, Grosvenor's brother Barton, lived near me here in Vermont. From this family, I was gained access to such a rich cache of letters, photos, scrapbooks and a family so entwined with American history that it astonishes me it has never been consulted by other historians.

A similar hunt led me to Stephen Elmer, son of Capt. Basil Elmer. When I tracked Stephen down, he asked what he could do for me. I asked if he had any letters. He replied, "You hit the gold mine." His father, who turned out to be Joyce Kilmer's commanding officer in the intelligence section, had often written two or three letters a day, now neatly bound in notebooks.

Finding the family of Sgt. Richard O'Neill, Medal of Honor recipient, took more than a year. Obviously, O'Neill is a common name, so I posted a query on the Internet. A long time later, after I'd forgotten I'd posted the query, I received an e-mail from Ireland. The e-mailer said he'd written a history of the O'Neills and had gotten a letter from a man in Michigan who said his father had won the Medal of Honor. It then took me fifteen minutes to locate William Donovan O'Neill—and his father's combat diary.

As in my first book, I want to acknowledge the help of these families whose relatives fought in the war. I think that I've treated their kin fairly and honestly.

Oliver F. Ames, cousin of Lt. Oliver Ames Jr.

Mrs. William Manice, daughter of Lt. Oliver Ames Jr.

Mrs. S. Hill, of the family of Capt. Charles Baker

Royce Barnes, nephew of Lindsey Barnes

Mary Commons Haeger and Michael Haeger, daughter and grandson of Pfc. Vivian Commons

Stephen "Buzz" Elmer, son of Capt. Basil Elmer

Karl Lindholm and his cousins, John and Jim Finn, nephews of Capt. Jim Finn

Ned Fanning, great nephew of Pvt. Philip S. Finn

Rev. Davis Given and John Kee, family of Lt. William B. Given Jr.

Jan and Joy Helmer, Star Holmer-Thornton and Gail Carstens, children of Cpl. Alf Helmer

Joseph Jones III and Jim Jones, family of Pvt. Joseph Jones

Miriam Kilmer, granddaughter of Sgt. Joyce Kilmer

Rosie Camp, family of Donnie King

Stephen P. Lawrence, grandson of Lt. Austin Lawrence

Julia L. Willemin, daughter of Maj. George Lawrence

Gerard Doyle, grandson of Pvt. Richard D. Leahy

Michael J. Fitz, grandnephew of Pvt. George Patrick McKeon

Grosvenor and Barton Merle-Smith, grandsons of Capt. Van S. Merle-Smith

Grayson Murphy III, grandson of Maj. Grayson Murphy

William Donovan O'Neill, son of Sgt. Richard W. O'Neill

Ralph and Elizabeth Whitehead, family of Pvt. Ernst Otto

Nathan Rouse, grandson of Pvt. Nathaniel Rouse

Carolyn Atkinson Hotchkiss and Richard C. Ryan, the family of Capt. Richard Ryan

Marion T. Silliman, the family of Lt. Harper Silliman

Ed Spencer, son of Lt. William Spencer

Victor Van Yorx Jr., son of Victor Van Yorx

W. T. Van Yorx Jr., son of W. T. "Ted" Van Yorx

Edie Heiss, family of Sgt. Bill Heiss (150th Machine Gun Battalion)

Sally Parsons Oriel, daughter of Lt. Livingston Parsons (167th Infantry)

William M. Semans, son of Dr. William O. Semans (166th Infantry)

I apologize to the kind folks from the 150th Machine Gun Battalion of Wisconsin, who had provided splendid material about their families. Although the letters and diaries were wonderful, they did not advance my story on the Sixty-ninth as I had hoped. I'm sorry. Someday someone must write the 150th's history. It needs to be told.

I want to thank a heap of others who helped in my research, read all or parts of the book, and went the extra mile for me.

The first is my family—my wife, Sue, our son Mark and his wife, Leigh, and their son, Connor. They had to put up with me.

My publisher at Potomac Books, Don McKeon, who not only pushed me to a higher standard, but whose comments in the margins of my manuscript made me grimace or made me laugh, and to Jennifer Silvia, a masterful copy editor.

Mitchell Yockelson at the National Archives in College Park, Maryland, gets a special thank you. Whenever I needed anything, even at a moment's notice, Mitch was right there.

Joe Hourigan, one of the most knowledgeable persons on the Sixty-ninth, did a yeoman's job and read my entire manuscript, and his comments and suggestions were ever valuable. Joe maintains the best webpage on the regiment. Also, Jim Tierney has taken over as historian of the Sixty-ninth since the death of my good friend Ken Powers. Jim read my manuscript and provided some rare photographs.

Alice Quist saved me time and money by digging through the Library of Congress and pulling out the letters of Col. Frank McCoy.

The staff at the Middlebury College Library once again came through. I'm especially grateful to Fleur Laslocky, now retired, Rachel Manning, Joanne Stewart, Richard Jenkins, and Andy Wentink, who obtained material from Middlebury's Sheldon Museum of Vermont History; to Mike Knapp, who's moved on to the Military History Institute (welcome back from Afghanistan, Mike); and to Mary Cheney at the Bixby Library, Vergennes, Vermont.

Others I must thank—and there are so many—include Phyllis Lane, an expert on Col. Michael Corcoran and the early years of the Sixty-ninth; Sister Marguerita Smith, archivist for the Archdiocese of New York; Susan H. Brosnan, archivist for the Knights of Columbus Supreme Council; and Father Daniel Gatti, president of New York's Xavier High School. I also owe thanks to Mary Ellen Ducey, at the archives and special collections University of

Nebraska-Lincoln Libraries; Nancy Merz, associate archivist, Midwest Jesuit Archives; James W. Zobel, archivist at the MacArthur Memorial in Norfolk, Virginia; Michael Finn, who provided information on the Rev. George Carpentier; Scott Kelly, assistant director of the American Irish Historical Society; Ellen Seiber, curator of collections at Mathers Museum of World Cultures at Indiana University; Beverly Nelson of the Choctaw Indian Nation; and Michael Aikey of the New York State Military Museum and Veterans Research Center.

And as always, Sheila H. Biles and C. Hather Scalf at the United States Military Academy, West Point, New York, and the folks at Princeton University's Seeley G. Mudd Manuscript Library, Cornell's Division of Rare and Manuscript Collections and Yale's Manuscripts and Archives Collections.

I'd also like to thank my neighbor John Quinn who stopped by every evening for a glass of red wine and to ask, "Well, didja amount to anything today?" Then I had to admit how many words I'd written.

On a sad note, John Howe of Albany, who helped in my last book, *Harlem's Hell Fighters,* and led the ongoing fight to get Sgt. Henry Johnson his deserved Congressional Medal of Honor, passed away in the spring of 2005. John, a war hero in his own right, will be missed.

"The War Was the Making of Me"

A lexander Woollcott, the celebrated wit of the Algonquin Round Table and columnist for the *New Yorker,* remembered the "cool, candle-lit dusk" of St. Patrick's Cathedral on that sad Wednesday, 29 June 1932. He remembered, too, how the thousands of mourners, so thick and tightly bunched, made St. Patrick's seem a tiny chapel rather than the huge cathedral that it was. On the steps outside the great church, a thousand others pressed against the entrance for a glimpse inside or unabashedly knelt in prayer. More of the crowd, estimated at 25,000, spilled down the steps and on to Fifth Avenue, where police had been forced to cordon off traffic. In the crush of people, one woman tried to stake out a small section of sidewalk when, as absurd as it sounds, a big burly police officer ordered her to move on because it had been reserved for another. She protested, claiming to be a friend of the deceased. Replied the officer, "That is true Ma'am of everyone here today."[1] From all walks of life and from every neighborhood in the city and even from the far reaches of the country and from across the Atlantic, they had come to bid good-bye to America's most famous priest, the late chaplain of the Fighting Sixty-ninth New York Regiment, Father Francis Patrick Duffy.

The chaplain had died three days earlier at five-thirty in the morning. He suffered from colitis, and for three months leading up to his death had been in and out of St. Vincent's Hospital. Described by a newspaper editor at the time of his passing as a man with a "salty personality, full of force and flavor,"[2] Duffy confided to a friend that he did not want to live as a "tottering old man." As he drifted in and out of consciousness, he sighed that he was "so near heaven . . . that the pearly gates almost opened to let me in." Moments before he lapsed into his final sleep he drew a friend close and traced a cross on his forehead.[3]

Duffy was sixty-one. He left an estate worth twenty-five hundred dollars. Perhaps the most valuable items, at least sentimentally, were a watch, chain, and pendants, given to him after the war by the old soldiers he had once comforted on the battlefield.

At first, Duffy's funeral was to have taken place in his own church, but it had been deemed too small, and St. Patrick's Cathedral had been chosen. One of the first mourners to arrive was Woollcott. The drama critic and now radio personality picked a good spot from which to watch the proceedings. A non-Catholic who, "ankle-deep in the Argonne mud" in 1918, had formed a lasting friendship with the chaplain, Woollcott looked around at the growing grief-stricken crowd. He saw former soldiers of the Sixty-ninth and other National Guard outfits, some in musty uniforms they had long outgrown; priests in somber black robes, two hundred fifty of them; one-hundred monsignors; parishioners from Duffy's own Church of the Holy Cross, who had trudged up from Times Square and the adjacent neighborhood of Hell's Kitchen; and more parishioners from his old parish in the Bronx. He noted a number of Tammany Hall politicians and Republican bigwigs. Behind his thick glasses, Woollcott studied "gnarled fingers" as they worked their rosaries. He watched lips move reverently in silent prayer. It occurred to him then that without a doubt Duffy had been *the* first citizen of Gotham. "This city is too large for most of us," Woollcott would write later when reflecting on the funeral. "But not for Father Duffy. Not too large, I mean, for him to invest it with the homeliness of a neighborhood. When he walked down the street—any street—he was like a curé striding through his own village. Everyone knew him."[4]

The chaplain had early figured out why it was that he saw New York as a small village—his village—and not an impersonal metropolis. "I cannot claim any special attribute except that of being fond of people," is how he had put it. "Just people."[5]

Among the throng closest to the open casket, Woollcott spotted the familiar face of William Donovan, the colonel known as "Wild Bill," not yet fifty years old. Seeing him, Woollcott recalled an incident that occurred soon after Donovan had been wounded during the Argonne offensive and carried off the field in a blanket. When he reached a dressing station Donovan had shaken a fist at Duffy. As Woollcott, then on the staff of *The Stars & Stripes,* remembered it, Wild Bill had said, "Ah there, Father, you thought you'd have the pleasure of burying me!" Duffy had shaken his own fist. "And I will yet."

The Columbia University football star, lawyer, and Medal of Honor holder Donovan delighted in his friendship with the priest. In France they had engaged in a friendly game of one-upmanship about which of them was the more famous. Each time one of them got his name mentioned in a newspaper he waved the article in front of the other. Eventually, Wild Bill was forced to concede that, of their two names, Duffy's appeared most often in the newspapers.

Donovan had outlived not only his chaplain but also his equally famous sergeant, Joyce Kilmer, the poet who before the war had been Woollcott's colleague at the *New York Times.*

For the Algonquin wit, the thought of these men and the sight of Donovan brought forth a flood of war stories about France and the Rhine, where priest and reporter had met many times. Woollcott recollected them all.

> [Father Duffy] would always have tall tales to tell of his Irish fighters, who, with death all around them, heard only the grace of God purring in their hearts. It delighted him that they spoke of the Ourcq as the O'Rourke, and he enjoyed their wonderment at the French presumption in dignifying so measly a creek by calling it a river. He loved the story of one wounded soldier who waved aside a proffered canteen. "Give it to the Ourcq. It needs it more than I do." And he loved all stories wherein the uppity were discomfited. On the Rhine he relished the spectacle of Pershing vainly trying to unbend a bit and play the little father to his troops. The Commander-in-Chief paused before one Irish doughboy who had three wound stripes on his arm. "Well, my lad," asked the great man in benevolent tones, "and where did you get those?" "From the supply sergeant, Sir," the hero answered, and Father Duffy grinned from ear to ear.[6]

Another member of New York's press corps, Martin Green of the *Sun,* was also at St. Patrick's that day. He described it as "filled to the suffocation point." Green had reported on the fighting on the Western Front. He had witnessed Father Duffy's courage on the battlefield. In his mind's eye he saw him once again at the battle of the Ourcq River comforting two dying brothers as "each [clung] desperately to one of Father Duffy's hands." He had first met the chaplain on St. Patrick's Day, 1918, dining with him and other war correspondents at the officers' mess while the rumble of artillery failed to drown out the "recitals of his [Duffy's] experiences with members of the Sixty-ninth."[7] Now, like Woollcott, Green had lost a dear friend. "It was a fixed belief of

Father Duffy," he reported, "that New York is the friendliest city on the face of the earth. New York proved the truth of Father Duffy's belief today by giving him a tribute which would have been memorable for a national hero; for a parish priest and an army chaplain it was an astonishing display of respect and grief."[8]

Near the altar of St. Patrick's, Duffy lay in the purple robe that he had worn so often for mass at the Church of the Holy Cross, a black biretta upon his head. On either side of his bier stood the six-man color guard from the 165th Infantry, the old Sixty-ninth.

That morning his body had been carried to the cathedral atop an artillery caisson draped in black and pulled by six brown horses from his church in Times Square, where all through the night twenty thousand people had trooped by to pay their respects. Along the entire Fifth Avenue route, storefronts were draped with American flags, and onlookers, unable to push their way onto the sidewalk, peered through windows or gazed down from rooftops. Accompanying the caisson was Duffy's horse, Captain, with empty saddle and empty boots—Duffy's own—in reversed stirrups. Leading Captain was Sgt. Michael Shea Jr., formerly of D Company, who during the war had transferred into the Sixty-ninth from the old Seventh Regiment. Behind the horse, Phil Malone, another veteran, marched alone, reverently holding his chaplain's army cap. A special guard of honor—boys and girls who earlier in the week had graduated from Duffy's parochial school, followed Malone. The priest was to have signed each student's diploma; instead, on their graduation day, he had been on his deathbed in St. Vincent's Hospital.

As the procession moved up Fifth Avenue it was led by fifty mounted police officers, followed by the Sixty-ninth Regiment band playing "Nearer My God to Thee." Then came veterans of Duffy's regiment, nearly all of whom had fought with him on the Western Front: firemen, the clergy, chaplains from all faiths, and behind the caisson, an army of dignitaries. One of them, grim-faced and erect, was Wild Bill himself, soon to be the Republican candidate for governor of New York. Among the missing were the current and former governors—Franklin Delano Roosevelt and Al Smith. Both of these politicians were in Chicago at the Democratic National Convention, where in a few days Roosevelt would be nominated the Democratic candidate for president of the United States. Amid the hoopla of the convention, Roosevelt dashed off a statement.

> In Father Duffy's death the nation has lost one of its great spiritual leaders, a real battler for a higher moral sense among

men. I saw him during the war and knew his bravery and his helpfulness. . . . He leaves behind a cherished memory in the hearts of all who knew him and a space in the ranks of the leaders of religion which will not soon be filled. I feel a sense of great loss for myself as well as for our State.[9]

He then dispatched his adjutant general, Franklin Ward, to stand in for him at the funeral. Meanwhile, back in Chicago at the same hour as the New York funeral, the Empire State's convention delegation, led by Tammany Hall Boss John Curry and Lt. Gov. Herbert Lehman, went to Holy Name Cathedral to kneel in prayer and hear a solemn requiem mass for Father Duffy.

Patrick Cardinal Hayes was also out of town. The leader of the New York Archdiocese was in Dublin, attending the worldwide Eucharistic Congress. The moment he got word of his priest's death, he wired home: "Shocked at the news of Chaplain Duffy's death. Personally I shall miss him greatly. He was a tower of strength. New York will without doubt pay him worthy tribute. The church will long mourn the loss of a most devoted son."[10]

Also missing were a number of ex-Sixty-ninth soldiers who had joined up with the Bonus Expeditionary Force. For the past month these so-called bonus marchers had been gathering in Washington, demanding from the government money they felt was rightfully theirs— a bonus of about five hundred dollars each. The day before Duffy's funeral, seventy veterans from New York City's Gashouse District ferried across the Hudson en route to their nation's capital. In all likelihood, if he had lived, Duffy would have sided with them. "While I do not take on any very definite color politically," he had once said, "still in economic questions, I stand with the class of people that by birth and association I belong and love in the directions of organized labor and social reform."[11]

Still, there were plenty of the old Sixty-ninth Regiment warriors at the funeral. Martin Green was astounded at their sight. "They never have turned out before in such numbers, and they never will again," wrote the sixty-two-year-old reporter, who had covered the city for thirty years on three different daily newspapers. In the procession from the Church of the Holy Cross to St. Patrick's they had marched two abreast. The leader was James Dooley from Duffy's old parish in the Bronx. Green stared at Dooley's face, "deeply scarred by German machine gun bullets." He noted how very pale many of the others looked.

He saw a number of them leaning on crutches or canes, and thought they had slipped out of hospitals to be at the funeral. "A few wore their old mud-stained khaki uniforms and one private wore his camouflaged iron helmet." He saw tears streaming down the cheeks of those battle-hardened men. They were not ashamed to show their grief, he wrote. "Those were the men who knew Father Duffy best. They went to confession to him on the field of battle. They went to him for comfort and advice, and they never were turned down. It is no wonder that the eyes of quite a few of them showed traces of tears."[12]

Richard O'Neill was there, although neither Green nor Woollcott had singled him out among the veterans. New York's most decorated hero of the Great War, O'Neill owed much to Duffy. The chaplain had indeed comforted him on the battlefield, heard his confessions and later, after the war, had gone against the bias of his church and married the young sergeant from Harlem to his protestant sweetheart. Duffy said to her at the altar, "You're a Christian and a good woman." And that was all the priest needed to know. He later christened their son; whom they named after the child's godfather, William Donovan.[13]

When the caisson bearing Duffy's body stopped in front of the cathedral, soldiers still on active duty with the Sixty-ninth, almost the entire regiment, lined up on the west side of Fifth Avenue in front of the construction site of Rockefeller Center with its half-completed spires rising out of the concrete like monstrous steel skeletons. Atop the scaffolding, workers stopped what they were doing—the bark of their pneumatic drills suddenly still—and solemnly took off their hats and bowed their heads. The veterans then snapped to attention as battle flags from the Civil War and Great War flapped in the morning air.

At ten fifteen, the coffin was carried up the steps and into St. Patrick's. There the Right Rev. John Dunn, auxiliary bishop of the Archdiocese of New York, received the last remains of the beloved chaplain. He and Msgr. Michael Lavelle, the cathedral's ancient rector, and a group of priests then escorted it down the aisle to a specially built stand. Bishop Dunn opened the casket and gently placed the biretta on Duffy's head. In the meantime, a delegation of high-ranking New York National Guard officers was approaching behind the escort. It was led by Brig. Gen. John Daniell and included Col. Latham Reed, who in 1917 had temporarily commanded the Sixty-ninth and who at first had not been a favorite of Duffy's. A delegation of veterans followed. In it were five former and current regimental commanders. Donovan was the most prominent among them; the others were Maj. Gen. William

Haskell, the West Pointer who in 1916 took the Irish troops to the Mexican border; Gen. John Phelan of the Ninety-third Brigade, known for the rules he devised for the sport of boxing; and Lt. Col. Alexander Anderson, who stood vigil at Duffy's bedside the day he died.

Other Sixty-ninth veterans, along with police and firefighters, were unable to find seats and during the service stood shoulder to shoulder in the cathedral's vestibule. Nearest the altar sat Hugh Duffy and Margaret Bird, the chaplain's brother and sister. Close by them, representing the Irish Free State, was Col. James Fitzmaurice. A swashbuckling soldier, Fitzmaurice had co-piloted the first plane to fly across the Atlantic Ocean from east to west. He and two crewmen performed the daredevil feat a year after Charles Lindbergh had made it going the other way, flying solo. Duffy, who always championed Irish causes, had befriended Fitzmaurice in 1928 following his transatlantic flight, and they had stayed close ever since.

Another close friend was Msgr. Michael Lavelle, for nearly fifty years the rector of St. Patrick's Cathedral. It was his task to give the eulogy. The seventy-six-year-old monsignor had known Duffy since the young priest had joined the faculty of St. Joseph's Seminary at Dunwoodie in Yonkers, where Lavelle also taught, and had worked together again at the Catholic Summer School at Cliff Haven, NY. It was Lavelle who in 1914 had urged John Cardinal Farley to recommend Duffy, then the pastor of the Church of Our Savior in the Bronx, for appointment as chaplain of the Sixty-ninth Regiment. A spellbinding orator, Monsignor Lavelle was often Cardinal Hayes's voice at official functions around the city, state, and country.

The eulogy was short. Lavelle took for his text a verse from the chapter of St. John, "I am the good shepherd: the good shepherd giveth his life for his sheep." As the monsignor's words floated out across the congregation, he felt himself choking up.

> With aching hearts and streaming eyes, we have just offered the holy sacrifice of the mass for the repose of the soul of dear Father Duffy; a priest, a scholar, a soldier; unique in our generation. His name . . . a household word, not merely on the tongue of those of our own faith, but among others, not only in New York, but throughout the nation and abroad, because of the valor and the value of his deeds.
>
> Father Duffy, though born in Canada, was an American. And every drop of his blood was Irish. It was no wonder that

the army had a lure for him that was enhancing and encom-
passing—not that he loved war, but that his soul went out to the
men who must fight. It is some consolation he can live on in our
hearts by keeping alive our love for the things he loved—his
love for the church, the nation and for human souls.[14]

Now and then, as Lavelle spoke, the near utter silence of the estimated four thousand mourners jammed inside St. Patrick's was broken
by a heart-rending sob. Even Woollcott, the acerbic critic, fought back
a tear. He thought then of Duffy's smile. "A mutinous smile, the eyes
dancing, the lips puckering as if his conscientious sobriety as a priest
were once more engaged in its long, losing fight with his inner amusement at the world—his deeply contented amusement at the world.
I thought that smile one of the pleasantest sights in America, and I find
unbearable the thought that I shall not see it again."[15]

What flashed through Martin Green's mind was not the smile, but a
pair of muddy army boots at a makeshift altar high on a hill in France on
St. Patrick's Day, only hours after he had first met the chaplain.
German shells had struck there a few weeks before, burying a platoon
of boys from E Company. Joyce Kilmer scrawled a poem about the
calamity and called it "Rouge Bouquet." The war correspondent remembered how he had accompanied Duffy and some officers at daybreak to the hallowed spot and, with the sound of big guns far to the
east for background "celebrated a hurried mass at the tomb of some of
the first New Yorkers who gave up their lives. . . . Every time [Father
Duffy] raised his hands the hem of his cassock would lift, revealing his
muddy boots." To the old reporter, that scene symbolized the chaplain
he knew best. "The warrior-priest."[16] Now he would never again see
the man who had worn those muddy boots into the front-line trenches
every day to buck up his troops.

Lavelle closed his eulogy. "Farewell then, Father Duffy, true priest,
noble American, ardent lover of the land of your fathers, self-sacrificing
colleague of the clergy of this archdiocese. Farewell until we join you in
the happy reunion that will come. . . . You were a good shepherd and you
laid down your life for your sheep."[17]

Duffy's body was taken outside and placed back on the artillery
caisson for a trip to the Bronx, to the old cemetery of St. Raymond's
Church at Castle Hill. It was believed that his burial there, not too far
from where the East River rushes into Long Island Sound, would be
temporary—that soon he would be moved to Arlington National

Cemetery; Secretary of War Patrick Hurley had already offered a plot for the priest, and several high-ranking officers within the regiment were conspiring to have his body shipped south as soon as it was convenient.

As the funeral procession moved north up Fifth Avenue, thousands of mourners, including the many veterans of the old Sixty-ninth, again fell in behind the caisson. Watching from the packed sidewalk with his mother, little Billy O'Neill, six years old, shuddered, believing that his father was marching off to war. But Richard, his father, spotted him and left the procession, scooped up the boy in his arms and took his wife's hand, and rejoined the marchers. When the caisson rolled past St. Thomas Episcopal Church at Fifty-third Street, a reporter for the *Times* noted the "unusual honor" paid by a protestant church to a Roman Catholic priest when "the carillon in its tower rang out in the slow toll of the dead, blending with the funeral music being played by the band."[18]

At the Plaza at Central Park, the coffin was transferred to a hearse. Cars waited to carry special dignitaries to St. Raymond's, about a ten-mile trip. Along the way, children at a Bronx public school and their principal stood quietly beside the road as the hearse drove by. Further on, somber firefighters stood at attention outside their station. By the time the body arrived in the Bronx, another five thousand people were there waiting. A squadron of airplanes flew low across the cemetery and over Duffy's final resting place. Green noticed that many of the new mourners were Gold Star mothers who had lost their sons on the Western Front. Police officers ushered these women to folding chairs in the shade of some tall, stately trees. In time, the coffin was lowered into the ground. Lavelle delivered the committal service. A twenty-gun salute was fired over the fresh grave, "Taps" was played—one bugle sorrowfully answered by another.

As the last note faded across the cemetery, those still at the graveside were witnessing the end of a military epoch that had made New York City's role in the Great War more glorious than any other metropolis in the country. For as long as the tall, angular priest strode through the streets of his parish, or was seen, as he once was, giving the last rites to a dying man in Times Square, he served as a reminder to Gotham's citizens of the bravery of their doughboys. And not just those of the old Sixty-ninth, but others as well: the wealthy boys from the Upper East Side's Silk Stocking District who signed on with the Seventh Regiment, the African-American youths of the Fifteenth New York, who earned the title "Harlem's Hell Fighters," and those draftees of the 308th Infantry, the heroes of the "Lost Battalion." There is no more vivid example of this than an entry in Duffy's diary in which he recounts an eerie meeting in France on a night in June 1918. The men of the Sixty-ninth were marching out of the Lorraine Sector on "our hunt for new trouble," Duffy had written in his diary, when they ran into troops from the 77th Division, the all–New York City outfit of which the 308th was a part. In the moonlight, amid the sound of treading feet, greetings and insults had been tossed back and forth. The chaplain described how one voice called for John Kelly. A chorus sang back, "Which one of them do you want?" Two brothers broke ranks, dropped their backpacks and "grabbed each other awkwardly and just punched each other and swore for lack of other words until officers ordered them into ranks and they parted perhaps not to meet again." The New Yorkers then sang old favorites as they passed by. "The last notes I heard as the tail of the dusty column swung around a bend in the road were 'Herald Square, anywhere, New York Town, take me there.' Good lads, God bless them, I hope their wish comes true."[19]

Now, fourteen years later, almost to the day, the men of his regiment and the men of his church laid their warrior priest to rest—far from Herald Square and an ocean away from the killing fields of the Western Front. It was Duffy himself who, when reminiscing about his experiences in battle, had, unknowingly perhaps, come up with his own epitaph. "The war," he had said, "was the making of me."[20]

1

"Give Me A Man's Job"

In the winter of 1916, six months before President Woodrow
Wilson called out federal and state troops for deployment along
the Mexican border to protect American citizens and corral
the outlaw Pancho Villa, Father Francis Patrick Duffy, the chaplain of the Sixty-ninth New York National Guard Regiment,
begged for a transfer. Not out of the Sixty-ninth, but from his small
parish in the Bronx, where in 1912 he had been sent into exile by
the New York Archdiocese as punishment for being too liberal.

Tall and lean, gaunt in his flowing priestly robes, forty-five-
year-old Duffy now felt that life was passing him by in his Bronx
outpost. For a scholar who before his banishment had taught for
years at the renowned St. Joseph's Seminary in Yonkers, Duffy
missed the give and take of the classroom, the philosophical dis-
cussions with students and other priests, the chance to expound his
own thoughts on God and religion. He especially missed his days
as an editor of the influential, but controversial *New York Review:
A Journal of Ancient Faith and Modern Thought*. A student of his
at St. Joseph's had once remarked that he was "something of an
Irish Socrates, not a lecturer, but a teacher who probed the mind
of each student, sometimes in a disquieting fashion."[1]

On the cold Wednesday of 12 January, with a storm rushing
toward the city, the discouraged priest sat in his rectory in the
modest Church of Our Savior, a converted store at the corner of
Washington Avenue and 184th Street. The newspapers that day
carried reports on the European war, the endless troubles in Ireland, and the slaughter in Mexico of sixteen American engineers,
their bodies left to rot along the railroad tracks near Chihuahua
City. In long hand, Duffy wrote to his Eminence, John Cardinal
Farley. Like the approaching weather, the relationship between

the Irish-born Farley, the fourth archbishop of New York, and the Canadian-born Duffy was stormy. This dated back to Duffy's days on the faculty of St. Joseph's. Farley had been wary of Duffy's circle of friends there. They were too "modern" for the cardinal. The rift between them, which led to Duffy's exile, had grown with each issue of the *New York Review*.

At first Farley had supported the popular journal, an outgrowth of the Modernism Movement within the Roman Catholic Church—an attempt to reconcile historical Christianity with modern science and philosophy. In the United States, St. Joseph's, under the presidency of the Rev. James Francis Driscoll and its rector, Edward Dyer, was at the heart of this enlightened movement. One of Driscoll's disciples was Duffy. Driscoll, Dyer, Duffy and several other like-minded priests had founded the innovative *New York Review* to circulate their controversial views.

Pope Pius X took a dim view of Modernism. In 1907 he condemned it with his encyclical, *Pascendi Dominici Gregis*. Meanwhile, believing they had the support of Cardinal Farley, Driscoll and Duffy continued to publish the *New York Review*—although their colleague Dyer had warned them that the archbishop was a "well-intentioned prelate whose ambition and lack of moral fibre would make him an uncertain ally in a crisis."[2] His characterization had proved true. In the summer of 1908 the journal ceased publication. Driscoll was relieved as president of St. Joseph's and sent to St. Ambrose Parish in Manhattan. His replacement was the Rev. John Chidwick, a seminary alumnus who had been a chaplain aboard the USS *Maine* when it blew up in Havana harbor in 1898. Duffy also was ordered away, but was spared at the last moment. For the next several years he worked on the faculty, prowling the long, wide corridors, conducting mass in the spacious chapel, still teaching—and certainly listening to Chidwick's tales of his days as a military chaplain. Called "Father John" by American sailors, Chidwick had been the last man off the *Maine*, had comforted the sick and wounded in the sweltering jungles of Puerto Rico, and had resigned from the Society of United Spanish War Veterans when he learned that some of its members were Ku Klux Klansmen.

Duffy's reprieve lasted until 1912, and then he was sent packing to the Bronx, where he founded the parish of Our Savior. Soon afterward, Farley gave this revealing answer to a Spanish prelate who, as an apostolic delegate to Canada, asked him if he thought

Duffy's Canadian roots might qualify him to recommend someone for a bishopric:

[Father Duffy] is a priest of good parts and very intelligent, but to his judgment in the matter of the choice of a bishop, I should hesitate to attach much weight to his opinion. He has shown for years a strong leaning towards the liberal tendency of the time called Modernism. . . . As he has been attached to this diocese as student and priest for more than fifteen years, I should think his knowledge and experience of the clergy of Peterborough would not be of much value.[3]

Francis Patrick Duffy was Canadian Irish—not American Irish, as some thought. His grandparents on both sides had been driven out of Ireland during the great potato famine of the 1840s. His father's family came from Carrickmacross in County Cavan. His mother's family was from County Roscommon. Once in North America, they settled in the struggling mill town of Cobourg on the north shore of Lake Ontario. There his father, Patrick, worked as a weaver in one of the mills. Mary, his mother, stayed home, trying as best she could to raise eleven children. Ella Flick, who knew the family well enough to write Duffy's biography, described Mary as "An intellectual woman, possessed of a quick active mind, good health and a very praiseworthy ambition to give her children every advantage in her power."[4] But in those hard times, five of her children did not survive to adulthood. Another died as he prepared for the priesthood. Frank, born on 2 May 1871, was frail and sickly. For him it was always touch and go. One of his instructors later described him as "not very robust of health."[5] Yet he inherited his mother's quick mind. Flick noted that he was "so clever from the start that he rather startled his mother."[6] Mary enrolled him in school at age five. Frank excelled in his studies, went on to college, and in 1893 followed his boyhood friend, Matthew Fortier, a Jesuit priest, to New York City. He taught for a year at Manhattan's College of St. Francis Xavier.

It was there that Duffy decided to become a priest. He entered St. Joseph's Seminary in Troy with the class of 1897. In his final year, St. Joseph's moved to the Dunwoodie neighborhood of Yonkers. After his ordination as a priest and then after a summer helping out at a parish in Haverstraw, New York (where one of his altar boys was Mike Donaldson, later a war hero), he went to the Catholic

University in Washington, D.C. Then in the autumn of 1898, not yet twenty-eight, Duffy got his first experience as a chaplain.

The Spanish-American War was over. The fighting in Cuba had ended, and troops were returning home. Disembarking at Montauk Point on the far end of Long Island, scores of men, including Teddy Roosevelt's Rough Riders, were ill with malaria and typhoid fever. Colonel Roosevelt remarked, "One of the distressing features of the malarial fever which had been ravaging the troops was that it was recurrent and persistent. Some of my men died after reaching home, and many were very sick."[7] Duffy had volunteered to bring some solace to those sick and dying soldiers. For more than a month he could be found among them and it was not long before the once frail child came down with typhoid fever. He was brought back to St. Joseph's and there spent many months as a hospital patient. "He used laughingly to say," Flick wrote, "that his brief experience and a bad dose of fever were all he got out of the Spanish War."[8] When he recovered, Duffy stayed at St. Joseph's. For more than a decade he was an influential faculty member. At Dunwoodie he devoted his life to scholarship—until Farley sent him away.

And so for Francis Duffy, in the last days of summer, 1912, after his years as an esteemed teacher, there was no lonesomer a place in greater New York than that corner of the Bronx picked out for him by the Catholic Church. Here Duffy knew he would be tested as never before as he began life as a parish priest. Here he had no brilliant minds to exchange ideas with, no eager students to impart knowledge to, no influential journal to edit. He had no church, no congregation—just an empty wood-frame store with a vacant lot next door and a prayer that in this working-class neighborhood there were enough souls to be saved.

It took Duffy a month to convert the store into the Church of Our Savior. There were few parishioners huddled inside when he said his first mass. Afterward, he stood on the sidewalk and spoke smilingly to passersby. At first, non-Catholics glared at this audacious priest. He later noted, that "the looks might be taken as signs of resentment." But every day he was there smiling, and after a bit, a smile was returned.[9]

The number of parishioners grew and some of the boys later joined him in the Sixty-ninth. The parish blossomed. Duffy built a church and school and opened a nursery for mothers so they could attend mass without worrying about their children. Writing about why he started the nursery, a forerunner of today's day care centers, he explained, "If one can check a hand-bag or an umbrella, why not a baby?"[10] Yet in spite of his success in the Bronx, he worried about the value of his life's work. He missed Dunwoodie. Even in his role as chaplain of the Sixty-ninth, a position given him in 1914, he had no crisis to deal with, certainly nothing as notable as the sinking of the *Maine*. The moment he saw an opening in a larger parish, he decided that enough time had elapsed that Farley might be ready to bring the prodigal priest back into the mainstream of the church. On that stormy day of 12 January, Duffy pleaded for a transfer.

In his letter he assured the holy leader that he was happy with the work that he had been sent to do and was contented "amongst my devoted people in the Bronx." But he pointed out that, although he didn't care whether his parishioners were "rich or poor, educated or the reverse, I just hoped you would give me a man's job—one big enough to tax my energies to the full."

> I am by no means unhappy or restless in my present parochial appointment. But I reason this way about it. I am at the prime of my activities. My strenuous work as organizer and builder is at a standstill. The nature of the Parish does not call for any great concentration of mind or effort. And I have an abiding horror of growing rusty. I would like to put in work in a fresh field of labor which would call out the best that is in me.[11]

A transfer was not forthcoming. And neither was the man's job Duffy so desperately wanted. Disappointed, he stayed on at the Church of Our Savior, resigned to his fate as an obscure priest in an obscure parish.

World events followed each other quickly in 1916. The fighting in Europe intensified, although without direct American participation yet. President Wilson threatened to break off diplomatic relations with Germany if American merchant ships were not guaranteed safe passage on the high seas. Roger Casement, the Irish rebel leader, was sentenced to death while Sinn Fein freedom fighters battled British soldiers in the streets of Dublin in the Easter Uprising. In the southwest, Pancho Villa's men crossed the border into New Mexico, killing seventeen Americans. A punitive expedition, led by Gen. John Pershing, was ordered and National Guard troops from nearly every state poured into the Southwest. In New York, Governor Whitman mobilized the Sixth Division and by 27 June the first units were on their way to McAllen.

Suddenly, the "man's job" that Duffy thought had passed him by was thrust upon him, and it started out with a crisis when a change in command threatened the Irish character of the Sixty-ninth, a change that Duffy himself would not rectify until the end of the Great War. Other issues would crop up once the regiment made it to the border. The worst was a newspaper article by an anonymous soldier in the Fourteenth Regiment that portrayed Duffy's men as riotous, hard drinking "insulters of women."

But first, before entraining for Texas, the Sixty-ninth's Irish colonel and lieutenant colonel had been let go because of health. Duffy had to soothe the anger of his Celtic soldiers—especially when a West Pointer and a 30-year-old protestant stockbroker replaced the officers. The command change had come as the Sixth Division, comprising almost nineteen thousand National Guard troops from across the Empire State, was in the midst of mobilization. Throughout June and July, at an upstate staging camp named for Governor Whitman, regiment after regiment clambered aboard trains and set off for the mouth of the Rio Grande. The departure of the Sixty-ninth had been held up when military surgeons, after examining every soldier, ruled that the regiment's two senior officers, Col. Louis Conley and Lt. Col. John Phelan, were unfit for duty, Conley because of a suspect heart, Phelan for being too stout. Former U.S. Army Chief of Staff, Maj. Gen. Leonard Wood, now head of the Department of the East, relieved them of command.

At first no reason had been given as to why Conley failed the test. At Camp Whitman, a reporter for the *New York Times* described how the "whole camp was thunderstruck by the news, but the men of the Sixty-ninth were more than that—they were in despair."[12] Another reporter, writing for the *Sun,* chronicled the anger felt by the regiment. "Men and officers alike raged at the situation. Some wanted to resign, others wanted to strike, and all wanted to fight."[13] Conley promised to fight his dismissal, which he believed political. He was buoyed by the fact that New York's congressional delegation and most city newspapers supported his reinstatement—all believing that politics had been involved. The angriest lawmaker was U.S. Senator Thomas O'Gorman, who already had little use for General Wood and President Wilson. He was damned if he would see the general tampering with the regiment by tossing out its Irish officers. As for Wilson, he disdained the president for his blatant pro-British stance that, unwittingly perhaps, was propelling America toward a war with Germany that many of his constituents did not want to fight. But in an effort to get Conley reinstated, O'Gorman met with the president. When the parley ended, the senator emerged confident that both officers would get their jobs back. Secretary of War Baker called for a special inquiry. The *New York Post* editorialized that the investigation meant "the President and Secretary Baker openly repudiate General Wood." The editorial chastised the administration as well. "The whole transaction is rapidly coming to smell of politics; politics juggling with military matters, politics overruling army officers, politics dictating appointments, promotions, reinstatements."[14]

Wood, a national hero who had earned the Medal of Honor as an Indian fighter and commanded Roosevelt's Rough Riders, brushed off the investigation. He trusted the judgment of his surgeons. He said he regretted the action taken against the commander of the Sixty-ninth.

> For Colonel Conley, both as an officer and man, I have the greatest respect, but the matter was one for the surgeons to decide, and my only course was to approve what they recommended. The action was not taken until every phase of it had been carefully considered by . . . the Surgeon General and by myself. . . . My duty was clear, and I had no choice but to order the rejection of Colonel Conley and Lieut. Col. Phelan.[15]

In the midst of the dispute, Conley swung aboard the train that was to take the Sixty-ninth to the border, claiming he had earned the right to lead his men to Texas. (Phelan had decided not to challenge his dismissal.) As the train ground toward the southwest, rumors spread about who would command the Sixty-ninth if Conley was let go. One of the names that emerged in the press was William Haskell, a 1901 graduate of the United States Military Academy. The thirty-seven-year-old captain was cavalry inspector-instructor for New York and Vermont, which included Manhattan's elite Squadron A. He had been adjutant of the Seventh Cavalry. He had fought in the Philippine jungles against the Moros and there had caught

the eye of Pershing, then commander of the counterinsurgency campaign; the ubiquitous General Wood, then governor of the Moro
Province; and Wood's aide-de-camp, Capt. Frank McCoy.

Conley, however, clung to the hope that he would stay in charge
of his old outfit, that Secretary Baker's investigation would vindi-
cate him. The forty-two-year-old manager of the Conley Foil Company had gained the Sixty-ninth's colonelcy in 1910. To do so, he
had had to beat several contenders. One of them was H. H. Rogers
Jr., the son of the president of the Standard Oil Company. Rogers's
candidacy had rankled the outspoken Irish nationalist, Jeremiah
O'Leary, who at the time was regimental adjutant. What angered
O'Leary, according to Capt. Mike Kelly, had been the fact that
Rogers was "rich and powerful, with no Irish blood" and had used
his "wealth and influence [to secure] the support of a large number of officers in the Regiment." Recollected Kelly, a County Clare
man, "O'Leary, anxious to preserve the Regiment's Irish traditions, and affronted at the idea of an outsider becoming its Colonel, organized with my assistance and co-operation, the young
officers in bringing about the selection of Louis D. Conley, a man
of Irish blood."[16]

O n 12 July, in spite of political pressure from the president and
Senator O'Gorman to reinstate Conley, Baker concluded that
the colonel *was* unfit for duty. He refused to make the results of his
investigation public because he did not want to embarrass Conley
or Phelan. "No question is raised as to their zeal, military capacity
or character as officers," he assured everyone, "the only consideration being their own welfare and their ability to perform active
military duties."[17]

The new commander of the Sixty-ninth turned out to be Wood's
friend from the Philippines, Captain Haskell.

Once in command, Haskell transferred outsiders into the regiment. When they arrived Duffy liked one of them right away, especially his "keenest dryest humor." He was Capt. Walter Powers,
a veteran of the Seventh Cavalry. Haskell had installed him as
adjutant. Wrote the chaplain, "He entered the Regular Army out
of high school, out of short trousers, I tell him. . . . If he had not
run away to be a soldier he would have made a successful lawyer or
journalist."[18] But another transfer bothered Duffy: Haskell's friend
from Squadron A's Troop C, Latham Reed, slotted to replace
Phelan as lieutenant colonel. A stockbroker, he was non-Irish and

non-Catholic and traced his family to Plymouth Colony. His father, a well-known attorney, had studied law at Cambridge University and upon graduation served in England as a barrister. When the father had returned to the United States, he organized Troop C and became its first captain. The thirty-two-year-old Reed used his influence to bribe several noncommissioned officers in his troop with lieutenancies if they came along with him to the Sixty-ninth to ensure that at least he had a few allies in the regiment.

Two of the young troopers were graduates of The Hill School and Princeton University and had been a part of the Plattsburgh Experiment in which promising young American men had been trained to take military leadership roles in case of war: Sgt. Charles Baker and Cpl. Van Santvoord Merle-Smith. A bachelor, Baker was the son of the president of the Bank of Manhattan. He taught Sunday school at St. James Episcopal Church on Madison Avenue. The newly married Merle-Smith, he stood a towering six-four, was of Dutch-English stock, had been a student of Woodrow Wilson while at Princeton and, like the president, was the son of a Presbyterian minister. He had accepted Reed's bribe, not because he saw it as an easy way to a commission, but because he believed he could do more good for his country if he prepared for war with the scrappy Irish regiment rather than with the bluebloods of Squadron A. Duffy agreed, recalling that "From the time [Merle-Smith] joined us he has felt that the best opening for real soldier work is in this regiment."[19]

At first, the arrival of the Squadron A men had bothered the chaplain. He feared that if Haskell ever went elsewhere then Reed could end up commanding the regiment and thus be able to place more of his non-Catholic, non-Irish cronies from Squadron A in positions of power. Duffy dispatched a letter to Cardinal Farley, worrying him that the unique religious and ethnic make up of their regiment had been threatened. "I am at present searching for a high class Irish soldier to recommend for a vacant position as major," he wrote. "If I can get the right man, we can make him the next colonel without any fuss or row."[20]

As soon as this apparent thinning within the ranks of Celtic officers became known it drew the ire of the powerful Irish newspaper, *The Advocate*. Its outspoken columnist, John Coyle, under the heading "Irishmen, Save The Sixty-ninth," found it unforgivable that following Conley's dismissal "no junior officer of Irish blood was promoted to command it, nor was an officer of Irish

blood assigned to its command." He complained about the transfer into the regiment of the young men from Squadron A. To Coyle,
a renowned lecturer on Irish topics, it was an outrage. "This historic regiment is in danger of losing its traditional, distinctive character," he argued. "For more than half a century it has been a
distinctly Irish regiment in its personnel, Irish in its spirit, Irish
in its associations, and Irish in its deathless courage, and in its
sacrifice. But a conscious effort is under way to rob it of its Irish
character."[21]

While Duffy fretted over the arrival of the new officers, the regiment, after reaching Mission, Texas, strung its tents alongside the
Fourteenth Regiment, from Brooklyn. And that meant more trouble—
trouble that would test the chaplain and his new commander.

By late summer, the Sixth Division was spread along a sandy
stretch above the Rio Grande River from Brownsville west
to McAllen, where Maj. Gen. John O'Ryan had set up his headquarters, to Pharr and then Mission. In Mission, the First New
York Infantry Brigade—the Second, Fourteenth, and Sixty-ninth
regiments—was encamped north of the tracks of the St. Louis,
Brownsville, and Mexico Railroad.

With the arrival of almost twenty thousand troops, it appeared
that O'Ryan was more wary of saloons and brothels than armed
conflict. He did not like his men drinking and, later, in 1917, when
the National Guard was refederalized, he did not allow them to
smoke while on the streets of New York if in uniform. In Texas, he
issued General Order 7, which prohibited the soldiers from "using
intoxicating liquors in any form" or to enter "houses of prostitution or places where liquor was sold." To enforce his order, he
posted military police at the front and rear entrances to every
brothel and saloon. He boasted that within three weeks "we had
driven out of our territory every house of prostitution but one and
this closed down a week or two later."[22]

If what happened next was true, then General Order 7 was not
the ringing success boasted by O'Ryan. On the night of 11 August, according to newspapers, drunken guardsmen from the Sixty-
ninth had rampaged through Mission. The Brooklyn *Daily Eagle*
reported the affair on its front page, describing it as an act of
"wildness."[23] The most damaging story had appeared in the Brooklyn *Daily Standard Union*. Written by an anonymous Fourteenth
Regiment soldier, it had enraged the Irish community and led to

a front-page assault in *The Irish World and American Industrial Liberator*, which called the article "venomous," "malignant," "anti-Catholic and anti-Irish."[24]

The unknown author gave a blow-by-blow account of the incident, describing that for two nights saloons were "filled with the men of the Sixty-ninth." Rowdiness had been kept in check by military police. On Friday night they cleared a saloon and arrested an Irish soldier. A Corporal Slocum, also of the Fourteenth, marched the prisoner to the Chamber of Commerce building, used as headquarters for the military police. Word of the arrest reached a detachment of the Sixty-ninth on guard elsewhere in town. With fixed bayonets, the detachment went after Slocum. As it followed the corporal and his prisoner down the main street of Mission, three hundred men of the Sixty-ninth joined in.

"[They] demanded that Slocum give up his prisoner," the reporter had written. "Slocum refused, whereupon the guard and mob tried to force their way into the building. Slocum threatened to shoot the first man who entered the door." The mob fell back, jeering and throwing rocks. A call to the brigade commander brought the Fourteenth on the run. Fifteen men were arrested. According to the reporter, the adjutant of the Sixty-ninth then showed up with thirty men, also with fixed bayonets. The prisoners were turned over to him, and the miscreants were taken back to camp in trucks.

"Many of the men of the Sixty-ninth were found in a helpless condition and had to be taken to camp in vehicles," the reporter had charged. "Drinking continued all day Saturday." When they could not get back into saloons "a number of Sixty-ninth men staggered into camp. These men had been in homes of Mexicans, where they could get liquor." The reporter had also written that while on a work detail a squad openly drank beer in front of its captain. He ended his tale:

> The residents of Mission are asking that the Sixty-ninth be sent away from here. Houses have been entered and women insulted. The Fourteenth and Second Infantry are also anxious that the Sixty-ninth leave camp, as they are suffering from the disorderly conduct of the Sixty-ninth men. Before the arrival of the Sixty-ninth the residents of Mission were pleased that the soldiers had been sent here, but since then they are anxious that they be sent away. They say they would rather take the chance of a raid by the

Mexicans than have the soldiers here, if the Sixty-ninth is one of the organizations to stay.[25]

The article hit the streets of Brooklyn on 14 August, two days after other newspapers throughout the city had published briefer reports. The impression was that while these guardsmen had been carousing on the border, insulting decent women and spending their measly pay on hard liquor and beer, back home their neglected families were having a hard enough time putting food on the table. What else could you expect from the Irish Sixty-ninth? No doubt they were guilty.

If what one read in the newspapers had been true then the Sixty-ninth was a gang of drunken thugs—officers as well as men. No discipline, no decorum, no honor. They had frightened the citizens of Mission, who wanted them sent away.

Duffy and Haskell knew better. A report signed by Haskell and sent to O'Ryan, read in part:

This [article] is an absolute fabrication. . . . and I request that the correspondent of the Brooklyn Standard Union be removed from this military district. He is a menace to military discipline here, inasmuch as he seeks to take away from the members of the Sixty-ninth N.Y. Inf., the self-respect and pride in their regiment which is my purpose to instill.

Haskell included a letter of rebuttal by Duffy. The colonel requested permission that it be sent to the Brooklyn newspaper and other publications so that "justice" be given to the "men of this regiment."

The chaplain called the article a "bitter assault made against the good name of our regiment."

The mob of 300 soldiers, the hissing and the pelting, the ready gun and the flashing bayonet, the ruse of the wily Adjutant (like the side sketch of our detail drinking beer at a spot where they never worked and on a day, Sunday, when nobody labored) all this moving picture stuff, which your correspondent presents as facts is the product of empty boyish bragging, and rumors growing as they ran together with a desire for sensation and, who shall say, perhaps prejudice against the Sixty-ninth Regiment or a feeling of jealousy at its prestige. . . . It seems absolutely intolerable that a body of men, who stand in arms for the defense of their country, should be subjected to the pain of reading this vile and wanton attack on their reputation, which is given forth to the public without investigation; that gentleman who sits snug and safe at home, while they sweat in the field, should present them to the world as if their regiment, officers and men, were largely made up of brawling drunkards, rioters, insulters of women—a scandal to their more proper brethren, a disgrace to their uniform, a menace to the very community which it is their right to defend. Is this reward for their services? Is this the solace for their hardships? Is this the stimulus for their patriotism? Have we traveled 2,000 miles to the outposts of the nation in order to receive this stab in the back to our good name from fellow citizens at home?[26]

O'Ryan sent Haskell's report and Duffy's letter on to Maj. Gen. Frederick Funston, commander of the federal troops on the border. Funston ordered that the anonymous author, if a soldier, be disciplined, and the chaplain's letter forwarded to the *Standard Union*. But by the time the general acted, the Fourteenth had been withdrawn from Mission and was on its way back to Brooklyn.

The incident never blew over. It festered until nearly a year later when the regiments were at it again.

For Duffy there was one more mind to put at ease. "The Catholic spirit is very strong in the New York Division and all our boys have their chests out when they speak of themselves as Catholics," he wrote Cardinal Farley. He described to his eminence one particular moving service that had been held at night. "The big fringe of soldiers around the village church and the Knights of Columbus building during mass is one of the most enjoyable sights in the world, and the only one around here that is more so to see a lot of husky soldiers standing in the moonlight outside a tent in all men's view waiting their turn for confession."

He told him how he had overheard a preacher say to his boys, "If you want an example of how you ought to worship God, go over to the Sixty-ninth. You'll see hundreds of sturdy men kneeling on the ground hearing mass."[27]

Father Francis Duffy in McAllen, Texas, where he defended his regiment from scurrilous allegations of drinking and riotous behavior. *Courtesy of Julia L. Willemin*

In the meantime, other troubles pestered the National Guards-men. Three of its own died. Pvt. Clarke Martin died of pneumonia and Pvt. Peter Murtaz of heart failure. Second Lt. Hans Stevenson Whalen, a lawyer whose regimental roots went back to the Civil War, perished of tubercular meningitis. As his body was shipped home for burial, his brother, Grover, and brother-in-law, the antiwar firebrand and former adjutant of the Sixty-ninth, Jeremiah O'Leary, used his death to squabble publicly amongst themselves about whether the United States—if it was drawn into the European war—should fight Germany or stand up against England and stay home. The family rift was emblematic of the rift within the Celtic community in general—and the Sixty-ninth in particular—about the coming war and what should be done. Were Irish Americans ready to take up arms in defense of England? It was a question that needed answering, especially as the winter of 1916–17 faded away and the Sixty-ninth, one of the few distinctly Irish regiments in the United States, rattled back home aboard a convoy of trains.

On the cold, slate gray afternoon of 6 March 1917, after eight months of trial and tribulation—the controversial change of command, thinning in the ranks of its Celtic officers, and slander-ous allegations lodged against it—the Sixty-ninth pulled into the ferry slip at West Twenty-third Street. In the dreary afternoon the famous Manhattan skyline was all but gone; there was only the closeness of the tall buildings pressing down on the citizen-soldiers, a sharp contrast from the hot, open land of the southwest. Gray slush collected in the gutters of Twenty-third Street, packed with families who had come down to the pier to search among the men trooping off the ferry for the face of a loved one. The deposed senior officers of the regiment showed up, too. Colonel Conley and Lieutenant Colonel Phelan greeted their former troops while bands played marching tunes and skittish horses stepped reluctantly down gangways. Crowding the pier were hundreds of represen-tatives of the Society of the Friendly Sons of St. Patrick, led by New York State Supreme Court Justices Victor Dowling, a former sachem of Tammany Hall, and Daniel Cohalan, a virulent antiwar adherent and member of the secret Clan na Gael whose goal was the militant overthrow of English rule. These Friendly Sons of St. Patrick slapped returning friends on the back while nearby children from the Catholic School of the Guardian Angels stood on the stone steps of their school and waved American flags. The Seventh Regiment was there, ready to escort the Sixty-ninth over to Fifth

Avenue and then up past the public library at Forty-second Street where city dignitaries, including the governor, awaited their arrival. The plan was for the Irish soldiers to march behind the men of the Twelfth Regiment, who had landed in the city a few hours earlier. A detachment of cavalry from Squadron A was to accompany the Twelfth. At the end of the parade the two regiments would split off, each marching home to its respective armory.

At four-fifteen some two thousand National Guardsmen marched off, the bands with the Sixty-ninth playing "The Rocky Road to Dublin." On the sidewalks, family and friends marched along with their regiments. At Eleventh Avenue, the Sixty-ninth broke away from the Twelfth Regiment, hiked north to Twenty-fourth Street, crossed over to Tenth Avenue and, with its band striking up its regimental tune "Garryowen," marched through the Irish neighborhoods where many of the National Guardsmen lived. From the red brick tenement buildings, windows flew open and heads craned out. There were sharp cries of joy.

"Tim, my boy, ya darlin'!" one mother yelled over the din.

A *New York Sun* reporter saw many a woman holding up young children and many a marching soldier with "gauntletted hand" briskly rub away a tear.

Up through the Irish neighborhoods they went. "And when they finally condescended to let Fifth Avenue see them they came down the long slope from Fifty-seventh Street with a lifting swing that showed they were proud of themselves. . . . They rolled down the avenue with the ease of well oiled machinery, brown and hard and alert, with a snap that caused those on the sidewalk to snatch off their hats and cheer in a way that hasn't been heard here in many a day."[28]

Joyce Kilmer, not yet a member of the regiment, wrote, "There were old women there in whose eyes was the eager light that only the thought of a son can cause to glow; there were proud old men—some of them with battered blue garrison-caps, and badges that told of service in the War Between the States—there were wives, mothers, children—all waiting, in jubilant and affectionate expectation."[29]

It was almost six o'clock when the Sixty-ninth marched past St. Patrick's Cathedral. The city was in deep shadows by then, and the street lamps cast a strange glow upon the soldiers. The cathedral's bells chimed "Home Sweet Home" and the regimental band answered with "Tara's Halls." Outside in the cold, Cardinal Farley and Bishop Patrick Hayes blessed the soldiers, while among the marching men, Duffy most certainly cracked a smile.

At that moment, the chaplain, to whom history had delivered the man's job he had so wanted, could not have been happier or prouder of his boys—knowing, too, that his Eminence, the Cardinal, was happy and proud as well.

But as night closed tight around the city and the Sixty-ninth continued its march in the gathering gloom toward its armory on Lexington Avenue, its weary soldiers wondered, with war looming, whether they would be called out and if so, who among the Irish in the regiment would balk at taking up arms in defense of a country they hated with all their hearts and souls.

2

"Shall We Fight for England?"

Two days after the Sixty-ninth had tramped up Tenth Avenue in the slush, as war with Germany bore down heavily on the United States, the *Irish World and American Industrial Liberator* asked its 35,000 readers "Shall We Fight for England?" It was a question New York's Celtic community was now asking—and arguing about. The editors of one of the most important pro-Irish newspapers in the country warned of what would happen if the United States, especially its Irish-American citizens, went to war. "The function of a vassal is to fight for the interests of his suzerain and not for his own," they wrote. "He fights that he may be retained in vassalage. So England has drawn upon her Hindoos and Gorkhas and her Irish and Scottish serfs. The more they suffer and die for their over-lord, more their chains are riveted. So it is with us."[1]

The editors found many sympathizers in the ranks of the Sixty-ninth. One of them was John Prout of F Company, the supply officer when the regiment had been in Texas. Prout was Irish born and a supporter of Sinn Fein. In the 1920s, he went back to his native country to fight in its Civil War. He became a major general in the army of the Irish Free State and was credited with founding Ireland's version of West Point. He once explained to the Friendly Sons of St. Patrick his feelings about England. "To the English," he had told them, "Ireland means a happy hunting ground for the adventurer, the confiscator, the hangman, the tax collector, penal laws and servitude." And sounding much like the editors of the *Irish World*, Prout said he did not care what others thought of the Irish and their bloody rebellion against king, the parliament, and the people of England. "One hour of freedom, accompanied by poverty and suffering, was better for the soul of

Ireland than ages of material prosperity, with subserviency to any alien government."[2]

It was this hatred Irish Americans felt for England—with roots going back through generations and embraced by Prout and others—that had brought about the creation of their own regiment.

In the early nineteenth century, before there was the Sixty-ninth, New York had been a city of explosive ethnic change. The Irish had provided much of the fuel firing that change. With famine and repression driving them out of their native country, especially in the 1840s, they spiked the population of Manhattan—raising it from just over 300,000 to more than 800,000. In the decade leading up to the American Civil War they had played the most dramatic part in turning Gotham into the country's largest metropolis. Soon one in every four New Yorkers was Irish born. Yet they were humiliated, shunned, and discriminated against by an establishment that had been losing too much ground to them too fast. The door of opportunity had been slammed in their faces. They found refuge amongst their own in the crowded wards below Fourteenth Street. They found political power there, too, in the wards. In time the Irish would govern most of the city, spreading out from the wards to the wigwam of Tammany Hall, where they grabbed control in 1872 when Honest John Kelly took over—the first of ten successive Irish bosses. In the meantime, the monarchs of the ward ruled with iron fists. They paid off city officials, bought votes, and doled out prize jobs—from fire fighting and police work to street cleaning and sanitation.

Another place of refuge for the Irish was the neighborhood militia. In Ireland they had been denied the right to bear arms or take part in any form of military training unless they did so in the British army or navy. In New York and other urban centers where they had settled, volunteer militia units soon appeared, bearing names like the "O'Connell Guards," the "Erin Guard," or the "Irish National Grenadiers." In the neighborhoods around Manhattan's Prince Street, the city's newest citizens had gathered at the headquarters of the Ancient Order of Hibernians, a local tavern known as Hibernian Hall. There they had argued politics, the fate of the old homeland, and what had to be done, and then organized companies of militia. They had elected officers and sergeants and had drilled; and many had dreamt of a day when they could, as Prout did nearly a century later, use their military skills in defense of Ireland. One of the companies, the Tenth, called itself the "Irish Rifles." Another, the First, actually traced its lineage back to the Revolutionary War. By 1851, there had been enough companies to merge into a single regiment, which was then mustered into the state militia as the Sixty-ninth New York.

Capt. Mike Kelly, who was in F Company with Prout and his friend, the fiery nationalist Jeremiah O'Leary, knew the history of the regiment thoroughly. He knew the British army as well. Although he was from County Clare, he had fought as a British soldier in the Boer War and in Burma. "Captain Kelly is a soldier first, last and all the time," Father Francis Duffy wrote of him. The chaplain saw how F Company "[stood] in awe of him and boast[ed] of him to others."[3] About the origins of the Sixty-ninth, Kelly wrote, "American sympathy for Ireland ran high, and so pronounced was it, that the Sixty-ninth was formed as a distinctly Irish Regiment for the express purpose of aiding in the liberation of Ireland. The finest types of young Irish-Americans joined it and drilled assiduously in the ardent hope that by becoming proficient in military tactics they might be better equipped to strike a blow for Ireland."[4]

Another officer, the writer Rupert Hughes whose poor hearing would keep him out of the war, agreed with Kelly. "All sorts of young Irishmen, when they left Ireland for the next best place, joined the Sixty-ninth Regiment of New York," he wrote. He added that they were "educated up to the meaning of the Sixty-ninth in the history of the nation, the achievements of its child, the Irish Brigade, in the Civil War, and other matters that have given the regiment a place all of its own."[5]

The regiment's first colonel had been Charles Roe, a lawyer. Its second commander had been James Ryan, from County Kilkenny. But if there was one man who truly symbolized the Sixty-ninth back in the mid-1800s, and whose legacy is still felt today, it was Michael Corcoran.

At the age of twenty-two, Corcoran fled Ireland for fear that if he stayed in his country he might be hanged as a traitor to the English crown. Although his father had served as an officer in the British army and he himself had been a young constable hunting down distillers of unlicensed whiskey, he had felt the anguish of his people starving in the midst of the potato famine. The famine was as deadly as any plague ever was. Bodies were strewn along country roads or left to rot in stone farmhouses or church graveyards. The stink of decaying flesh rolled across Erin like a foul fog. In the end, more than a million Irish died—one in every nine. Corcoran had witnessed how the British kept food out of the mouths of desperate men, women, and children by charging exorbitant prices for crops spared by the potato blight. Unable to pay for food—which was therefore exported to England and the continent—they had simply given up. And because there was no money for burial hundreds of thousands of the Irish dead were left out in the open, where they had crawled off to die. Rage grew in Corcoran, until he joined the Ribbon Boys, a clandestine gang, as a double agent. Then, a year later, in 1849, he sailed for America.

In New York, Corcoran landed a job at Hibernian Hall as a bookkeeper and general assistant. Inside the tavern on Prince Street, he listened to the local men argue, organize, and plot. Eager to be one of them, he enlisted in 1851 as a private in the Ninth Company of the Sixty-ninth. Almost eight years later, in 1859, he was sworn into the Fenian Brotherhood, whose goal was to liberate Ireland from England's oppressive clutches—by force of arms if necessary. Popular among the men of the militia, nearly all of them Fenians, Corcoran was elected colonel of the Sixty-ninth.

In 1860 Corcoran put the Sixty-ninth squarely on the international map with an act defiant enough to endear him to Irish patriots everywhere. In the fall of the year, Albert Edward, Prince of Wales, on a tour of Canada and the United States, had booked New York for one of his stops. When he landed in Manhattan in October he had been treated so royally it was as if America had never fought a war for independence. Newspapers reported that Broadway, from the Battery to Grace Church at 10th Street, was "one vast trough of humanity, animated, glittering, good-natured and bent on making the best of all possible greetings to the coming Prince." The *Times* reported that at the Battery "now in the occupation of peaceful immigrants, there were assembled within and without the houses at the very least, 200,000 human beings."[6]

As the princely procession worked its way up from the Battery to city hall, something was amiss. The state militia had been ordered out, to stand in review along Broadway. The city's regiments, with bayonets affixed, stood at attention. Regimental bands alternately played "God Save the Queen" and "Hail to the Chief." The Twelfth New York had been designated as honor guard to Albert Edward, who looked dashing in the scarlet regalia of a British colonel as he sat next to Mayor Fernando Wood. The wealthy soldiers of the Seventh caught the prince's attention; later he would comment on how resplendent they looked in their long gray uniforms. But Wood was fuming. The entire Sixty-ninth Regiment was nowhere to be seen. Corcoran, who earlier had declined an invitation to a ball to honor Albert Edward, stating, "I am not desirous of joining in the Festivity,"[7] had given his men the choice of snubbing the prince or joining forces with the other regiments and standing in review. In his heart he did not want them to march behind the heir to the English throne the dozen blocks to city hall as if they were loyal subjects of the royal whelp, but he had left it up to them. They had voted no, and he had ordered them away from the festivities.

After the procession, Corcoran was arrested. On 12 April, as he awaited his court-martial, Southern secessionists fired on Fort Sumter, triggering the start of the Civil War. Eleven days later, his affront to the Prince of Wales forgotten, still sick and looking thin and drawn, he led the Sixty-ninth gloriously out of New York toward Bull Run—the first of many battles for the regiment, including the battles of Antietam, Chancellorsville, Fredericksburg, Gettysburg, and the Wilderness.[8] At Bull Run, Corcoran was wounded and fell into Confederate hands. For the next thirteen months he rotted away in a Southern prison. His captors threatened to hang him but never carried out this threat. Finally released, the colonel returned to New York a hero. Promoted to brigadier general, he organized and recruited Corcoran's Irish Legion. But on 22 December 1863, a fall from his horse killed him. He was buried in New York's First Calvary Cemetery, known as the "City of the Celtic Dead."

Now, a half century later, nothing had changed. The loathing of all things British still gnawed at the Sixty-ninth like an incurable ulcer. It had become obvious that numbers of Gaelic guardsmen, like John Prout, Mike Kelly, and Martin Meaney, had no quarrel with Germany. It was England they hated. They had first-hand experience of the centuries-long political and religious repression of Ireland. If there was to be war, they wanted to stay home—let the Allies fend for themselves and, if England were defeated as a result, so be it. Perhaps then their homeland would be free. The most vociferous of the anti-British, antiwar rabble-rousers was Jeremiah O'Leary, the former regimental adjutant. Pounding Gotham's streets, from one end of the island to the other, and stumping as far west as Chicago and St. Louis, the charismatic O'Leary fomented antiwar sentiment so strident that his rhetoric bordered on sedition. The repressive administration of Woodrow Wilson—which he regarded as his number one enemy and which he saw personified in the president—was breathing hard down his Irish neck, ready to bury him in the Tombs jailhouse as soon as it amassed enough evidence against him.

O'Leary, from upstate New York, had never set foot in Ireland. His first taste of Irish nationalism had come when he joined the Harlem Gaelic Society after he had moved to Manhattan and become one of the city's most effective trial lawyers. The Society taught him about Irish history, and as a fervent member he learned the Irish language and Irish literature, music, and dancing. And its politics. To him, Irish freedom was all that mattered. "I always approached the Irish question from the American standpoint," he argued. "The Declaration of Independence is the gospel of my Americanism. The American of Irish blood or of any other racial extraction who wishes for Ireland a lesser measure of liberty than that which America enjoys is not in harmony with the spirit of real Americanism."[9]

During his Celtic education, O'Leary had married into the Whalen family, an Irish clan from the Lower East Side. His father-in-law, Michael Whalen, had fought in the Civil War as a captain in the Sixty-ninth, as had one of O'Leary's cousins, who fell in battle fighting with Meagher's Irish Brigade. O'Leary took his inspiration from both men, enlisting in the regiment as a private in 1905. Because of his judicial experience, he had been promoted to adjutant.

Kelly was proud of their friendship. "He was always popular among the men and active on their behalf," he wrote. "He never lost an opportunity at smokers and public affairs to remind the men of its traditions or to portray the Regiment as a constant reminder of what America owes to Ireland and what the American of Irish blood owes to America." Kelly recalled:

[O'Leary] narrated frequently how Thomas Francis Meagher, later commander of Meagher's famous Irish Brigade, the fighters par excellence of the Union Army during the Civil War, of which the Sixty-ninth was a part, had been tried for treason in Ireland and sentenced to death, how his sentence was subsequently commuted to imprisonment in the penal colony at Van Dieman's land, how he escaped, came to America to organize the Irish Brigade which won for the Irish in America imperishable glory upon the battlefields of the Civil War.[10]

Jeremiah O'Leary, adjutant of the Sixty-ninth in the early 1900s, fought to keep the United States out of the war because he did not want Irish Americans defending England. *From* My Political Trial and Experiences

O'Leary became more involved as a leader of Irish nationalism—firing off angry telegrams to President Wilson. He organized and ran the American Truth Society and edited its house organ, *The Bull*. His ultimate aim was to keep America out of the war. But when he exploited the death of his brother-in-law, Hans Whalen, on the Mexican border to further his cause, he opened a wound within his family and, in doing so, found out that not all the men in the Sixty-ninth were dead set against the war. Rather, they saw themselves as American patriots ready to shed their own blood to make the world safe for democracy.

Lt. Hans Stevenson Whalen, a lawyer, had enlisted in the Seventh Regiment and then transferred into the Sixty-ninth before its departure for Texas. He had died on the border of tubercular meningitis. O'Leary used the death of his wife's little brother to attack the president. Prior to the 1916 presidential election, he showed a telegram from Wilson to five thousand roaring antiwar protestors, among them many Americans of German descent. The president despised O'Leary and his ilk. "I would feel deeply mortified to have you or anybody like you vote for me," O'Leary quoted from the cable. "Since you have access to many disloyal Americans and I have not, I will ask you to convey this message to them. WOODROW WILSON."

Waving the telegram in the air, O'Leary said that it revealed the real man, an anglophile whose family had come from England. "'You and your kind,'" he repeated. "My kind were fighting that the Union might live when his kind were trying to destroy it." He added,

> Only recently Lieutenant H. Stevenson Whalen, an officer in the gallant Sixty-ninth Regiment of New York, was murdered at the border because Woodrow Wilson sent him there without providing him with proper hospital equipment or medical supplies. At the same time the equipment that he needed, that would have saved his life, was being sent in large quantities to the Allies in Europe. Lieutenant Whalen was my wife's brother, the uncle of my children, my companion, and my friend. . . . [Wilson] was only concerned with that one idea . . . which is born of every man who worships at the shrine of the British Empire, who believes that democracy is a failure, who shows the contempt for republican institutions by the way that he has controlled Congress . . . and that his hatred for the Irish people because they love liberty, because they have never ceased to demand it as a birthright not only in Ireland but in the United States, because they have been sympathetic with their fellow citizens of German blood who have been abused by the newspapers and have been tortured by the cruel neutrality that has been maintained by this Administration because they have revolted in Ireland against conscription.[11]

O'Leary's speech had upset his other brother-in-law Grover Whalen. With strong and historic ties to the regiment as well, Grover was a trusted sachem of Tammany Hall. His cousin was New York State Supreme Court Justice Daniel Cohalan, the leader of the Friends of Irish Freedom and the Clan na Gael and a columnist for the *Gaelic American,* the newspaper of John Devoy, the legendary exiled Irish freedom fighter. Cohalan wrote editorials every bit as strident as O'Leary's orations. The *Gaelic American* gave O'Leary's speech attacking the president front-page treatment, describing Wilson's reply a sign of his "uncontrollable anger" as well as the "worst mistake of his career." The author, either Devoy or Cohalan, added, "Every intelligent man who reads his [Wilson's] telegram to Jeremiah O'Leary can see for himself that it is an expression of hatred for the Irish and a contention that every citizen who refuses to take the English side in the European war is disloyal to the United States."[12]

It would seem then that Whalen and O'Leary, with their common bond as in-laws and a rebellious cousin in their midst, would be in agreement when it came to the war and the Irish American role in it. They were not. Grover was more cautious, and the more O'Leary used his brother's death to push the antiwar cause the angrier Grover had become.

"Everyone who knows us is aware that our political views are diametrically opposed," he finally said, and underscored the fact that he had never been a member of any Irish organization or society in which O'Leary was a member. "It is true that Mr. O'Leary married my sister and I resent and I believe all decent people will resent the attempt to create a political situation out of a family relationship."[13]

Meanwhile, O'Leary stepped up his assault on Wilson. He cabled him again on the eve of the presidential election, responding to the president's telegram in which he, Wilson, called O'Leary and his "kind" disloyal Americans. First, to prove his loyalty to America, he informed the president that three of his uncles, Union soldiers, had been killed in the Civil War. He scolded Wilson for using, for the first time, the hyphenated description Irish-American. "It has remained for you to break new ground as a President and to seek to divide your countrymen into racial and religious groups. The word 'hyphenate' was never heard in American public life until you coined it to insult your hosts, real Americans of Irish blood." He

scolded him, too, for his foreign policies—his misguided adventure
in Mexico and his "truckling" to England.

> I stand, as men of my blood have always stood, in favor of
> America as against every foreign power. Do you? More par-
> ticularly, I stand against the present aggressions of that power
> from which we wrung our freedom in the Revolution and
> which has ever since, by force and guile, attempted to take
> it from us. . . . I warn you that you are being weighed in the
> balance and that adherence to your policies will carry you
> down to deserved defeat on Election Day.[14]

But when Wilson was reelected, the disenchanted O'Leary was
dangerously close to being arrested for treason. That arrest would
not be ordered until the last days of winter, 1918, after hundreds
of other antiwar agitators, including Emma Goldman, had been
rounded up. By the time government agents got around to chasing O'Leary, the Sixty-ninth's former adjutant had hightailed it
west and was hiding out on a chicken ranch.

As Irish leaders such as O'Leary and his cousin-in-law Justice
Cohalan railed against the English and a war in which it tried
to drag in the United States—a brilliant "bunco" job—a scam
concocted by British propagandists, according to one newspaper,
Irish-American patriotism was in question. War was right around
the corner: would the Celts fight?

A typical Irish soldier at the time who raised concerns within
the Sixty-ninth was nineteen-year-old Patrick McDonough, a corporal in D Company. His American patriotism was not in question, and certainly not his fighting spirit. But how would he, and
others like him, take to fighting alongside British soldiers?

McDonough had been two years old when his family arrived in
lower Manhattan from Johannesburg, South Africa, with Maj. John
McBride, who had fought in the Boer War as a leader of an Irish
brigade that had been raised specifically to battle the English on the
side of the rebellious South Africans. McDonough's father, born in
County Kerry, had helped organize that Irish brigade, which then
harassed the Brits with deadly hit and run operations. After McBride
had returned to Ireland and been executed for his role in the Easter
Rebellion, Patrick asked his father, a member of Clan na Gael, if he
could enlist in the Sixty-ninth. Reported the *Irish World,* "The

father, with memories of the South African battlefields surging within him, cheerfully gave consent, and Mrs. McDonough, with tears in her eyes and also with memories of South Africa, declared that she was proud to have a son manly enough to fight for his country."[15]

But that was against Mexico and not Germany. Now, in 1917, would soldiers like McDonough stay with the regiment?

On St. Patrick's Day, eleven days after the Sixty-ninth had arrived home from Texas, Daniel Cohalan's fellow justice on the State Supreme Court, Victor Dowling, answered that question. Although Dowling ignored or perhaps had not known of the St. Patrick's Brigade that in the Mexican War had deserted from the United States Army to fight on the side of the enemy, he told the Friendly Sons of St. Patrick, "Ireland has never bred a traitor to America, and there is no divided allegiance among us. However we may differ on questions of Irish policies, there is no division among us when America is concerned. The Irish lad who landed here within a year is ready to lay down his life for the flag of this Republic as the man whose Irish ancestors came here in Revolutionary or famine days. We have but one flag and one country, and we love and will defend both while life endures."[16] Almost three weeks later, President Wilson went before Congress and asked for a declaration of war against Germany. He argued, "The world must be made safe for democracy." On 4 April, Good Friday, Congress voted overwhelmingly for war.

Father Duffy knew the Sixty-ninth was ready, although its troop strength was well under one thousand—a far cry from the 2,002 officers and men now required by the War Department for a fully equipped and armed infantry regiment. The War Department would soon raise that figure to thirty-six hundred. Yet the chaplain, knowing full well the controversy of fighting on the side of England, had confidence in his Irish lads. Perhaps thinking back to the days of the Civil War and the ghosts of Corcoran and Meagher and the Irish Brigade, he wrote in his diary, "An Irish regiment has its troubles in time of peace, but when the call to arms was sounding we knew that if they let us we could easily offer them an Irish Brigade for the service."[17]

Still, other questions had to be answered. Would enough of Gotham's Irish Americans be willing to step forward to fill the ranks of the Fighting Sixty-ninth and then march off to war? Or, for want of men, would the regiment be forced to stay home?

3

"Rainbow—There's the Name for the Division"

I n the spring and summer of 1917, the United States was not prepared for a world war. It had a standing army of fewer than six thousand officers and not more than one hundred and twenty thousand men. The National Guard had almost as many troops—a total of 101,174 citizen-soldiers under state control. Of that number, 66,594 had seen service on the Mexican border. New York had shipped the most men to the southwest, the only state to provide a whole division. Maj. Gen. John O'Ryan estimated the size of the division at nineteen thousand officers and men—more than a quarter of the National Guard troops that had been encamped along the banks of the Rio Grande. Only one other state at the time, Pennsylvania, had the manpower to field a complete division. When war had been declared, nearly every National Guard regiment was woefully undermanned. Getting these state militias ready to sail for France and the blood-soaked Western Front would take months, a year at least—maybe longer.

The United States government knew that the Allies wanted troops sent quickly to shore up weakened lines of defense, even if they were untrained and underequipped. Bodies were what they wanted. France was so tired of the killing that its own soldiers were in a state of mutiny. Former President Teddy Roosevelt offered to raise a volunteer division, akin to his old Rough Riders, and get it overseas in short order. Thousands of men from every walk of life wanted to be part of Colonel Roosevelt's division. While Congress debated his tempting offer, which his bitter rival, President Wilson, summarily turned down, Gen. John Pershing took command of the American army. One of his first tasks was to scrape together a fighting outfit all his own—starting with the First Division. Units of the First were in

Paris before the Fourth of July. The first four divisions of what were known as the American Expeditionary Forces were soldiers from the regular army. In those days, the size of a United States division had been increased to about thirty thousand men. After unfit veterans had been culled from the rolls and able-bodied recruits added, those four divisions were all the federal troops Pershing had at the ready. He looked warily to the National Guard to supply him men while he built up his own armies. In too many instances, however, the Guard was in deplorable shape—so much so that only a few division commanders made it through the war without being replaced.

Because the Empire state could immediately offer a full division officered by many of the country's influential businessmen and because it had earned a reputation for discipline while serving on the border, the War Department believed that the New Yorkers were ideally suited to be the first of the guard to head for the war zone. The only other state with troops in consideration was Pennsylvania, although New England could have combined troops from its six states and offered a division of its own.

Yet the fact that there were no other states with division-sized guard outfits posed a potential public-relations problem for the War Department.

"If we sent the New York National Guard Division first, we might have encountered two kinds of comment," Secretary of War Newton Baker recalled when explaining how the federal government handled the National Guard. "First, from the people of New York who might have said why send our boys first; or, we might have had comment from other states charging that we were preferring New York and giving it first chance."

Pondering this dilemma, Baker sought counsel from one of his military aides. A brash, headstrong young major from West Point, Douglas MacArthur had been with Baker only a short time and served as his press censor. He suggested a multistate division, made up of surplus units within the National Guard. Baker liked the idea and called for Brig. Gen. William Mann, then the foremost expert on the nation's militia. Mann mulled over the idea and told Baker and MacArthur there were enough Guard units around the country to piece a division together. Twenty-six states and the District of Columbia could be represented, he said.

Baker recollected what MacArthur said about the makeup of the proposed division, "Fine, [it] will stretch over the whole country like a rainbow."

In MacArthur's version he said, "In the make up and promise of the future of this division it resembles a rainbow." Then a correspondent piped up, "Rainbow—there's the name for the division—I shall call it the Rainbow in my dispatch."[1]

Later, two soldiers in the Fighting Sixty-ninth quipped about the nickname.

"Rainbow, my eye!" cracked 1st Sgt. Billy Heaton of C Company. "Tis a fancy noime for sogers. Rainbow Division, eh? Full of colors with the green predominatin."

"But with no yellow back or front, Sarge!" added Cpl. Frank Curtis, lately of Princeton University.[2]

In New York nobody had been aware of any of this. Instead, everyone had it on good authority that O'Ryan's Sixth New York had been handpicked to be the first National Guard division for duty in France. And within months, too. It was only days now before orders would come down from the War Department.

At the Sixty-ninth's armory on Lexington Avenue, as in other armories all over the city, a recruiting race was off and running. Each regiment wanted to be the first to reach the wartime strength of 2,002 officers and men, later expanded to thirty-six-hundred soldiers. Seventeen-year-old Martin Hogan, who lived at 415 East Fifty-second Street, was dazzled by the rush to recruit soldiers, the splash of colorful posters. "Men from the National Guard regiments spoke on street corners, from automobiles and motor trucks all over the city. . . . The call for men was sounded in theaters, in motion picture houses and even restaurants," he wrote. "It was impossible to escape hourly reminder of the urgency of Uncle Sam's demand."[3]

Like all regiments, the Sixty-ninth, its strength below one thousand men, nailed up posters everywhere.

ENLIST TO-DAY
IN
THE 69TH INFANTRY
JOIN THE FAMOUS IRISH REGIMENT
THAT FOUGHT IN ALL THE GREAT
BATTLES OF THE CIVIL WAR
FROM BULL RUN TO APPOMATOX
GO TO THE FRONT
WITH YOUR FRIENDS
DON'T BE DRAFTED INTO SOME REGIMENT

WHERE YOU DON'T KNOW ANYONE
MEN WANTED FROM 18 TO 40
APPLY AT THE ARMORY
LEXINGTON AVENUE AND 25TH STREET

John Cardinal Farley called upon every Catholic of war age in his diocese to enlist or at least register for the draft. He warned Catholics that the "quality of our patriotism will be tested."[4] The Catholic Laymen's League conducted recruiting drives in parishes on the East Side, from Fifty-sixth Street south to Fourteenth Street. Its aim: "To maintain the present Irish-American character of the [Sixty-ninth] regiment."[5]

During a sermon at St. Patrick's Cathedral, a cassock draped over his uniform, Father Francis Duffy issued a call to "race and blood."

> The Sixty-ninth has never hesitated to do its duty when the call came and it is ready now as ever. Not alone, the members of the Sixty-ninth, but the members of the Irish race all over this state and in other states have been loyal and patriotic Americans whenever the call to service of this, their adopted country, came. And we all cherish the hope that Ireland, one of the small nations, will be represented at the peace council after the war by America. We trust America will see to it that the rights of Ireland and of all other small nations are safeguarded.[6]

Duffy rightly sensed that the Irish would not let America down in time of war, and would heed his call. Recruits poured in from city neighborhoods like the Gashouse and Hell's Kitchen and from across the East River in Brooklyn, Queens, Long Island City, Coney Island, and the Far Rockaways. They came from the Bronx and from Duffy's own parish. They left Staten Island in droves. Dozens of orphans from the Mission of the Immaculate Virgin at Mount Loretto, led by Herbert McKenna, showed up, ready to fight. Another orphan was Hogan whose parents had been dead for some time. A footloose teenager, he confided that there were "no responsibilities to hold me back." At a theater one night he listened to a recruiter, who had marched out on the stage and spoke convincingly to the audience. He asked for volunteers. Hogan leaped up on the stage and joined the Irish regiment.

"Many and odd motives brought us together in those first days of the war, when America was calling for volunteers," he wrote. "Some joined to escape drudging work at home, others because their friends had joined, but most of us volunteered unknowing why."[7]

Jimmy Minogue from Brooklyn knew why. "The Sixty-ninth, you see, was quite a thing to the Irish kids, narrow backs and greenhorns alike. We'd hear about their record in the Civil War and Francis Meagher and Michael Corcoran. So I guess it was natural that when war came, I would want to go over with them."[8] An Arizonan, Harry Horgan, who had been with the Sixty-ninth in Texas but left to punch cattle, dropped by the armory and rejoined, surprising even Duffy. Horgan had previous military experience, having served with the British army in Egypt before he had enlisted in the Irish outfit as it headed for the border. William Lee Bailey, who came from the Morris Heights section of the city, had been a blockade-runner during the Spanish-American War and then a guerrilla fighter in the jungles of Central America. Another enlistee was Martin Carroll, an undertaker. He went in as a cook. Edward Riley lived at the Waldorf-Astoria where he toiled as a chef. His special pastries and flapjacks soon endeared him to the men of A Company. In B Company, the men there may not have had a great chef, but boasted instead Thomas O'Kelly, a famous opera singer from Dublin with a deep baritone voice.

Joyce Kilmer, who did not join the regiment until later in the year, recalled the type of men the Sixty-ninth desired. "Men who would, in every purpose and way—physically, mentally and morally—keep up its ancient and honorable standards. . . . strong, intelligent, decent-living men, whose sturdy Americanism was strengthened and vivified by their Celtic blood, men who would be worthy successors of those unforgotten patriots who at Bloody Ford and on Marye's Heights earned the title of 'The Fighting Irish'."[9]

The Hearn twins from County Mayo, Arthur Patrick and Patrick Arthur, who found themselves privates in B Company, were exactly the type of soldiers Kilmer had in mind. "After we've beaten the Germans," Patrick told his father, who had moved his family to Brooklyn from the Emerald Isle six years earlier, "we are going to visit the old home in Ireland and tell the folks there how happy we are in America."[10]

When antiwar agitator and former regimental adjutant, Jeremiah O'Leary, saw the type of recruits who were filling up the

Sixty-ninth's armory now that war had been declared, he softened his stance. Although he still resisted sending troops to Europe, he trumpeted in his diary, "I have always been with the boys. I want them to win. If the American soldier gets there he will beat Germany and win the war in a short time."[11]

Every night the armory was packed with men taking physicals. Duffy noted in his own diary, "Our 2,000 men were a picked lot. They came mainly from Irish County Societies and from Catholic Athletic Clubs. A number of these latter Irish bore distinctly German, French, Italian or Polish names. They were Irish by adoption, Irish by association or Irish by conviction. The 69th never attempted to set up any religious test. It was an institution offered to the Nation by a people grateful for liberty, and it always welcomed and made part of it any American citizen who desired to serve in it."[12]

They carried names like Donohue, Donovan, and Doyle. There were almost forty Kellys and nearly as many Sullivans as Smiths. Four Murphys were crowded into one company—twenty-two in the entire regiment. You could fill up a company with just O'Briens, O'Connors, O'Connells, O'Neills, and O'Reillys. There were McCarthys and a multitude of Murrays. Duffy had been right about the Irish by adoption, association and conviction. Sprinkled throughout the roster, especially after the arrival of transfers from the city's other regiments, were such names as Blaustein from Brooklyn, Bernstein, Bruno, and Winestock, and Second Lt. Miguel DeAguero. There was an Ernst, a Munz and a Goldmunz. Also there was a Zarella, a Copozoli, and a Guggenheim, and two Van Yorxes from Mount Vernon. And then there was Cpl. Louis Doan, from Brooklyn. Doan was not his real name. It was Domb. Because he was Jewish, he had figured the Irish regiment would not want him, so he had changed his name and enlisted without a hitch.

As the regiment swelled with new recruits, pockets of resistance cropped up here and there. Not only did the pro-Irish *Advocate* call for all American troops to be kept home, but as the ranks of the Sixty-ninth filled up with new men, the newspaper's foremost columnist, Dr. John Coyle, had seen something very disturbing. The regiment's Celtic character was changing and, unlike Duffy, who had no problem opening up the ranks—except perhaps officers' ranks— to all, Coyle took a dim view of this metamorphosis. He had already lamented the loss of Col. Louis Conley in an earlier column. Now on 28 April, he called upon Gov. Charles

Whitman and General O'Ryan to "Keep the Sixty-ninth Irish!" He argued,

> Everybody knows the Sixty-ninth is an Irish regiment. It has been, as well, an overwhelmingly Catholic regiment. But Catholic or non-Catholic it has been Irish in blood. . . . But, of late, there have been signs and evidences that men desiring commands but not of Irish blood have sought or have been selected to take commands in the Sixty-ninth Regiment. . . . When, as has been recently the case, a considerable percentage of officers are not Irish blooded, it cannot be laid at the door of chance. . . . It is to assure the continuance of the Sixty-ninth Regiment as a distinctively Irish-blooded regiment to be officered by Irish-blooded men that the Irish societies of New York are requested to take formal and effective action. Not one but all should make the welfare of the Sixty-ninth Regiment a matter of earnest consideration and prompt action. Every Irish-blooded man or woman is proud of the Sixty-ninth Regiment. . . . Its Irishism must be kept as an integral part of the regiment's character.[13]

The character of the Sixty-ninth was indeed changing. Three days after the regiment returned from Texas, a disappointed Col. William Haskell had been mustered out as commander and assigned to his old duties as inspector-instructor of the cavalry. Lieutenant Col. Latham Reed, the transfer from Squadron A, then took over as acting commander. No one knew if Reed would get the post permanently. A number of officers in the regiment were not happy with him, and he sensed their dislike. After the war, in a letter to Kate Merle-Smith, the wife of one of his best friends, he railed against Duffy and three majors—Alexander Anderson, Tom Reilley, and Mike Kelly, the crony of rabble-rouser O'Leary. "The little inside gang," he called them. "No one will ever know what I went through with that crowd and the powerful people behind them." He told Kate that he "knew most of the tricks of that crowd" and almost had them when they got him bounced out of the Sixty-ninth for a desk job with the War Department in Washington.[14]

Meanwhile, Duffy had gone on record in a letter to John Cardinal Farley saying that he did not want the "squatter" from Squadron A in command, but that a young major of Irish blood and a Catholic had to be brought in and groomed as Haskell's successor.

The chaplain told Farley that he was actively searching for the right man. That search would take more than a year and end on the banks of the Rhine River.

H e was called Wild Bill, from his days as an athlete at Columbia University. He was Irish. He was Catholic. And in mid-March 1917, William Joseph Donovan, then thirty-four, joined the Sixty-ninth Regiment. He had transferred in from I Troop of the First Cavalry from his hometown of Buffalo, an upper crust National Guard outfit that he had organized in 1912. The citizens of Buffalo called these troopers, a number of them lawyers like Donovan, the "Silk Stocking Boys." As captain, Wild Bill led the troop and had been with it during the disturbances on the Mexican border. A few days after the Buffalo boys had returned home, he was ordered to New York City, where he was promoted to major and assigned to command the Sixty-ninth's First Battalion.

When he walked into the armory on Lexington Avenue with his aide, Trooper J. Livingston Wadsworth from Geneseo, New York, nephew of a sergeant in the Rough Riders and cousin of U.S. Senator James Wadsworth, Donovan thought the colonelcy of the regiment would be his. He certainly had the bearing of a regimental commander. When Al Ettinger of Headquarters Company saw him for the first time he muttered to himself, "God!" Ettinger, son of New York City's superintendent of education, recalled that Wild Bill "had eyes like blue ice that drilled straight through you."[15] A writer for the New York Herald reported that around division headquarters Donovan was affectionately referred to as "Blue-eyed Billy."[16]

Duffy took to Donovan right away. "He is cool, untiring, strenuous, a man that always uses his head," he recorded. "He is a lawyer by profession, and a successful one, I am told. I like him for his agreeable disposition, his fine character, his alert and eager intelligence." Instinctively Duffy knew that here was the man he had been looking for. He convinced himself that it was "almost certain that Donovan would be appointed Colonel after the efforts to get Colonel Haskell had failed, as he was our next choice, and General O'Ryan knew that there were no politics about it, but a sincere desire to find the best military leader."[17]

Donovan was every bit as Irish as Duffy or any of the men in the Sixty-ninth. Like so many of their families, his family had escaped the potato famine of the 1840s. His grandparents headed

Maj. Wild Bill Donovan, Medal of Honor winner, boasted that he had been born to be hanged rather than killed in battle. *Signal Corps/National Archives*

for Buffalo because of its promise of a new life working at the huge port there. Ships and railroads crowded the hectic waterfront. Mules pulled barges along the Erie Canal. To many Americans Buffalo was the gateway to the West. His grandfather landed a job as a scooper in the grain holds of ships and then toiled in the rail yards. He led the fight for temperance. He sided with the Fenians, and it had been rumored that in his home he had harbored some of the more than eight hundred Fenians who, in 1866, undertook an ill-advised armed invasion of Canada to drive out the British government. Donovan's own father had started out as a greaser on train locomotives and later took over as yardmaster at Buffalo's main terminal. He wed Anna Letitia Lennon. Their first four children died. The fifth, born 1 January 1883, was William Joseph.

Outside of his family, which was run by the iron hand of his father, a major influence in Donovan's life was the Catholic Church. Donovan once considered becoming a Dominican priest, and his brother, Vincent, joined the order as a friar. Wild Bill settled on a law career and went off to New York City and Columbia University. While studying to be an attorney he played football, ran track, and rowed on the crew team. In the 1905 season, he was a one-hundred-sixty-pound starting quarterback on a so-so Columbia eleven. If there was a silver lining during the football season, it was the arrival on the gridiron of another law student. Tom Reilley of Harlem, later one of Reed's infamous "little inside gang," was ineligible because he had played at New York University. He was a stalwart performer of the New York Athletic Club and colleague of the great all-around athlete Martin Sheridan. Duffy described him as "an imposing figure. He stands six feet three or so and fills the eye with seeing any way you look at him."[18] Reilley's role at Columbia was that of student-coach. He and Donovan became friends, first on the turf of Baker Field, then in the classrooms atop Morningside Heights and finally in the ranks of the Irish regiment where, at the time of Donovan's transfer, Reilley served as captain of B Company.

Back in Buffalo, the recent law graduate joined a small firm for a few years and then, with Columbia classmate Bradley Goodyear, formed the law office of Donovan & Goodyear. Goodyear's father was Charles Waterhouse Goodyear, Grover Cleveland's law partner. Society's doors, usually closed to Irish Americans, especially Catholics, suddenly swung open, and the up-and-coming lawyer found himself dating the daughter of the late Dexter Rumsey, who had been the richest man in Buffalo. The Rumseys were Episcopalians, yet the daughter, Ruth, a girl with natural platinum blond hair, and blue eyes every bit as riveting as Wild Bill's, and who at seventeen had traveled throughout Europe with her family, three servants, twenty-eight trunks and a private, chauffeur-driven limousine, fell in love with the Irish-Catholic attorney. Ruth's mother begged her not to marry Donovan. But on 14 July 1914, just seven months after meeting him, she did so anyway. The Catholic wedding must have set Mrs. Rumsey and her proper Protestant family on edge.

Around the time he had met Ruth, Bill and his partner merged their law firm with that of John Lord O'Brian, one of the country's most distinguished attorneys. The new partnership of O'Brian Hamlin Donovan & Goodyear was another stroke of political savvy. Donovan's sphere of influence soon extended far beyond Buffalo, and by 1916 he was on assignment in Europe for the John D. Rockefeller Foundation. His task was to broker a deal between the warring nations of England and Germany so that food could be shipped into famine-stricken Poland. Because England refused to ease its blockade of German ports, the deal failed. Stuck in London for the time being, Donovan met Herbert Hoover. The wealthy Iowa mining engineer was directing a U.S.-sponsored program to feed millions of hungry Belgians. While Donovan assisted Hoover with the help of the Rockefeller Foundation, he inexplicably traveled throughout Europe, in Austria, in German-occupied Belgium, and in Germany itself—Aachen, Berlin, and as far east as Vienna. Was he on an intelligence-gathering mission? It's never been clear, but if so, then it was most likely the first such foray into intelligence for the man who was later known as "America's spymaster" for his leadership at the Office of Strategic Services (OSS).

But when trouble on the border between Mexico and the United States forced the president to call out federal soldiers and the Guard, those surreptitious rambles throughout Europe abruptly ended. Donovan was summoned home to join his Silk Stocking Boys of I Troop, already in Texas. A telegram from them was waiting when he docked at New York harbor.

THE WHOLE TROOP IS OUTSIDE THE TELE-GRAPH OFFICE. IT SENDS YOU GREETINGS AND BEST WISHES AND HOPES TO SEE YOU SOON.[19]

Donovan spent a few days in Buffalo with Ruth and then packed his gear, loaded a bay horse named Trivet and a black stallion named Andrew on the train, and with his gangly Great Dane, Nat, headed for the border.

Now, in 1917, soon after his transfer to the Sixty-ninth, Donovan described the politics of promotion in a letter. He told Ruth that Col. Harry Bandholtz, chief of staff of the New York division, "sent over my unqualified recommendation" as Haskell's successor as colonel of the regiment. The *Herald* reported that the Sixtyninth was "without a colonel and Major Donovan is so popular in the New York division that there would be little surprise at division headquarters if he was nominated for the command of the famous Irish regiment before the troops start for France. While no one would talk officially about the suggestion yesterday, several officers of the division smiled knowingly when the matter was mentioned to them."[20]

However, the Department of the East had other plans. Promotions from major to full colonel were not permitted within a regiment. That meant either Reed had the job or a new colonel had to be brought in. Donovan could deal with a new colonel. Reed was another matter. When Bandholtz broke the news that the Department of the East would not jump his rank from major to colonel, Wild Bill told him "I [do] not wish to go under Reed, but would rather go as a major under a good man than be Colonel." He comforted Ruth, saying, "Lucky for me I am not too keen for the place as I should now be quite disappointed knowing that a little wisdom would have given it to me."

Yet Donovan, in fact, relented and agreed to be Reed's major. He let the lieutenant colonel know that he would do his best in this role. Perhaps his change of heart resulted from his belief that Reed would never get command of the regiment. He made a prediction. "Hines [*sic*] for Colonel, Hines for Lt. Col. Your husband for the junior major."[21]

The Hines he referred to was Charles De Lano Hine. A middleaged West Point man, a lawyer and veteran of the Spanish-American War, Hine was one of the most knowledgeable railroad men in the country. Even though he held degrees from West Point and the Cincinnati Law School, he preferred the life of railroader and had started his career as a brakeman on the Cleveland, Cincinnati, Chicago, and St. Louis Railroad. At the time, he was in command of the New York division's field trains, under General O'Ryan.

As the plot thickened as to the next commander of the Sixtyninth, among the veteran officers in the regiment there were several with strong enough credentials to lead it and who ought to have been given the chance, irrespective of the regulations of the Department of the East about jumping rank. Capt. James Gregory

Finn, a native of Maine, was one of them. Another was Capt. James McKenna Jr., whose father had been postmaster of Long Island City, and whose brother Bill, a first lieutenant, was a battalion adjutant. Both Finn and McKenna were prominent attorneys in New York City.

The writer Rupert Hughes, a Sixty-ninth captain, knew firsthand the leadership qualities of Jim Finn, a bespectacled figure whose bookish looks belied a powerful man. In Texas, Finn had served as Hughes's first lieutenant in H Company. "He was a real soldier—six feet two—just George Washington's height—and strong as an ox," Hughes said of Finn. All the soldiers in the regiment who knew Finn, a star football player for Bowdoin College, remarked upon his size and strength. Hughes, whose own frail health and bad hearing forced him to give up his captaincy to Finn, recalled a moment in the Texas heat that summed up the big lieutenant's strength.

> I always remember Jim Finn as I saw him once down near the Rio Grande on a frightful test-march in which nearly half of that huskiest of regiments fell by the wayside with sunstroke and heat prostration. The alkali dust most of the way was so thick that you could hardly see the back of the man whose heel you trod on. Toward the end, I was so exhausted that I was holding the thin strap of my field glasses off my chest since the weight of it impeded my breath. Wondering if I could make the last hundred yards to my tent before I fell over [*sic*]. I looked back and saw First Lieutenant Finn striding along magnificently and carrying two rifles for soldiers who could not have made camp otherwise.[22]

Duffy also was in awe of Finn's strength. Describing him as an honest, manly man and devoted soldier, the chaplain said nobody would ever call Finn a liar. "Not after taking one look at him. He is a broad-shouldered, big-chested fellow, one that the eye will pick out of a crowd, even in a congested crowd, for he stands above the heads of ordinary mortals. . . . [T]he Captain has thews like the son of Anak."[23]

Finn's Irish family, a clan of men of size, had immigrated to Lewiston, Maine, from Cork sometime after the American Civil War. Daniel and Joanna O'Donoghue Finn had five children, all born in Lewiston. The youngest, born in 1879, was James Gregory. At the start of the Spanish-American War, when he was nineteen,

Jim had enlisted in the First Maine Volunteers. Before he was mustered out in 1901, he had been made an officer. He then went to college, first at Bates and then Bowdoin, where he had been the mainstay of the football team's line. He weighed over two hundred and twenty pounds. After graduating from Bowdoin he had earned his law degree at St. Lawrence University. He came to New York City in 1908, starting a career there with the Corporation Counsel.

"I envied Jim Finn, who became captain in my place," regretted Rupert Hughes, forced to resign because of his health. Hughes never made it overseas as a soldier and he was grateful in a way. As he wrote, "I have a poltroonish feeling that my deafness was the most fortunate affliction, the most blessed curse that anyone ever had. It may have saved me from what happened to Captain Finn."[24]

Like Finn, Capt. James McKenna was an attorney. As a former accountant, he specialized in banking law. When a summons to war required him to take a leave of absence from his legal practice in Manhattan's financial district to be a soldier, he wrote a message for his clients and stuck it on the office door. "I'll be back when we lick the Hun!"[25]

McKenna was born in Long Island City on 24 September 1885. The family lived in Hunter's Point and Jim's father was politically connected. During the Cleveland administration he had been postmaster for Long Island City. He had also served as an assemblyman. Jim's brother, William, was a lawyer, too, and when the war ended he worked as assistant district attorney for New York County. Jim had studied at Cornell and Harvard and got his law degree from Fordham University. He and William, a graduate of Holy Cross, became soldiers in the Seventh Regiment. A month before the New York guard headed for Texas, the McKenna brothers transferred into the Sixty-ninth.

When Duffy got to know Jim he found him a "fellow of great ability, ambitious, energetic and enduring." He figured that the young lawyer would be successful in any line of work and that as a soldier "he will score a high mark," adding that "he has fine ideals and fine sentiments which he chooses to conceal under a playfully aggressive or business-like demeanor."[26]

Although McKenna did not get the colonelcy, he did move up a notch to major and was placed in charge of the Third Battalion, which he nicknamed "Shamrock." Martin Hogan, the seventeen-year-old orphan, observed that the new major would be an ideal officer. Once he figured out the kind of man McKenna was, he wrote, "The men of the battalion would have followed him into the worst muss on earth."[27]

A high-ranking outsider that Duffy took an immediate liking to was Lt. Van Santvoord Merle-Smith, the lanky, blue-eyed Squadron A trooper who had transferred in with Latham Reed. The fact that he was Reed's friend did not grate on the chaplain. Duffy confided in his diary, "If I had to pick out one man to spend a year with on a voyage to Central Africa, there is the man I would select. A big fellow—he and Reilley and Finn are prize specimens—and big like them, all the way through."[28]

If Merle-Smith was not the wealthiest man in the regiment, he came pretty close to the title—if you count both his own family's wealth and that of his bride of a few months, Kate Fowler (who had picked him to be her husband over Capt. George Patton Jr., Pershing's impulsive new aide). Merle-Smith's grandfather, a Staten Island Dutchman known as the Commodore, had made a fortune off the Hudson River the same way as another Staten Island Dutchman, also known as the Commodore—Cornelius Vanderbilt. Alfred Van Santvoord established the Hudson River Day Line during the Civil War. Merle-Smith's English-bred father once remarked that the Van Santvoord side of the family, which claims lineage back to William of Orange, gave his son a "Dutch steadiness . . . sometimes called obstinacy."[29] Van's unusual hyphenated last name came about when his father and uncle, who were twins and sons of a justice of the New York State Supreme Court, decided that Smith was too common a name for them. They each took their middle names, and affixed them to their last name to create new surnames for the family. The Rev. Wilton Smith was now Merle-Smith. His brother was Lloyd-Smith. As a minister, Wilton, a Princeton graduate who, in the baseball lore of the university, is credited with developing the curveball, presided over New York's Central Presbyterian Church. Like his father, Van studied at Princeton. One of his law professors there was Woodrow Wilson, and after taking his course he went off to Harvard Law School.

The crisis along the Rio Grande hastened many a marriage in the summer of 1916. Big gala affairs planned for months had been scrapped for small, private weddings, usually witnessed by family

Capt. Van S. Merle-Smith of L Company joined the Sixty-ninth in 1916 while the regiment was stationed in Texas. Wounded at the Ourcq River, he compared the hopelessness of the attack to the charge of the Light Brigade. *Courtesy of Grosvenor Merle-Smith*

and only the dearest of friends. Such was the case for Van and his sweetheart, Kate. Instead of the social event of the year in Pasadena, set for 1 August, the couple was married in New York at the Merle-Smith home at 29 West Fifty-fourth Street on the evening of 20 June, hours before Squadron A was to be sent to Camp Beekman to prepare for service on the border. As the *New York Times* reported, "It was a small family wedding, as it was only possible to send invitations to a few of the immediate friends of the families in this city. It was, however, characteristic of military activity, as a number of Corporal Merle-Smith's friends from the squadron were present."[30] Reed attended as a member of the wedding party.

Soon after the wedding, Kate received a letter from her old beau, George Patton, pursuing Pancho Villa down in Mexico with General Pershing. Patton wrote in his peculiarly illiterate way that because she was one of the only female friends who in his youth had interested him he wanted to meet the man she had just married. "I am delighted that Mr. Merle-Smith is in the cavalry for besides the fact that you selected him the fact of his choice of an Arm prooves him very superior. Just fancy had he been a Doughboy or a Wagon Soldier?" Patton also feared that while he had been in Mexico for the past five months his wife, Beatrice, "might have fallen in love with some one else."[31]

Like many wives of the well-to-do officers and men, Kate followed her husband to Texas. When she settled in she discovered that her living quarters and the small town in which they were— Hildalgo, south of McAllen—were not so bad. The stores were surprisingly good, and fresh fruit and vegetables were abundant. She prepared meals for the troops. To her mother she wrote, "It's a joy to see the men eat. There are usually two extra each evening, and if one just puts food quietly on their plates they eat enormously." In the evenings there were "stylish" parties. She met wives of soldiers from other regiments. There was Mrs. Auchincloss, who never took to the heat and returned to New York. And there was Mrs. Ruth Donovan, "who is the quiet reserved young wife of Capt. Donovan on the 1st Cav. which comes from Buffalo. He is one of the nicest men here and one of the best soldiers, simple, frank, kindly and Irish."[32]

A few months after the Sixth Division arrived, Reed was promoted from first lieutenant to major and transferred to the Sixty-ninth. His leaving, Kate wrote home, "hit Van pretty hard because of his friendship, personally, and because of what he has meant to the Troop—been the head, backbone, heart and spirit of it and Van has pride and affection enough for the troop to worry about its future."[33]

After Reed's promotion, Merle-Smith had been offered a commission in the Twelfth New York. Kate was relieved when he turned it down. "It would have been an interesting experience and a good chance to try his hand managing men of that type, but the work would have been hard and disagreeable, somewhat dangerous. There are about twenty 'Diamond Dicks' and New York gangsters in the Company, and they are drunk and angry most of the time." She added that "selfishly" she was glad he had not taken the offer because, with Squadron A, "He's with his own kind."

But in November Reed held out a lieutenancy in the Sixty-ninth to his closest friends, and they accepted—Merle-Smith, of course, Charles Baker, Ewing Philbin, son of a New York State Supreme Court justice, and Sherman Phelps Platt. Platt was the grandson of Thomas Collier Platt, who before his death in 1910 had ruled the New York Republican Party as the "Easy Boss" with a power so absolute that an alcove in the Fifth Avenue Hotel in Manhattan where he held sway had been dubbed the "Amen Corner."

Kate viewed the Sixty-ninth the same way she did the Twelfth— "another tough proposition of Irishmen. . . . But all I care about is that Latham wanted him."[34] Van was promoted to second lieutenant on 16 November, honorably discharged from Squadron A and on the 19th, along with his horse, Forager, a nine-year-old bay, reported to D Company. To her in-laws, Kate wrote,

> Were you here you would feel and appreciate the difference between first the spirit of Van Cortland [Park], the natural slump of the last two months and the new life now sprung from this determination to accept a commission. And feeling it you could not help but be glad too, because it will give him a chance to be true to himself. . . . And were you here you would feel how unfinished and unsatisfactory is this attempt to do what one believes to be one's duty. . . . It seems so certain that during Van's life time there will be armed trouble . . . that the preparation for life of this generation is twofold—to learn how best to protect as well as develop our country.[35]

Another officer from outside the Sixty-ninth who would have an impact on the fortunes of the regiment, including the early days when undesirables had to be weeded out, was George Lawrence, a transfer from the "gangster-ridden" Twelfth New York. A physician, Lawrence arrived in May 1917 and, having the rank of major, took over as top medical officer.

Not yet thirty-six, Lawrence was the son of an eminent doctor, Enoch Lawrence, who in 1884 had been one of the founders of Flushing Hospital. The elder Lawrence used to make his rounds in a horse and buggy, always making sure to stop at the St. Joseph's Orphan Asylum to provide free care for the children there. George had three brothers and two of them, Austin and Andrew, also wound up in the Sixty-ninth. He attended the College of St. Francis Xavier, then, in 1907, he got his medical degree from the University of Pennsylvania, where he had starred in football and basketball. His mother wrote about his final season in her diary. "This fall George played Quarterback on the University foot-ball team, in the last three games of the season, where he made a great record for himself. Quarter-back was a very appropriate title for him, for when he returned home after the last game, on Thanksgiving day, three quarters of him must have been left on the gridiron, judging by the rack of bones brought home to me." When her youngest son, Austin, had graduated from Pennsylvania as a dentist in 1913, she wrote, "Thus the last of our dear sons has finished at college or School. And now all four are equipped for their life battles."[36]

In 1908, George joined the Tenth Regiment, as did all his brothers. When the New York Guard was sent to the Mexican border, he transferred to the Twelfth as chief surgeon at the camp hospital in McAllen. After the Guard's return to New York, George was promoted to major and sent to the Sixty-ninth. His arrival pleased Duffy.

> Major George Lawrence of the Sanitary Detachment is one of the best acquisitions of our Border experience. He is well educated, a product of St. Francis Xavier and Pennsylvania, a competent physician and surgeon, a famous athlete in football and basketball in his day, and an athlete still; and one of the most devoted and most reliable men that God has made for the healing of wounds of mind or body. When I think of what we shall have to go through it makes me feel good to see George Lawrence around.[37]

With the summer of 1917 fast approaching and the nation astir with war fever, the ranks of the Sixty-ninth were soon

Maj. George Lawrence, the 165th's chief medical officer, on the steps of the Tenth Regiment's armory in 1916. Behind him is his father, Dr. Enoch Lawrence, one of the founders of the Flushing Hospital. *Courtesy of Stephen Lawrence*

swollen with enough soldiers to form a full regiment of 2,002 men and officers. The only vacancy left was at the top. Who would be colonel? Latham Reed, unpopular among most of the officers? Or a complete stranger, another non-Irish, non-Catholic outsider? The

War Department was moving slowly, perhaps because it had to make another decision that would affect every regiment in New York City. Word had now reached Gotham that a new division of National Guardsmen was to be organized that once completed and trained would be the first of the country's militia to sail for France. For the new division, dubbed the "Rainbow" and described by one of its top officers as the "arch of patriotism," New York would have the honor of furnishing one of its infantry regiments.

Several of the city's regiments were worthy of selection. Certainly the Seventh had earned that right as the oldest National Guard regiment in the country. The Sixty-ninth also had an inside track. Its record in the Civil War, when Gen. Robert E. Lee called the regiment the "Fighting Sixty-ninth," gave it a more than even chance for the nod.

Once Secretary of War Baker had made the decision to form the Rainbow Division, he had named General Mann to head it. Colonels Michael Lenihan and Robert Brown were promoted to brigadier generals and selected to command the Eighty-third and Eighty-fourth Brigades, respectively. Fifty-year-old Col. Charles Summerall, a former artillery instructor at West Point, was promoted to brigadier general and put in charge of the Sixty-seventh Artillery Brigade. Next, Major MacArthur left his position as Baker's aide and, with the rank of colonel, took over as Mann's chief of staff.

According to Col. Henry Reilly, commander of the 149th Regiment Field Artillery, two principles governed which units got into the division. "The first was that every unit must be one which had established a record for efficiency. The second was to insure as many states as possible as widely scattered throughout the union as possible, being represented."[38]

But as for the regiments that would be part of one of the infantry brigades, one of the four had to come from New York. Mann had already made a survey of the National Guard units he could pull together from across the nation for reassignment to his division. In time, the roster did resemble a rainbow that stretched from east to west, north to south, and the multistate representation started with his seventy-three-member staff. The officers and men hailed from twenty-six states and the District of Columbia—the same number as the various units themselves. New Yorkers made up the largest group on Mann's staff. There were thirteen of them, including nine from the city.

For his headquarters troop, he picked the Second Louisiana Cavalry. The military police were out of the Virginia Coast Artillery

Corps. The 117th Field Signal Battalion was from Missouri, the 117th Ammunition Train from Kansas, the 117th Supply Train from Texas, and the Fourth Pennsylvania Infantry made up what was later renamed the 149th Machine Gun Battalion. The 117th Engineer Regiment was from California and South Carolina and the 117th Engineer Train from North Carolina.

He selected for his Sixty-seventh Artillery Brigade the 149th Regiment Field Artillery (First Illinois), 150th Regiment Field Artillery, Heavy (First Indiana), 151st Regiment Field Artillery (First Minnesota), and 117th Trench Mortar Battery (Maryland Coast Artillery Corps). The four companies of the 117th Sanitary Train came from Michigan, New Jersey, Oklahoma and Tennessee, while the four field hospital sections were from Colorado, Nebraska, Oregon, and the District of Columbia.

His major fighting force, the Eighty-third and Eighty-fourth Brigades, each comprised two infantry regiments as well as one machine gun battalion. It was decided to tap the Sixty-ninth first and rename it the 165th United States Infantry Regiment.

"We are . . . full of excitement," exclaimed Duffy, "at our selection among the National Guard Regiments of New York to represent our State in the selected 42nd or Rainbow Division which is to go abroad amongst the very first for active service. It is an undeniable compliment to the condition of the Regiment and we are pleased at that as well as at the prospects of carrying our battle-ringed standards to fly their colors on the fields of France."[39]

Joining the Sixty-ninth in the Eighty-third Brigade were the Fourth Ohio, now the 166th Infantry, and the Second Wisconsin from Appleton, Oconto, Oshkosh, and Fond du Lac, now the 150th Machine Gun Battalion.

The Eighty-fourth Brigade comprised the Fourth Alabama, now the 167th Infantry, the Third Iowa, now the 168th Infantry, and the Second Georgia, now the 151st Machine Gun Battalion. The Fourth Alabama had a history going back to the Seminole Wars and had fought at Bull Run, Gettysburg, Sharpsburg and Chickamauga. It had battled the Irish Brigade, and the animosity between it and the Sixty-ninth had not been forgotten by either regiment.

At about the time it organized the Rainbow Division, the War Department also devised numerical designations for each division. Regular army divisions would be numbered one through twenty-five. National Guard divisions, beginning with the "Yankee"

Division from New England, would start at twenty-six. The New York "Empire" Division, the Sixth, now became the Twenty-seventh. The renumbering had been done regionally. The highest-numbered region came from the Pacific Northwest, Forty-one. Because the "Rainbow" was not regional but represented many states it was tagged the Forty-second. Higher numbered divisions were then made up of draftees, which later rankled the African-American Fifteenth, whose men were all volunteers and chafed that their outfit had been dumped into a provisional division with the highest number of all, the Ninety-third.

As well as renumbering the divisions, the War Department had increased their size considerably, which meant that each regiment would now nearly double, jumping from 2,002 to 3,600 men and ninety-five officers. By a stroke of the pen, the Sixty-ninth found itself suddenly undermanned. It now needed at least sixteen hundred new recruits. And it still had no colonel.

4

"Did You Ever Go Into an Irishman's Shanty?"

In the dog days of August 1917, the Sixty-ninth found itself in a bind. It still had no commander and all of a sudden was woefully short of soldiers, even though men and boys, many of them not even of age, banged on the door of the Lexington Avenue armory for a chance to enlist. Within weeks the regiment, loathe to refer to itself as the 165th Infantry (Rupert Hughes complained that the rechristening had been done "sacrilegiously"[1]), had to pack up and head for Camp Mills on Long Island to start training as part of the Forty-second Rainbow Division. Because it would head for France in a few months, it had lost the luxury of recruiting the type of men it desired. Like a thunderclap that resounded throughout greater New York came the War Department's order that Gotham's other regiments surrender three hundred and fifty of their own men to the Irish—more than seventeen hundred soldiers found fit to fight. The order hit the proud regiments hard. The Fourteenth was furious, and so was the Twenty-third. The Seventh was stunned. And the Sixty-ninth ground its teeth at the thought of accepting all those outsiders.

"We would have been glad to have done our own recruiting as we could easily have managed; but these are the orders," Father Francis Duffy jotted in his diary. "We shall give a royal Irish welcome to our new companions in arms. They are volunteers like ourselves and fellow townsmen, and after a little feeling out of one another's qualities we shall be a united Regiment."[2]

Before the unpopular order had been issued, Duffy had been determined to personally transfer into the regiment a special soldier, one who he believed would "confer upon [the Sixty-ninth] the gift of immortality."

On 4 August, for the first time, Duffy met Joyce Kilmer, then a lowly private in the highly esteemed Seventh Regiment, a poet

Poet Joyce Kilmer wanted to be a fighting sergeant and not a clerk safe behind the lines. *Courtesy of James Tierney*

of note, especially for his popular verse "Trees," and writer for the *New York Times*. When they met, Kilmer was in anguish over the slow, bitter death of his nine-year-old daughter Rosamonde, or as he called her, Rose, by infantile paralysis. Kilmer impressed the chaplain, who had expected to find in him an effeteness that might be disconcerting among the rough and tumble men of the Sixty-ninth. "Nothing of the long-haired variety about him—a sturdy fellow, manly, humorous, interesting," Duffy wrote

As Duffy and Kilmer chatted, the poet startled the chaplain by telling him that he had truly wanted to serve in the Sixty-ninth. He claimed that he had gone to the armory several times to enlist but had not found a recruiting officer there. On 23 April, two weeks after the United States declared war, he and Louis Wetmore—a fellow *Times* man, who as an editor there first accepted Kilmer's literary work—had signed on with the Seventh. "I told him that if we could not have him in the 69th the next best place was the 7th, but he still wants to return to his first love, so I shall be glad to arrange it."[3]

Kilmer had two reasons for joining the Sixty-ninth. As much as it distressed his mother, Annie—a zealous Episcopalian who had named her only son after the ministers of Christ Church in East Brunswick, New Jersey, the Rev. Alfred Taylor and Rector Elisha Brooks Joyce—Kilmer had turned his back on their church and converted to Catholicism. The Sixty-ninth, therefore, with its roster reputed to be ninety-five percent Catholic, was the regiment for him. It must have relieved his mother when he joined the Seventh instead. He again upset his mother, who traced her family's lineage back to seventeenth century England, when he remarked that he was half-Irish. And the second reason was that in his heart he was—although some critic had quipped that he was not half-Irish, in fact had no Irish blood at all. Kilmer had shrugged it off and said to his wife that he had never been a good mathematician. Kenton Kilmer, the poet's son, commented that long before the United States entered the war his father had been "enamored of Irish history, Irish legend and literature, and Irish and Irish-American poetry. . . . Dad used to frequent the company of Irish patriots, eager for Ireland to break free of British rule."[4]

After their first meeting, Duffy started the paperwork to get Joyce transferred into the Sixty-ninth even though he believed that Kilmer's rightful place was at home looking after his family. He wrote, "I shall be glad to have him with us personally for the pleasure of his companionship."[5]

Born on 6 December 1886 in New Brunswick, Kilmer was the son of Dr. Frederick Kilmer, a chemist for the Johnson & Johnson Company credited with developing one of its best products, baby powder. Annie Kilburn, his mother, doted on her son with an almost suffocating love that is evident in the letters she and Joyce wrote back and forth over the years. In those letters, he endearingly called her "Brat." When Joyce was a child, Annie's "dearest pleasure [was] to arrange his wealth of golden hair into their natural curls. And I could see the intelligence and that promise of his later years in his dark brown eyes."[6]

Also enchanted by Kilmer's eyes, as well as his smile, had been Christopher Morley, the well-known essayist, novelist, editor of *Bartlett's Familiar Quotations* and a founder of *The Saturday Review of Literature*. "His smile, never far away, when it came was winning, charming," Morley wrote. "It broke like spring sunshine, it was so fresh and warm and clear. And there was noticeable then in his eyes a light, a quiet glow, which marked him as a spirit not to be forgotten."[7] Another friend had recalled his remarkable head with a broad high forehead and a prominent bulge at the back covered with dark, reddish hair.

> But his eyes were his most remarkable feature. They were of the unusual color of red, and they had a most peculiar quality which I can only inadequately suggest by saying that they literally glowed. It actually seemed as if there were a fire behind them; not a leaping, blazing fire, but a steady and unquenchable flame, which appeared to suffuse the whole eyeball with a brooding light. And this brooding and somewhat somber light never left his eyes even in his most weary or most care-free moments, so that they gave the impression of a brain behind them working intensely every hour of the waking day.[8]

Annie used to haul her son to England, where she schooled him in their family's Anglican heritage. In 1905, at a church in Cambridgeshire, she had a window dedicated to their ancestor, Thomas Kilburn, who had been a warden there in the early 1600s. Joyce read the dedication and Annie had been "so proud." She was even happier that year when he informed his father that he planned to become an Episcopal minister. "All this time," Mrs. Kilmer wrote, "he had been a regular communicant of the Church where he was christened. At eighteen he was a licensed lay reader, and it made me very happy to hear him read the Lessons from the old Oak Lectern, brought from England, in Christ Church on Sunday." Yet a year later Joyce had "astonished" his mother when he "brought home to me . . . a Rosary of Garnets." Kilmer studied at Rutgers University, went on to Columbia, and in 1908 married Aline Murray, a poet and writer and the stepdaughter of the editor of *Harper's Monthly*. Soon afterward, according to his mother, he "lost all interest in his Church."[9]

His son, Kenton, remembered years later that because his father was a socialist Joyce felt obligated to be an atheist, bidding farewell to the allegiance he had held to the Protestant Episcopal Church, in which he had been a Lay Reader.

Long after the passing of this phase, my mother told me that for a time, when she said her accustomed night prayers, she had to pray in silence and secrecy, lying in bed under the covers. Dad had forbidden her to pray, so, lying beside him in bed, she prayed fervently for him, as well as for all other people and causes dear to her. For the time being, his hand had found the Marxist principle, "Religion is the opium of the people."[10]

By 1913, Joyce had apparently rediscovered God and, in spite of Kenton's recollection of his father's atheism, finally converted to Catholicism. In a 1914 letter to his confidant and fellow writer, Father James Daly, Kilmer explained, "I am beginning to understand [my conversion]. I believed in the Catholic position, the Catholic view of ethics and aesthetics, for a long time. But I wanted something, not intellectual, some conviction not mental—in fact I wanted faith." He went on to tell the priest that while agonizing over becoming a Catholic he used to drop into the Church of Holy Innocents near the *Times* building just off Broadway every day on his way to work. "I prayed in this church for faith. When faith did come, it came, I think, by way of my little paralyzed daughter. Her lifeless hands led me; I think the tiny still feet know beautiful paths. You understand this and it gives me selfish pleasure to write it down."[11]

Although his conversion had hurt the young poet's mother she let it be known that it had "never brought a cloud between us, and neither did his father ever utter a word of disapproval. As for me, I bless the day when he became a Catholic."[12]

Kilmer's first book of poetry, *Summer of Love*, was published in 1911. Then in the August 1913 issue of *Poetry* magazine

"Trees" appeared. A year later the poem led off his second book, *Trees and other Poems.* A critic for a Catholic magazine observed, "He saw the Hand of God in everything, in the trees of the forest, in the roar of the world, and in the midnight train that brought him safely to his cottage in the Jersey hills."[13] In his poem "Trees," it is certain Kilmer saw the hand of God.

> I think that I shall never see
> A poem lovely as a tree.
> A tree whose hungry mouth is prest
> Against the earth's sweet flowing breast;
> A tree that looks at God all day,
> And lifts her leafy arms to pray;
> A tree that may in Summer wear
> A nest of robins in her hair;
> Upon whose bosom snow has lain;
> Who ultimately lives with rain.
> Poems are made by fools like me,
> But only God can make a tree.[14]

After the publication of "Trees" Kilmer's fame stretched worldwide. And hours after the Germans torpedoed the *Lusitania* on 7 May 1915, killing 1,198 people, among them 124 Americans, he penned another memorable poem. An editor assigned the task of writing the eulogy to Kilmer the moment the news of the ship's sinking and the terrible loss of life was cabled to the *Times.* Gulping down his lunch, Kilmer composed "The White Ships and the Red." He contrasts the *Lusitania* to other sunken ships, particularly the *Titanic*, all resting at the bottom of the sea when the doomed ship joins them.

The sinking of the *Lusitania* had a profound affect on Kilmer, and afterward he wanted to attend the Plattsburgh Officers Training Camp where hundreds of young men, most of them college graduates, learned the rudiments of military leadership. To his mother, he warned "I might go to the training camp at Plattsburg for a month. I think it will do me a lot of good to go to Plattsburg, and it will also be enjoyable."[15] But after mulling it over from a socialist's viewpoint, he decided against camp. He explained, "I was going to Plattsburg to try for a commission, but for many reasons—one of them being that I didn't want to be an officer in charge of conscripts . . . I gave up the idea. So a month ago I enlisted as a private in the Seventh Regiment, National Guard, New York."[16]

Kilmer drilled day and night with the citizen-soldiers of the Seventh while continuing to work at the *Times*. "I passed my Federal physical examination yesterday, and tomorrow all the Regiment is to be mustered into Federal service," he informed his mother on 14 July. "I drill about four hours a day, and also have guard duty and such things." He kept his mother scrupulously updated on his soldiering duties in endless dispatches, even letting her know that he had lost weight. "Well, I got weighed yesterday and the scales showed 178 pounds—only two pounds less than I weighed last winter! So either I've lost fat or I've gained muscle." In another letter he had warned that the Seventh was soon to be sent south and that "I find I'll have to get a lot of stuff to take to camp with me—I only learned what I would need last night. Will you please give me an order on Rogers Peet, 34th Street store, or telegraph it (not signing the telegram 'Gerber') to get some truck—chiefly hussifs and towels and similar things." He wrote again, urgently, "Very soon I'll be in camp, and ready to receive such things as boxes of cigars, cans of tobacco, cans (or, if you prefer, tins) of ginger snaps, and pipes and such things." Finally, the things arrived and he fired back a thank you, along with the news that "I may find out tonight where I'll be stationed. I think we'll be in New York at the Armory for a month yet, but I'm not sure." He closed, complaining about Maj. Gen. John O'Ryan's edict that National Guard troops not to smoke or drink. "Have to go on the wagon Sunday when we get mobilised. Terrible isn't it? Also, we can't smoke on the streets when we are in uniform, and we are always to be in uniform."

He also kept Annie abreast of his status with the Sixty-ninth, expecting any day to be transferred. "If, or when, my transfer to the 69th goes through, my address will be Private Joyce Kilmer, Company K, 165th Regiment, Camp Mills, Mineola, Garden City, Long Island, New York. You see, or rather don't, that the 69th is now the 165th. But I'll let you know when, or if, the transfer occurs." And again, "The transfer has not yet gone though, but it may this week. It is certain to go through in the course of time."[17]

While Kilmer worried about his transfer, the Sixty-ninth worried about the sudden arrival of nearly two thousand men from Gotham's other National Guard regiments. One of the first regiments to cull men from its own ranks turned out to be the

Seventh. Because recruiting had diluted the blue-blooded make up of the Park Avenue outfit it would have been easy to ship objectionable soldiers off to the Irishers. Some of New York's other regiments had done just that, forcing Duffy to remark, "A couple of our sister organizations have flipped the cards from the bottom of the pack in some instances and worked off on us some of their least desirables."[18] Martin Green of the *Evening World*, knew Duffy was right. He reported, "Other regiments of the New York National Guard, summoned to the aid of the Sixty-ninth, were not so ardent as the Seventh. In the high commands of these regiments there was displayed a degree of selfishness more or less excusable under the circumstances."[19]

The colonel of the Seventh, Willard Fisk, played it straight. In a move that proved unpopular at the Seventh, Fisk, a lawyer, had first asked for volunteers who might want to transfer to the Sixty-ninth and then, when that produced only a handful of willing soldiers, selected every fourth man to go, as directed by the War Department. For some, it was heartbreaking. Others just shrugged it off and accepted their fate.

One of the happy transfers was Albert "Red" Ettinger. A feisty lad, he had tried to enlist in the Sixty-ninth in 1916, while still in high school, so he could go to the Mexican border. His father squelched that effort, making him promise that when he was old enough to join the Guard the only regiment for him would be the Seventh. Ettinger did not like the Seventh—the "kid glove Seventh," he called it. When Fisk asked for volunteers, "virtually everyone in the 7th wanted to transfer," he recollected, although that was hardly the case. When he found out he was going to the Sixty-ninth, he rejoiced, saying it was a "wonderful day."[20]

In all, the Seventh sent to the Sixty-ninth three hundred fifty-five men, an average of twenty-eight from each company. They carried such non-Irish names as Lippincott, Swope, Titterton, Tiffany, Van Brunt, Van Pelt, Winthrop, and Pfc. Emmett St. Cyr Watson Jr., a commercial artist who later illustrated Kilmer's war poem, "Rouge Bouquet." A transfer from K Company was Vanderbilt Ward, a great grandson of Cornelius Vanderbilt. Also from K Company came Malcolm Robertson from Brooklyn, a Princeton graduate who had served as an ambulance driver in France and whose parents were well-known physicians. Malcolm's close friend, also in the same company, was Charles Holt, whose family were Brooklyn flour merchants. Ettinger thought Holt a

Finding himself underweight for military service, Pfc. Vivian Commons drank a quart of milk and then gorged on bananas before a medical officer would allow him to enlist. *Courtesy of Haeger Family*

"pampered momma's boy," and wrote how every Sunday his mother brought him fresh sheets for his bunk because she did not want him to sleep "between rough sheets" and how he once was so startled that he "soiled his undershorts."[21]

Vivian Commons from C Company was just out of Stuyvesant High School and needed permission to enlist from his father, who ran a wholesale drugstore known as the Commons Bros. When he signed up to be a private in the Seventh, he was thin and underweight, and the recruiting officer at first turned him down. He rushed home to gorge on bananas and a quart of milk and then sped back to the armory.

"You're still a few pounds underweight," the officer said. "Do you really want to be a soldier?"

"Yes, sir!" blurted Vivian.

"Okay then. In you go."[22]

Unlike Commons, Philip Schuyler Finn, raised down near the Battery, was Irish through and through, and it probably would have rankled his father, "Battery Dan" Finn, had he been alive, that his son had hitched his soldiering star to the swanky Seventh, not the Sixty-ninth. "Battery Dan" had been one of Tammany Hall's most colorful sachems. A native of Limerick, Ireland, he had led the First Assembly District, run a saloon, and fought in the Civil War, and he had been a city magistrate at the time of his death in 1910. He had been so beloved by the people of the Battery that a thousand mourners passed by his coffin. Philip enlisted in the Seventh on 1 August at age thirty. Two weeks later he was in the Sixty-ninth, with his brother, Leonard, a private in K Company, and "Battery Dan" rested easier.

Another Irish American from the Seventh, eighteen-year-old Joseph Paxton McKinney, hailed from the Richmond Hill section of Queens. His father was the police captain there. The McKinneys had come to America in the early 1700s, and played a part in Kentucky history, claiming that one of Joseph's great-great grandfathers had been a trusted friend of Daniel Boone. In the Civil War, a great grandfather had captained the Seventeenth Kentucky Regiment that fought on the Union side. Joseph enlisted a month after graduating from high school, where for several years he had been one of the city's best tennis players.

Dutchmen Victor Van Yorx and his brother William T. Jr., called Ted, both transfers from G Company, were suburbanites. They grew up in Mount Vernon, New York. They were high school football stars. Victor loved to sing, a trait he picked up from his father who conducted the Mount Vernon Men's Glee Club. He also fancied himself a poet and when he was a boy wrote

When I get through with school and toys,
I'm going to join the soldier boys.
We'll march about with fife and drum,
With a rub a dub dub, and a bum, bum, bum.[23]

Victor, who had worked for Remington Arms in Bridgeport, Connecticut, when he was fifteen, became a Seventh Regiment soldier on 4 May—five weeks before his eighteenth birthday. After Duffy got to know the Van Yorx brothers he wrote their mother. "When

Ted Van Yorx, from Mount Vernon, New York, who, along with his brother Victor, were among the 355 transfers from the Seventh Regiment. Between them, they fought in all of the 165th's engagements. *Courtesy of Van Yorx Family*

I am fond of people I always want to know their mothers and I certainly do like those two fine sons of yours of Company K."[24]

When the list of transfers was issued, the reaction in the Seventh Regiment armory was one of dismay.

Cpl. Ben Franklin of A Company lamented, "Many are the familiar faces that we will see no more until the war is over. Veterans in service grown dear to the hearts of A Co. men, and the new men with the promise of great futures have been torn away from us by the exigencies of the greatest war in the history of mankind." He singled out James Tiffany as one of the transfers, calling him "the one and only." And he added, "May they ever reflect the spirit of the Seventh."[25]

Cpl. Thomas Kerr snapped, "We regret very much losing so many of our fine fellows and wish that it could have been arranged in some other manner. But the Government knows best." Sgt. Earle Grimm described the order as a wallop and a punch, but noted the regiment was still on its feet. Scribbled Cpl. Billy Leonard, a former news editor from Flushing, "It cannot be said that the order drafting our men into another regiment was received with great joy, but the men upon whom the choice of fortune fell accepted the situation with fine spirit, and in many instances other men volunteered to take the places of those reluctant to go, inspired by the prospect of early service in France."[26]

On 16 August, the transfers marched from the Seventh Regiment Armory on Park Avenue down to the Sixty-ninth Regiment Armory on Lexington Avenue. One soldier commented, "The welcome accorded the Seventh men at the 69th Armory . . . will live forever in the minds of those who witnessed it."[27]

At two-thirty in the afternoon, the regiment assembled in its huge drill shed, the 355 transfers snapping to attention as soldiers of the Seventh for the last time. They were dressed in full uniform, packs slung on their backs, rifles on their shoulders. Colonel Fisk called the entire regiment to attention and then ordered them out of the armory and onto Park Avenue. The transfers followed those who were to stay in the Seventh. More than two thousand soldiers headed south. The sidewalks were crowded with well-wishers, cheering the departing men. When the parade turned east on Twenty-sixth, the regiment split in two, forming a line on both sides of the street. As the transfers marched between their former comrades, rifles were snapped up to present arms. In the distance, the Sixty-ninth's band came out of the armory, the strains of its own regimental song, "Garryowen," welcoming the new troops. The crowd, by now in the tens of thousands, and among them the former commander of the Irish, William Haskell, roared as the two regiments merged. The transfers were visibly moved.

"The meeting of the bands was the signal for vehement outburst at the doors of and within the armory," wrote the Seventh's

Eugene O'Brien. "Bugle calls, band music and commands all were drowned in the friendly pandemonium which made the 7th's men feel that the long friendship between the two regiments was cemented into a union which will carry the best traditions of the two organizations into the trenches 'over there'."[28]

"The ovation the smart Seventh got from the proud and admiring New Yorkers wasn't anything compared to the reception the Sixty-ninth extended," noted a reporter for the *Times*."[29]

As the newcomers mounted the steps, the Sixty-ninth's band played the old tune, "Did You Ever Go Into an Irishman's Shanty?" Inside the armory—the Irishman's Shanty—soldiers packed themselves along the walls or sat precariously on the steel girders above. Acting Commander Latham Reed greeted the nervous arrivals as they stepped into their new military home. Recalled Ettinger, "As we entered those Irishers of the 69th gave us a rousing welcome. Men were up in the balcony and hanging from the rafters, and they cheered and cheered, because we were the first troops from the other regiments in New York to make the transfer."[30] Duffy, who had wanted to give the soldiers from the other regiments a "royal Irish welcome," was taken aback. "Our 2,000 . . . cheered and cheered and cheered till the blare of the bands was unheard in the joyous din—till hearts beat so full and fast that they seemed too big for the ribs that confined them, till tears of emotion came, and something mystical was born in every breast—the soul of a regiment. Heaven be good to the enemy when these cheering lads go forward together in battle."[31]

For some citizen-soldiers of other regiments there would be no royal Irish welcome as warm and as rowdy as for the Seventh. For those who were sickly or showed no military promise, their commanders gave them train fare and sent them packing, unceremoniously, over to the "Irishman's Shanty."

And once the Sixty-ninth reached Camp Mills troubled followed.

5

"Good-bye Broadway, Hello France!"

The Sixty-ninth stopped on its way to Camp Albert Mills to visit with Martin Sheridan, in his glory days arguably America's finest athlete. Then it was on to the Polo Grounds for a rare Sunday baseball contest sponsored by the Friendly Sons of St. Patrick to benefit the regiment's needy families, with John McGraw's Giants taking on Christy Mathewson's Cincinnati Reds. And from there a trip across the East River and then by train to Hempstead Plains, with the last leg on foot—"farmland inhabited by rabbits and skunks," observed Al Ettinger.[1] But first the boys had to hear a pep talk from Sheridan and other standouts of the Irish-American Athletic Club.

The fact that Sheridan, a New York City police detective, had amassed nine Olympic medals, five of them gold, and had once held the world record in the all-around, was not the only reason Irish Americans loved this native of County Mayo. They loved him for the stirring words he had uttered before the opening ceremonies of the 1908 Olympic Games in London and for what had occurred the next day as the U.S. team marched past the king of England. Although the modern Olympic Games were new, it already was customary for all countries parading before the host country's head of state to dip their flags. The night before, the Irish on the team, who held no love for England, had argued about what do with the American flag, which was to be held aloft by massive shot-putter, Ralph Rose. Sheridan, who would win two gold medals, stood among his teammates, and convinced them that "this flag dips to no earthly king!" The next day, as teams from more than thirty countries tramped past King Edward VII, the very same royal who when he was the Prince of Wales in 1860 had been snubbed in New York by Michael Corcoran's Sixty-ninth

Regiment, all flags dipped respectfully—until the American contingent strode by. Rose held the Stars and Stripes high, with one hand. Since then the United States has never dipped its flag at the Olympic Games.[2]

Sheridan and other members of the Irish-American Athletic Club too old to fight had two reasons for getting together with the Sixty-ninth. The first was to instill in the minds of the young new recruits the gallant history of the regiment—most importantly how it had been organized to strike back against England's ill-treatment of Ireland. The second, and less political, reason was to honor Capt. James Archer, one of America's fastest sprinters and one of the club's own outstanding athletes, who was marching off to war. On behalf of club members, Sheridan presented to Archer a service revolver, field glasses, and a wristwatch.

The G Company commander (and track star) was a popular club member. The world war had taken away from him any chance to compete in the Olympics. Now he had active duty to contend with. A few weeks earlier, at a muster in the regimental armory, Archer, thinking about himself as much as his own troops, remarked to the *Irish Advocate*, "Look at that bunch of fightin' Irishmen! . . . Hard as nails. Fully eighty percent of the outfit are Irish through and through, the remainder being of a 'semi-Irish' mixture that will lend a dignity to the unit. . . . Every county in Ireland is represented in the regiment, but I think Tipperary has the heaviest score." Then he had said, "All the fellows I have spoken to are anxious to get out and show the world that the Irish can still fight."[3]

The next day, a Sunday, the regiment, two thousand strong, ferried around Manhattan, from the East River up the Hudson to West 157th Street. There, the men scrambled off the *William J. Gaynor* and hiked to the Polo Grounds. Missing from the festivities was L Company, now under the command of Latham Reed's friend, Capt. Van S. Merle-Smith. It was in Hempstead Plains, readying Camp Mills for the arrival the following day of the rest of the Sixty-ninth.

As the boys traipsed across town they buzzed about their meeting with the great Sheridan and the even bigger news—they now had a colonel to be their permanent leader.

Reed was out, much to the delight of the older officers of the regiment. In letters to Ruth, Maj. Bill Donovan told his wife of the men's dissatisfaction with Reed. He described how the lieutenant colonel had gone to Maj. Gen. John O'Ryan to outline the reasons he deserved the colonelcy. By taking such action, Donovan thought, Reed had made a "fool of himself." After O'Ryan had rejected Reed, Donovan's name had come up. Unlike Reed, however, Wild Bill was not about to make a fool of himself. He would not ask for anything, but instead would do whatever the general requested.[4] O'Ryan then made his decision. The commander who now awaited the men at Camp Mills happened to be the man that Donovan had predicted would get the post, Charles De Lano Hine.

A West Pointer, the fifty-year-old Hine was more interested in railroad management than soldiering, and that interest would be put to good use later in the war. He had been out of the army since the end of the Spanish-American War. At the time of his appointment to head the Sixty-ninth, the gray-haired, slightly paunchy officer was serving on O'Ryan's staff. He said he knew all about the glorious deeds the Irish had done while in Cuba because, in Cuba, Hine had met Michael Emmet Urell, a native of Henagh, Ireland, who in the American Civil War had earned the Medal of Honor. Hine had mistakenly thought Urell had served in the Sixty-ninth. "I was brought up on stories of the Fighting Sixty-ninth," he had boasted. "A brother Major in the Santiago campaign of 1898 was Michael Emmett Urell. . . . So you can see how I have been wrapped up in the traditions of the old organization and what a double honor it appears to me to be its commanding officer."[5] In the Civil War, Urell had been with the Eighty-second New York Volunteers, not the Sixty-ninth. Still, the veteran had filled Hine with romantic tales of Irish battlefield valor.

At first, the new commander failed to impress Father Francis Duffy. In his diary, which he later rewrote for posterity, the chaplain praised Hine, saying "We like our new Colonel. . . . He is a man of ideas, of ideas formed by contact with life and business. He is a tireless worker, and demands the same unflinching service from every man under him."[6] Yet in a letter to Cardinal Farley, when comparing Hine to the departed Haskell, he had said otherwise. "The new Colonel is not a Catholic—nor is he the soldier that Col. Haskell is. But he is the Colonel and as good soldiers we are all getting behind him to support his administration and make the regiment an honor to the race and the nation."[7]

As far as the Sixty-ninth's troops were concerned, they were in no hurry to meet their new colonel at Camp Mills. They wanted to watch the Giants in a benefit game against the Reds and see one of the legends of baseball, Christy Mathewson. The man called "Big Six" had left the ball club in 1916, after seventeen years in New York. He had won 363 games before his trade to Cincinnati. Now he managed the Reds. Twenty-five thousand people were in the stands when the Sixty-ninth marched onto the grass of the Polo Grounds, led by its band playing "Hail, Hail, The Gang's All Here!" At home plate, the Interborough Subway Band greeted the soldiers with Irish tunes while a tenor sang "Good-bye Broadway, Hello France." Fans stood and roared. Reporting on the sound of the applause, a scribe for the *New York Sun* wrote, "There was a quiver to it that gripped one to the inward man, that caused the temples to throb and an old lump to rise in the throat."[8]

Marching to the left-field wall, the soldiers climbed into the bleachers. After they settled themselves into their wooden seats, Red's pitcher Fred Toney appeared on the field. The troops went wild, mistaking him for Mathewson. Then the old ace of the Giants' pitching staff strode to the left-field wall and pitched balls into the stands. It brought on more pandemonium, as boys in uniform dove for balls, fell out of the bleachers, and were laughingly pulled back in by their comrades.

The Friendly Sons of St. Patrick auctioned off a ball autographed by President Wilson. The ball had been donated by Dan Brady, younger brother of "Diamond Jim" Brady. It brought five hundred dollars for the regiment's families, purchased by the horse-racing sportsman James Butler. He gave the treasured sphere to Duffy with orders to carry it to France and in Paris auction it off again, with the proceeds this time to benefit French orphans. The *Tribune* called it the "most expensive ball ever turned loose on a baseball field."[9]

The Reds beat McGraw's Giants, 5–0. "Not all the cheering of the lusty-lunged soldiers, their sweethearts, wives, parents and neighbors could rally the tottering Giants," the *Tribune* commented.[10]

Duffy called it a great day for Ireland. "A fine game—plenty of people, plenty of fun, and best of all, plenty of money for the exchequer, which, after an ancient venerable custom, is going to have an ecclesiastical chancellor." The game raised twelve thousand dollars for the regiment. Reflecting on the responsibility of taking the autographed baseball overseas, he put down in his diary, "I am to auction it in Paris for the French Orphans' Fund. So

Mr. Brady says, though I wish I had his confidence that we shall ever get to Paris."[11]

The following Monday the Sixty-ninth departed Manhattan for Camp Mills.

Because five hundred men were already at camp, the march through Gotham to the ferry train proved to be an informal parade. There was no official reviewing stand, although the governor, mayor, and commander of the state guard showed up in a farewell gesture. Col. Willard Fisk of the Seventh Regiment was also on the scene to bid his former greyjackets, now with the Irishers, good-bye. Hine stayed on Long Island, allowing Lieutenant Colonel Reed to take the regiment to camp. Before the parade, Reed received a postcard from a well-wisher adorned with a dried shamrock and the words, "Glory and good luck to the Sixty-ninth Regiment."

Donovan, head of the First Battalion, stepped aside to let his friend from college days, Capt. Thomas Reilley, lead it. He told Ruth that because "Big Tom Reilly [*sic*]" had been acting commander of the battalion he, Donovan, asked Reed "to let him continue in command and I marched as one of Reed's staff."[12]

The regiment took its final leave of the armory at nine-thirty in the morning, after a blessing from Patrick Bishop Hayes. Drum Major John Mullins, son of the regiment's armorer, led the band outside. Throngs of New Yorkers crowded the sidewalks and overflowed onto Lexington Avenue as shouts and yells of "Here they come!" resounded off the cement and concrete. With the police clearing a path for the departing soldiers, the band struck up "Garryowen." Following the band strode Reed and Chaplain Duffy, Majors Donovan and Lawrence, and Adjutant Walter Powers.

Along with the marchers trotted two mascots: Billy, a goat brought back from the border, and Smoke, a dalmatian that had been the mascot of Fire Engine Company 55. Smoke had earned his name by entering burning tenement buildings on the East Side to rescue people given up for dead. Smoke had collected so many commendation medals he could no longer wear his collar. As he turned Smoke over to the care of Pvt. Michael Dineen, firefighter Joe Horack said, "The boys give him up with the sincerest hopes that he will prove a lucky mascot. We only hope that he will detect the whereabouts of the Germans for you boys as quickly and as surely as he has located one of us when we had become lost in the smoke of some fire."[13]

The guardsmen executed a two-and-a-half-mile march to the Thirty-fourth Street ferry slip. Along the way, sidewalks filled with cheering onlookers, family, and friends. Yet an observant Donovan was not impressed with the way the men marched. "They need a great deal of work," he wrote, showing again his disdain for Reed and his idea of the role he, Donovan, planned to play at Camp Mills to turn his battalion into a crack outfit. "I think many of the officers think the regiment is too good, Latham especially. There is needed a lot of work."[14]

At Thirty-ninth Street, a little girl atop her father's shoulders threw a bouquet of red roses into the arms of a young soldier as he swung close to the curb. "They're for you Danny," she cried. He tossed her a kiss and passed the roses to the soldiers beside him.[15] A reporter for the *Herald* wrote, "At times there were odd lulls in the cheering during which the sound of women weeping could be heard." He described tears steaming down faces. "Proverbially an emotional people, the Irish of New York were not ashamed to show that the occasion was one of mingled joy and grief for them."[16]

Joyce Kilmer, still awaiting orders to join the Sixty-ninth, recalled how wives and mothers looked upon the "bright ranks with smiling anguish." He reported that an old woman, unknown to any of the soldiers, burst from the crowd with a green flag embroidered with harp and crown, Ireland's centuries old emblem, and the words "Erin Go Bragh!" She gave the flag to Musician 1st Class William Evers, who hailed from Hell's Kitchen. Evers carried the flag to France and twice it went "over the top"—attached to the end of a bayonet.[17]

Martin Hogan, the orphan, fought back tears as he trooped along with Capt. John Hurley's K Company.

> The strong impressions that we men got from this march . . . were not those of the large, triumphant sort, of the cheering, of the affectionate calls of friends, of martial pride to know that we were on our way into a great, and probably glorious, adventure for home and country, but rather humbler impressions of a chastening sort, impressions of heartbroken mothers, wives, and sisters who tried to force their way by the police to kiss their "boy," a comrade in our ranks, goodby, of fathers who gulped out some choking word of love as their boys swung by with us.[18]

Across Fifth Avenue from the public library a group of women called to soldiers by name. They "frantically waved flags and handkerchiefs and shouted cheering messages," pointed out the *Sun*'s reporter. "Their efforts to be cheerful were even more moving than those of other women who made no secret of their weeping." The reporter went on:

> New York, at least that part of it which saw the "boys" on their way—and it was a goodly part—was thrilled and stirred in a manner it has not known since the days of the Spanish American War. The sight of those unflinching marchers, largely of Celtic descent, and the sight of mothers and fathers and sweethearts nobly giving up their most priceless possession gripped the imagination and tugged at the heartstrings as nothing else could do. One's thoughts turned involuntarily to England and France, especially France, which is already bled of its finest manhood, and wondered how these nations have survived the sight of millions of their sons travelling a similar road.[19]

At the ferry slip, the soldiers boarded the *William J. Gaynor* for the last time and crossed the East River. They jammed onto the deck and sang "Good-bye Broadway, Hello France!" Noted the *Herald*, "Every pier and roof in the vicinity was crowded with spectators who cheered and waved farewell until the boat reached Long Island City."[20] Most of the crowd that had cheered the boys along the line of march was not yet finished. Finding boats of all sizes and designs, they chased the ferry to the other side.

At Long Island City, amid more good-byes and more tears, the regiment was loaded onto special trains for the short trip to Hempstead Crossing. The *Sun* described how one girl, who was "more tightly clasped in her sweetheart's arms than the rest, managed to smuggle herself by the cordon of police thrown about the gates, but even her haven was short lived."[21] Duffy tried to soothe the heartbreak the women felt, consoling mothers and wives and girlfriends, their faces damp with tears. The chaplain assured them that their men would be well taken care of—both physically and spiritually.

As the trains pulled away, heads hung out of windows. Hands touched hands. One man lifted a girl up to a window so she could kiss her man good-bye once more.

The trip to Hempstead Crossing was quick and when the men climbed down from the trains they were met by a tremendous yell bursting from the throats of the more than one thousand employees at Camp Mills. Then a squadron of planes from a nearby airfield buzzed the Sixty-ninth. At that moment, Hine officially took command. He greeted his regiment, carrying a shillelagh—the cudgel a gift O'Ryan had given him along with a note that read, "Your regiment, my dear Colonel, should have at least one orthodox weapon."[22] Hine briefly addressed his troops, telling them, "The proud traditions of the regiment will be respected and perpetuated."

He had hardly finished his address when a sixty-one-year-old man, holder of the Medal of Honor, entered his tent and volunteered. Colonel Webb Cook Hayes, youngest son of President Rutherford Hayes, who had been wounded in Cuba during the Spanish-American War and had then in the Philippines won America's highest award, begged to go to France. He said he wanted to be a soldier in the Sixty-ninth more than any other regiment. Alas, Hine had to turn down the old warrior's request.

The New Yorkers were the first contingent of the Forty-second Division to arrive at the cantonment. Units from Wisconsin and Ohio, which along with the Sixty-ninth completed the Eighty-third Infantry Brigade, had been delayed. In the meantime, transfers from New York's other outfits, including men from the Fourteenth and Twenty-third Regiments, were due in a few days. Their arrival would mean trouble, and so would the arrival of the 167th Infantry, the old Fourth Alabama that had last met the Sixty-ninth on the field of battle in such places as Bull Run and Gettysburg.

6

"It's a Huge Regiment Now"

C amp Mills was named in honor of the late Albert Mills, who had served in the Spanish-American War and received a Medal of Honor for rallying his men after taking a bullet through the head and being temporarily blinded. After this, he had been superintendent of the U.S. Military Academy and before his death in 1916 had drawn up plans for federalizing the National Guard. The camp itself—one hundred twenty acres on what is known as Hempstead Plains—had been built on the site of another training cantonment, Camp Black, where troops headed for Cuba in 1898 had received their training. Several of the older veterans of the Sixty-ninth were familiar with the site because they had been sent there when the regiment had been mustered into service during the Spanish-American War. The task of remaking Mills into a place to drill thousands of untrained soldiers in the art of modern warfare had fallen to the Army engineers. Once it was ready, pioneer units from the 165th Infantry, mostly from the Third Battalion, went to work setting up tents for their comrades-in-arms back in the armory in Manhattan.

As Pvt. Al Ettinger, one of the Pioneers, put it, "It was laborious work, but we went at it with zeal, feeling rather proud to erect the first squad tents at Camp Mills." They ate boiled beans, pork fat, and canned corned beef stew. "Men soon sickened from the greasy pork, and we were assaulted with an epidemic of boils. However, we persisted, and it was a happy day when the last squad tent was in place."[1]

After the first night, Father Francis Duffy remarked, "We are tenting tonight on the Hempstead Plains, where Colonel Duffy and the old 69th encamped in 1898, when getting ready for service in the Spanish War. It is a huge regiment now—bigger, I think, than the whole Irish brigade ever was in the Civil War."[2]

As the regiment grew bigger, so did its problems.

Men from other regiments poured into Mills, many of them angry because they had been booted out of their own outfits. They had enlisted with friends and expected to stay with them in their regiments. Being unceremoniously shipped off to the Sixty-ninth had not been part of their plans.

One contributing regiment, the Seventy-first, had been organized in 1850 as the American Rifles (later called the American Guard) partly to counterbalance the militias formed by the Irish immigrants who flooded into the United States. The Seventy-first had a sterling record in the Civil War and the Spanish-American War, but that did not matter to the War Department. It emasculated the proud regiment, sending its men to shore up not only the 165th, but other regiments, most notably the newly created 105th and 106th Infantries.

"We of the 71st are spiritualists," said Robert Stewart Sutcliffe after the break up of his regiment. "We believe that the old 71st has a spirit—a tangible, live factor. That even though the regiment were wiped out of existence, by disbandment or disintegration, the spirit of the 71st, so interwoven with the history of the Country, the State and the City, would still live and have its influence." He stressed, "When the old 71st was disintegrated in 1917 at Van Cortland Park and at Camp Wadsworth, the soul of the old regiment went marching on."[3]

When the Seventy-first's men arrived at Mills, they strode through camp with a "flea-bitten" Airedale named "Paddy Owen" and belted out "Tipperary," claiming that from now on it was to be their marching song.

Arthur Totten was one of the singing transfers who paraded right into the open arms of the 165th. A resident of 206 West 103rd Street, he had been sixteen when he joined the Seventy-first. A descendant of Gen. Joseph Totten, for whom the fort at Willets Point in Bayside is named, Arthur's great-grandfather was Anthony Bleeker, who had owned a farm in what is now the corner of Bleeker Street and West Broadway.

Before the breakup, the men of the Seventy-first believed that because of its record, efficient discipline, and long history, it would be one of the first regiments to head for France. "This prophecy, however, was not to prove correct," Sutcliffe duly noted. When orders called for three hundred and fifty men to be transferred to the 165th, he recalled the bitterness his fellow guardsmen felt.[4] Yet when they reached the Western Front, transfers like Totten fought with a fury that earned great respect from the Irish regulars. Some forty-four men from the old Seventy-first would die in France while 139 would suffer wounds—for them a casualty rate of more than fifty percent.

Before the disgruntled troops from the Fighting Fourteenth, known in the Civil War as the "Red Legged Devils," had left their regiment on 24 August for the 165th, their commander, Col. James Howlett, a renowned horseman, spoke to them atop an automobile. He warned, "It hurts many of you to go, and many of us to see you go. We have been together, some of us, for years. But we are soldiers. We must be brave. These are the fortunes of war. We must obey orders. It may be for the best. God bless you, men."[5]

The *Brooklyn Daily Eagle* reported that those men selected for transfer had not been told until the last moment. "There was much dissatisfaction among the men in the Fourteenth. They said that they were ready for service in the trenches, but were opposed to leaving the regiment with which they enlisted to fight."[6] For many, their run-in with the Irish soldiers in Mission, Texas, still rankled them. As they left by train, one mother stood on the tracks, wringing her hands; another fainted.[7]

Among the transfers were Jewish brothers, Abraham Blaustein of D Company and Harry Blaustein of C Company, both living with their parents at 423 15th Street, Brooklyn. Another transfer was Alf Helmer, an eighteen-year-old, blue-eyed, blond-haired native of Bergen, Norway. After his switch to the 165th, Helmer believed he was the only Scandinavian in the Irish regiment. In France, he and Abe Blaustein became inseparable following the entombment of E Company at Rouge Bouquet.

On the heels of those from the Fourteenth, transfers from the Twelfth and Twenty-third regiments trooped into Mills. Bitter feelings were everywhere, even among the men of the 165th, who felt many of the new soldiers were inferior, physically and mentally. Duffy was among these, and he later recollected how company commanders and the medical staff of Maj. George Lawrence and his brother, Austin, the dental surgeon, devised ways to send them back home. They came up with "thirty-five distinct damnations," wrote the chaplain, "or almost that many, by which an undesirable can be returned to civilian life to take his chances in the draft. . . . We can get all the good men we want."[8]

An investigation conducted by an aide to Maj. Gen. John O'Ryan proved that the Fourteenth had sent many second-rate men to the 165th. Charges were brought against several officers for the "weaklings and slovenly soldiers" shipped to the Irish regiment. Those men were "undersized, improperly drilled and without regulation equipment."[9] As one newspaper had put it, by not adhering to the War Department's plan of selecting every fourth man, "some units" selected men "promiscuously."[10]

Even though officers of the 165th showed their anger over lowly specimens foisted on them by outsiders they ironically accepted back into the regiment Pvt. William Seiders, a convicted burglar. The 23-year-old Seiders had broken into a woman's home in the Greenpoint section of Brooklyn. He was arrested and convicted, but Judge John Hylan, running for mayor, had suspended his sentence and ordered the burglar to report back to his regiment.[11]

Danny O'Connell, a private in the Twenty-third Regiment's C Company, was one of the better specimens to arrive at Mills. Descended from the famous Irish leader of the same name, Danny had grown up on Rockaway Beach, gone to Public School 44, served as an altar boy at St. Rose of Lima Church, and, in 1916, when he was eighteen, had joined the National Guard for a chance to chase Pancho Villa.

Mary O'Connell, his mother, told a newspaper reporter, "Back in 1916, when we were having trouble with Mexico, Danny used to run to the newsstand the first thing in the morning to see how things were going. I hated to see it, for I knew before long [what] he would be asking to do. Sure enough, one day, he came to me and asked me to sign papers that would let him enlist."

Mrs. O'Connell scolded her son. "Danny," she had said, "You're just a boy and only seventeen and hardly that. Don't be foolish."

But Danny talked his mother into signing the papers anyway, saying that he would forge her name if she did not. "Why, it's only such a little while ago that he was just a slip of a boy," she reminisced.[12]

Leo Throop, of the Twenty-third's Machine Gun Company, had relics at his home in Flatbush that Duffy would have wanted very much to see if he had known about them. Throop's parents had led a pilgrimage to Lourdes in 1895 where his father had converted to Catholicism. Pope Leo XIII, obviously pleased by the conversion, had given Mrs. Throop a trove of religious relics.

As fantastic as it seems, according to the *New York Times*, a sample list included the veil of the Blessed Virgin, a cloak belonging to St. Joseph, and bones from a number of saints including Peter and Paul, Andrew, Augustine, and Francis of Assisi. She had also been given a piece of the true cross and a thorn from the crown of thorns.[13]

Throop, O'Connell, Helmer, and the Blaustein brothers, and a majority of other transfers, found a home in the 165th. Joe Pettit, a lad from Roosevelt, where he had been one of that Long Island city's great athletes, loved being in the old Sixty-ninth. "This fighting game is the best ever," he beamed over one of his first meals in the mess tent. "It was a sad blow to separate from many of the boys, but when I heard that we had been assigned to the 165th and would likely be the first regiment to go off, I felt that my choice was a good one."[14]

On an early Saturday evening after the regiment reached full strength of three thousand six hundred enlisted men (it was still far short of the required number of officers), Duffy conducted his first religious service, a general ceremony for all his men and their visitors. The next morning he held his first mass. He said it would take place rain or shine, commenting with a twinkle in his eye, "You know how the Irish like their religion, with just a little touch of hardship."[15] As the sun rose across the dewy cantonment there was no rain. Troops gathered around their chaplain. He spoke to them all—Catholics and others alike.

I come to you in soldiers' togs, with a message from the Church. I want to be your friend, whatever your religion may be. I know many of you are leaving families behind you and will have many worries. Come to me with them and you will find me ready with a wise word and a merry one. God grant you through this gruesome business of war. Whatever faults this old regiment ever had, it never yet lacked faith and courage. The sun has never been too hot, the rain too strong to drive us from the field when mass was being celebrated. We will be hearing mass before the war is over on ships where our lives will be none too safe; by the smiling streams and on the sunny fields of France, in the shattered cathedrals of the Old World, in the trenches and over the very graves of our own men. God be with us through all the days ahead. I know how you'll fight, men. I have an infinite faith in every one of you. You'll wage your glorious battles like the archangels of God who pressed the demons down into hell.[16]

But even after Duffy's sermon, beneath the shadowy flaps of many camp tents, hundreds of Brooklyn soldiers seethed from the harsh treatment they believed had been dealt them and plotted their way out of the damned Irish regiment.

Two grievances fueled what happened within four days of the merging of the Fourteenth and Twenty-third into the 165th. The newcomers claimed they had signed up with the promise they would fight with their friends. That promise had been broken. Now they felt unwelcome and discriminated against in their new home.

"You see, it's like this," complained one of the boys. "We were asked at the outset to enlist and be with our friends. In many instances, clubs of friends enlisted and wanted to stick together. They felt that if any of them were killed, their chums would send back the account of it to their friends in Brooklyn. In this way they did not mind enlisting, in the belief that they'd stick together through thick and thin. In some cases, brothers were separated when we transferred to the 165th."

The same soldier said, "We Brooklynites who went to Camp Mills found ourselves surrounded by New Yorkers who had been part of the original 'Fighting Sixty-ninth' and these men are treated in the finest fashion. They are looked upon as heroes and all that sort of thing, whereas we Brooklynites are discriminated against right and left."[17]

"None of the men get enough to eat unless they pay for their own food, and many of them are not in a position to do this," another transfer stated. "Non-commissioned officers have been summarily reduced in rank, and the indications are that other reductions will follow. This is the situation with regard to the Fourteenth and it is also true of the Twenty-third. We are all standing solidly together, and intend to fight for our rights if we are sent to the guardhouse to rot."[18]

"We want a square deal and we're not getting it," grumbled another.[19]

When he first drew his pay as a member of the 165th, Abe Blaustein, the Jewish sergeant from the Fourteenth, had reason to agree that transfers were not getting a square deal. The paymaster handed him thirty-six dollars—two dollars short of his buck sergeant's salary.

"Where's my other two dollars?" he asked.

"Don't block the line," the paymaster said. "You're down on the rolls as a corporal and you've got corporal's pay."

"That's what I call a rough deal," Blaustein griped. "They not only transfer me but they make me pay $2 for the privilege."[20] Behind his back and sometimes to his face, a few of the Irish soldiers called him a "Jew bastard." Ettinger was impressed that Blaustein never "turned them in. It was like water off a duck's back." Ettinger thought the Brooklyn sergeant "aloof," but remembered his every manner like that of a "trained soldier," and he would never forget Blaustein's heroics at Rouge Bouquet.[21]

Duffy patrolled the camp, trying to keep peace between the city neighborhoods and to raise the spirits of the soldiers. One day, as he walked among the men, his hands folded on his chest as if in prayer, he came across Bill Fleming of H Company. Fleming looked at him, noticing that the padre was "meditating on things not of this world." Duffy asked Fleming where he was from. The private, married to the daughter of the regiment's drum major, told him in a thick Irish brogue that he hailed from the Bronx.

"No, son," Duffy said. "But before that."
"Oh, Tipperary, Father!"
"I thought so. And your name?"
"Bill Fleming, Father."
"Well, Bill, the Tipperary men are all fine. God bless you."

Somewhat stunned, Fleming watched the chaplain walk away, "communicating with the Almighty."[22]

On 28 August, when other units of the Rainbow Division finally straggled into Mills, as many as two hundred soldiers from the 165th deserted. Three quarters of them fled back to the Fourteenth's encampment at Sheepshead Bay, begging to see Colonel Howlett. After listening to their grievances, he reprimanded them in such a "fatherly" way that, according to one report, "they [wanted] back, without guard, and on their honor determined to face whatever might be ahead of them."[23]

When word of the desertion, described by Brooklyn newspapers as "French leave," spread through camp an officer snapped, "The trouble with these Brooklyn lads is that they don't seem to realize this is war and not a football game. They wanted to be with their friends and have rebelled against authority from the time they became affiliated with the 165th. It is now time for them to prove their manhood and show that they are not Brooklynites first, but Americans and that their duty is to their country, regardless of the hardships."[24]

Sneered another officer, "War is not a game for slackers and whiners."

"Yellow bellies!" cried a third. "The regiment is well rid of these skulkers who are tied to their mothers' apron strings! Thank God we discovered them before our regiment landed in France!"

When deserters slinked into camp a day or so later, men hooted, "Mamma's darlings!"[25]

At least one soldier kept a sense of humor. He chained his dog, Chubby, to his tent. When asked why the pet had been chained up, he said, "[Chubby] took French leave last night, was away for three hours, so he's confined to quarters for three days."[26]

As taunts were thrown at the returning miscreants, military police rounded up the remainder of the deserters. Rumors abounded that many of them were headed for prison at Fort Leavenworth while, even worse, ringleaders, if found out, faced death in front of a firing squad. An investigation was launched. But the episode had hardly died down when the 167th Infantry, the old Fourth Alabama, barged into Mills. The proud regiment, which had battled the Sixty-ninth in the Civil War, showed up with a chip on its shoulder.

The 167th, under command of Colonel William Screws, had rattled out of Montgomery, Alabama, on 28 August, riding in eight special trains. The soldiers left quietly, with little fanfare. What happened when they reached Hempstead Plains almost started a second war between the states.

First Lt. Emmett Smith, the regimental chaplain from Auburn, who never got over his dislike for the Irish regiment, remembered how the boys from New York were standing by their tents when the Alabama troops strode into camp.

These Yankees . . . began to jeer at these Southern boys, calling them boll weevils and all such stuff as that. The first

I know then our ranks just melted and every fellow had them a Yankee. They pulled the tents down and gave 'em quite a whipping, and their colonel came out and found where our colonel was and he went up there and begged him to get his men out of there—out of his camp. Said they were tearing my camp up, but we got them out. They had a few bruises and some lacerations on their scalps, but they never did pick another row with the boys from Alabama.[27]

A few days later, two companies of the 167th broke past their own guards and attacked guards of the 165th. Reported the *New York Age*, an African-American newspaper, "The fight between the New Yorkers and the Alabamians raged fast and furious for several minutes and ended with the Southerners being forced back to the Alabama camp, carrying bruised bodies and sore heads."[28]

The Alabamians were ready to fight anyone, especially blacks, and within days of their arrival a number of them went into nearby Hempstead and attacked every dark-skinned person they saw. A reporter for the *New York Herald* described how the Southerners "engaged in pitched battle with as many negroes on the main street of Hempstead."[29] Later, they attacked black train porters, even gouging out the eye of one of them and tossing him out of the train.

Over in the 150th Machine Gun Battalion from Wisconsin, twenty-year-old Sgt. Bill Heiss of Appleton remembered the Alabama troops. "They're country the whole bunch. Got head lice and gray backs. Positively the dirtiest, filthiest gang of supposed to be men I ever saw."[30]

Alabama's William Amerine explained what had made his fellow soldiers so testy. An epidemic of measles and mumps and even meningitis had ripped through the 167th, forcing the Alabamians to be quarantined almost as soon as they had reached camp. "While the entire organization was confined to the limits of the camp," Amerine wrote, "several ugly rumors were maliciously circulated to the effect that the men were undisciplined and out creating trouble. The ban was not lifted for six weeks. Too, a very insignificant scrap of a personal nature, between small groups of Alabamians and New Yorkers started a lot of baseless criticism against the former."

It is said the men of the 165th . . . would tell incoming organizations: "The Alabamas are coming over and clean you out." A specific case is cited that when the negroes of the 15th New York arrived the whites from the same state ran out and embraced the blacks, repeating to the latter the warning: "The Alabamas are coming over and clean you out," which caused the 15th that night to have a call to arms, though men of the 167th at the time were all sleeping soundly.[31]

Ettinger recollected how "fist fights erupted at the taverns in Hempstead where the fellows hung out." He also recalled the attack against his own men and how the military police drove the Southerners back with bayonets, stating that "one of the Alabamians was killed. It was hell to pay, but finally the officers of both regiments and Father Duffy in particular, calmed down the situation."[32]

The epidemic that put the Alabamians on edge proved costly and a handful of their soldiers died. The division's assistant surgeon blamed the rampant illnesses that swept through the 167th on the fact that "nearly all the boys [were] from the mountains and rural districts and as soon as they hit camp they began to have their baby diseases."[33]

For the 165th, its first death might have been avoided.

Pvt. George Neff was a transfer from the Seventy-first Regiment. To get into the National Guard he had lied about his age, saying he was forty when in fact he was forty-seven. In civilian life he was a cashier at Tiffany's. He was married and had a four-year-old son. Rumors said he and his wife were estranged. He had gone to his home at St. Nicholas Place in Manhattan for a day's leave. When he returned to camp he told his "top kick," 1st Sgt. Bill Bailey of E Company, that he was glad to be in the Rainbow Division and was ready to go "Over There." Yet some of his friends thought him morose.[34] During drill he acted strangely. He was reprimanded several times. Finally he stepped out of the ranks, placed his rifle on the ground, barrel up, leaned his head over the barrel and pulled the trigger.

Still, there were many happy times at camp and Duffy noted one type of happy occasion in his diary. "I have become a marrying parson," he wrote. "Love and fighting seem to go together—they are the two staples of romance."

The chaplain had erected a church tent in which he conducted mass, heard confessions, and quietly married sweethearts. But not all weddings were quiet, as he described in his diary, particularly when Peggy O'Brien and Musician 3rd Class Mike Mulhern, a resident of St. Ann's Avenue in Manhattan and, according to the *Herald,* "th' swatest clarinet player that ever piped Garryowen," were hitched.[35] Before the ceremony, the band escorted the couple, along with Duffy, to his "canvas church." The music caught the attention of thousands of soldiers and camp visitors, and they followed the wedding procession. "So Michael and his bride were united in matrimony before a vast throng that cheered them, and showered them with rice that soldiers brought over from the kitchens of the lads battling with the groom for the privilege of kissing the bride."[36]

A similar wedding to the Mulhern-O'Brien affair took place after the 166th Infantry from Ohio set up camp. According to a newspaper account, "Mary Winter, a pretty young miss from Delaware, Ohio, came on recently to see her lover, Sergeant William Valentine. . . . and yesterday they were made man and wife. Both being Catholics they sought out Duffy, chaplain of the 165th, and were married in the open, on the hill between Clinton road and the first line of tents. The regimental Ohio band played Lohengrin's 'Wedding March' while several hundred soldiers from the Ohio and the 165th regiments witnessed the event. About 1,000 visitors also saw the ceremony."[37]

The chaplain also performed two weddings in secret, honoring the wishes of both grooms that no one be told of the marriages. One of the newlyweds was an aviator training nearby.

A wedding at which Duffy was not the celebrant but at which he assisted, took place in mid-September when Cpl. Joseph Dunnigan of the Bronx, who had grown up in the Gashouse District, married Margaret Crankshaw from Brooklyn. Dunnigan's older brother, the Rev. James Dunnigan, performed the ceremony. Another of Dunnigan's brothers, John J., was best man. John was one of Tammany Hall's political leaders in the Bronx, where for most of his career as state senator he represented that borough's Twenty-third District.

In one week, the village of Hempstead issued a dozen marriage licenses. Reported the *Brooklyn Eagle,* "Some of the brides have come from the Far West to make their soldier-lovers happy."[38]

And when four comely colleens appeared in camp on a Sunday looking for a Timothy Mooney of B Company, another soldier, not Mooney, spotted them and licked his chops. "Ladies," he asked, "can I direct you to any one?" They said they wanted to visit Private Mooney of 239 East 51st Street, Manhattan. "Timothy Mooney?" the poacher gasped. "Why haven't you heard about Tim? He's been made a sergeant and confined to the guardhouse for good behavior. He won't be out until Tuesday, ladies, and in the meantime, now that, you are out here and all, why just step into our tent and we'll tell you all about the war."[39]

In all likelihood, with happy young lovers getting married and romance in the air, Bill Donovan, whose wife was far away in their home in Buffalo, was touched. He begged Ruth to come down to see him, said he was "like a youngster" to see her. "Be well and strong, soon come to me and be a sweet virgin bride again. Learn before coming if we may safely renew our marriage vows. . . . Dearest, you are with me always."[40]

In other letters home, Donovan warned that it looked like the Rainbow Division would not be the first National Guard outfit to reach France. In an undated note to his mother, he wrote, "The rumor today is that the New England Division may precede us abroad and that in fact our ships have already gone to Boston to take them." Bitterly, he told her why. "This is due to the influence of New England gentlemen who wanted to have 'New England' first."[41] At the time he penned the letter, Donovan had no way of knowing that soon a handsome, privileged lieutenant from Massachusetts, the very son of those New England gentlemen, would arrive from the Officers' Training Camp in Plattsburgh, New York, and that, once in France, Oliver Ames Jr. would serve as Wild Bill's trusted aide—from Château Thierry to the costly crossing of the Ourcq River.

7

"The People I Like Best Are the Wild Irish"

"I look forward with dread to the next two weeks," Oliver Ames Jr. wrote to his mother in the summer of 1917. Ames was then an officer's candidate at the military training camp in Plattsburgh. "Commissions are to be decided pretty soon," he explained, "and the strain and worry is terrific and promises to be worse in the coming fortnight; rumors are flying fast, and it is all one can do to keep oneself from believing them." A graduate of Harvard University, Ames was among a group of privileged young men at the camp who, as soon as they had earned their commissions as second lieutenants, would go to the 165th Infantry. What he dreaded was assignment to a non-combat organization, not knowing, of course, that soon his military destiny would be tied to that of Bill Donovan. "I couldn't stand being an officer in the quartermaster corps or ordnance corps. I'd much rather volunteer as a private or else be conscripted."[1]

A handsome youth, the twenty-two-year-old Ames came from a family that it can truthfully be said changed the course of American history. It had provided much of the management, funding, and tools for the construction of the first transcontinental railroad. Ames's great grandfather, also named Oliver, had become president of the Union Pacific after his own business, Ames Shovel and Tool Company of Easton, Massachusetts, had bailed out the bankrupt railroad. A monument to him, the great grandfather, and his brother Oakes that commemorates their role in linking the East and West Coasts by rail, stands in Sherman, Wyoming. The Ameses trace their descendants back to the Mayflower and were related to Theodore Roosevelt and his family, and members of the clan have served Massachusetts as governor, and as representatives in both houses of the U.S. Congress. Thus a sense of duty had been instilled in the youngest Oliver since before his days at St. Mark's School. In college, he had joined the "Harvard Regiment" of more than one thousand student-soldiers—the precursor of the Reserve Officer Training Corps. In 1916, the summer before his senior year, he had set off for Plattsburgh. The following year, with the United States at war, he found himself back at the camp in up-state New York where thousands of men hoped to earn commissions so they could lead others into battle.

"My excitement and enthusiasm for the trenches is unbounded, and I'm keen to go too," Oliver confided to his mother. "And the best part of it is that it's not a morbid enthusiasm but a really constructive and happy enthusiasm; am pleased to death with myself."[2]

Plattsburgh that summer of 1917 was a sure path to a commission for bright, duty-bound men like Oliver who believed their responsibility was, as President Wilson had said, to "make the world safe for democracy." But these men also dreamed that the adventure of their lives awaited them on the other side of the Atlantic. Plattsburgh was an idea that had been shaped several years earlier by men who believed emphatically in military preparedness. Among the guiding forces had been Maj. Gen. Leonard Wood, the former President Roosevelt, and the planning genius Grenville Clark, whose quiet, persuasive demeanor had earned him the sobriquet of "Statesman Incognito." To turn the idea of military preparedness into reality a "Committee of Twenty-one" had been formed. Among its first members were Clark's law partner Elihu Root Jr., Theodore Roosevelt Jr., W. Averill Harriman, the great Princeton athlete Hobey Baker, and two other Princeton men, who on the Mexican border had transferred into the Sixty-ninth Regiment, Charles Baker and Van S. Merle-Smith.

Because he was a Princeton graduate, one of Merle-Smith's tasks had been to go after its alumni and students—to get those men off their duffs so that they would spend their hot summers playing soldier in woolen khaki rather than batting tennis balls or sipping drinks at high-society cocktail parties. The problem for Merle-Smith, as he saw it, was a feeling of "apathy" that had seeped through the entire United States. He described that apathy as "the alarming lack of a sense of responsible patriotism." He wrote that the Committee of Twenty-one "recognized that to bring racial and social groups of our Nation into unified co-operation in time of War, it was necessary to change the critical apathy of our pure blooded Americans to a sense of individual national duty in time of Peace. Talking would not do it. A realization of the personal relation between man and country had to come from action in its behalf. One act at the cost of convenience and pleasure was a large step toward the goal not only for the man himself, but through its vitalizing effect on his community, by example, its purpose and personal cost."

The committee had worked hard, and Merle-Smith was not surprised that when the first so-called "Plattsburg Business Men's Camps" opened in 1911, two thousand men responded to the call. "The most remarkable thing about the Camps was the spirit with which the men went," he wrote. "Everything was attacked with a deep sense of the duty involved, the value of the opportunity and the bigness of the meaning of the whole idea." Plattsburgh was "no place for excuses or a quitter or one who wished to sit critically by and kid the other man doing the work. It was action driven by a vigorous ideal." It made no difference who the recruits had been in civilian life. Rich men, privileged men, business leaders. "Men who had been accustomed to control the actions of a hundred men took orders, and sharp ones, from those half their age, and struggled on perhaps with aching feet and tired bodies. It was these same men who would sit with the light of a campfire, fighting sleep, to pore over books on Minor Tactics to find the mistake made during the day."[3]

In 1917, training in Plattsburgh was divided regionally. The first officer candidates came from New York City. Not all of them were natives of the city; many had come from some place else to work there as bankers, lawyers, and stockbrokers or as rising young businessmen. Some were sons of renowned families, including Theodore Roosevelt Jr. and his brother Kermit. The first contingent of fourteen companies arrived on 12 May. The second group started two days later, 14 May.

Out of the total number, eleven candidates wound up as first or second lieutenants in the 165th Infantry.

One of the eleven was Basil Beebe Elmer, son of a prominent professor at Cornell University, where he had recently earned his degree. A prolific letter writer, Basil, called "Bay" by his fellow students at Cornell, quickly formed a friendship with Oliver Ames when they were assigned to A Company. From his ship, as the regiment sailed for France, he told his parents in Ithaca that "Ames, the second lieutenant of our company, and I are becoming closer friends than ever. He is a fine fellow."[4] Elmer eventually took over the Intelligence Section and there commanded Joyce Kilmer.

Another Plattsburgher was Harper Silliman, the grandson of the publisher of *Harper's* magazine. A third was a Yale engineering graduate, Howard Arnold, son of the president of Arnold, Schiff & Company, manufacturer of parasols. Arnold was one of the few Jewish officers in the regiment. Other Plattsburgh officers were William Given Jr. (also a Yale man) Francis Joseph McNamara, Beverly Becker, Henry Crawford, Philip Lacy, Raymond Newton, Horace Stokes, son of the head of the publishing house of Frederick A. Stokes & Company, and Arthur Bunnell, a Williams College graduate and, at the time of his commission, an advertising representative for the *New York Tribune*.

Not all of New York City's graduates at Plattsburgh made it into a northern regiment. A few of them, like the banker Livingston Parsons, much to their chagrin, found themselves amidst backwoods Alabamians in the 167th Infantry. The Alabamians feud with the Irish threatened to put these new lieutenants at odds with their fellow New York officers now in the 165th. In a letter to his father, Livingston, at least for the moment, did not seem to mind. There were other aspects of his duty as a gung ho tenderfoot officer that occupied his thoughts.

"If anything should happen that 'I should be out of luck' as we call it in the army why you must feel proud and glad that one of yours had given the best he had in him in a good and just cause. I suppose that dying for one's country is about as much as they can ask provided you do it to benefit others."[5]

As more and more officers filled the ranks of the 165th, daily drill at Camp Mills intensified. And other units of the Rainbow Division rolled in, including the 166th Infantry from Ohio (the old Fourth Ohio Regiment) and the 150th Machine Gun Battalion from Wisconsin (three companies of the old Second Wisconsin), completing the make up of the Eighty-third Infantry Brigade. Michael Lenihan, a fifty-two-year-old West Pointer and spellbinding raconteur who had known the generals Ulysses Grant and Philip Sheridan, commanded the Eighty-third. He was the right officer to lead the brigade. For one thing, he was Irish and a devout Catholic, and he took his faith so seriously that on occasion he surprised Father Francis Duffy by serving him at a morning mass as altar boy. For another thing, his troops genuinely liked him. They called him "General Mike." Writing to Cardinal Farley, Duffy said that Lenihan was a "fine man, a thorough soldier and a Catholic to the manor born."[6]

Unlike the 165th, the 166th was a relatively new National Guard organization. It was headquartered in Columbus and commanded by Col. Benson Hough, affectionately called the "Old Man." The regiment had been formed in the mid-1870s as the Fourteenth Ohio in an effort of the state to stem the flood of civil unrest that was then sweeping across the Midwest. On 9 September, the soldiers of the 166th pulled into Camp Mills, stiff and tired from a miserable train ride in which they had been squeezed three to a seat inside Pullman cars. A *Tribune* reporter remarked, "It took eight trains of fourteen cars each to carry the Ohio soldiers and their equipment."[7]

When the 166th finally got to Mills it found itself tenting next to the 165th. A rawboned Ohio farm boy, seeing where the regiment had been billeted and noticing that droves of new officers were arriving from Plattsburgh and elsewhere, grumbled, "As if it ain't bad enough to be hooked up with that crazy Irish crowd from New York, they're goin' to shove off a bunch of them green trainin' camp birds on us fer officers."[8]

The 150th Machine Gun Battalion had pulled into Mills a few days before the 166th, arriving in three special trains. To make up the battalion, three companies had been plucked from the Second Wisconsin Infantry on 16 August—E from Fond du Lac, F from Oshkosh, and G from Appleton—all towns on the shores of Lake Winnebago. Afterwards G became the First Company, E the Second, and F the Third. Men from Oconto, about twenty miles north of Green Bay, served in the Headquarters Company. The commander was Oconto's Maj. William Hall, a former officer in the Second Wisconsin. For many of Hall's men, Camp Mills meant their first time in Gotham and its environs.

One of the machine gunners, Sgt. Bill Heiss, the son of German immigrants and valedictorian of Appleton High School's Class of 1916, who had enlisted in the Second Wisconsin while still in school, was overwhelmed by New York. He wrote to his younger brother about his first excursion into Manhattan.

We found Broadway and Fifth Ave. They are some streets. You might imagine Bdway as a big boulevard, but if you do you will be disappointed when you see it. It's a common ordinary street with lots of theaters and cabarets. At night it's all lit up and makes some sight. Fifth Ave. is some street. Here's where you see crowds and crowds. Autos so thick you can't see how they move. And is all packed with swells.

Heiss had taken the elevator up to the top of the Woolworth Tower, the world's tallest building.

The view of New York, New Jersey, Brooklyn, all the bridges and the harbor + steamship docks was wonderful. . . . It's a long ride up + down and you ought to see the elevators go. Whew but they travel. When they started down I thought my insides were going to come out on me.[9]

Another newcomer to New York was William Semans, a dentist from Ohio's 166th Regiment. In his diary, the twenty-five-year-old graduate of Ohio Wesleyan University wrote how on one of his first days at Mills he also left the camp to tour Manhattan. "Went to New York afternoon. Took bus up 5th Avenue to Polo grounds."[10]

Semans's counterpart in the Irish regiment was 1st Lt. Austin Lawrence, younger brother of Maj. George Lawrence and a dental surgeon. Austin started off in the Tenth New York, but when George took over as chief medical officer of the Sixty-ninth he transferred to that regiment as soon as possible. Austin was twenty-six, already a hero in Flushing, New York, since as a teenager he had twice saved youngsters from drowning in Flushing Bay. In 1906, riding a homemade vehicle he called a "pushmobile," he had captured the first William K. Vanderbilt Cup, a ten-lap race around a Flushing street.

A month after landing at Mills, Austin consulted with Duffy about when he should marry his sweetheart, Cecelia Agnes Rogers, the daughter of a master plumber and herself a third generation Irish American. Duffy, now a professional at romance counseling, advised him that he had better get married in a hurry before the regiment shipped overseas. Lawrence then asked Colonel Hine for a five-day leave beginning 24 September. That day, back in Flushing, he and Cecelia were married, a regular Catholic wedding witnessed

First Lt. Austin Lawrence, a dental surgeon from Flushing, married Cecilia Rogers while at Camp Mills. *Courtesy of Stephen Lawrence*

by close family and friends, including Austin's brothers George and Andrew, a captain in I Company.

After his wedding, Austin set up his dental office at Camp Mills, and he went to work patching up loose, broken, and missing teeth in the bloody mouths of the soldiers now taking rigorous boxing lessons—part of Wild Bill Donovan's instruction in how to defend themselves.

From the moment the 165th departed its armory to train at Mills, Donovan, the former Columbia University athlete, had been determined to whip the men of the First Battalion into prime physical shape. Duffy noted this in his diary. "He is preparing his men for the fatigues of open warfare by all kinds of wearying stunts. They too call him 'Wild Bill' with malicious unction after he has led them over a cross country run for four miles. But they admire him all the same, for he is the freshest man in the crowd when the run is over. . . . I certainly would not want to be in his Battalion."[11]

Joseph Fuhrman, a correspondent for the *Tribune*, alerted his readers that the course of training that had been decided upon would "send the 165th abroad with the fighting spirit of the old 69th strung to its highest pitch." He added that Donovan "has his course of sprouts all planned."[12] In one instance, he divided his battalion into two teams of five hundred men each. He had them strip off their shirts and attack each other. "The maneuver will be just like a great football game," the major informed Fuhrman. "I am having the men go through this thing shirtless so that they will get accustomed to the impact of flesh against flesh. There is lots of that ahead of them."[13]

Donovan also had a pair of tough officers along with an eccentric sergeant to assist him. The sergeant was Jay Casey of C Company. He pushed his men forward in training by cracking a bullwhip over their heads. One of the officers was B Company's Capt. Tom Reilley. The ex-football coach from New York University and Columbia took on the task of teaching the men rudiments of running and hurdling. In C Company, Donovan had the dashing Capt. William Kennelly, a real-estate tycoon who once had been listed as among New York's "handsomest bachelor millionaires."[14] A stickler for detail, Kennelly went so far as to dress down a lieutenant for wearing a wimpy Charlie Chaplin moustache, telling him that such a growth had to be "supplanted by a regular [moustache] or vanish."[15] Kennelly had three chores. The first had nothing to do with physical prowess: he organized French lessons for the men with Cpl. Frank "Watty" Curtis, another of the Princeton men, class of 1909. Kennelly's other chores fit his own sporting background as one of the leading members of the New York Athletic Club (which in later years he rescued from

While in training, soldiers also learned the ancient martial art of potato peeling. *Courtesy of Grosvenor Merle-Smith*

bankruptcy). "He had the build of a runner, clean-cut, trim, alert," Duffy wrote of him. "Brisk is the word that describes him, for the trait is mental as well as physical. . . . I never seen anybody who could get more snap out of a body of men with less nagging."[16] Kennelly organized football games and joined Donovan in teaching the men the art of self-defense. And although a captain, he sparred with his men.

To get started, Donovan ordered more than two hundred boxing gloves. He was anxious for them to arrive so he could strap them onto his men and commence teaching them the finer points of pugilism. According to the *Tribune*, the reason Donovan believed his men had to learn to box was that he "intends to lead the hard-fisted, hard-hitting battalion into the trenches, that will go over the top like back-fence cats and fight like wild ones."[17] Donovan himself explained, "Our men are going to learn that it's possible to fight after it begins to hurt. We want every man to be able to stand up and take punishment like a real fighter. And the bouts will do it. . . . These men will be sluggers who will laugh at bruises. They'll be prepared for that day ahead when they'll need every ounce of endurance and courage for the supreme effort."[18]

He told Ruth about the boxing lessons, but that on the first day the camp was belted by a tremendous storm that tore down most of the tents. A bolt of lightning flattened Latham Reed's tent and sent a flash of blue coursing through the electrical wires in Colonel Hine's tent. "We started our boxing this afternoon," Donovan wrote, "but in the midst of it a rain storm came and we had to streak it for home."[19]

One of the battalion's professional boxers was D Company's Richard O'Neill. Just nineteen in 1917, the five-foot-nine, gray-eyed resident of Harlem had won twelve fights before he enlisted in the Sixty-ninth in June of 1916. He was one of thirteen children, and lived near the Johnson family, Norwegians and non-Catholics, whose pretty daughter Estelle was his girlfriend. He later said of her, "I can't image any man amounting to anything as a soldier unless there is somewhere some woman he loves."[20] The O'Neills and Johnsons, in the words of a family member, were a "step under blue collar." On many occasions young Richard had taken refuge from his abusive father at the Johnson house. O'Neill's father was a ship's carpenter who more often than not was off sailing around the world. When he returned from the sea, he would have a few drinks and beat up his wife. One day, when O'Neill was seventeen, he walked into his house to find his father hitting his mother. O'Neill pummeled his father, his flashing prizefighter's fists knocking the old man into submission.[21]

Richard decided to join the Sixty-ninth because, as he put it, "there was something a little special about the old Sixty-ninth. . . . I think all of New York's Irish was proud of it."[22] Another reason had to do with blood. D Company's 1st Sgt. Edward Geaney was his brother-in-law. "[Ed] was a typical 69th-er," O'Neill said of him, "a strict disciplinarian—a 'top kick' in every sense of the phrase. Our relationship was in name only. It warranted no favors and I received none. Ed was a tough soldier."[23]

Years later O'Neill looked back on Donovan's training technique and said, "He surely worked us that summer at Mills. But I ask you, was there any other way to get us ready for what was coming? And it came fast enough."[24]

To help out with boxing and with all athletic training, the *Irish Advocate* had created a Gaelic Athletic Fund to raise money for the purchase of sporting equipment—but only equipment that would appeal to Irish lads. No baseballs, bats—nothing to do with tennis or any "other such American sports." Martin Sheridan contributed five dollars, praising the fund. The former Olympic champion declared the Irish to be a "vigorous and virile race," saying also that the "national games of a race are its distinctive badges, and when a people have neither national games nor national aspirations their racial deterioration has set in and their racial life is approaching its final termination."[25]

When Roosevelt heard about the First Battalion's instruction in the art of self-defense, he invited its commanding officers to his home at Sagamore Hill in nearby Oyster Bay for a party. The officers were Donovan, Kennelly and Reilley, and captains George McAdie from A Company and James McKenna from D Company. McAdie was a Scot and Duffy described him as "my kind of Scot—like a volcano, rugged to outward view, but glowing with fire beneath."[26] Roosevelt eyed Donovan's men and was comforted because he saw in them "good fighting stuff." He admitted to his son, Archie, that the major would have easily been a lieutenant colonel in his all-volunteer division, if President Wilson had let him raise such a division.[27]

As word of the boxing spread, George Higgins, a fight promoter and the owner of Brooklyn's Pelican Club, sent Duffy two pairs of battered and frayed gloves that had belonged to the late Stanley Ketchell. Dubbed the "Michigan Assassin," Ketchell had been one of the best middleweight champions ever. He had had enough power in his fists to knock out heavyweights, and he had. (But in 1909, while middleweight champion, Ketchell had battled Jack Johnson for the heavyweight title and lost.)

"When you get 'over there' don't hog the gloves," Higgins wrote Duffy. "There is a punch in every one of the four and four times 3,605 [number of men in the regiment] is a total of 14,420 K.O.'s, more or less, and a fair day's work. All take your turn with them and when you reach the enemy's jaw shoot them over straight. Easy work, boys, easy work. The Dutch were never much against the glove ammunition."[28]

In his letters to his mother Donovan described life at Camp Mills in detail. "The work here is hard but it is interesting to see them respond. They are good enough to give me a free hand in making out my scheme of instructions and I feel that I am doing at least a little good."[29]

One of the priorities that Maj. Gen. William Mann and Col. Douglas MacArthur set for their division had been physical fitness, and Donovan had set out to follow through on that priority the moment he set foot in camp.

While the First Battalion strained and sweated under Donovan's regimen, it seemed that the Third Battalion had it easy—so much so that Cpl. Martin Hogan found camp life "routine." In his memoirs he used the word "routine" in three successive sentences to describe what went on. He also noted, "We did practically no shooting all the time we were at Mills. I think the popular idea of the amount of training that we of the 'Rainbow' Division got over here was very greatly exaggerated."[30]

In his battalion's I Company, however, lurked a boxing menace who assuredly could have cleaned the clocks of any of Donovan's boys if he had ever gotten the chance. Big Mike Donaldson, from Haverstraw, New York, worked in the brickyards along the Hudson River. He was built solid as a ship, with shoulders as wide as anyone's in the regiment. As a kid he had tried his fists at boxing and had one day stepped into the ring with Ketchell. Big Mike so impressed the great middleweight that, according to local legend, he wound up as his sparring partner. Donaldson also had one thing that no other man in the old Sixty-ninth had. He had known Duffy longer than anyone—going back to 1897 when he had gone to St. Peter's Church in Haverstraw, Duffy's first assignment. Although he had stayed there less than a year, Duffy remembered the powerful youngster who, along with O'Neill, the other prizefighter in D Company, would distinguish himself in battle. "I have an old friend in Camp in the person of Mike Donaldson," he wrote. "Mike was an altar boy of mine in Haverstraw not long after I was ordained. We both left there, I to teach metaphysics and Mike for a career in the prize-ring, in which he became much more widely and favorably known to his fellow citizens than I can ever hope to be."

When George Higgins sent Ketchell's gloves to Duffy with instructions that they be used as "glove ammunition," he had given them to Donaldson who then brought them to his old priest. Recalled the chaplain, "I do not know exactly what [Mike] expects me to do with the relics but I rather feel after his [very moving] speech of presentation that it would be considered appropriate if I suspend them reverently from the rafter of my chapel like the *ex voto* offerings of ships that one sees in seaport shrines."[31]

If Big Mike had an antithesis, it had to be the poet Joyce Kilmer. After weeks of wrangling and wondering, his transfer from the old Seventh Regiment to the 165th Infantry came through—but at a time of terrible suffering, just after the death of his daughter, Rose.

"I am, as you know, a member of the 165th Infantry, U.S., formerly the 69th New York," he wrote to his friend Father Daly as soon as he had arrived at Mills. "I have recently transferred from Co. H to headquarters Co., and exchanged my 8 hours a day of violent physical exercise (almost deadening to the brain, a useful anodyne for me, coming as it did after my grief) for exacting but interesting statistical work. I am called Senior Regimental Statistician, but in spite of all these syllables still rank as a private."

To Daly, who had helped convert him to Catholicism, he added, "Her death was a piercing blow, but beautiful. . . . Certainly Rose makes Heaven dearer to us."[32]

"Poor Joyce brought her little body to us the next day," recalled his mother, Annie. "When I met Joyce I scarcely knew him, he was so changed! We buried her in our plot in Willow Grove Cemetery, and I placed a cross of pink roses over her little grave. Joyce came home with us, and had the last dinner he was ever to have with us! He left at 10:30 that evening."

At the time of Rose's death, Kilmer's wife, Aline, had been in the hospital awaiting the birth of another child. That child, a son the Kilmers named Christopher, was born three weeks after Rose's funeral. When Kilmer settled in with his new regiment his parents visited him at Mills. Wrote Annie, "It was my first experience of a military camp—I cannot write of it."[33] Kilmer, though, thrived on camp life. The poet explained to Daly:

> The people I like best here are the wild Irish—boys of 18 and 20, who left Ireland a few years ago, some of them to escape threatened conscription, and travelled about the country in gangs, generally working on the railroads. They have delightful songs that have never been written down, but sung in vagabond's camps and country jails. I have got some of the songs down and hope to get more—"The Boston Burglar"— "Sitting in My Cell All Alone"—they are fine, a veritable Irish-American folk-lore. Before I was transferred to headquarters Co., I slept in a tent with a number of these entertaining youths and enjoyed it tremendously. We sang every night.[34]

In another letter, Kilmer told Daly that he had learned how to be a typist, and that "I'm going to get Fr. Duffy to let me pinch-hit for his orderly at mass some mornings. So I'll be an accomplished cuss when I come back from the Wars—I'll know how to typewrite and serve Mass and to sing the Boston Burglar."[35]

And Kilmer was right, those wild Irish boys sang and fiddled and danced every night, long after "Taps" ordered them to turn in. Of an evening, with the company streets lit by a silvery moon and the white tents crowded along each way aglow with stove fires, the boys gathered. The fiddlers among them got the boys high-footing to Irish jigs. Dancing shadows flickered off the tents. And then, when the dancers had their moment, a tall lad, Irish born, stepped out from beneath his tent. Except for the fiddling, a hush settled over the company streets, and the tall lad sang.

Tom O'Kelly of C Company, his voice compared to that of the popular Irish tenor, John McCormack, always quieted the boys, and soothed them with their beloved ballads. "Here, boys, wind me up," he began. "The Lootenant is callin' for his phonograph." And then he sang "The Old Boreen," "Limerick Girls," "Father O'Flynn," "Molly Brannigan," and other songs. The "Lootenant" was Henry Kelley of Brooklyn, and he called O'Kelly his "phonograph." O'Kelly had arrived from Ireland by way of England eighteen months earlier. He had fled the British Isles because he feared conscription. He had settled in Chicago and had made a living there. "I was treated right over here," he said. "The people were kind to me and received me well. I made money and the country seemed square. Then Uncle Sam went into the fight, and though I may not know what for, I'm going with Uncle Sam. The country goes in and I'm going with the country."[36]

The rumor Wild Bill had earlier passed on to his mother that the New England National Guardsmen, the Yankee Division, would beat the New Yorkers to France turned out to be true. He announced that fact to a friend on 12 September. "26 ships of New England troops left Friday."[37] Nearly six more weeks would pass before orders for the Rainbow Division to embark for Europe would come down from the War Department.

8

"A Willing, Bright, Strong, Clean Lot"

"Orders at last," Father Duffy exclaimed to his diary on 28 October.[1] "It was a welcome change, our move from Camp Mills," Martin Hogan remembered. He remembered, too, that once under way, the boys lost the restlessness that had pestered them throughout their training days on the Hempstead Plains. "Camp Mills was drudgery, not adventure."[2] Now the Rainbow Division was truly off to war, and once on the high seas there was no turning back.

Orders for the division's departure had the men leaving from the ports of New York, Hoboken, and Montreal, on different dates. Al Ettinger recalled how "Each unit had its own schedule and, without warning, would simply disappear overnight."[3]

The first contingent, including division headquarters and the 166th Infantry from Ohio, left on the night of 18 October, with scant training in weaponry and, in many cases, with barely enough uniforms to go around. Winter would soon close in and the soldiers still needed sweaters and mufflers and socks. The boots issued them, as became evident, were of inferior quality. Before leaving, Lt. William Semans went into Hempstead and bought supplies and warm clothing. In his diary entry that night, the Ohioan wrote, "Moved at 3:00 A.M. from Camp Mills to Long Island city by train. Took ferry up to Hoboken. Saw all points of interest along way. Passed under Belle Isle, Williams, Brooklyn bridges and saw the Statue of Liberty for the first time. Embarked on ship Castereus. Sailed from port at 8 P.M. Passed the Statue of Liberty at 8:50. Anchored in the bay."[4]

The Division's Chief of Staff, Douglas MacArthur, sailed on the *Covington* for St. Nazaire. Part of the voyage was "bleak and nerve-racking." There were endless drills, space was cramped, he later reminisced, and because of the threat of attack, at night lights were forbidden. "In a running sea it is a real sensation to grope around decks in the darkness."[5]

By the time the entire 165th had cleared out it was near the end of October. Duffy recalled how Maj. William Donovan's First Battalion "slipped out quietly in the night," bound for Montreal. He accompanied Donovan's men to Canada and then returned, to sail a few days later from Hoboken. On the way up he had observed that they were "in gleeful spirit, glad to have the wait over and to be off on the Long Trail."[6]

Before the Irish troops left Long Island, families and friends had come to Camp Mills for a last good-bye. A farewell dance took place at the Garden City Hotel. Officers and their wives and sweethearts, wearing scented gloves, held tightly to each other, dancing slowly round and round the crowded ballroom.

Before the dance started, Capt. William Kennelly, the dashing millionaire bachelor, addressed them all, especially the lovers to be left behind:

> We leave you, our friends, with a smile on our faces and joy in our hearts. Music is in our ears, and as we go into battle we shall hear your ringing laughter and fight the harder. Our farewell dance will be our last good-bye. Make it happy as you can for us, and always remember that last dance—'Send Me Away With a Smile.' It is a time for rejoicing—not sorrow. We are happy in the thought that before long we have done our duty, licked the Kaiser—and then you can welcome us home with a dance. On with the dance! Strike up the band! It's our last good-bye!

At eleven a bugler strode into the ballroom and blew "Taps." For a moment confusion came over the dancers, until Col. Charles Hine ordered the orchestra to play "Send Me Away With a Smile." When the song ended, "Taps" was played again. The throats of the soldiers tightened. Girls cried, dabbing at their eyes. They removed their scented gloves and gave them to their men. And as the soldiers departed the ballroom, they pressed the gloves to their hearts.[7]

The departure of 2nd Lt. Harper Silliman of F Company left his wife, Gertrude Silliman, alone to raise four children. When Harper had told her he was off to join the army she felt abandoned. Both her mother and her father-in-law had recently died. She thought to herself, "Would you really go and leave me like this?" Harper had said, "It is an unfortunate time, but war is war, and cannot wait upon convenience."

"But what shall I do?" she cried.

"Oh, you'll get along," he said.

Now that he was leaving, Gertrude, with a nursing baby in her arms, rode the night train from Manhattan and then took a car to the camp. Her aunt and uncle went with her and took care of the child so she could find her husband. "It was like hunting for a needle in a haystack, to find one khaki clad soldier among the hundreds swarming in all that sea of tents." She feared he had already sailed. "Then all at once he came and stood before [me], so handsome in his uniform." Gertrude said she could hardly believe her eyes because "they were too full of tears to see him clearly." They walked together back to the baby. Harper then held his youngest child.

After a moment, he said to Gertrude, "I must go back now. I may not see you again."

They embraced silently for a long time and then as he pulled back he said, "Oh, you don't know how I love you." They were the last words Harper spoke to her. He turned and walked away.

When she got home, Gertrude wrote to him. "The wide deep dangerous ocean will soon be between you and me—but oh! I love to think that our spirits are closer & closer together & that we love each other more & more thru' all the dangers & trials & sorrows that we have passed thru' & are now passing thru'."[8]

Joyce Kilmer's wife, Aline, their son, Kenton, and his parents arrived separately to Mills to see him off. The parents arrived first and found him in his tent. When it was time for all of them to go, the Kilmers offered to drive Aline and Kenton to Grand Central Station where they would catch the train back to their home in Larchmont Manor. Kilmer's mother recalled,

> Before I got in the car I said, "Aline, you may kiss him last," though had I known it was to be the last time his dear lips would touch mine, I doubt if I could have been brave enough to have said it, though I thought it was her right. He kissed me as had been his custom for many years,

first on the mouth and then on the left cheek—always that cheek! Then I got in the car. He kissed Aline and she got in beside me; as we were taking her to the 42nd Street Station. He stood at the window of the car. I can see him so plainly as I write! His dear brown eyes looked so steadily in mine—then at his wife—but last, at me, thank God! There was something in that look which sent a cold chill all through me, though I would not let myself realize what that look meant. A handshake with his father, and I saw him no more. No more!![9]

Kenton's recollection was different. "When my father was at Camp Mills . . . expecting to sail for France with the Rainbow Division he said a farewell to my mother and me. Kissing me goodbye, he said, 'Don't let any other man kiss you until I come home and kiss you'."[10]

Basil Elmer's parents did not come down from Ithaca to bid him good-bye. The first lieutenant sent them a letter, telling them of the "exciting" secrecy of the orders. He warned, "Don't expect to hear from me for two months at least. . . . For me the whole game is the best sport every minute. The life is ideal from every viewpoint, and agrees with me perfectly." In an earlier letter he had talked of the "great adventure, the whole thing teeming with excitement and romance."[11]

On 29 October, Dental Surgeon Austin Lawrence wrote in his diary, "Entrained at 11:30 A.M., train to L.I. City, Ferry to Hoboken. On board ship at 3 P.M. Old H.A. Line 'Amerika' now 'America.' Stateroom with [Alfred] Landigran & [John] Rowley of 'M.' Had good supper. Bed about 10 slept solid."[12]

Joseph Jones, whose Headquarters Company was headed for Montreal, departed camp on a sour note. He and his sweetheart—who had the grand-sounding name of Amelia Veronica Magdelena Fatthauer, but who simply went by Helen—had an argument when they said good-bye. Because her parents had been born in Bavaria, she had been upset that he was sailing away from her to kill Germans. Their good-byes said, fretting over whether Helen would wait for him, he wrote in his diary for the first time on 5 November in a staccato style like a machine-gun burst. "Reveille 4 A.M. Entrained 8:11 A.M. Two Co's Alabama guard. L.I. City. Doubled back on N. tracks. Springfield. New Hampshire. Vermont. Beans. 'Sandwich'. 2 A.M. Police the Train! Montreal 6 A.M. 6:55 Ascania.

Drift out about 11." The next day he wrote, "Lay all night in the middle of St. Law."[13]

D Company's Richard O'Neill, the former boxer, also left a sweetheart behind, Estelle Johnson. He carried a photograph of her always, keeping it pressed against his heart. As part of Donovan's First Battalion he had gone to Montreal before Jones. "Left Camp Mills Oct. 25th, '17," he noted. "Crossed Canadian border 26th, boarded ship Tunisian morning of 28th, 3 A.M. Left 7 A.M. from Montreal. Sailed down St. Lawrence."[14]

Also in Montreal, Donovan left without an embracing good-bye from his wife. He had written his mother, telling her "I am crazy to see Ruth before I leave. It will be impossible for me to get to Buffalo or even to New York." He had hoped Ruth might go to Garden City, where there was an "excellent old time hotel." But he added, "Above all, I don't want her here when we pull out! It will be done at night and she would awaken and find me gone."[15]

George Patrick McKeon from Brooklyn had neither a girlfriend nor wife to fret over. Instead, the twenty-three-year-old E Company soldier fretted over his eldest sister Daisy, who had been taking care of the family ever since their mother died in 1914. Their father was blind and had not been able to offer any support for twenty years. Daisy was unable to come to camp to see him off, so he wrote her. "Dear Sister, Just a line to let you know we are going on our way. So goodby till I return. And light a candle in the church so that we get over safe. Lovingly, Brother George." He signed off with x's—four rows of seven—for Daisy and his other siblings and relatives.[16]

The last out of Mills was Hogan's Third Battalion, commanded by Maj. Timothy Moynahan. Duffy liked Moynahan, describing him as the "ideal of the Irish soldier, as he comes down to us in history and in fiction. . . . A soldier born—trim, erect, handsome, active in his movements, commanding and crisp in his orders. . . . A vivid interesting character in our drab modern life. He has one fault—a flaring Irish temper when military discipline is violated or high ideals belittled."[17] Ettinger liked him as well. He had found him a "strict, but good-natured officer who was quite the dandy, with a black, waxed moustache turned up at the ends. Moynahan spoke with a loud distinctive brogue that could be heard a block away." Ettinger tells the tale of how, on guard duty one midnight in France, he saw a man came around a turn in a trench. Ettinger ordered him to stop. It was Moynahan, and he snapped at Ettinger,

"My God, man. Don't you recognize the footsteps of your own major?"[18]

As Moynahan's men entrained for Long Island City, Hogan felt a "buoyant spirit about us as we made ready to take up the 'long, long trail.' The men were in high fettle, full of that American merriment that enlivens the American man when bent on taking a chance."[19]

Part of the merriment spilled over in L Company, when the soldiers there said good-bye to the sons of their captain, Van S. Merle-Smith. Instead of calling them by their Christian Dutch and English names, Van Santvoord and Fowler, they affectionately gave them the Irish monikers of Pat and Mike respectively, and for the rest of their lives they were always known by those names. In a farewell letter to Van Santvoord, Merle-Smith referred to him as "young Pat." He wrote, "Dear Pat this is a note of greeting and goodbye from your big soldier father to his little son who must follow in his father's footsteps and fight each battle to the finish whether its to be won or lost." He told the toddler that he must never quit, must look after his mother and love her as hard as he could, and must "always tell the truth." Then, "Don't forget your father. . . . Good bye little tyke, your father's life is bound up in you and your mother so take good care of yourself and her for his sake."[20]

The Shamrock Battalion boarded the *America*, a captured German transport originally named *Amerika*. When it left the pier in Hoboken, the transport sailed up the Hudson River and then dropped anchor opposite Ninety-fourth Street, and stayed there. Chortled one comedian, "They're going to take us to the Catskills and send us after old 'Heinie' Hudson and his gang."[21] Lawrence jotted down, "Stopped in bay till about 9:00. Then went on. Supposedly 7 destroyers, 1 dreadnaught, & 2 armored cruisers, convoying this ship, the Agememmon, Powhattan, Mt. Vernon & one other ship. Did nothing much all day. Went to Confession tonight. Bed at 10."[22]

When the troops awoke, the next morning the *America* was at sea with no land in sight.

And so the entire "Rainbow" Division plowed across the North Atlantic, setting sail on different dates and in different convoys, in some cases even with regiments divided and plying separate sea-lanes—under some of which German U-boats lurked. Several transports headed for Brest or St. Nazaire, others pushed on to Liverpool. But in the end they all met up on the other side.

As the *Tunisian*, a passenger liner and not a troop transport, churned toward the mouth of the St. Lawrence River, Donovan got to know its captain. "He is a short plain agreeable Scot who has been handling troop ships at Salonika and the Dardanelles. A gentleman all over." Accompanying the American soldiers were an Indian prince who looked "as old as Indian civilization" and was attended to by a young man in Indian garb; a Canadian general and a British naval captain; a nurse; and the young chaplain of a regiment from Newfoundland. On the first Sunday out, Donovan had the chaplain say mass for the men.

Donovan found the ship's small size a drawback. "It is difficult to drill and discipline the men" he complained. "I have insisted that the officers give their entire time to the men at the sacrifice of their own." Another problem on board was the scarcity of deckhands and waiters. Most of the crew were teenagers, and Donovan had been forced to use some of his own men in the galley to help dish out food. At least he had someone to wait on him hand and foot. "I have a striker, a man who was valet for Col. Vincent Astor for 12 years. My clothes are kept clean."[23]

Although the ship was small, Donovan insisted on boxing lessons for his men. "I have been taking up boxing and enjoy it," Elmer informed his parents. "The major knows it scientifically, if I can use the term, and is a good teacher. We spar together every afternoon."

In the meantime, Elmer felt that he and the men in his platoon were getting to know each other "very well." He knew them all by name and by their characteristics. "They are young, but a willing, bright, strong, clean lot, and it is a pleasure to have them mould into my idea of soldiers, under my own hands. There are many mischief makers and jokers sometimes. None in my platoon are vicious or stubborn. All are just sturdy + typical American boys between the ages of 18 and 28 and are most dependable. I have absolute confidence in them + there will be no reason to shake my confidence."

And, Elmer said, when British and Canadian veterans spun their war stories late at night—especially one gory account of the battle for Vimy Ridge given by a major in the Toronto Highlanders— "We officers just eat up such tales."[24]

Eager to get into the fight, D Company commander, Capt. James McKenna, had told a New York newspaperman before climbing aboard ship that he firmly believed he was not coming

back, "There are a lot of boys here . . . who will never see old
New York again." McKenna continued: "All I ask is a chance to
get six Germans. I am entitled to it. I can lick six Germans in a
stand-up fight, one after another or all in a bunch. This isn't boasting. I can name dozens of men in the regiment who can do the
same thing. . . . The American soldier thinks as well as fights. He
is a natural born fighter, and the average soldier is a general in
any kind of mix-up."[25]

A storm struck the *Tunisian* on 5 November. The ship rolled
from side to side. Waves poured over the decks. Elmer was with
Donovan when the major was "thrown down on the deck and
cut his nose so that four or five stitches were necessary, but the
doctor said he couldn't touch [Donovan] until the sea quieted
down."

Elmer deepened his friendship with 2nd Lt. Oliver Ames Jr.,
who was in his company. "Baron Waldorf Astor is a great friend of
his family and if we can get away while in [censored], he and I are
going to the Baron's castle outside of [censored] for a [censored]."
Before the voyage ended, he sent a letter to his girl friend. To his
father he confessed, "Today I wrote to K. telling her that it was
the last she would receive from me. I told her not to wait. It was a
hard letter to write. . . . Remember that I shall always love her a
little."[26]

As for Ames, he thought the heavy seas looked forbidding and
the *Tunisian*, even if it was a refitted liner, left a lot to be desired.

> If you ever want to appreciate your family and friends, just
> try a three-thousand-mile trip across the ocean in a rotten
> little tub, a huge life preserver with you every minute, and
> a feeling every minute that you may have to swim for it,
> and the water looking oh! So cold, to say nothing of the
> glorious future of participating in an allied drive in the spring
> which may bring you glory and martyrdom; I wonder how
> I like to be a martyr; my chief occupation on the trip has
> been one long attempt to persuade myself I'll like it.[27]

The recollections of Spencer Rossell, a New York University
man who had shipped over to the old Sixty-ninth from the Seventh into A Company, differed. It was a voyage of "ideal [weather
conditions], sunshine and calm," he wrote to a friend in Brooklyn.
"The breezes were warm and sea behaved so well that not a man

was seasick." Rossell slept in a stateroom, although he said it was a second-class cabin. He found it comfortable. According to Rossell, there was an English convoy guarding the *Tunisian* made up of "monsters of the deep."[28]

A board the *America*, Hogan observed that there were four transports, the "reassuring battleship South Carolina and a few sharp-visaged, wasp-like submarine chasers. The smaller boats were stationed one on each side ahead and one on each side behind, and thus they danced along with us day after day, merrily, arrogantly, scornful of the German sea-adders said to be infesting all the deeper waters of the North Atlantic."[29]

"Absolutely black on deck tonight," wrote Lieutenant Lawrence. "No lights or smoking on deck. Great precautions taken. All matches & flashlights taken from men. Change course & speed every 8 minutes. Phosphorous in water a great sight. Especially in wake of ship."[30]

"The seas were calm, and sailing on the *America* was like taking a trip on the end of the dock—you had to look over the side to realize she was in motion," Duffy wrote. "No submarines, though we were on constant watch for them."[31]

Soldiers pulled submarine lookout duty, watching for telltale signs of enemy U-boats. Ettinger hid from officers so that he would not be detailed as a lookout. "The fellows not on lookout were either singing, playing cards, or shooting craps when the officers weren't around," he recollected. "You'd have thought we were on a grand picnic."[32]

T he whole time the Forty-second Division was on the high seas, events in Europe were changing the course of the war and even threatening the Allies' chances for victory. The Bolsheviks had gained control of Russia. Lenin, now in power, had negotiated a separate armistice with the Germans. By December, the Germans would begin to shift divisions from the Eastern Front to the west to gain numerical superiority over England, France, and Belgium. When they finished they would have 136,000 officers and three and a half million men of other ranks. They planned to strike hard and fast before the Americans built up enough forces to be a factor in the war's outcome. From 24 October until 12 November, a combined Austrian-German army had inflicted severe casualties on the Italians at Caporetto. Afterward, the dismayed Allies realized they needed a supreme war council to give them unity of command. It would not be until spring that Gen. Ferdinand Foch would be named commander-in-chief of all Allied forces.

And on the drizzly, cold morning of 6 November, the blood of American soldiers was spilled for the first time in combat on the Western Front. A German raiding party slipped into the Yankee trenches in the Sommerviller sector near Bathelémont, a supposedly quiet chunk of land. The Germans captured eleven soldiers of the Second Battalion of the Sixteenth Infantry but left three dead, their throats slit so deeply by trench knives that their heads were nearly severed.

All this happened before the New Yorkers reached Europe, ready and eager to fight but unaware of the horrors that lay in wait.

9

"Not a Gloomy Man in Town"

The moment the Forty-second Division hit the shores of Europe in the first weeks of November it was sent toward the city of Nancy; to the training area at Vaucouleurs—to be billeted in the surrounding villages; among them Broussey, Naives, Sauvoy, Vacon, and Villeroy-sur-Meholle, each about forty miles west of the Lunéville sector and twenty-five miles south of the Argonne forest. The arrival of these twenty-seven thousand Rainbow soldiers gave Gen. John Pershing a total of 125,000 men on the ground in France. He was caught in a struggle with the desperate Allies as he tried to build an army of his own. They were pleading with him to provide fresh men to buttress their weakened armies. For the most part, Pershing refused their pleas, so that he could hold onto his divisions until there were enough American troops to form an army that could then join the war in full force.

The split-up New Yorkers landed in England and France. Major William Donovan's First Battalion arrived in Liverpool on 10 November. They were hustled off to Southampton by train and did not have a chance to look around England's busiest harbor. Two days later most of the rest of the regiment, including Joyce Kilmer, with Col. Charles Hine and his staff and Father Francis Duffy steamed through a thick fog into Brest.

Recalled Spencer Rossell, "We left the boat, much to our pleasure, to be on land again, and for [censored] days our detachment traveled across to France. We were in second-class coaches, but a la freight." On the way "people would try to overcharge you if possible, but that is one thing I will never stand for."[1] The trip south through England had been so fast that Vivian Commons, formerly of the old Seventh Regiment, informed his mother that he "didn't have time to see Grandmother on the way."[2] Yet Bill

Oligive of A Company, who lived on Prospect Place in Manhattan, found the time to attend church services in Southampton, although to do this he had to slip past marines. When services were over he walked around the city.

From Southampton, the men crossed the English Channel to Le Havre, boarded cramped French troop trains and, on the 15th, after a two-hundred-and-fifty-mile trip, rolled into Vaucouleurs for training.

In Brest, meanwhile, when the *America* nosed into the foggy, crowded harbor, the men on board went up on deck to see the sights. On guard duty, Ted Van Yorx peered into the thick mist when, as he wrote to his mother, "all of a sudden I heard a familiar buzz and then two planes came out to meet us. One of them whizzed right over our boat and you should have heard the boys yell." "The aviator leaned out and waved to them. They kept yelling for about 20 minutes. You should have seen the colored porters. They went crazy. Some of them were crying and others yelling, 'Hurrah. Praise the Lord!'"[3]

According to Harper Silliman, they stood with "open mouths and wide-eyed to drink in all the strange sights." Writing to Gertrude, he said, "I know none of us will deny the relief we all feel to be once more in a safe harbour behind the sheltering guns and destroyers of the Allies. We sleep in pajamas tonight."[4]

Because of the fog, however, the soldiers were held on board for over a week. "Quarantined," growled Martin Hogan. "Marooned in a fog bank in a chill and dreary harbor."[5]

Knowing that the troops were stuck on ship for at least a week, Duffy gained permission to go into the city to "get some necessities for my church work." The chaplain found his way to the nearest church, looking for communion wafers and other necessities. The curate, a very short, heavy-set man with a limp, escorted him to a convent. A "cultivated, balanced and perfectly serene" mother superior invited Duffy to dinner. During the meal the chaplain was grilled about America and what he thought of President Wilson and former President Roosevelt. On the way back to the curate's church, Duffy stopped at a number of stores to purchase the things he needed. Along the way the curate introduced him to people in the street, telling them that here was an American chaplain.

"He has crosses on his collar," the curate said. "Also on his shoulders. If I were taller I could see them. I saw them when he was sitting down."[6]

On ship, Duffy conducted a mass for Catholics and a non-denominational service for Protestants. Kilmer helped, as he wrote to his mother, "Your friend, Father Duffy, would send his love if he knew I were writing to you. He has been doing the work of about twenty chaplains, but seems to thrive on it. Yesterday afternoon he held a service for Protestants, and I typewrote some hymns for distribution—'Jesus, Lover of My Soul,' 'Nearer My God to Thee,' 'Onward, Christian Soldiers' and the like. The service was well attended and the daily masses have been crowded."[7]

When all the troops had finally set foot on French soil they looked around the strange country and recorded their thoughts in letters and diaries—even as they rattled across France in troop trains with the famous "40 Hommes 8 Cheveaux" painted on the sides of the boxcars. Or as the men soon called them "hommies" and "chevoos." Quipped Hogan, "I don't know how forty hommies make out in a French box car, but I do know that forty men find it fairly crowded."[8] For the long ride, soldiers received rations for three days of corned willie and hard tack—smelly corned beef out of a tin and unleavened bread—water, and a pinch of salt.

In Headquarters Company, Sgt. Abraham Blaustein efficiently herded his men into boxcars, although one of them, Al Ettinger, wanted to make friends with the French ladies lingering near the soldiers. Casting a lustful eye at the women, Ettinger and his fellows "definitely wanted to demonstrate Irish-American goodwill toward our French allies. Unfortunately, it was not to be."[9]

Cpl. Leo Throop, whose parents had converted to Catholicism after a pilgrimage to Lourdes years earlier, announced his safe arrival in France.

> Well, after landing we traveled for seventy-two hours in freight cars. (You remember the French freighters, not as big as moving vans in the States.) Well, forty-two humans were thrown into each car and away we started. We passed through [censored], but not Paris. One thing I must say, the train was very fast all the time. At various points along our route we were allowed to get out for exercise (once a day) for fifteen minutes, and twice a day for hot coffee, but when we got it it was cold, and three times we got none.[10]

Kilmer portrayed the train trip as "Three days and three nights of such travelling as no soldier of the 69th can ever forget."[11]

Sanitary Detachment's John Grady, a private from the Greenpoint section of Brooklyn, wrote to the Jefferson Democratic Club of the Seventeenth Ward. "We were constantly seeing new people and new scenery. We were royally received all along the line, and the attitude of the people showed us that we were indeed welcome." When the train passed railroad stations, Grady spotted "groups of French soldiers returning from the trenches and others going to them. The people in some of the little towns are indeed quaint in appearance. They recognized the 'Old Glories' carried by our men and cheered at them."[12]

Basil Elmer told his father, "The contrast between France of today and France as we knew it back in 1909 is marked, but all are cheerful in their righteous cause."[13]

Cpl. Robert Emmett Coughlin of I Company, a transfer from the Twenty-third Regiment, complained of the rain. "The country in France is beautiful and I only wish we had a few days of sun to show it up. One thing I have noticed particularly is the scarcity of men working in the fields. Women are seen almost entirely working in the open at heavy work, and this seems strange enough to us Americans."[14]

After the long, wearying trip from Brest to Vaucouleurs, L Company's Pvt. Harry McLaughlin, a Harlem lad, and his brother Danny, were happy to be off the packed trains, although the view from the train they were in had been "fine." Writing to a friend in Brooklyn, Harry said, "It took us three days and three nights from when we got off the ship until we arrived at our destination, which is a small town with a church and about 10 houses, and half the houses are vacant, but we are living in them and when the rest of the company gets here they'll take the rest of the vacancies."[15]

Throop recalled the arduous train ride and how, after reaching their destination, the men were held inside the car overnight. "When morning came it brought with it the worst rain I ever saw or felt, and we had to march (with our baggage) eight long miles in it. Believe me, a mile never looked so long before, but it is all part of the game."[16]

The weather on the ride had been bad enough for Ettinger later to remember how the wind and water howled up through the floorboards and swept in through open doors. And at the end of their journey, when they climbed down from the boxcars they "tumbled into the pouring rain." It took Ettinger two weeks to dry out, because it was "that long before we got any sunshine, and we were prohibited from having any kind of fire in our billets."[17]

When Donovan arrived at the training area, he set up his temporary headquarters in a home owned by a war widow with a son at Verdun and a niece at home who, the major felt, was "partly eaten away by cancer." The widow was "very agreeable and old and motherly." Around him in the small village his troops were billeted in barns in groups of from ten to as many as thirty. With the weather already turning cold and damp, the major asked Ruth to take his fur coat to a good military tailor, and have it turned into something "snappy" along the lines of an English trench coat. He wanted it to reach to his knees, but also wanted the fur collar to show on the outside.[18]

Throop informed his family that the billets were "hay lofts of barns. I am in charge of Billet No. 9—ten men, including myself, and a splendid bunch of fellows they are. With us live three horses, two cows, two pigs, rabbits, chickens and a dog." He described the barn as having a roof with holes in it large enough to stick your head through.[19]

The villages the men now occupied were close enough to the front lines for the men to hear and feel the rumble of artillery, a reminder of how close the war was to them. In spite of that constant threat, once they settled down in their new surroundings they sought out the little pleasures in life: candy, cigarettes, and wine.

"Tobacco and sweets are next to impossible [to find]," grumbled Sgt. W. C. Comstock, " but I think things will pick up by and by." He discovered that wine was cheap. "We are allowed to go in these wine halls and get whatever we want, and I was surprised at the way the boys drank." The wine he tried "so far tastes just like the old claret we used to get in New Orleans, and a glass of it now and then goes pretty good."[20]

One soldier wrote gloomily to the *New York Sun* that "the wine has given out and all you can buy is French beer, so it looks like a quiet winter, with the lid clamped down tight."[21]

It did not take Commons long to write home, saying, "I nearly forgot something important. I wish you would send a few cigarettes over with some pipe tobacco. The French tobacco is black and strong. I exchanged a gold Franc for a French cigarette with the money and the fag nearly choked me."[22] Kilmer, a prodigious smoker himself, who loved receiving pipes as gifts, begged his wife to send enough tobacco to "fill a bedsack." When he heard that the tobacco was on the way he admitted that he had smoked all of Duffy's cigars and that "I'll be glad to get the cigars my father has sent me."[23]

As the 165th Infantry got more familiar with the small-town life of the French countryside, the troops came to feel a certain warmth for the place and its people. "The village is small, but the most picturesque and romantic I ever seen," wrote Elmer. "To live in such a place is to live in a village described only by French authors and formerly believed by me to exist only in books."[24]

His friend, Oliver Ames, felt the same. "This town I'm in is just like the one I've read about in Dumas, and always been crazy to visit; from my bedroom window I can see a remnant of an old tower and of the old fortified town wall and the irony of it is that I haven't possibly the time to explore it, which I'm crazy to do."[25]

"Dearest," wrote Wild Bill to Ruth, "It does not seem real somehow that I should be here in the land of romance and chivalry."[26]

Longing for his wife, Kilmer wrote, "I am having a delightful time out here—absolutely beautiful country and nice people. I love you very much indeed and see you clearly always and have a conviction that I will be with you soon—sooner than you expect."[27]

Duffy, however, took a more realistic view of his new rural surroundings. "The dung heap occupies a place of pride outside the front door; and the loftier it stands and the louder it raises its penetrating voice, the more it proclaims the worth and greatness of its possessor." A letter from a soldier to his family bemused the chaplain even though he had to censor it. According to Duffy, the soldier wrote, "There are three classes of inhabitants in the houses— first, residents; second, cattle; third, soldiers."[28] Kilmer seconded that view. "[B]illeting, in the European sense of the term . . . meant that certain householders, in return for the payment of a few sous per man per twenty-four hours, were obliged to allow soldiers to sleep in their stables, barns or other outhouses. They were not obliged to furnish any food, light or heat. They were not obliged even to mend the roofs or walls of the shelters."[29]

Mechanics Edward Lacey and Edward Unger from Hunter's Point co-wrote a droll letter to Miss Mary Smith, a Red Cross volunteer in Brooklyn, letting her know they had been lucky enough to move from the hayloft to a "room on the first floor where the ploughs are stored alongside the horses. It is warmer there. The reason for the move was that the roof leaked and the janitor refused to turn up the heat."[30]

Livestock roamed the narrow streets and when the wind came blustering through the village, Cpl. Victor Denis of Brooklyn had been surprised to see that the "chickens can't even go across the street in a straight line; they are half way up the block."[31]

Observing the townspeople slaughtering a pig, Throop wrote, "That is all the meat in this village for a certain period of time. The French Government keeps a record of every animal killed for food, of every stick of wood, of every bag of grain, and everything else. The war bread is all they have, and that is sold by the pound. Only a loaf a day for four people is what they are allowed to buy each day."[32]

Yet the hardships the villagers faced, sharing their quarters with soldiers in addition to pigs, chickens, and cows, did not seem to faze most of the city-bred men. In a letter that caught the attention of Pershing, James McKenna described how "All through the village I hear men singing, playing the various musical instruments they carried from home, joking and discussing the news or work of the week. There's not a gloomy man in town, not a homesick soldier or sorry soldier, and not the slightest semblance of intoxication."[33]

Ames revealed to his mother, but not to his new wife of a few months, now pregnant, "My French is getting excellent; I'm getting so self-confident in it that I've got to the stage of addressing the young ladies with '*Mais vous êtes charmante, Mademoiselle*,' with such astounding success that I've found it necessary to retrace my steps for safety sake; I always knew I had a charming accent, the French girls fall for it; to-morrow I shall try out a couple of 'r's' with a rolling accent."

While Ames impressed the ladies he also impressed the commander of the First Battalion. In the same letter to his mother, he boasted that he had been put in charge of a detail of sixty-two men to make sure the soldiers were fed and clothed and had dry billets. He elaborated, "Major Donovan was darn nice to let me have it, and if I don't manage it well I shall never be able to look him in the face again. . . . So things are working out pretty well, but I don't dare preach till I'm out of the woods." The Harvard graduate had to pinch himself now and then as he ordered strapping young men around. He confessed of having to stifle a laugh every evening when he forced his sergeant and four corporals to stand at attention around his paper-strewn desk awaiting orders. Then he gave them either "hell" or "encouragement" and orders for "the morrow." One day, feeling as "proud as a general," he marched his detail of sixty-two men, with soap and towels in their hands, "down to the French shower baths and personally [saw] that every man took a shower, the first they had had since leaving Mineola four weeks before."[34]

The young lieutenant did not know it at the time, but the sterling way he had led the detail would so impress Donovan that the major would select him to be the adjutant of the First Battalion.

As the friendship between Ames and Elmer grew tighter, Oliver suggested that they hike over to Gondrecourt, a training area close to Vaucouleurs. The First Infantry Division was there, and Ames wanted to visit his cousin, Archie Roosevelt.

After meeting the son of the former president, Elmer bragged "Archie is a nice chap and I like him a lot." He did not expand on these remarks, but a few weeks later, Archie dropped by to have supper with Oliver, and they invited Basil to join them. Roosevelt had just come back from a successful trench raid, according to Elmer. "There was nothing to it, [Archie] said. Of course, there were no casualties and he accomplished his mission without any difficulty and returned to his own line safely. He is an active officer, judging from his actions."[35] Ames later rode to Gondrecourt alone to see Roosevelt for lunch. "We talked over old times, and got quite homesick."[36]

In a rash moment Elmer broke up with his girlfriend, K. He felt sorry for her, "poor girl." Yet to his parents, on a lonely, rainy Sunday, he rued the fact that "I haven't even brought a picture of her with me." That Sunday he also missed Ames, who had been sent to a training school. "Ames is away this week on special detail, but is expected back tomorrow. He is a very nice chap and I am very glad he is with us."[37]

About the romantic life, one doughboy grumbled, "That newspaper stuff about the pretty French girls running up to kiss you in the streets is a lot of bull. In the first place there aren't any pretty French girls, or anyway they have all gone to Paris."[38]

Pvt. Billy Mehl of the Detachment Company felt the same and had assured a Miss Gertrude Wagner from Brooklyn that French girls could not hold a candle to the New York girls. "The girls wear wooden shoes, milk the cows, clean the stables, etc., so you can imagine what they look like. You couldn't talk to them if you wanted and every time I try to speak French I get into an argument so I've decided to give it up as a bad job."[39]

"Life dragged here," Martin Hogan later wrote. He recalled how they drilled twice daily, once in the morning and again in the afternoon and then hiked through villages, wearing their own trails into the mud. Another soldier piped up, "We have been drilling some, but most of the time the company is on detail cleaning up the town. I don't believe the place has had such a housecleaning since Joan of Arc's time."[40]

November passed and in the first weeks of December, as training intensified, so did the weather, an omen of the winter to come. Kilmer described "a freezing wind [that] blew through the great holes in the tumble-down sheds where the men slept, covering them, night after night, with snow. They learned many soldierly things. How to make blouse and overcoat supplement the thin army blankets, for instance. How to keep shoes from freezing by sleeping on them. How to dress and undress in the dark—for lamps were unknown and candles forbidden."[41] Writing to Aline, Kilmer announced, "I got a Sing Sing haircut recently and am growing a corsair moustache. This is the pleasantest war I ever attended—nothing to do but fall in, fall out, pound a typewriter 13 hours a day and occasionally hike across France and back carrying a piano."[42]

"Nothing out of the ordinary," Lt. Austin Lawrence put in his diary on the 16th. "Went to Mass & stood near door. Almost froze. Nothing extra today."[43]

When snow fell at first, it came as a blessing because the ground froze over and the mud disappeared. Officers and men came down with colds. And everyone wondered when orders would come and where would they go next. Would they be moved up to the front? Would they see action at last? As Christmas approached, changes were brewing, that was certain.

Then on 19 December, Maj. Gen. William Mann was replaced as commander of the Rainbow Division by Charles Menoher, an artillery colonel and West Pointer, class of 1886. Rumors abounded that Colonel Hine was next. Duffy's initial sense that Hine would not measure up as successor to Col. William Haskell had perhaps been right. A report criticizing his command showed that he had been lax in discipline, supplying his men inadequately and not properly preparing them for battle. Also, their uniforms, including their hobnailed field shoes, were in wretched condition. In his own defense, Hine countered that equipment including articles of clothing such as extra buttons that were to have been shipped overland by train and wagon, had been slow in reaching his troops. "Because of lack of transportation much time was consumed in walking from village to village," the colonel had written bitterly to Brig. Gen. Michael Lenihan, his brigade commander. "The weather was rainy and many men had severe colds. Transportation was lacking and every effort was made to rush supplies and equipment to the proper stations." He pointed out that soldiers had to hike a mile or two into the forest to collect firewood. In response to accusations of allowing his troops' rifles to rust, he pointed out the "failure of the Ordnance Department to provide gun oil." The gun oil had been shipped out from Camp Mills along with the regiment and, at the time Hine penned his report, still had not arrived.[44]

A number of officers, Duffy included, hoped that if or when Hine was replaced, Haskell would be his replacement. He was nearby in France, serving on the general staff; and he was well liked by nearly all. There was a rumor that Lt. Col. Latham Reed was out, as well.

But when orders came, they were more of the same: training, training, and more training. This time, the division would shift from the Fifth Training Area at Vaucouleurs to the Seventh Training Area at Rolampont. But first it would go to Grand, about fifteen miles southwest of Vaucouleurs, and stay there until after Christmas. For the 165th Infantry, the departure date would be on the day after Christmas. The hike to the latest campgrounds around the villages of Longeau and Langres, south of Rolampont, an eighty-mile trek through the foothills of the Vosges mountains to the banks of the Marne River, would be long, cold, and legendary.

In his diary entry for 1 January 1918, Duffy wrote, "I cannot tell just what hard fates this New Year may have in store for us, but I am sure that no matter how trying they may be they will not make us forget the closing days of 1917."[45]

10

"Most Pitiful and Unsightly Bunch of Men I Have Ever Seen"

Father Francis Duffy wanted to make sure that the men got off on the right foot in the new year by closing out 1917 well. To this end, he held midnight mass on Christmas. "If there is one day in all the year that wanderers from home cannot afford to forget it is Christmas," he entered in his diary on 25 December. The chaplain knew he had to give his "parish," as he called the men of the regiment, a "religious celebration that they would remember for many a year."[1]

In a letter to John Cardinal Farley, Duffy informed him that he planned a midnight mass in an old, old church that had seen better days. He promised the cardinal that it would be a great celebration. He had already held a mass in that church, he told him, and it had been "so full that a cat could go from door to altar from head to head without touching the floor. You may imagine the joy of the curés. And after pay-day the collection—ah! How good, how generous your Irish soldiers."[2]

Although the church in Grand was small, Duffy felt most of the regiment could squeeze into it. "I knew that confessions and communions would be literally by the thousands," he wrote. The church was seven hundred years old with a watchtower made of stone seven-feet thick, an impressive edifice. With the assistance of Joyce Kilmer and Pvt. Frank Driscoll, an ex-Jesuit novice from Duffy's parish in the Bronx, Duffy placed the regimental colors in the chancel, flanked by the French tricolor. He called on the regimental band to provide the right music and added several French violinists to the mix. Knowing he could not handle confessions and communion for so many soldiers by himself, he enlisted the aid of the church's curate and another priest, as well as a chaplain from an artillery unit. When the church was ready, Duffy asked a soldier how he felt about making his confession to a French priest who could not speak English. Replied the soldier, "Fine, Father. All he could do was give me a penance, but you'd have given me hell."[3]

On Christmas Eve a heavy snow fell in the Meuse Valley. Cpl. Martin Hogan looked at the snow. "It was though a kindly disposed Fate was to make this last Christmas that many among us should know a good old-fashioned one."[4]

Basil Elmer wrote of the Christmas spirit so strong among his men. "I can see it in their actions toward one another." When he walked past the billet where the men in his A Company platoon were quartered they hollered out, "Merry Christmas, Lieutenant." He saw that they were all smiling and happy and cheerful, and later, before attending midnight mass, they were "singing all the songs."[5]

A touch of homesickness came over Oliver Ames. "Here I am in a little town in France writing home by candlelight," he told his mother. "Just through the walls of my room (very thin walls) is the barn where about forty of the men are billeted. They seem to be homesick, too, because I can hear them singing, and the most mournfully sentimental songs; and I don't blame them, Ma, because no matter how hardened to it, no man will ever become hardened to spending Christmas Eve in a cold barn with nothing but straw to sleep on and no lights to see by, and thousands of miles from home."[6]

A new lieutenant assigned to Capt. Richard Ryan's I Company, George Benz from Conshocken, Pennsylvania, reported how privates Tommy O'Brien and Dick McLaughlin slipped into the woods and chopped down a little cedar tree—"a horrible offense if some Frenchman had caught them at it." Benz described how they buried it in the mud at the foot of their bunk, trimmed it with colored paper torn from a magazine, and then placed candles, stolen from the kitchen, around its base and lit them. On the tree they tied one cartridge. Next to the cartridge they hung a cardboard sign that read, "For the Kaiser, damn his hide." The men had made a fire with green logs; the smoke inside the barn was thick, and the only light besides that of the fire came from sputtering candles. When Benz walked in he saw that "The boys, true to old Christmas customs, were going 'visiting' from one bunk to the other. A few, a mighty few, had received Christmas packages and boxes. If there was something to eat in them, they were muchly visited that night."[7]

With two companions, Al Ettinger wandered around Grand. They went into a deserted old church. "There were the most unusual stations of the cross I had ever seen," he recalled. "They were carved from wood and painted, and the paint had peeled quite a bit. But it was really the age of this little church that impressed us so much." Afterward they met the owner of a butcher shop, a Madame Bouvier, who served them lunch and then invited the trio back for Christmas dinner. The dinner of rabbit, veal pot roast, turnips and potatoes and "all the wine you could drink," was the best meal Ettinger had yet eaten in France.[8] When the dinner was over, he and his stuffed and happy companions, singing Christmas carols, walked through a light, falling snow to the church for midnight mass. Hogan, also attending the service, saw that it was "crowded with men until I thought its sides would be pushed out."[9]

Kilmer recollected that "all the town came to see these strange, gentle, brave, mirthful, pious American soldiers, who, coming from a new land to fight for France, practiced France's ancient faith with such devotion."[10] Up front in the sanctuary sat Brig. Gen. Michael Lenihan with Col. Charles Hine and their brigade and regimental staffs. After Duffy preached, the soldiers sang "The Little Town of Bethlehem" and "The Snow Lay On the Ground." Then everyone, French and American alike, sang "Oh, Come All Ye Faithful," wrote Duffy, "until the vaults resounded." Communion, even with three priests hard at work, took until two in the morning. When it was over, the chaplain felt "happy with the thought that, exiles though we are, we celebrated the old feast in high and holy fashion."[11]

Austin Lawrence had sat in the sanctuary with his brother, Maj. George Lawrence. In his diary, he observed that the church was "very pretty & packed. French priest read Mass. Fr. D. preached & gave communion. Great little bit with incense lamp. Very nice service."[12]

Many soldiers had to stand outside the church for lack of room inside. One of them observed that the "dim lights from the altar could barely be seen by those on the outside steps. In the stillness of the night the voice of our beloved Father Duffy could be distinctly heard as he recited the mass and his words brought consolation to the hearts of all his listeners who were thinking of their loved ones so far away."[13]

In the room he shared with Ames, Elmer sat in front of a big
fire with the lights out, hearing the Christmas carols. "It was lovely
gazing into the fire to hear them and think of you," he wrote his
parents. "First they sang 'Onward, Christian Soldiers'—then 'Lead
Kindly Light' and then they sang 'Noel.' At this last, I acted like a
big baby and cried like a two-year old."[14]

Richard O'Neill, the D Company sergeant from Harlem, also
felt a touch of melancholy. "Nothing worse than Christmas," he
put in his diary. "We went to Mass in a cathedral Christmas Eve
and the next day had one tiny meal, that rotten coffee again, and
some kind of meat, and a small portion at that."[15]

On Christmas day, after he "patiently waited in line for this
well-advertised, glorious dinner and filled our mess kits with turkey, mashed potatoes, squash, and giblet gravy," Ettinger bit into
his meal and gagged. "The turkey was awful. Taking so long to
reach us, it had spoiled."[16] Martin Hogan, on the other hand, felt
that the turkey dinner "made everything complete."[17]

In Hogan's Third Battalion, Sgt. Paddy Rogan from Brooklyn, a doorman at the Biltmore Hotel in civilian life, collected
extra food for the men of I Company. He commandeered a French
wagon and drove to a French commissary in the next village and
brought back raisins, nuts, figs, and small oranges. "The feast that
day was a wonder," Benz said. "And there were 'seconds,' too, for
any man who wished them."[18]

Throughout the day the snow continued, and unpromising
weather was forecast for the following day, when the division
planned to march to Longeau and environs—a hike that would
take four days and nights.

Looking back on that time, Hogan mused, "It was from this
Christmas that the 165th, the old 'Fighting Irish,' got its collec-
tive nose pointed for the front."[19]

On the morning of the 26th, when the Rainbow Division broke
camp for its long march to its final training area, snow swirled
heavily around the shivering soldiers and temperatures plummeted
to near zero degrees. Although the hobnailed field shoes fit snugly
on most of the troops, everyone prayed they would last through
the miles and miles of rough terrain that loomed in front of them.
The Vosges mountains, with their worn, rounded tops and pine-
forested slopes, did not look as threatening as the Alps, but they
were rugged enough, just the same. The division's route would

take it into the high country and test the endurance of every one of its men. When the hike was over the Irish regiment would remember it as their "Valley Forge."

"I don't believe half a dozen men of our outfit had two pairs of socks with him," recalled Benz, still getting to know the men of I Company. "And so many had worn out shoes that we left something like twenty-five behind to follow us by train or wagon later. All the cripples, those recovering from disease or with flat feet, were left behind, too."[20]

The first indication that the march was going to be anything but a lark occurred on Christmas day, when Capt. John Mangan's Supply Company pulled out of Grand to begin a trek that would run through the villages around Longeau in three-ton French wagons piled high with fresh meat and vegetables and pulled by teams of mules. Mangan rousted Cpl. Charlie Hennings out of bed early in the morning and gave him fifteen minutes to roll his pack and get into one of the wagons. The Lexington Avenue resident had the job of putting the chains on the wagon wheels when the mountain roads turned hazardous. The route kept him wide-eyed and holding his breath the whole way. To his parents he wrote, "From three that afternoon until five the next morning we boosted the froggies over the hill."[21]

Traveling with the Supply Company, Duffy hopped onto one of the wagons. "The roads we were to take," he said, "were mean country roads over the foothills of the Vosges." Duffy realized that "the situation for Captain Mangan's braves looked desperate from the start." First of all, the mules weren't shod for winter weather and the harnesses did not fit. "A mile out of town the wagons were all across the road, as the lead teams were not trained to answer the reins. The battle was on."[22]

Colonel Hine reported that most of the mules had not been broken and that the "heavy grades and snow and ice caused trains to lose all semblance of order. In some cases 30 men were required to get wagons up difficult hills en route."[23]

Some of the men in the Supply Company were veteran hands when it came to working with animals. Wagoner Roland Ferdinando from Jersey City had been in the circus. Sgt. Harry Horgan, the Arizona cowboy who had left the old Sixty-ninth on the Texas border, could, according to Duffy, "get anything out of mules that mules could do." Duffy also cited Wagoner Jim Regan, a tough veteran of the Spanish-American War who hailed from

Harlem. "[Regan] had his four new mules christened and pulling in answer to their names before a greenhorn could gather up the reins." He described the work of nearly all the boys in the Supply Company, pointing out that "Charles Hennings of the commissary, and Joe Healy, cook, [actually it was David Healy from the Gashouse District] made themselves mule-skinners once more and worked with energies that never flagged."[24]

At midnight, after nine hours navigating the treacherous roads, Mangan's convoy struck a steep grade four kilometers long. Hennings's wagon slipped in the snow and spun to a stop. Driver Sgt. Ambrose Steinert, who worked for the city of New York, snapped, "Stuck!" Swearing at the mules, he growled, "Frenchie wants to quit! We go through and all hands out to work."

Hennings slapped the chains on his wagon and then on another. "Whipping a skid chain under the wheels of a three tonner is fair work. Gosh, I certainly kept warm. Well, we pulled him out and then went back after his partner."

When Mangan's troops reached the Longeau area they looked over the billets that would house the rest of the regiment that was just then marching out of Grand. Hennings's new job was to collect straw for beds. His search carried him five miles into the snowy hills until he located a farm with plenty of straw. He negotiated with the farmer, relying on his own "rotten French" and the "broken English" of "one of the sweetest French girls I've met yet." The farmer promised to deliver the straw the next day, but failed to show up. Hennings went back to the farm and ordered the farmer to give him at least some straw. "Hiked the Frenchy back with some wood. Sore and disgusted because I knew the boys would sure need that bedding. . . . All told, I traveled twenty miles on foot to get a half ton of the stuff." Then he begged his folks to send Harry Horgan "some smoking tobacco and some of the other boys also." The ex-cowboy had just received a new pipe. "Say, dad, I'd have written sooner, but I've had a job that didn't any more than give me time to sleep."[25]

Back in Grand, with Christmas now a memory, the 165th Infantry shouldered packs and rifles, and set out for Longeau in a blizzard.

"It had been snowing for three days," recalled Hogan, "and this morning [26 December] the roads were knee-deep. It was still snowing when we broke camp at nine o'clock, and a head-on wind blew the sharp crystals into our faces and eyes."[26]

"It was bitter cold and snowing," Ettinger wrote, "and a fierce wind lashed at our gloveless hands and faces. Going up those slopes, the Lead Company had to break through snow up to their knees, while the Rear Company slipped on packed-down icy snow."[27]

"We plodded along in the snow, making fairly good time, and with the men in good spirits," is how Benz remembered that first morning. "It was so cold that snow made a mound on one's hat and stayed there and water froze in one's canteen."[28]

In his diary entry for the 26th, Lawrence commented, "Snowing hard. Ready for the hike at 8:30. Stood out in cold & snow for one hour waiting for rest of regt. to come up. Finally got off. Snow stopped but started again later. Pretty cold & hard walking. Passed thru La Fuche, Prig La Fach, Clefmont & spent night at Consigny. Distance 24K or 15 miles."[29]

The New Yorkers had only gone a few miles when their hobnailed shoes began to fall apart. Kilmer described how desperate the men became. "They would crush their bleeding feet into their frozen, broken hobnails of a black morning, and breakfastless, start out, with a song on their lips, to climb the foothills of the Vosges Mountains through the heart of a blizzard. At noon (shifting their feet about to keep the blood moving) they would (if it was one of the lucky days) have a slice of bread or two pieces of hardtack for noon mess. At night they would have sleep instead of supper."[30]

Soon the hobnails turned into a major problem, a disaster that threatened the long march and the very health of the regiment. The biggest problem was that they absorbed water quickly and, when dried out, shrank and turned hard as iron. At night the men pulled them off, but in the morning they had a miserable time trying to get the stiff shoes back on. Capt. George McAdie, the Scottish commander of A Company, reported that "practically one half" of his company was late for reveille every morning on the march "due to the length of time it took to put their shoes on."[31] Jim McKenna, over in D Company, agreed. "When drying out after having been wet, or when frozen during the night as was often the case, it was very difficult to get the shoes on. Many men worked a long time, in some cases more than one hour, before they were able to get into their shoes."[32] First Lt. Horace Stokes described the soles of the hobnails as "brittle and unserviceable, resembling papier mache. They flake off and large pieces drop off. . . . Unless soaked in grease the stiffness of this shoe causes blisters and footsores. . . . The shoe is over-heavy for long marches."[33]

Capt. Tom Reilley saw every night that his men in B Company, "despite admonitions and precautions [persisted] in drying wet, cold feet before open fires and from my experience this causes the shoes to crack across the soles more easily than the old issue of shoes did."[34]

During the night many of the troops took their hobnails to bed, hoping body heat might keep them from getting stiff. In the morning they still had to knead their unforgiving shoes in an effort to make them pliable. When nothing worked, they pounded down the back of the shoe and then cut open the toes with bayonets. Thus, they exposed their toes to the bitter cold, snow, and ice. Duffy remembered how some of the boys stuffed straw or paper into their shoes and burned the paper, hoping to warm their shoes. So did Ettinger, who added that the fire not only warmed the shoe it burned the thread around the soles "and within a day the soles would fall off." Ettinger suffered from frostbite and a big black blister that tore open. The medics, he said, could only help with iodine.[35] "Men hiked with frozen feet, with shoes so broken their feet were in the snow," said the chaplain. "Many could be seen in wooden sabots or with their feet wrapped in burlap. Hands got so cold and frost-bitten that the rifles almost dropped from their fingers. Soldiers fell in the snow and arose and staggered on and dropped again."[36]

Benz wrote, "That was some job, watching some hardly pushed man, full of grit, trying to keep up the pace, falter and then fall face downward into the snow. It was your job to run up, see if he really was sick and then give him his little card permitting him to leave the column. He would be picked up later by the ambulance men."[37]

"In other companies, some men just fell on their faces and stayed there. They couldn't move," recalled Ettinger. Then, most likely quoting rumor or hearsay, he added, "During the four days of that march, five men in our regiment died of exhaustion. They were placed alongside the road to wait for an ambulance, but the mule drawn ambulances also had trouble on the grades and by the time they arrived, it was too late."[38] Other than Ettinger's words, however, there is no record of any member of the 165th Infantry dying by the roadside.

On the third day out, Lieutenant Lawrence had to stay behind "to look after sick men with bum feet. Tagged them all."[39]

As the frozen, tired soldiers trudged through the deep snow, the wind whipping against their numbed cheeks, they looked for distant church steeples, a sign that they were approaching a town and that maybe their hike for the day was done. Declared Walter Reynolds of Hempstead, "Oh how we would look for that church nights when hiking."[40]

The mess wagons had a hard time keeping up with the marchers and arrived in the villages hours after the men had found their billets and crashed for the night. Captain Mangan saw his wagoners alternate driving so they could walk along with the mules, stamping their feet to get the blood flowing. At night, wrote Hogan, "when we had reached the small town which was our destination mess call was blown but there was nothing to eat. Our kitchens had stuck in the soft mud and snow far behind us."[41]

Because of the deep snow, the mule-drawn mess wagons kept falling farther and farther behind. The first day it was six miles, the next day ten.

"The mules dropped dead on the road," said Maj. William Stacom, who led the Second Battalion. "And that meant a lot to us, for at that time we didn't have any rolling kitchens. . . . When our mules died we couldn't get our stoves. Besides we had thrown some of our food away in the effort to save the mules by lightening their loads. And there was no way to get other food up to us."[42] For the men on foot there were no reserve rations.

It meant the soldiers went hungry. When the wagons finally clattered into the streets of the villages where the men were holed up in attics or barn lofts or in stables, stretched out on cold stone or wooden floors or smelly straw, exhausted, trying to warm up, it was one or two in the morning. Most of them were too tired to eat, and waited until four when breakfast was served—rice mixed with a syrup, bacon, bread and coffee. Benz remembered a night when the mess wagons had been so late that he and several officers scrounged up twelve loaves of bread from the villagers. "After the men were sent into their stables and pigpens for the night's rest we walked around with the bread and a bayonet. We'd stick our head in a door, ask how many men were there and then cut off a portion of the loaf. It was just like feeding so many animals. Twelve loaves of bread for 230 men! They grabbed at it as if they hadn't seen food for years."[43]

One night Hogan found shelter in a shed with no roof. "I lay for a long time, fully dressed, with my blanket over me, staring at the cold stars. When I woke in the cold, dark morning the same stars were staring idly back at me. Mess call was sounded again that morning, but there was nothing to eat."[44]

On the march, the tramping soldiers begged for morsels of food from the French villagers who lined the way to watch the first American soldiers they had ever seen pass by. They cannot have been favorably impressed by the ragged, shivering, and starving army.

Each day's trek covered between fifteen and twenty miles, and each leaden step took a heroic effort. One soldier in or near Headquarters Company lifted the spirits of his struggling fellows high through song. His wonderful voice was so comforting to them that they shouldered on, joining him boisterously in singing that rang from one end of the regiment to the other. Stable Sgt. Harvey Constantine—called "Dad"—a minstrel if ever there was one, was a spry fifty-year-old veteran of the Spanish-American War.

Lt. Richard Larned declared him "famous as a singer of Irish songs and as a yodler years ago." He watched how the men took to Constantine's voice, keeping an eye on one particular soldier: the poet Joyce Kilmer. "The hikes did not come easy to [Kilmer]. But no matter how hard or long they were, he always finished them. He was game, that boy. I've known him to hike mile on weary mile with blistered feet, hardly able to move, finishing purely on his nerve. If any one offered to carry his rifle or ease his load in another way, Joyce became indignant. He'd stick it to the bitter end if it killed him. And never a complaint from him." And one of the reasons for this, Larned believed, was the "cheer" that "Harvey and his songs brought to Kilmer and the rest of us."

Kilmer himself was so moved by Constantine's singing that later he penned a poem in honor of the stable sergeant. He called it "The Singing Soldier." His ode ran for thirteen verses. He told of how the packs of the men seemed lighter because of the singing, and how they thought of home and how proud their families would be when the Sixty-ninth came marching up through the heart of old New York. The poem ends,

> And no better singing soldier under Heaven can be seen,
> Than yourself if you will lead us in the "Wearin' of the
>   Green."
> With your rifle on your shoulder and helmet cocked a bit,
> And your Yankee independence and your native Irish wit.

Let the Colonel give us "Route Step" when we're on
    Fifth Avenue,
Let us rest and take it easy till we sing a song or two,
And they'll know what all the silver furls upon our flag-
    staff mean,
When they hear old Harvey lead us in "The Wearin' of
    the Green."[45]

When the regiment finally strode into Longeau, the men ended their march with their voices ringing off the houses on the main street with "In the Good Old Summertime!" Wrote Kilmer after the march, "The Regiment that arrived in Longeau on the afternoon of December 29th looked different from the Regiment that had left Grand four days before. To judge by their gait and their faces, the men had aged twenty years. But their hearts were unchanged. As they stood in the deep snow, the ice-crusted packs still on their bruised shoulders, they had a laughing word for every pretty face at a Longeau window."[46]

Regimental Adjutant Walter Powers, who had served with General Pershing on the Mexican border, had been moved by his men's attitude. "The morale has been that of veteran troops—any commander who knows and appreciates pluck and endurance in men little used to the rigors of winter marching can appreciate the standard attained during the entire march," he wrote in a New Year's Eve report. "Personally, I have had considerable experience with troops in the field under all conditions of service . . . and I have yet to see or serve with troops that I consider the superior of the troops that I now serve with."[47]

A corporal in the Machine Gun Company, John Flint of Brooklyn, was proud that the boys had come through "all right, not losing a man. You can't kill this bunch," he boasted.[48]

But when Capt. Thomas Burcham, an assistant to the Forty-second Division's sanitary inspector, saw the Irish soldiers three weeks after their arrival in Longeau, he blanched, wondering how any of them had survived. In an angry report to his commander, he painted a grim picture of the New Yorkers.

The men are very dirty, their clothes are worn out, covered with grease and dirt, the most pitiful and unsightly bunch of men I have ever seen, either in the Army or out. A man found in this condition in Civil life would be a case to be

taken care of by a Charitable organization. Two men,
Thomas Harris and James R. McCabe, both privates in F
Company, 165th Inf., told me they had only the clothes
they were wearing on their person, having been left in the
U.S. when their organization came over and they were
sent later with the 168th Inf. Reg., without overcoats, mess
kits or Blankets, which have not been supplied them up to
this date. They had not had a change of underwear or uniform since leaving the U.S. on Oct. 28th, 1917.

Burcham warned of "trench foot," bringing up the deplorable
condition of the hobnail shoes. "One man," he wrote, "had a blister on his foot and could not get his shoes on, and was wearing one
old worn shoe on one foot and a wooden shoe on the other."
Burcham said that the fungi that causes trench foot "grows best in
a cold, wet and muddy earth . . . entering through some lesion in
the skin, such as a blister or abrasion on the feet." And there was
more. He had found that eighty percent of the soldiers in both the
165th and 166th Infantries suffered from body lice, which, he said,
"cannot be eradicated unless these men are provided with a change
of clothing, as only a few of the organizations have their Barrack
Bags, at this date."[49]

In his diary, Duffy mused, "But one thing we all feel now—
we have not the slightest doubt that men who have shown the
endurance that these men have shown will give a good account of
themselves in any kind of battle they are put into."[50]

Hine's fate had been sealed eight days before Burcham's report landed on the sanitary inspector's desk. In what was the
darkest hour of his life, according to a friend from their West Point
days, the commander of the 165th Infantry was transferred to the
headquarters of Service of Supply, where his expertise in railroad-
ing would come in handy. The transfer "broke his heart," claimed
the friend.[51] Along with Hine, Latham Reed also departed. And so
on 10 January, the Irish regiment got yet another commander.
Many of the officers had been hoping for Hine to be replaced by
Haskell or even Bill Donovan, one of their own.

Donovan had been away at a field-officers' school for five weeks
and had missed the long, miserable march. There was a good chance
that when he completed his courses he would get a promotion,
and the colonelcy would be his for the asking. On his first days

away studying, he had been thrown in with some men not to his liking and complained to Ruth. "A hundred different human frailties now assert themselves. Jelousies [*sic*] and pettiness and selfishness. And then out of it stand a few strong figures who are true and patriotic and unselfish. This school should be good to teach humility." He had worked hard, and had turned down chances to go to Paris, telling his wife that on the first weekend after Thanksgiving one hundred students had headed for the French capital. "No Paris for me. I want to put in some good licks here." The commander at the school appreciated Donovan's hard work. "He said that it would not be forgotten," he crowed, "and that I would never regret having worked as I have."[52]

Haskell also had high hopes for the colonelcy. Languishing on Pershing's general staff in Chaumont, twenty miles up the Marne River from Longeau, the former commander wanted terribly to return to the 165th, if not as the colonel, then at least as a lieutenant colonel in place of Reed, now being shuffled back to the United States. Henry Reilly, then colonel of the 149th Field Artillery, later recalled Haskell's disappointment when he got neither promotion. The reason that he was passed over, according to Reilly, was a shortage of trained general staff officers.

Instead of Donovan or Haskell, charge of the regiment went to Col. John Barker, also a member of Pershing's general staff. Barker was forty-six, another graduate of the U.S. Military Academy, class of 1894. A hero of the Spanish-American War and the Moro uprising in the Philippines, he had already earned three Silver Stars. In Cuba yellow fever had struck him down. After recovering he had been posted to the Philippines. On his second tour in the Pacific he had been severely wounded and spent six weeks in a hospital. In 1914 he went to France to study military tactics. But upon the German invasion he had been named attaché to the United States ambassador to France. Later, President Wilson selected him as a neutral observer of the war and Barker spent many months on the Western Front. When Pershing reached Paris in the summer of 1917, Barker was there to greet him.

After learning that he now had a new commander—actually two of them, because Maj. Gen. William Mann had been replaced at the division's top by Charles Menoher—Donovan assured Ruth that "The line is the real place. And truly the Major has the best job in the war. It is low enough so that you still have touch with the men and high enough so that you use your intellect."[53]

Duffy commented on the change of divisional leaders. "There is evidently to be no regard for feelings or established relations of dependency or intimacy, but just put men in where they will be considered to fit best." He wrote that he would miss Hine and even Reed, a soldier who had eventually earned his respect. As for Barker, he described him as a "Manly man, strong of face, silent of speech and courteous of manner. We have learned to like him already—we always like a good soldier."[54] Yet in a letter to Cardinal Farley, he once again expressed his disappointment that the regiment's new colonel was "not one of us." However, he held out hope that because Barker's wife was a "French Catholic lady" he had a chance to convert him. "I told him to start preparing Mrs. Barker for the news that he would have to send for her some day, that we had made a Catholic of him."[55]

But Barker had a more important worry than fending off the chaplain's religious overtures: he had to clean up the mess that he had inherited from Hine. His men needed thorough washing and delousing, and clean, new uniforms. And in seeing to this, the West Pointer who, as Duffy pointed out, was "not one of us," would learn soon enough that, like Eugene Field's dueling gingham dog and calico cat, the Irish and anything English did not mix—even when it came down to a thing so mundane as uniforms.

11

"We Are All Volunteers in This War"

One of the first things Col. John Barker had done upon taking command of the ragged 165th Infantry had been to inspect his new troops and investigate their deplorable condition. The officers ordered by Brig. Gen. Michael Lenihan to look into the plight of the men and report back to him were Majors George Lawrence and William Stacom. Lawrence was the regiment's top medical officer, recently returned from officers' school where he had witnessed the death of twenty-one British soldiers in a German bombing raid. Stacom led the Second Battalion, which had suffered the worst on the march across the Vosges.

Lawrence found that the enlisted men had been without a change of clothing, including underwear, for two months. "Shoes of about 40 % of command have been worn to shreds, and at present time there are none to replace them." Lawrence blamed this on the fact that the men's barracks bags had been shipped by rail from Vaucouleurs to Rolampont and "In most cases this freight has not been delivered." And when a few of the soldiers finally got their barrack bags, they discovered that "they had been rifled in transit, of shoes, personal belongings and the like." He emphasized the "necessity of Division Supply Off. of doing all that is possible to fill immediately requisitions for clothing and shoes for this command."

Barker sent Lawrence's report up through the chain of command—first to Lenihan and then to Maj. Gen. Charles Menoher at division headquarters. At the bottom of the report, he typed, "From personal investigation I find this report not exaggerated. . . . The men lack the bare necessities for keeping clean, and many are not sufficiently shod to keep up with the training."[1]

A day later, on the 17th, Stacom handed in his report. He noted that conditions had been "improving steadily," especially the cleanliness of the men since the battalion bath had opened. "Upon arrival many men were infected with Lice but in three days time will have all bathed and with the arrival of Barrack Bags it will permit change of clothing." Although he reported that firewood was scarce and billets always cold, a number of cots had arrived and the men were no longer sleeping on straw-covered floors. He said, however, that the condition of the clothing was "poor," blaming this on the overcrowded ships that had carried the men to Europe as well as on lost and late barrack bags. "Since July the men have had to wear the same clothing without any change. The same were wet almost daily and owing to cold, were worn also at night."

The major ended his report on an upbeat note, focusing on morale, which he declared "very good."

> The experiences of the past month have been sufficient to test the spirit of the men. Cold weather and snow, cold billets, worn shoes and in many cases no shoes, no change of clothing, underwear or socks whatever for several weeks owing to the failure of Barrack Bags being sent forward during that time. Drills every day except Sunday during all the daylight hours, returning wet each night with no possibility of drying clothing, nevertheless giving the closest attention to instructions and returning from drill in the best of spirit.[2]

A year later, Stacom stated that for "two days men marched with feet literally bleeding. I used to see their bloody footprints in the snow. . . . It took us pretty much the whole month of January to get the men's morale back."[3]

In his final report to the new division commander, Barker focused on four things: living conditions, clothing, cleanliness, and morale. The Spanish-American War veteran termed the living conditions as "hard war conditions, but not unbearable." Clothing he called "generally serviceable," although he once again cited "shoes in many cases in unserviceable condition—burned soles, cut uppers, and ill-fitting." The men, he felt, were too filthy, although showers had been erected for them and baths were under construction. He complained that too many men had long hair. "Barbering equipment lacking. Canvas equipment very greasy. Washing underclothing hanging in several billets."

As for morale, all the new commander had to say was "apparently not bad." He added, "Officers state that the lack of clothing and facilities for general cleanup following a painful march under severe weather conditions had taken much out of the men, but that the arrival of some supplies and an improvement of the mess was reviving their spirits."[4]

Sgt. Richard O'Neill knew that the problem, as far as uniforms and gear were concerned, had been transportation. "It wasn't that we didn't have equipment in France," he told a writer. "They just had trouble getting it to us, that's all. But how the boys did suffer."[5]

While Barker and his officers mulled over how best to re-uniform their men, training went on, but not without a hitch. In fact, the situation was all too familiar: the 165th Infantry was ill-equipped in all areas.

"In this place we really started training—that is as far as we could without grenades, without gas masks, without auto rifles, or in short, without any modern weapons of war," Lt. George Benz admitted. "We wasted almost a month telling them about new weapons because we had none to show them. Finally the arms started coming in, and then we could train. We received everything but rifle grenades, and they came a few days before we started toward the front."[6]

Then, along with the new weaponry, came new uniforms—and with the new uniforms, a new problem.

Enough uniforms to clothe most of the regiment had been shipped in from the British zone. When the crates were opened, the Irish Americans examined the new uniforms, muttered oaths, and threw them on the ground. They were British. Their glistening, brass buttons had the crown of England imprinted on them, and every time the men buttoned up their uniforms their fingers would touch those buttons.

"Now the men born in Ireland were really steamed," recalled Pvt. Al Ettinger. "They didn't like the idea of wearing anything made in England, and they refused to wear the new uniforms. For them, those buttons were the hated symbol of their former oppressors."[7]

Father Duffy happened upon H Company the day the British uniforms were issued. The company was billeted in the village of Cohons. It was unnerving for him to see the entire company lined

A platoon of New Yorkers pull one-pound cannons into firing positions while training with the French prior to its first engagement against the Germans. *Signal Corps/National Archives*

up on the main street in angry groups. In each group there was much arguing and "gesticulating." When Duffy asked what had them so upset, a supply sergeant yanked one of the uniforms out of a pile on the ground. He dangled it in front of the priest.

"Look at the damn thing!" he said. Softening his voice because he was addressing his chaplain, he added, "Excuse me, Father, but you'll say as bad when you look at it. They want us to wear this!"

Duffy recognized what was an English tunic with brass buttons. He also recognized how volatile the situation was, how fervently the men now pressing around him were hoping for his support.

Nodding toward the uniform, he said sardonically, "Got nice shiny buttons."

Pvt. John Thornton from Manhattan's West Side, clipped a button off the uniform. "They look betther this way," he said in his Irish brogue. Duffy had to admit that they did, but warned them not to destroy government property. East Sider Pvt. Martin Higgins then growled that he would rather hang than "put wan of thim rags on me back!"

The English uniforms foisted on his men sank Duffy into a black mood. When dining that night in the officers' mess, with Barker seemingly unconcerned but Major Lawrence and Captains Alexander Anderson, John Mangan, and Jim McKenna raging, the chaplain "exploded." Barker, already worried after investigating the inferior field shoes that had fallen apart on the long hike through the Vosges, quipped, "Well, at least they wouldn't object if they had to wear English shoes, would they?"

"No," the priest shot back. "They'd have the satisfaction of stamping on them."

Barker was taken aback by the anger of his chaplain and the other officers and felt that Pershing had dumped him into a nest of Irish malcontents. Here they were dressed in filthy rags and worthless shoes and grumbling about new uniforms. Sensing Barker's uneasiness, Duffy felt it his duty to instruct the colonel about his new regiment. His lecture is worth repeating:

> We do not want you to feel that you have a regiment of divided loyalty or dubious reliability on your hands. We are all volunteers for this war. If you put our fellows in line alongside a bunch of Tommies, they would only fight the harder to show the English who are the better men, though

I would not guarantee that there would not be an occasional row in the rest of the camp if we were billeted with them. There are soldiers with us who left Ireland to avoid service in the British Army. But as soon as we got into the war, these men, though not yet citizens, volunteered to fight under the Stars and Stripes.

We have our racial feelings, but these do not affect our loyalty to the United States. You can understand it. There were times during the past two years when if England had not restrained her John Bull tendencies on the sea we might have gotten into a series of difficulties that would have led to a war with her. In that case Germany would have been the Ally. You are a soldier, and you would have fought, suppressing your own dislike for the Ally. But supposing in the course of the war we were short of tin hats and they asked you to put on one of those Boche helmets?

Barker "whacked the table, stung to sudden anger at the picture." He assured his chaplain that "I'll see that they clothe my men hereafter in American uniforms."[8]

The following day some of the Irish in the regiment built a roaring fire in the street, ready to set the uniforms ablaze. Ettinger felt they were close to mutiny. To his relief, Duffy "calmed the rebels down with a great speech on how their indiscipline would shame the regiment, and how we had to prove in this war that Irish volunteers were the best fighters in the Army—and that couldn't be demonstrated around a bonfire in Longeau."[9]

The mutiny, if it was one, was quelled when officers and men struck a compromise. With their men begging to keep their own tattered uniforms, Benz and other officers in I Company ordered them to cut off all buttons from the English tunics and replace them with American buttons. The switch settled the men down.

In the midst of this button insurrection, new officers arrived to bolster the 165th Infantry. First Lieutenant Charles Baker was a friendly face from the Texas border days of the Sixty-ninth, but the banker's son and ex-sergeant of Squadron A was able to thrill his old comrades with the tale of how he reached Longeau. A *New York Times* reporter, writing of Baker's adventure to rejoin his regiment, compared it to "stories of the sea by Jack London."

Baker, a 1913 Princeton graduate often mistaken for another Princetonian, the renowned athlete Hobey Baker, had transferred into the Sixty-ninth while it was in Texas. However, he was not with the regiment when it sailed for France, but in the south on special assignment. He did not leave for Europe until January, and of all the transports he could have found himself on, he wound up on a ship filled with sixteen hundred mules and horses stowed below decks like sardines. The neighing and braying, the stench of dung mixed with the salty ocean air, all combined with the rolling of waves, promised a long, agonizing voyage. Still, the soldiers and sailors crammed on board had counted on tedium, just not the terror produced by the foulest of weather—and sabotage.[10]

Before the mule transport had left its port of embarkation as part of a thirty-ship convoy, German espionage agents or sympathizers had removed almost every bolt that held the coal ports shut, ensuring that they would burst open in rough seas. The transport would be swamped with water and likely sink, according to the ship's captain, who described the mules as already "half mad." Three officers, one of them Baker, were in charge of the animals.

In the middle of the Atlantic a "storm blew up," said the captain. And this man who had spent almost all of thirty years at sea added, "I never saw anything like it in my life." Winds reached ninety miles an hour. "Great waves slapped us about as though we had a tonnage of 12 pounds instead of 12,000 tons." As the transport rocked in the raging storm, the poor animals slid and toppled across the steel-plated flooring. "Many of them were literally torn to pieces by the tossing and rolling. Their screams of agony were something awful to listen to. I never heard a horse or a mule actually scream before, and it sounded like a human being in terrible agony." The transport was sturdy enough to ride out the storm. But the tampered coal ports ripped open and water gushed in, drowning animals and putting the ship and the men on board in peril. To make matters worse, the starboard propeller snapped off and disappeared beneath the waves. The convoy, already in the German submarine zone, scattered.

"Lieutenant Baker," the ship's captain said, "took command as though tending sick and dying mules in a leaky ship in a gale was the most natural thing he did."

Baker assigned everyone a task. He put together bailing squads and had other men hold back the dead and dying animals so they would not roll over the bailers in the bucking waves, crushing them to death. In the midst of this battle to save the transport, a German U-boat off the port side torpedoed one of the ships in the convoy, sinking it. Two other ships had also been lost. But ignoring the menace outside, Baker kept his men battling the massive leak. Miraculously, concrete had been stored on board, and the quick-thinking Baker used it to erect a kind of dike to shore up the hole just enough to stanch the flow of seawater into the ship.

When the storm had subsided and the transport hobbled into port, four hundred mules were dead. It took the crew a week to clean up the gore.

"You cannot put the courage of Lieutenant Baker and his men high enough," the ship's captain said, admitting he had been scared throughout the entire ordeal. "They were green and they were landsmen, and never a peep of fear or discouragement did anyone hear out of any of them. They're the sort that will lick Germany or I miss my guess."

One of the crew said of Baker, "The young man came aboard a quiet, unassuming chap and left it with every man on board ready and eager to lay down his life for him." For his heroic action, Baker received a formal commendation from the Navy Department.

Once on shore, he wired his parents that he was safe, and then resumed his journey to rejoin the 165th Infantry. On his travels he wrote a letter home that modestly skipped over his adventure, revealing the true nature of a hero. "I am moving around slowly and expect to join my regiment. Of course, I have a great deal to tell you which would be most interesting, but which cannot be written. You know already by my cable that I am safe and well. We had a very rough voyage, but I didn't miss a meal."[11]

After Baker found the regiment, several changes took place that affected lieutenants Basil Elmer and his friend, Oliver Ames Jr., and eventually Joyce Kilmer. Elmer had been told to organize the regiment's Intelligence Section. Kilmer became one of the last to join Elmer's fledgling outfit. Ames was reassigned to Maj. William Donovan's First Battalion as adjutant.

Elmer wrote to his parents that he and Ames had been transferred out of A Company—he to Headquarters and Ames first to the Supply Company for a miserable four days and then on to serve under Donovan. Elmer knew he would now see less of Ames, but he discovered a new friend that would help to make up for the

At Camp Mills, L Company officers Capt. Van S. Merle-Smith and Lt. Charles Baker, both Princeton men, stand alongside Lt. Joseph Carroll (right). Baker's heroics aboard a troop transport earned him a commendation medal from the U.S. Navy. *Signal Corps/National Archives*

disappointment—a dog. "I have a dog whom I have adopted or
rather he has adopted me," he scribbled home. "We understand
each other perfectly." Also, his new position, which he felt was the
"best job in the whole regiment," one he was ideally suited for and
honored to get, came with a horse. However, he had occasion to
write, "I am supposed to be mounted, but the horses haven't yet
put in an appearance."[12]

Ames, while toiling in supply, had complained to his "Ma" of
how he hated the job. He termed it "a lot of bull." His dream had
been "so set to be in the line, in the infantry with handling of
troops, that I thought I would commit suicide." While Ames made
the most of a "miserable" situation, behind the scenes Donovan
and Capt. George McAdie were hounding Barker to turn him over
to the First Battalion. Donovan had had his eye on Ames ever
since the lieutenant led that sixty-two-man detail in Vancouleurs.
Although Ames had made light of the assignment in a letter to his
mother, Donovan knew the men he had put Ames in charge of
were undisciplined, lacked a strong work ethic, and had even cowed
their own noncommissioned officers. Donovan commented that
he had selected Ames for that job because "I felt he would have
the courage and intelligence to take hold of these men and to see
that the work would be properly done." A week later, Wild Bill
inspected the work. "He had done a really fine job," he said. "He
had obtained new clothing and equipment for his detachment.
The men's billets were in good order and well cleaned. There was
a good spirit among the men. He was getting food for them, and
all of the Divisional Staff officers with whom I spoke were most
commendatory of the way in which the work was being handled."[13]

When Barker gave in to Donovan's request, making Ames acting adjutant, the lieutenant was delighted.

And what do you think the Major then did, he made me
his adjutant, which is the greatest honor I've ever had; it
could n't [sic] be so great with any other major but Bill
Donovan, but he, to my mind, in fact to every other who
really knows him, is the 'livest' officer in the American Ex.
Forces, and some day when people at home begin to hear
about him you ought to be proud that your son was once
his adjutant. Perhaps you wonder why, if he is such a 'live
wire,' he is not more than a major; the answer is that for
the last two months general headquarters have been trying

to get him on the staff, but he hates the staff and has his heart set on having the best battalion in the U.S. Army, and with the most wonderful management has succeeded in 'ducking it,' at the same time keeping in good graces. I'm awfully afraid, however, we will lose him soon, which would be a calamity.[14]

As Ames was writing to his mother, Donovan was writing to Ruth. He wondered whether he should go after a staff job. "Perhaps I'm foolish to stay here. Perhaps I should seize the opportunity of getting in that new school where I know both the Commandant and the director but I want to stay by these men here and finish the job. I told the Colonel that I did not expect promotion, that I was content to serve as a major and that I was going to turn out the best battalion in the entire army."[15]

While Donovan worked hard to turn out the best battalion, Elmer worked hard to create the best intelligence section.

"I have never been so busy in my life," he wrote. "Every minute of the day is taken up. The great responsibility of my new work makes it more interesting. I cannot tell you my duties, but I can tell you that I am much more independent than before, being responsible only to the colonel himself." The Cornell graduate explained that he had started out with no organization, no staff and just the sketchiest of plans. "Just to see something mould, or rather to mould into some shape under my hands is its own reward, in satisfaction. If I can but build the scheme into a perfect working machine, I shall indeed be a happy boy."[16]

The Intelligence Section was small. The staff Elmer collected was an eclectic group. He reported that his men were fine. "My new work gives me selected men, men chosen for their intellect, the best men in the regiment. My regret is that I only have eight in all—eight men. It is a shame that they are clerks because they would make good men anywhere."[17]

One of them, Emmett St. Cyr Watson, who in his civilian days had been a magazine illustrator, later recollected that, "Except for Sergeant [John] Kerrigan, an old-time Guardsman, there wasn't a real soldier in the bunch." Among the others were John Livingstone Mott, part of the 165th's growing clan of Princeton men, who had enlisted while in Paris where he worked for the YMCA; Leonard Beck from Hasbrouck Heights, New Jersey; Edwin Titterton from

Orange, New Jersey; and Bill Levinson, whose hometown was actually Paris and who spoke French fluently. Watson, Beck, and Titterton were Seventh Regiment transfers. Watson likened their job to the newspaper business. "All of us had routine duties which took us to the front line, occasionally out into No man's land," he explained. "A member of the Intelligence Section accompanied each night patrol outside the wire. Daily we visited the battalion and company posts of command gathering items on happenings of the day and night, much like reporters assigned to cover a designated beat."

They were a close-knit bunch when Kilmer showed up, did their dangerous work without unnecessarily increasing labor or danger, and stayed out of trouble. According to them, Elmer was an informal officer, treating each of his subordinates as a social equal—even turning a blind eye sometimes when every once in a while they slipped into a nearby village for a glass of wine or a beer. Kilmer did not join them for several months, and they resented the intrusion of the famous poet. They disliked the fact that they had been privates first class when Elmer had assigned them to the Intelligence Section and had gotten no promotions for it, while Kilmer marched in sporting new sergeant's stripes and, as they saw it, taking his rank too seriously.

"It was part of his romantic nature that he visualized himself as a hard-boiled non-com in the best military tradition," Watson thought. "He at first thoroughly disapproved of the easy informality existing between us all, and on duty he insisted upon the observance of promulgated regulations." Watson's impression of the *New York Times* writer had been formed when they had met on the voyage over. At the time, several soldiers, including Watson and Kilmer, were making plans to put out a ship's newspaper. "I still can recall him sitting quietly, puffing at the old blackened pipe which he smoked ceaselessly, taking no part in the discussion."[18] Watson did not know then that Kilmer had no desire for newspaper work. He wanted to be a combatant, not a clerk, and he detested sitting behind a typewriter.

Kilmer had made this clear in his letters to Aline and his mother and to friends in the States. In a missive to his wife he broke the news that he was to be transferred as a sergeant, "although I was willing to give up my stripes for the sake of getting into this work. So henceforth I'll be peering at the Germans through field glasses from some observatory instead of toiling in a dugout or crowded office. You wouldn't want me to come back round-shouldered and near-sighted, would you? Well, that would be the result of keeping on this statistical job much longer. The intelligence work is absolutely fascinating—you'll be glad I took it up."[19]

To his mother he wrote, "I am having an absolutely Heavenly time since I joined the Intelligence Section. I wouldn't change places with any soldiers of any rank in any outfit. This suits me better than any job I ever had in civil life."[20] Once he got to know the soldiers and they got to accept him, he wrote, "I want you to meet all the Regimental Intelligence Section—a fine bunch of brave men, and good comrades. We have taken big chances together, and it has made us the best of friends."[21]

In the meantime, Kilmer's boss, Elmer, had finally gotten his horse. "He is a beauty—a bay with as fine a neck as you ever saw. And the best part of it is he didn't cost me a cent." Also on Elmer's mind, always it seemed, was Ames. "I want to enclose a picture of Ames," he wrote. "I forgot it in my last letter. He's about the only real friend I have outside of Major Donovan, but he's enough, believe me. He's a wonderful boy."[22]

The relationship between Donovan and Ames grew tighter with each passing day. The major worked his young adjutant hard, as he did all men in his battalion. His pace was fast and furious, and he kept Ames up until one or two every morning. In the first days under this regimen, Ames became fatigued—"all in." He had never come across anyone with an intellect so quick; it jumped from one thing to another with a speed that astonished the Harvard graduate, himself no intellectual slouch.

"Donovan has a wonderful mind," he raved to his mother. "The result of years of training, his energy is untiring, his personality is the strongest I've ever come in contact with, and with it all he combines the most consummate tact."

But Ames spotted what he perceived as a flaw in Donovan's makeup: ambition. In a frank letter to his mother, he observed that Donovan's ambition

has no limits, and I'm afraid he may overreach himself: not that he can overreach himself as far as ability goes because he can't, his ability is tremendous, but with conditions as they are now over here, with every inefficient officer fighting to cover himself up, with no system yet developed, with more or less jealousy between officers of the regular army, National Guard and reserve, with ability rather held in suspicion than recognized, to my mind, he may run his head against a rock. Somebody told me if ever he got back alive from this war he would be sure to be governor of New York.[23]

Donovan's feelings toward Ames were equally strong. In a letter to his adjutant's young wife, Anne, he said that her husband had endeared himself to all the battalion officers and that his work was done well, conscientiously, and tactfully. He said that he was full of energy and spirit, attributes that Donovan thought a man should have. "There is no doubt of his courage and more—his good sense," he continued. "He has been recommended for promotion both to regimental and division headquarters. He is known and respected in both places.

"Be proud of him. One day we shall send him to you full of health and honor."[24]

Around the time Donovan wrote to Ames's wife, Duffy sent a letter to the major's brother, a priest himself, Father Vincent. He let him know that he had been trying to get his brother to "go again to the sacraments. And he says he will in a few days. He keeps his word, so I am satisfied."

I have no place for backwardness or politeness about this matter of the sacraments over here. Everybody simply has to go. And everybody goes. That policy suits Bill, whether applied to himself or others. He sends men on trial for offenses to me for confession. And he likes to see me back the shy or the recalcitrant into a corner and uncord a confession. Of course, I have the whole regiment back of my methods, and when I line up a company for confessions, those up first go after the others. . . . I can hear a score of voices shouting "You didn't get Brady, Father" or "Throw Mullins off the cot, and send him up to Fr. Duffy" or "Come on Kane, you may be in hell next week." There is no credit in getting results with such zealous assistants.[25]

In mid-February, in the midst of training in the Rolampont area, the Forty-second Division received orders attaching it to the French VII Army so its men could experience actual trench warfare. Officially, the division was part of the First U.S. Army Corps under Maj. Gen. Hunter Liggett that included the First, Second, and Twenty-sixth Divisions. The French army was made up of four line divisions dug in along a chunk of the front extending from the village of Lunéville to the village of Baccarat. Coincidentally, the numerical designations of the French divisions nearly corresponded with those of the American regiments. The 165th along with one battalion of the 149th Field Artillery reported to the 164th French Division. That part of the sector assigned to the New Yorkers was about thirty kilometers southeast of Nancy and included Lunéville itself and a subsector called Chaussailles-Rouge Bouquet.

Lunéville was the largest village the regiment had yet seen in France. To get there it would have to double back across the Vosges, a trek of more than one hundred and fifty kilometers. This time the men had the luxury of riding in the small boxcar trains. The trains pulled out of Langres on the 16th and arrived in Lunéville the following day. The troops' first taste of combat was days away.

In his diary, Duffy wrote, "The trenches at last!"[26]

Before boarding the troop train from Langres to Lunéville and the trenches, privates Tom Shannon of County Clare, Ireland, and Frank Hays of Brooklyn, both I Company boys, decided that shots of "Palestine," a special concoction Ettinger likened to cognac, were in order. They wanted to slake their thirst before another long, dreary train trip cramped inside what every doughboy called a "side-door Pullman." Neither Hays nor Shannon—whose life story unfolded on the big screen in the 1940 movie "The Fighting 69th," in which James Cagney played a character based on him— had thought that the potency of the home brew would land them in big trouble, drawing down a court-martial against Shannon that, if he were convicted, might end in his execution by firing squad.

Local priests sold "Palestine" in the villages around Langres. In fact, priests in Baissey ran a popular distillery, and the commanding officer of I Company, Capt. Richard Ryan of Watertown, New York, was forced to place it off limits to his men. Ryan was a tough soldier, a Canadian who had fought in the Boer War. (In South Africa his arm had nearly been sliced off by a Boer who attacked him with a saber. Ryan threw up his arm to ward off the blow and suffered a deep gash at the elbow.) To keep his men out of the priests' distillery he posted guards nearby.

On the 15th, Hays went to buy liquor from one of the priests. But when he did not have enough money the priest refused to give him what he thirsted for. Hays went back to his billet and told Shannon, who since first arriving at Camp Mills had earned three convictions for being absent without leave. Grabbing his rifle, Shannon, who was already drunk, staggered into the street. The corporal of the guard, James Sullivan from Brooklyn, heard the bolt of the rifle snap shut and saw Shannon aiming in the direction of the priest. Sullivan pushed Pvt. William Corbett and a girl they had been chatting with inside the guardhouse. A bullet winged past the priest who then gave the two soldiers the liquor they craved. They returned to their billet with Sullivan and Corbett following. Sullivan snatched Shannon's rifle, opened the chamber, and discovered a spent shell. Shannon fell back on his bunk in a drunken stupor. Captain Ryan had him arrested and court-martialed. The officers of the court found Shannon guilty and determined that he should be dishonorably discharged. But legend has it that Duffy intervened on Shannon's behalf, pleading that he stay in the Sixty-ninth.

In the movie, Cagney portrayed Shannon's character, called Jerry Plunkett, as a wisecracking coward whose fear in the front lines led to the death of a number of men, but who, after Duffy's defense of him, died a hero's death. Ettinger described the real man as "stocky and strong as an ox. He had bright red hair, blue eyes, a busted nose, and a cauliflower ear; one tough-looking hombre."[27] If there is one true fact in the movie it is that Shannon died a hero's death. An eyewitness described how during the Battle of the Ourcq River, Shannon advanced under heavy machine-gun fire, suffering severe wounds. He added, "Soldier was of excellent character and was admired by the men of this Company for his fighting spirit."[28] Duffy wrote, "Tom Shannon, being carried in, got off his stretcher and wanted to give his place to another man who, he said, was worse wounded than himself. An officer ordered him back on the stretcher and he was carried in, and since then I have heard he has died of his wounds."[29]

Shannon's drunken deed on the cobbled streets of Baissey and subsequent court-martial served as an omen of the dark days that would soon follow "in the wood they call the Rouge Bouquet."

12

"In the Wood They Call the Rouge Bouquet"

Rouge Bouquet Chaussailles, also known as Point d'Apui Rouge Bouquet, was a subsector of the larger sector of Lunéville, about twelve kilometers west-by-southwest, in the Department of Meurthe-et-Moselle. It was a wooded slice of land with twisted trenches, the bottoms of them duckboarded over so soldiers would not sink up to their knees in mud. Enclosed within the trenches were deep dugout shelters shored up by timber and packed with crude bunks that could house up to a single platoon at a time.

Before hiking off to the front line, the regiment stayed a week in Lunéville, an old city famous for its glazed earthenware pottery and for being the home of the exiled seventeenth-century Polish king Stanislaus I. Father-in-law to King Louis XV, Stanislaus had been given the province of Lorraine to rule until his death. He set up court in Lunéville, where he built a magnificent stone castle and barracks. The Forty-second Division, when it arrived there in the hard winter of 1918, was grateful for the use and warmth of the castle and barracks.

The 165th Infantry's headquarters company and staff were assigned to the castle, and the regiment's line companies were placed in the barracks—better accommodations than smelly stables and lofts. "There was a superstition among us by this time that all of France was composed of nothing but shabby little towns, where pigs brooded in melancholy in the muddy streets and cows parked themselves on the sidewalks," Martin Hogan recalled. "Lunéville was a sensation to us. It was quite a respectable village, with more life in it than any place in our French experience."[1]

About the days in Lunéville, Father Francis Duffy quipped, "We have been having the unwonted joys of city life."[2]

A rolling kitchen from K Company nears Camp New York in the Lunéville
Sector on 2 March. *Signal Corps/National Archives*

Al Ettinger discovered one of those unwonted joys. "We
encountered our first ladies of the night since landing in France,"
he wrote. "And some of us had an introduction to sex with a capital 'S'." In fact, after his first time spent in the arms of a "lady of
the night" he was smitten. She was a war widow and supplemented
her meager pension by "favor[ing]" certain soldiers. Ettinger had
been one of the favored and "managed to visit her several times."[3]

George Benz, also, noted the "immoral houses," reporting that
"there were quite a few in town."[4]

Basil Elmer wrote, "We are having lots of fun here . . . the best
time we have had since we landed in France." Although not billeted
in Stanislaus's old castle, he had located a furnished apartment with
kitchen and electric lights. While he slept in a bedroom, his orderly
bunked in the kitchen. "He takes care of our rooms, makes the
beds, etc., and cooks our breakfasts for us. We go to the hotel nearby
for the other two meals. Best of all we have a real live water closet
with running water. It is quite luxurious." At the restaurant he discovered another luxury, native beer. "It is wonderful. We drink it at
meals instead of the red wine we have been having." The only down

side that he mentioned was that "Ollie Ames is around but I haven't seen him for a week."[5]

One soldier not having a grand time was Joyce Kilmer. Soon after the regiment reached Lunéville he began to smart from a "muscle strain" and landed in a "charming" hospital. He "sojourned" there for twelve days.[6]

The 165th's stay in Lunéville was short. It was ordered to go to Camp New York in the forest around Croixmare, prior to entering the trenches under French supervision. According to Benz, Camp New York was "buried in a little forest." Flooded was more like it. Duffy likened the place to a floating "Noah's Ark in a sea of mud."[7] Hogan said it was the muddiest place in France. "It oozed, slopped, quivered and trickled. It slipped down our backs, matted our hair, got into our eyes and savored our food. We floundered and splashed and chunked through its wallows. We reveled in mud like turtles and ground hogs."[8] Benz agreed. "You didn't know if you were going into a camp or a batch of lakes." Cracked one of his boys, "Why they ever called it Camp New York I don't know. [The place] shames even New York."[9]

The trip to the trenches was to give the doughboys a taste of warfare. Each battalion would spend ten days there, mixed in with French units, and then be relieved. They would experience artillery fire and enemy raids and, if they proved themselves worthy, the French might allow a company to undertake a raid into no-man's-land.

The first in was the First Battalion.

In the early morning of 27 February, Bill Donovan's men, led by Capt. Jim McKenna's D Company, took over for a battalion of French chasseurs. The French machine-gun company stayed to enlighten America's citizen-soldiers on the ins and outs of trench warfare. The night before the Americans moved in Donovan had issued a memorandum to his commanders instructing them in how he expected his men to conduct themselves. The major reminded them that they were headed for the trenches "courtesy of the French and are under their instruction, guidance and direction." He warned them that their men must "conduct themselves quietly and with thought given to the fact that they are in the presence of the enemy." The memorandum went on:

We are here to accomplish a definite purpose. We shall set out to do that cheerfully and willingly, each man

Capt. Jim McKenna's D Company marches toward the trenches in the Lunéville Sector. His company was the regiment's first to enter the front lines. *Signal Corps/National Archives*

doing as best as he can the day's work, and each man being held responsible for performing that work faithfully, and at the same time of keeping himself, his uniform and equipment in a clean and soldierly condition. It may be that the French Command shall, before we leave our position, determine that we are in fit condition to attempt a small operation. The best preparation for that day is to meet fairly and accomplish thoroughly each day's task.[10]

Then, Donovan instructed his platoon commanders to ask themselves six questions.

1. Do I know my particular job here?
2. Do I know the amount of reserve ammunition I have on hand?
3. Do I know the use and purpose of each and every signal at this post?

4. Have I instructed my men in, and do they know
   A. The place of each in time of attack?
   B. The use and purpose of the signals?
   C. The use of the new hand grenades?
5. Am I doing my utmost in looking out for the men in my platoon so
   A. That they receive their food at the same hour?
   B. That this food is served hot?
   C. That every effort is made to give them 7 hours sleep?
6. Can I conscientiously say that I am giving the best attention to the feet of my men, insisting
   A. That socks are changed at least once a day or if no extra socks that socks are changed from one foot to the other?
   B. That each man bathes and rubs his feet each day?[11]

While the First Battalion hiked into the trenches during the night of the 26th and 27th, with rain and sleet pelting off their steel helmets, they heard the big guns up close. Thomas Johnson of the *New York Evening World* climbed up a tree to watch the men go in. He described the leafless forest that gave the place a sinister appearance. "The forest looked dark reddish brown, the color of rusted iron or it might be old blood stains. Down on the ground it looked black and forbidding."[12]

In reserve, the soldiers of the Second and Third Battalions watched the orange and red flares light the sky while beneath their hobnailed shoes the ground shook. "Over there before us was the enemy," wrote Hogan, "and to those of us with imagination his guns seemed to be calling to us tauntingly."[13]

Hunkered down inside the trenches, Donovan's boys felt the fierce overhead pounding of artillery. Almost to a man they shuddered and trembled. The section they were in looked like a "sinuous line" with duckboard paths zigzagging in different directions. Trees toppled by shellfire lay across the trenches "like slain giants, while brushwood tossed about by the same force plucked at one's trench coat like the hands of unseen goblins or wood spirits."[14] For the most part the soldiers lived in "mean little dugouts thinly roofed, poorly floored, wet and cold."[15] Near Donovan's command post a first aid station was set up. Before anyone in D Company got settled, McKenna, a detailed-oriented officer like Donovan, cautioned them to keep down, be quiet and not let curiosity get the best of them. "[We] are in the presence of the enemy, . . . there are sentinels on

Maj. Bill Donovan's First Battalion enters the trenches near Rouge Bouquet. The soldier overseeing the troops, with hand on hip, is most likely Donovan. *Signal Corps/National Archives*

watch at all times and in all places throughout the territory, and that the danger of being fired upon when appearing unexpectedly, even by our allies or neighboring American troops, is not to be minimized."[16]

But in A Company, Joe McKinney, son of a New York City police captain, bragged that the boys "don't care what happens to them. When the shrapnel bursts overhead we all duck and trust to our steel helmets and to good luck."[17]

Two companies away from McKinney, Edmond McCarthy, a Brooklyn lawyer, survived that first day. "I have heard the song of the big ones and can now almost distinguish the various brands from the sound." He confessed that he had been jumpy at night and living in the muck had been "very hard on an ex-law clerk who never lived very much in the open." McCarthy had been as- signed to Capt. William Kennelly as a "liaison agent," which meant, he said, that he was a "confidential man for his captain and also he must be able to run like the wind."[18]

Another Brooklyn boy, Earl Pierce, wished his mother had seen the night bombardment. "First, you see a star shell pierce the dark- ness, illuminating the whole works, that is followed by the sharp rat-tat-tat of a Boche machine gun. Then the bullets whine over one's head only to splat against a tree, then various colored lights would burst from the Boche and the indescribable whistle of a shell would come to us followed by the roar from the fragments of steel, stones, mud and other stuff, falling around us. Then a gas signal shows and we don our gas masks. So much for life in the trenches."[19]

McKenna retrieved a hunk of shrapnel to keep as a souvenir. "It is a fragment of the first German shell to explode over this regiment. I picked it out of the hole myself within a minute of the explosion, so you need not doubt its authenticity. Incidentally, it got two of my men, but both will recover." He said he was proud that those two men—Cpl. Arthur Trayer of Freeport, Long Island, and Pvt. John Lyons of Cedarhurst, New York—had been the division's first casualties. "You do not know how much we are envied by the others, but you can imagine how every company and every soldier hungered for the honor of being the first in line and how pleased I am to have had my company gain the boon, and then exceed expectations."[20]

At an outpost in the Lunéville Sector, sentries peer into the woods. Moments later, a German artillery shell destroyed the outpost, drawing first blood against the New Yorkers. The two men are probably Cpl. Arthur Trayer and Pvt. John Lyons, the Forty-second Division's first combat casualties. *Signal Corps/National Archives*

The German artillery assault was relentless. Shells rained down on the entire division, in the trenches or back in reserve positions. On 5 March, Oliver Ames sent an intelligence report to company commanders in Donovan's battalion, announcing the Rainbow's first combat deaths. During the night of the 4th, a heavy bombardment had hit the 168th Infantry. "One captain, one corporal and 5 men were killed and 10 wounded," he typed out. "The Germans then attacked the position, but were repulsed with heavy losses, and were unable to take one prisoner."[21]

Although the First Battalion suffered its own casualties while in the trenches, no one was killed. Perhaps the worst situation it had to deal with was the lack of gun oil. Tom Reilley pleaded for Wild Bill to apply pressure on the supply company to furnish gun oil for the troops on the firing line. "Since our occupation of the sector . . . it has rained or snowed every day, and although the men have endeavoured to keep their arms in proper condition . . . we have found it impossible to keep them in good shape. This should be remedied so that the other Battalions who are about to come up will be able to maintain their armament in proper condition. The company of French troops on our left have been furnished more oil per squad than we have received for our entire company during our period of occupancy of the trenches."[22]

Earlier Donovan had come across a soldier shouldering a dirty rifle. He was ready to order the man not go into the trenches.

"Sure Major, don't be sayin' that," the soldier had groaned. "Twill be the killin' of me. If I go into the trenches I get kilt maybe by them Boshes, but if ye kape me out, sure I'll die av a broken heart. Aren't ye goin' to give me a chance for me life at all?" His plea softened Donovan and he let him go in with his company.[23]

Two days after Reilley had pleaded with Donovan, the Second Battalion relieved the First. Maj. William Stacom's Companies E, F, G, and H left for Camp New York on 1 March. The men carried two days' reserve rations and one blanket each. Officers were allowed one bedding roll. Six days later the battalion settled in, awaiting its fate in the subsector of Rouge Bouquet. Like the boys of the First Battalion, the troops of the Second were jumpy, on edge, wondering what it would be like in the trenches.

As the companies took their places at nine on the morning of 7 March, some of the boys, like the typical New Yorkers they were, tossed wisecracks back and forth. But the night before, when they reached Camp New York prior to moving in, they had been serious. There they had seen Duffy standing in the muddy square of one of the small villages. Sergeant Major Michael Bowler, from County Cork, and his battalion boys went up to the chaplain. "No ceremonies," Bowler said. "He put his arm around each man, it required but a few a seconds for each one of us and then we turned into our barn for the night." The next morning, as they marched out of camp they passed a crude altar Duffy had erected. "All the regiment received Holy Communion," Bowler reported. "Immediately afterwards we moved in on our sector of the line, and by evening occupied the trenches and looked across no-man's land at the Boche. The Sixty-ninth were in the trenches!"[24]

The subsector assigned to E Company, commanded by Capt. William Cavanaugh, a former battalion adjutant, had names like Rezonville, Patte d'Oie, and Rocroi. Here E Company relieved A Company, under George McAdie. Rocroi was an eight-hundred-yard front that ran uphill to an observation post. Along that stretch of front were four dugouts built early in the war. Three of them were in poor shape and held together by rotting timber. Not only were the dugouts in disrepair, they had been constructed on the forward side of Rocroi hill—facing enemy guns—not on the reverse slope where they would be out of sight of German artillerymen and snipers.

As E Company marched into the trenches in single file it was met by McAdie's platoon commanders and noncommissioned officers, who, acting the role of wily old veterans after their turn in the trenches, escorted the greenhorns to their posts. Once they had them in position they instructed them on their duties as front-line soldiers with an enemy that watched and waited just across no-man's-land.

One of the escorts was Sgt. Danny O'Connell, the former Rockaway Beach altar boy who had broken his mother's heart when he enlisted. After arriving in France he had assured her that there was no need to worry. "I am feeling fine and hard as nails, and you bet I sleep every night without rocking." If Mary O'Connell had seen her boy now, guiding soldiers through the serpentine slit of slimy earth in this patch of the Western Front she would have been thrilled. She had no idea he had been promoted to sergeant. Later she told a newspaper reporter "I am proud and happy and somehow glad he went and I feel sure he is coming back."[25]

Inside the trenches, O'Connell waited until E Company's First Platoon, led by 1st Lt. John Norman, a Swede described as "Lincolnesque" because of his lean and lanky frame, passed by and then followed. "I went along and assigned the men to their different positions and fire bays. The men were mixed up in different arms—automatic, rifles, etc—which caused slight confusion," he recalled. Because Norman was not sure what to tell his men, O'Connell took charge. He explained how they should hold their positions in case of attack and what arms to use. His own company commander then attached him to Norman's platoon until it had settled down and learned from him what it had to do.

His first task was to divide up Norman's platoon, assigning thirty men to Dugout Number One, the largest of the underground shelters, and fifteen men to Dugout Number Two. Dugout Number One was the worst of the lot—a decrepit forty-foot-deep hole, lit by a half-dozen "guttering candles."[26] The air stank of dank earth, stale mustard gas, and dirty men. Richard O'Neill complained that the "worst thing about [the trenches] was the living conditions—the mud, the cooties, the rats—just lousy living, that's all."[27]

When O'Connell had them organized in the dugouts, he reported back to Norman. He took the lieutenant and his platoon sergeant on a tour of the fire bays and posts. He explained in detail what they were for and how they had to be manned and the responsibilities of each soldier at his post. Norman took down notes, and after the tour he seemed pleased.

"Come along, Sergeant, to the post commander's dugout," he said amiably, "and sit and have a smoke."

As they headed to the post command, O'Connell noticed that the men he had just placed in the dugouts were now outside, airing their straw bed sacks on top of the trench wall. He warned Norman that he had better tell his men to remove the bed sacks and get back inside the dugouts. He said the bed sacks would give away their location to the enemy, explaining that there were snipers in the woods who could easily pick off his men. "Also," he said, "they were violating an order which was that no men were allowed to be above the skyline or in the trenches except when on duty."

The consequences of the airing out of the bed sacks would soon be felt.

A shaken Norman ordered the men back to their dugouts, then, grateful for O'Connell's sage advice, invited him to mess with his platoon. O'Connell accepted, and after lunch ran into Spencer Rossell, a fellow sergeant temporarily attached to E Company's Second Platoon. Rossell suggested they head back to the YMCA canteen for candy and cigarettes. O'Connell asked Norman if it was all right for him to leave.

"Why certainly, Sergeant," he said. "Go right ahead." Leaving with Rossell saved O'Connell's life.[28]

Among the First Platoon men inside Dugout Number One were Alf Helmer, the native of Bergen, Norway, and Philip Schuyler Finn, the son of the late Tammany sachem, "Battery Dan" Finn." Finn had just written to his brother, assuring him that "some day in the near future [I'll] relate some of my experiences to you, and then you will look upon me as a real soldier."[29] The last thing he had said to family and friends, after giving away many of his personal belongings: "They'll get me, but I'm going to get some of them first."[30]

Another soldier inside the dugout was William Drain, a "freckle-faced, skinny East Side kid."[31] And there was Frank Meagher, whose brother-in-law, Douglas MacKenzie, was also in E Company; John Legall Jr.; and Elwood Raymond. Legall's brother, Leonard, was in K Company. Two men were from Headquarters: Art Hegney and Edwin Kearney. Another Headquarters man was Joe Jones, who had argued with his girl before leaving Camp Mills. He had been assigned to E Company, but at the last moment wound up in a different sector. In his diary for 7 March, he wrote, "Life saved by being switched from Rocroy to Chausildes. And two killed. E. Kearney and Hegney."[32]

Helmer remembered that before the First Platoon entered the dugout in the midst of a German artillery barrage, he and his fellow soldiers had been as eager as a football team before a kick-off to get at the enemy. "Soon rifles were cracking along the whole Rouge Bouquet front," he said, "and almost without exception at imagined targets in the wide expanse of no-man's land."[33]

In fact, the platoons in E Company fired away, the heads of the soldiers fully exposed above the rim of the trench. In some cases, they stood atop the trench in view of the Germans, who sniped at them. They shouted at the Germans to come out and fight like men.

First Lt. Oscar Buck, whose A Company had been relieved by Cavanaugh's men, turned back when he heard the clatter of rifle

Alf Helmer, a native of Norway, was one of the few survivors of the cave-in at Rouge Bouquet. *Courtesy of Jan Helmer*

fire. "Enemy infantry was firing a few long range shots," he reported. "Our infantry at Rocroy firing freely. Men were circulating above ground in small groups. Two small groups (4–6 men) could be seen in the woods in rear of our wire at Rocroy. I counted four men in one fire bay, looking toward the enemy lines, their mess kits on the parapet in front of them." He found Cavanaugh and ordered him to "correct this carelessness."[34]

Around two in the afternoon, the Allies began shelling German defenses. The men of the First Platoon dashed out of their dugout to witness the spectacle. "None of us missed the show," Helmer recalled. But an hour later, at three, the Germans fired back. "A screaming, banging hurricane of hardware, high explosives, shrapnel and *minenwerfers* [muzzle-loading mortars]. Yet the storm of projectiles did not drive us to cover. Almost to a man we watched the rain of potential death in fascination, some running to examine new shell craters as they were made, suggesting puppy retrievers chasing firecrackers on July fourth."

Lieutenant Norman, who had been momentarily buried in debris and slightly wounded in the barrage, ordered his platoon back inside the dugout. The men, "fighting game-cocks," according to Helmer, grudgingly retreated, jumping down the steep stairway that made several right angles as it descended forty feet beneath the ground. Helmer obeyed Norman, but not until he had watched a German projectile wail over his head and strike one of his regiment's one-pound cannons. A black cloud rose where the cannon had been and then chunks of earth and bits of metal and what was left of a tree stormed down around the awe-struck corporal. When the show was over, he dropped into the dugout, the last man in.

The artillery bombardment lasted through the afternoon and evening, and with each explosion the dugout shuddered. Rotten timbers quaked. Dirt broke lose from above. Private Drain looked up anxiously at the shaky earthen ceiling. Not liking what he saw he slipped under the bottom bunk of a row of bunks stacked against the dugout wall.

Norman reminded his men to make sure that when the shelling ended they get up into the trenches. No sooner had he issued his order than a shell hit the dugout roof. The thud was ominous. The ensuing explosion rocked the ground. Rotten beams gave way, and the ceiling fell. "Tons of earth and stones cascaded," Helmer wrote. "I remember only the crash. Thoughts ceased. I only know that I found myself in the doorway of the forward entrance, hands extended over my head."[35]

When O'Connell and Rossell reached the YMCA canteen they found it closed. Heading back to their command posts, they ran into Lt. Arthur Cunningham, who informed them that the telephone lines in that sector had been destroyed. The sergeants bolted into the trenches to work their way back to where E Company was holed up. Rossell and O'Connell were "met with a fire of shrapnel." They continued "through the trenches as best we could, for the shrapnel was coming fast," Rossell later testified. When they got to the command post they saw that it had been heavily damaged, and the dugouts had caved in. Their own equipment—packs and weapons—had been destroyed. At one of the dugouts they each grabbed a rifle and a cartridge bandolier and then, as artillery shells exploded around them, rushed toward the dugouts where O'Connell had placed the First Platoon.

Also dashing toward the stricken dugout was William Moore, another A Company sergeant. He had been ordered by Buck to find out what had happened. When he reached Rocroi he ran into Rossell who gave him the bad news that Norman and his men were trapped under tons of earth and timber.

O'Connell discovered that all fifteen men at Dugout Number Two were alive, if dazed and agitated. Over the horrific noise of exploding shells, the former altar boy barked at them not to lose their heads, to keep quiet, that everything would be all right. Then, from one of the platoon sergeants, he heard the grim details of the destruction of Dugout Number One.

To a surviving sergeant, O'Connell said, "You hold all the men here and have them ready to position, so that when the barrage lifts they will be ready to come out of the dugout." He next worked his way to the demolished dugout. A few men were outside, and they said that Norman and every single one of his men inside was dead. If Norman had been killed O'Connell was now in charge of that subsector.[36]

Inside Dugout Number One, half the soldiers had survived the cave-in, but there was no way out—the two entrances were blocked. The darkness was absolute. The survivors moaned and wept. Helmer found himself in the front stairway, arms over his head. There was enough air there for him to breathe, yet he was held fast by a broken hunk of timber that had fallen on his foot. Dirt drifted down on him and slowly filled the dugout. In the turmoil and fear he seemed to recognize the voices nearest him as those of "slight boyish Private Raymond and gentle, gray-haired Private McCormack." Helmer realized that his body was shielding them from the rising dirt. He felt a body touching his and knew it was William Ellinger. One of the heavier beams had dropped on Ellinger's shoulders. He struggled to hold it up so it would not fall on the men trapped below him. A strong lad, Ellinger held the beam for some time, then his legs gave way. He prayed aloud and proclaimed his "gallant fight" to his mother as he no longer had the strength to hold the beam. "And then there was a crash and silence," Helmer said, "as the gaining weight above forced him down to death."

Deeper into the dugout, Norman, his stomach pierced by a fallen timber, had curled up on a bunk. Some of the frightened survivors huddled around him in the pitch dark, the stench of earth and gas filling their nostrils.

"We are fighting for a good cause," Norman said. "It is worthwhile. Let us die like men."

Under his bunk, Drain, his leg broken, encouraged the men. He claimed they would be saved; that the men outside would not let them suffocate; that in no time they would be dug out and brought up into the fresh air.[37]

Even though the barrage was endless, there were lulls in the firing, and at those moments the Americans poured out of the dugouts that had withstood the assault. With rifles at the ready, they lined up along the trench walls to repulse any attack. In the first lull, O'Connell, seeing that many of the men in his sector were in disarray, got them organized properly. He then stood on the fire steps and searched across no-man's-land for the enemy.

Later in the afternoon, Donovan showed up, an officer's walking stick clutched in his hand. That morning he had observed how the men in the Second Battalion had been more nervous than his own and, worse, "did not have as good discipline, displaying themselves too much; and the officers did not seem as well informed as to their duties." He was in Major Stacom's command post with Maj. Marion Battle, the division's assistant adjutant, when word reached them that Norman's platoon had been wiped out. Donovan asked for permission to go there and make an accurate assessment of the damage. He wanted to make sure that panic did not overcome the men, and he wanted to be in charge of any rescue attempts. Battle refused to let him go. Majors were not expendable, he said; instead, send a lieutenant. When Battle left, Donovan said to Stacom that he ought to send him up to Rocroi. Stacom agreed.

When Donovan reached the subsector amid the continued enemy shelling he came across Cavanaugh sitting at his post, stunned. Another officer, 2nd Lt. Marshall Tarr, seemed frozen with fear. According to Sergeant Moore, Donovan went up to Tarr, cane in hand, looked at him hard, and asked if he had "his guts with him."

"Yes Sir!" Tarr replied.[38]

Donovan ordered him and Moore to locate entrenching tools, put together a rescue party and start digging out the buried men.

The lack of air inside the dugout had taken its toll. "Choking dust and gas stench filled the suffocating darkness," said Helmer. "Cries and moans at first were a blur of sound, with agony the keynote."

Pinned at the stairwell, Helmer, a Lutheran, prepared to die. "I gave myself to prayer, prayers for my parents, the Lord's prayer. Making my peace with God I was no longer afraid."

One by one, Helmer heard his trapped comrades die, some whimpering, others fiercely cursing, and still others going "quietly, nobly, with religious resignation." As each of his comrades died, Helmer saw something in the pitch dark that he kept to himself for years. He later swore that a faint purple light rose slowly from the body of each dead soldier, up toward the ceiling of the dugout, where it disappeared.[39]

Above the cave-in, men dug with a fury to save their fellow soldiers. The shelling continued as the late afternoon gave way to the eerie light of an early March evening. Flares burst overhead, illuminating the clawing figures bent at their work. The Germans lobbed gas bombs toward the rescue effort. With mustard gas now creeping through the trenches and over the ground of Rocroi, the men donned their gas masks; but then they went right back to their task to somehow open the dugout.

Among the frantic diggers was Abraham Blaustein, the Jewish sergeant from Brooklyn. He had been one of the first men to reach the blown-up dugout. As he later recollected, no one, it seemed, had yet done a thing. They stood around "dumbfounded." Blaustein saw a gaping hole in the ground about twenty feet deep. He slid into the hole. "Here I came upon dead men and men smothered, yelling for help. After laying on my back for eight long consecutive hours I succeeded in rescuing quite a few of the men with the aid of a shovel and small pick." He described how the shells kept coming "thick and fast" and when morning broke he was "deserted and left alone. I could no longer dig. My strength was sapped away and I collapsed."[40]

Ettinger was also there. He watched as his Pioneer unit labored all night long. "It was terrible as they tried to lift those shattered timbers, all the while hearing the survivors plead for help forty feet below. Of all the men there, however, it had been Blaustein, according to Ettinger, "who really took charge and led by example. The men worked in relays, but Blaustein always took the most dangerous position." Meanwhile, men from other E Company platoons begged to pitch in to save their friends. "Plenty of help," Ettinger observed, "but my God, only a few men could work in that narrow opening, and the Germans were shelling constantly during the rescue attempt."[41]

Down in that opening, they dug with their helmets, filling them as fast as they could and then passing them up like an "old-fashioned fire bucket brigade, slowly, o how slowly."[42]

Even Donovan got into the act. He slid down into the hole and "got them organized a little better." Meanwhile, German and French flares turned night into day. Realizing there was nothing more he could do, Donovan climbed out. He spotted a frightened guard peering over the trench wall. He put his arm around the soldier. "You going to let those damned Dutchmen get your goat?" he said. The soldier said "No Sir," and "grasped his gun a little more firmly, and resumed his watch more intently." Donovan realized that too many troops were at risk and had them moved out of harm's way. He then rounded up ten men and marched them into the woods just as the bombardment intensified. He ordered everyone to lie flat on the ground. Shells flew past the trenches to where they were with a "whistling, penetrating noise and seemed to be seeking us out individually. They were striking around us and lighting up the dead trees. In the blaze of the explosion you could see the twigs and the branches and sometimes the trees crash down." He got the men out of the woods and into the trench system and headed them back to the command post. The bombardment kicked in again and with it the klaxon horn, warning of another gas barrage. One of the soldiers became "obnoxious" with fear. Rushing up to him, Donovan "handed him a good punch in the jaw. That quieted them all down."[43]

Inside the dugout, Helmer felt the deadly grip of dirt around his body loosen and fall away. A hole finally opened up and he was almost free—except for his foot, still pinned by the fallen timber. But now there was enough room to pull out McCormack and Raymond. As they were lifted out, their bodies brushing by him, Helmer feared he would not make it. He thought his only chance was to cut off his foot, and he had a pocketknife that could do the grisly job. But just before Raymond was pulled clear of the dugout, he pulled back, refusing to be rescued until he found a way to free Helmer's foot from under the timber.

"It was quite a struggle he had, tugging and pulling with all his slight strength to free me," Helmer recalled "But success at last crowned our efforts and after some twelve hours of horror I crawled upwards to again breathe God's fresh air."[44]

As he and three men were transported back to the company command post, Helmer thought his nightmare was over. But a shell exploded next to him, killing Pvt. Edward Kelly from the East Side and wounding Pvt. Stephen Navin from the Bronx. Navin admitted years afterward that even though there was not much left of Kelly, he ran toward him. "I saw a pale purple blob of light rise from Kelly's body." The purple light, like the lights Helmer had seen inside the dugout, continued skyward, and passed through a cloud. "I always figured that must've been Kelly's soul rising up into heaven."[45]

After escorting Navin to a medical clearing station, Helmer reached the command post and reported to Cavanaugh. Then he broke down. His body trembled. He wept uncontrollably, blurting out, between sobs, the tragedy that had occurred back at the dugout. Pulling himself together, he requested permission to go back to try to save any survivors that were left.

"I knew that unless I saw the thing through," he admitted, "I would never again be able to look my comrades in the face."

By now Lieutenant Tarr had returned to supervising the rescue. But the constant shelling thwarted the work, and with each explosion the ground shook and more of the dugout collapsed inward.

As Helmer rejoined the men digging at the slight opening that had been made, he prayed that at least Drain would be saved. He spied the row of bunks under which the private had crawled. He yelled that they had to get Drain out first. But Drain, still clinging to the hope that everyone would be saved, yelled back, "Don't bother with me, get the other fellows!"

Another shell then rocked the ground and an "avalanche" of earth closed up the opening, entombing the men once again.[46]

At the First Battalion command post, Donovan slumped down at his field desk and started a letter to Ruth about the tragic events of the day. He described his encounter with the young guard and how he had comforted him and then, later, come across his body. The boy had been hit in the head with shrapnel. "I hope, Ruth, that if my day should come here I would be lucky enough to die as he did." He put his pencil down, unable to continue while there was unfinished business out in Rouge Bouquet. He headed back to the cave-in.

Working his way through the trenches, Donovan saw O'Connell ahead of him in the gloom. The sergeant led him to the front entrance. The shadows of men with picks and shovels and entrenching tools, still struggling to break a new hole into the dugout, flickered in the light of a single candle. They toiled without end. From beneath the tons of earth, came the muffled, despairing whimpers of the few men left alive. One voice cried out, "Come on, come on, fellows!" And then the voice changed to a murmur. "Mother!"

Donovan shouted down to them, "We will get you out! We will get you out!"[47]

O'Connell later remembered the major's shouts and how he ripped off his gas mask and coat and joined the digging. Donovan later told Ruth, "Took off my gas mask, coat, climbed in there myself where this earth was falling, thought again of you and the youngsters, wished I had finished my letter, and then made up my mind that the one thing to do was to go to work. Had only a little entrenching tool."[48]

As he dug he was conscious of the men around him, "tense and white and tired, and while willing to face all personal dangers, rapidly losing their nerve at the cries of the poor devils and the absolute futility and hopelessness of it all." And then Donovan knew that "nothing more could be done and that this must be their tomb." He wished that more dirt would fall in and that he might be buried there with those poor souls. Climbing out of the hole, dirty and tired, he saw standing atop the dugout the three sergeants from his own battalion, O'Connell, Moore, and Rossell. Maybe there was one last chance!

Addressing O'Connell, he ordered him to take some men and find the rear entrance—maybe they could get in from that side. He said he wanted the dugout open by daybreak. Helmer volunteered to go with O'Connell. He wanted to save Drain. They took off through the trench, but had not gotten far when a thick mound of earth brought them up. In the endless barrage, the trench, like the dugout, had collapsed. The only way past was to put their lives in danger by crawling into no-man's-land. Risking sniper fire, the two men leaped over the rim of the trench, their bodies exposed to the enemy. They rolled quickly along the muddy ground, bullets now cracking over them, until they had reached the other side of the dirt barrier and dropped back into the trench. In a moment they stood at the rear entrance, or at least where it had been. It had been reduced to a mere hole, but it held promise. Helmer worked his way down, praying there was a chance to free the last of the trapped men, those who might still be alive like Drain.

"There I found the dirt piled solidly against the bottom stairs," Helmer bitterly wrote afterward. "I called for Drain and the others, again and again."[49]

Instead of directing Helmer to clear the entrance, O'Connell had him work on the barrier that blocked the trench. He said he would go back, get some help and start digging from the other side. Once there was an opening then more men could be brought quickly and used to break through dugout door. It had to be cleared by morning, he said. Rolling across no-man's-land again, O'Connell slid back into the safety of his own trench. As his feet hit the bottom of the trench, a hand thumped hard into his chest, stopping him in his tracks.

"Who is that?" said a trembling voice. "I came very near to shooting you."

"Sergeant O'Connell. God damn it!"

A flare lit the sky and in the flash O'Connell found himself staring into the face of Marshall Tarr. He brushed by the lieutenant, found two men and ordered them to work on clearing the trench.

Snipers peppered the ground around them with bullets. The men looked anxiously at O'Connell.

"Keep on digging," he said.

Tarr complained that it was too dangerous, that O'Connell was putting the men's lives at risk. "Lieutenant, I have an order from the battalion commander in the front-line trench and it must be obeyed." But Tarr was adamant that they leave.

"Lieutenant, will you take the responsibility?" O'Connell asked.

"I will take the responsibility," Tarr said. He said he would go back to the command post and send up another officer. O'Connell watched Tarr disappear down the trench and throughout the rest of the night no officer came to help.

"Then I knew," O'Connell testified, "it was up to me to still hold the trench." The only thing left for O'Connell to do was organize a defense against possible attack. All night he went from post to post, instructing soldiers as to what they had to do in case the Germans came. It wasn't until five in the morning that a lieutenant showed up. And when he got there he refused to relieve the exhausted sergeant.[50]

By now Helmer had rejoined O'Connell. Instead of following him from post to post, he went back to the front entrance, where Blaustein still pawed at the earth with an entrenching tool.

"Fear gripped me as I stumbled and slid down the broken slope into the black tomb for the last time," Helmer wrote. "Again I called, until the empty echo of my own voice suddenly overcame me with a lonely terror." He seized a rifle and then, leaving Blaustein alone, "scrambled in mad flight from the chamber of awful horror," the last words of Bill Drain screaming inside his head, "Don't bother about me, save the others."[51]

Twenty-one men had been killed in the cave-in. The dead who had been pulled out of the dugout were buried in a small cemetery beside the road that led out of the village of Croixmare. The rest were left where they had died.

"We have our sorrows, too, in a railed-in plot," Sgt. Maj. Bowler wrote to the editor of the *Irish Advocate*. "Some of our pals were sleeping their last sleep. Taps have sounded for them. They lie in trim little rows with the tricolor and Old Glory entwined at the head of each."[52]

The body of Philip Schuyler Finn had been taken to that railed-in plot at Croixmare. The youngest son of "Battery Dan" never got his German, as he had boasted he would to family and friends. In New York, the board of alderman named the slice of land in the First Assembly District where West Broadway and Varick and Franklin Streets merge, "Finn Square." A reporter for the *Sun* noted how, while he was growing up, it had been Finn's nature to laugh and sing his way into the hearts of the community.[53] He was the first soldier from Gotham to be honored by the city for his sacrifice in the Great War.

Duffy felt grateful that before the boys had gone into the trenches he had heard their last confessions and that some of them had then stayed for a "little friendly personal chat." In his diary he wrote, "We have had our first big blow, and we are still reeling under the pain and sorrow of it." He went down to the caved-in dugout, read the services of the dead and blessed the spot where his boys were now entombed.[54]

The graves of the first soldiers of the old Sixty-ninth to fall in battle. Most of them are from E Company, casualties of the Rouge Bouquet cave-in. *Signal Corps/National Archives*

Finishing his letter to Ruth, Donovan penned, "To-day in a little promontory in a Lorraine forest, a Lieutenant and his men have done with the war. For my part, I think it is a fine thing for the regiment to have them meet so honorable a death, revenge for which is determined upon by their comrades—and really it is only that they have got a little sooner what each of us always expects."[55]

After his release from the hospital for "muscle strain," Joyce Kilmer thought about the death of those men, and then immortalized them in a poem he entitled, "Rouge Bouquet."

> In a wood they call the Rouge Bouquet
> There is a new-made grave to-day,
> Built by never a spade nor pick
> Yet covered with earth ten metres thick.
> There lie many fighting men,
> Dead in their youthful prime,
> Never to laugh nor love again
> Nor taste the Summertime.
> For Death came flying through the air
> And stopped his flight at the dugout stair,
> Touched his prey and left them there,
> Clay to clay.
> He hid their bodies stealthily
> In the soil of the land they fought to free
> And fled away.
> Now over the grave abrupt and clear
> Three volleys ring:
> And perhaps their brave young spirits hear
> The bugle sing:
> "Go to sleep!
> Go to sleep!
> Slumber well where the shell screamed and fell.
> Let your rifles rest on the muddy floor,
> You will not need them anymore.
> Danger's past;
> Now at last,
> Go to sleep!"
> There is on earth no worthier grave
> To hold the bodies of the brave
> Than this place of pain and pride
> Where they nobly fought and nobly died.

Never fear but in the skies
Saints and angels stand
Smiling with their holy eyes
On this new-come band.
St. Michael's sword darts through the air
And touches the aureole on his hair
As he sees them stand saluting there,
His stalwart sons;
And Patrick, Brigid, Columkill
Rejoice that in veins of warriors still
The Gael's blood runs.
And up to heaven's doorway floats,
From the wood called Rouge Bouquet,
A delicate cloud of buglenotes
That softly say:
"Farewell!
Farewell!
Comrades true, born anew, peace to you!
Your souls shall be where the heroes are
And your memory shine like the morning star.
Brave and dear
Shield us here.
Farewell!"[56]

13

"Quiet Sectors Are Not Necessarily Quiet"

When news of the death of twenty-one men in E Company rippled along the trenches, where other companies of the Second Battalion were now posted, soldiers became anxious, scared, jumpy. At night every shadow turned into an enemy. Peering across no-man's-land, a number of edgy soldiers fired blindly into the darkness.

In Capt. Mike Kelly's F Company, this mood turned deadly.

In the trench at the subsector of Souchet, Pvt. Bernard Corcoran of Long Island City had been placed on sentry duty. With gunfire popping off near him, he was afraid that a German raid was about to burst out of the inky night. In the shadows he spotted two men coming toward him. He was certain one of them wore a German helmet.

"Who is it?" he challenged.

When there was no answer, Corcoran fired at the shadows. The man in the strange helmet dropped. Corcoran yelled at Cpl. Theodore Hagen that he had shot a man, believing he was from a raiding party. Hagen said that he thought the man was an American.

Corcoran's bullet had hit Pvt. Oscar Ammon of College Point in the chest, killing him instantly. Only eighteen, Ammon was a broad-shouldered six-footer whose father had immigrated from Switzerland. It is not known why Ammon had not responded to Corcoran's challenge. He and Pvt. Joseph McCarthy had been ordered by 2nd Lt. Harper Silliman, their platoon commander, to distribute bandoleers of ammunition to the men in the trenches. Ammon had already received one warning for sneaking around. When Corcoran challenged him, he had turned to McCarthy to say something and had then been shot. Corcoran was exonerated. Because Ammon had been on orders from Silliman, he was listed as killed in the line of duty. Back home, it was believed a sniper had picked him off.[1]

A tragic fate also befell Pvt. William Wassis, another F Company man, on the night of the cave-in.

Wassis simply ran away. During the heavy bombardment, he bolted out of the trench and took off down the road that led from Rouge Bouquet. Sgt. Peter Crotty and a squad from K Company went after him. Crotty, who had served as a regimental water boy in the Spanish-American War when he was but twelve years old, had joined the Seventy-first with three pals from his Chelsea neighborhood—Cpl. Jack Gibbons and Pvts. Jim Corrigan and John Quinn. They became known as the "Four Musketeers" because they were inseparable and scoffed at danger. But for Crotty, the father of three, going after a deserter was no laughing matter. His orders were to do whatever was necessary to capture "that Wop, Wassis."

The deserter was hidden in a grove of trees near Camp New York when Crotty's squad showed up. He fired at them. Crotty formed a skirmish line as one of his men fired back. Wassis returned fire. Crotty's men replied in kind, hitting the private. Crotty then went into the woods and found Wassis dead, a rifle clasped in his hands.[2]

Two senseless killings. In less than twenty-four hours twenty-four men of the old Fighting Sixty-ninth had been killed and a score wounded, and there wasn't a dead German to show for it. The New Yorkers wanted revenge. The green flag with the harp and crown and "Erin Go Bragh!" embroidered on it was taken out. The words "Rouge Bouquet" were sewn on, along with the names of the dead. The flag was affixed to the end of a bayonet, ready to lead the first wave of Irish Americans into no-man's-land.

But first there was St. Patrick's Day to celebrate.

Father Francis Duffy chose St. Patrick's Day as a time to commemorate the fallen at Rouge Bouquet.

"What a day this would have been for us if we were back in New York!" the chaplain reflected in his diary of 17 March.

> Up the Avenue to St. Patrick's Cathedral in the morning, and the big organ booming out the old Irish airs and the venerable old Cardinal uttering words of blessing and

encouragement. And in the afternoon out on parade with the Irish Societies with the band playing Garryowen and Let Erin Remember and O'Donnell Aboo, as we pass through the cheering crowds. And how they would shout in this year of Grace 1918 if we could suddenly be transported to New York's Avenue of Triumph. But I am glad we are not there. . . . There is only one place in the world where the old Irish regiment has any right to celebrate [St. Patrick's Day], and this is on the battle line.[3]

Duffy asked Austin Lawrence to select a place for him to say mass near where the Third Battalion under Maj. Timothy Moynahan was experiencing its first stint in the trenches. Afterward he would hold mass for Stacom's battalion, which had limped back to Camp New York and Donovan's First.

Lawrence had been in a sour mood since disaster had hit E Company,. In his diary for the 12th, he wrote, "This war is all wrong!" That day he and 1st Lt. John Dooley Lyttle, a Cornell man, had gone down to Rocroi to post several of their medics from the Sanitary Detachment. "Some scared. I'll tell the world." That night he slept in a "little cubby hole" that was "forty-seven steps down." Spooked by what had happened to Lieutenant Norman, Lyttle slept outside in the trench. "He's welcome to it. Not for me."[4]

Over the next few days Lawrence got used to the roar of artillery. He was glad, though, when Duffy came to him to ask for a spot for the St. Patrick's Day mass. He selected a place among the trees so that Duffy's bright vestments would be concealed from enemy spotters.

The chaplain had gone down to the trenches to spend the previous night with Moynahan, who, he said, "gave me a true Irish welcome." He did not know that during the night, Moynahan had sent Sgt. Howard Emerson from M Company and Pvt. Edward Dittman from K into no-man's-land to "bag" a few Germans for St. Patrick's Day. Throughout the night the Brooklyn boys wiggled through the mire, but captured no enemy. For their trouble machine-gun fire raked them. Although satisfied that his boys had returned safely, Moynahan was disappointed there were no prisoners to show off.[5]

The next morning, at the spot Lawrence picked out, Duffy said mass, and those soldiers in the trenches who could get away "slipped up" to hear the service. When he had finished he moved to Camp New York for a second mass and a concert by the regimental band. He described his "altar" at Camp New York as a "grove of young birch trees on a hill slope, the men being scattered singly over the slope."[6]

"A humble altar," said Pvt. Peter Rogers, a native of Ireland who had come out the trenches with the rest of the boys from F Company. A bugle sounded "church call." Many of the soldiers now gathering on the slope had dried shamrocks pinned to their helmets, most likely sent to them by loved ones or carried to France. As Rogers watched he recollected life in the old country.

> Many a time during the days of my childhood have I climbed hills and mountains in Ireland. Many a time have I stood upon some lofty crest to survey the surrounding beauties—some broad silvery streams winding in the valley below or some antiquated castle whose dilapidated condition bespoke days of chivalry. Many a time have I pictured the apostle of Ireland preaching to and converting pagans assembled on hillsides, but never in all my life have I witnessed or pictured a more impressive or edifying scene as the one I saw on St. Patrick's Day on a hillside in France. . . . Father Duffy, the beloved chaplain of the Sixty-ninth I may call him and rightly, too, the apostle of the Sixty-ninth, stood erect on the hill-top beside his little improvised altar, and from there overlooked the columns of men as they approached.[7]

"Top o' the mornin' boys!" Duffy said in his thickest Irish brogue, looking straight into the "sparkling eyes of Erin's fighting sons." Every head, so many adorned with green shamrocks, bowed. To Rogers the scene was as "solemn as it was sublime."

Overhead, an observation balloon, moored to the ground by ropes, kept watch for German planes.

Martin Green of the *New York Evening World* reported on the steady rumble of artillery in the distance—the only sound heard save that of the voice of the priest. "The Germans had a good chance that morning to wipe out a fighting unit which was going to give them a lot of trouble later on."[8]

In his diary, the chaplain mentioned how he had talked of old St. Patrick days and how it was better to be in France than Gotham.

New Yorkers would talk more about them, think more about them. "Every man in the town would be saying he wished he were here and every man worth his salt would mean it." He reminded them that they had been called upon to "fight for human liberty and the rights of small nations, and if we rallied to that noble cause we would establish a claim on our own country and on humanity in favor of the dear land from which so many of us had sprung, and which all of us loved."[9]

Rogers's blood rushed through his veins, and he knew every soldier, Irish or not, felt the same pounding in their hearts.

"What your forefathers have done in the past I feel confident you will do in the future," Rogers repeated the chaplain's words. "The Irish love Right and Liberty, and they have fought and always will fight and fight valiantly when either Right or Liberty is at stake." Pointing toward the sound of the big Germans guns, he exclaimed, "You will uphold on that front the name and reputation of the Sixty-ninth of which I am proud to be chaplain."[10]

At the end of Duffy's sermon a huge explosion to the north rocked the ground they stood upon and broke most of the windows in Lunéville, fifteen miles away.

In the afternoon, the regiment held a concert under the trees. Duffy recited Joyce Kilmer's newly penned, "Rouge Bouquet." As the chaplain read the final words of the poem, Sgt. Patrick Stokes from Brooklyn, the bugler standing next to him, played "Taps" while in the woods a distance away another bugler, Eugene Egan, answered.

"Before I had finished," the priest wrote, "tears had started in many an eye especially amongst the lads of Company E."

Al Ettinger saw this, too. "Several hundred of the roughest, toughest men in New York stood by with tears rolling down their cheeks. I will never, never forget that beautiful service or that poem."[11]

Having known in advance that the poem would rouse sorrow, Duffy followed it up with a medley of rollicking Irish tunes, including "Garryowen" and "The Minstrel Boy." "We can pay tribute to our dead," judged the priest, "but we must not lament for them overmuch."[12]

In the line that St. Patrick's Day, Moynahan's battalion, having attending the earlier sermon, holed up in the trenches while German guns pounded them. Lawrence, at the time, had stopped by to visit with Van S. Merle-Smith, commander of L Company. They were in Rocroi, hunkered down near the E Company tomb, when they heard the huge explosion that had rocked Duffy's service and blown out the windows in Lunéville. A French shell had hit an ammunition dump. This angered the Germans and they bombarded the Third Battalion with the same ferocity they had used against the Second Battalion. Along the length of the meandering trench, shells fell one after the other, each explosion deafening. A shell struck twenty feet from Lawrence and Merle-Smith. The two officers ducked into a dugout, but Lawrence knew he would eventually have to make a dash for it. When the time felt right, he broke for safety, crawling and sliding through the mud like a rat. He finally got far enough away to be out of danger. Lawrence admitted to himself that he had been scared but kept his nerve until "I realized what I had gone thru & then nervous all day & evening. Ears ringing & head aching all the time, can hardly hear. Think one eardrum broken, but am thankful to be alive. Never will go visiting again during this war." His ears rang for a week. "Ear & head still at it. Also still quite deaf."[13]

The war would not wait for Lawrence to recover. A raiding party from the First Battalion was set to enter no-man's-land while, unbeknownst to them, the Germans were preparing to give the Third Battalion its first taste of mustard gas. And then Austin Lawrence, his brother, George, and 1st Lt. George Patton from the Bronx would be pressed into work under the worst of conditions.

The French selected Donovan's battalion for the 165th's first raid into no-man's-land, a *coup de main*. The mission was simple: take prisoners, gather information and blow up dugouts. The raiding party was to be made up of three officers and fifty handpicked men. Pvt. John Duffy boasted to his parents in Long Island City that everyone in C Company wanted to go. All hands went up with "so many cries of 'I go' . . . and I was one of the picked men."[14]

Commanding the party was Henry Bootz, a towering six-foot-six-inch first lieutenant from B Company. Bootz was from Woodbury, New Jersey, but had been born in Germany. His mother still lived there, and several of his brothers had died fighting on the Kaiser's side. The tall lieutenant impressed Donovan, who said, "I noticed from the first day in camp he was a genuine soldier. He kept pretty much to himself, but I guess that was because he had a bit of a German accent when he spoke."[15] Bootz later impressed

Col. Charles Howland when he marched the regiment to the Rhine River. "Bootz," he said, "is a soldier, every inch of him."[16] Ettinger called him a "fabulous character" who spoke with a thick German accent. His troops called him Papa Bootz. This gang of Irishmen just loved that Dutchman! . . . He was so brave, and he always led his men."[17]

The handpicked soldiers reported to Croixmare on 9 March. For the next ten days they trained with the chasseurs. Mixed in with French veterans, the Americans worked at close-order drill and competed in strenuous athletic contests; they ran and jumped. Every day they were instructed in how to read maps, and they learned every inch of the ground they would cover in their attack. Duffy was amused at their training, "They go through all sorts of athletic stunts to get into perfect condition."[18]

Bootz reported, "It was brought home to every man, by drawing on the blackboard, just where his position would be and what his particular job was upon gaining the position. Every soldier was thoroughly practiced in the handling of his special arms, including the use of grenades and pistol." Once the men knew their assigned tasks, they practiced the raid day and night. They went through simulated bombardments, advanced through every conceivable obstacle and were taught how to cut through wire entanglements. The French divided the Americans into two groups of twenty-four men, led by second lieutenants. Each group was then split into subgroups, with a sergeant in charge, aided by two corporals. "Each little group of 12 men," wrote Bootz, "was composed of 4 hand grenadiers or moppers-up, 8 rifle grenadiers and the balance riflemen."[19]

At seven thirty-three on the evening of 20 March, at a sector known as Ouvrage Blanc, the first wave of the joint French-American raiding party eased into no-man's-land. Private Duffy thought the boys "went over without a flinch, just like oldtimers." He said they were all "happy because we were going to get a real German."[20] One of the Irish soldiers, Cpl. Bob Foster of D Company, carried the green flag with harp and crown and "Erin Go Bragh!" and "Rouge Bouquet" and the names of the dead from E Company.[21] He fastened the flag to the barrel of his rifle. An observer from division headquarters, down to watch the raid—a young officer full of himself—claimed that the flag was inappropriate.

Papa Bootz glared at the officer. "What are you doing in these trenches?" he demanded.

"I came here to observe."

This Irish Flag that Went Over the Top.
Presented by Capt. J. P. Condon, Co. L, 69th N.Y.

Two unidentified veterans hold the Irish flag that went over the top. The flag had been given the regiment by an old woman when it marched off to war. *Courtesy of James Tierney*

"Then you had better climb a tree and observe there because we are here to fight, and that Irish flag is going over the top!"[22]

After the raid, Foster wrote to his cousin in Brooklyn, Emma McGeehan, "You may have read about the fellow who carried the Irish flag 'over the top' with the boys of the Fighting 69th. Well, I am the fellow. I held on to that old green flag and went right 'over the top' with my comrades. I feel mighty proud of the feat, too."[23]

As Sgt. Eugene McNiff, a freckle-faced, rangy boy of twenty-four from Bay Ridge, crept forward, he felt dazed. He was a transfer from the Fourteenth Regiment, described as "wiry as if built of spun steel, and with an honest, smiling face." McNiff still wore on his uniform collar the Fourteenth's insignia; he had promised himself to wear that insignia up to the day of his death. At the moment, though, he was concentrating on the task ahead. The one thing on his mind, he later said, was "You're going to get some of those damned Germans and you don't care what else happens."[24]

The men with him were also in a daze as the French opened up a creeping barrage which the Americans followed, staying fifty yards behind the exploding shells. As the barrage moved closer to the Germans, they answered with a bombardment of their own. Their shells fell just beyond the advancing soldiers, cutting them off from their own lines.

Crossing no-man's-land did not take the first raiding party long and soon Bootz and his men had reached the German side. The size of the trenches surprised the lieutenant—eight feet deep in places and up to fourteen feet wide. But the two days of constant shelling leading up to the raid had taken their toll. The trench was demolished—the entrance to every dugout caved in, not an enemy to be seen anywhere. "When we entered their trenches they were blown to pieces," Private Duffy wrote, "along with the Germans that were in them."

As at Rouge Bouquet, the Americans were certain the Germans had been buried alive. They "reconnoitered" the trench system, but came away empty-handed.

They also came away with fewer of their own men. The German barrage, which, according to Duffy, "hit the mark every time," had taken its toll: two men killed and one missing.[25] The French suffered casualties as well, and their wounded were out in no-man's-land with the fallen Americans. The missing doughboy was Pvt. Edward Maher of B Company. Bootz believed a shell had "scattered" his body. After a thorough search, nothing was found of him.

The second wave, led by Lt. Raymond Newton, then moved into no-man's-land. They crawled up to the enemy's trench line and waited in the dark. Very lights kept going off, but were far enough away not to reveal the party's position. It was the shellfire that hounded the men unrelentingly. After making certain that the trenches were empty, they headed back. Fifty yards away, a shell hit them. The explosion killed another soldier and wounded two more, along with a score of chasseurs.

Moments later, Bootz saw Newton struggle out of the darkness, a body slung over his back. When he reached the trench, Newton handed the wounded man to French stretcher-bearers. He said no-man's-land was littered with wounded.

Knowing that their men needed aid fast, Bootz and Joe Pettit ran to where the wounded lay moaning in the mud, most of them with head injuries. Fred Almendinger's eye had been smashed in. Shrapnel had ripped up Patrick Grogan's entire back, from his neck to his legs. Sergeant Joe Scully's right leg above the knee was held on by bloody strips of flesh, mangled muscles, and torn tendons. Bootz cut away the leg and hoisted Scully, a 190-pounder even without the leg, onto his back. To get him back to the trench, Bootz dropped into a shell hole, tore off his own helmet and heavy clothing—belt, pistol, gas mask, anything that weighted him down. Again scooping up Scully, he rushed through the churned up mud. Pettit, meanwhile, had carried three men to safety. That meant making three trips under the rain of artillery fire to bring them back.[26]

McNiff also went out three times, according to one of his comrades. "They were out there in front of the trenches and to go after them seemed to mean almost certain death," said Marlow Plant. "He just laughed at the barrage and said he was going to get them or never come back."[27] Marlow himself was no slouch, administering first aid to the wounded in no-man's-land and then lugging back a chasseur.

When the wounded had been accounted for, except Maher, Bootz got ready to go back into no-man's-land once more. One of his men said, "You're not going out again?"

"Of course I am," Bootz answered, as he headed off. "I'm going back for my stuff. Do you think I'm going to leave it there and let the Germans get it?"[28]

The dead Americans were Bill Ellwood from Brooklyn, Joe Miller from Manhattan's East Side, and Tom Minogue from Hell's Kitchen. Minogue had been killed in the rescue of the wounded. After hanging twenty-four grenades on his belt and climbing out of the trench, he had turned to a lieutenant and said, "All I hope is that I will never be taken prisoner." Those had been his last words. The lieutenant watched in awe, and, perhaps, later embellished the heroics of the B Company private. "For several minutes he crawled along the ground—we could see him by the rockets the Germans were sending up. Suddenly their machine guns stopped firing, but still a wall of steel confronted him. Standing up he started forward, blazing away with his grenades, and whenever a rocket went up he would drop into a shell hole. Determined to get through the barrage Tom dashed forward and a 20-pounder hit him. The poor boy—he was gone." When word of Minogue's death reached his pals in B Company who had not been picked to go over the

Lt. William Given Jr. had been impressed by the bravery of a German aviator and his spotter in the Lunéville Sector, unaware that they were directing a gas attack that moments later decimated the Third Battalion. *Courtesy of Given Family*

top, they took up a collection for Tom's mother and promised that when they returned home they would erect a tablet in his honor at his neighborhood church.[29]

Although the *coup de main* yielded little except eight American casualties and an untold number of dead and wounded chasseurs, Private Duffy knew its significance. To his "Pop" he wrote, "This raid that we made was the first real action by our regiment and it started the ball a-rolling. The cannons have been roaring ever since we started out on our party."[30]

On the night of the raid, the Germans had dropped more than explosives. Father Duffy recorded that they "suddenly began to bombard the entire sector . . . with mustard gas shells and shrapnel."[31]

Second Lt. William Given Jr. of L Company likely saw the spotter who called in the rain of mustard gas and shrapnel. He later wrote that the airplane had come in so close that the black crosses on its wings were clearly visible, and he had been astonished at the courage the pilot and his observer displayed. "You could see the observer leaning forward for a look—giving us the once over, so to speak. With all solemnity I take my hat off to that man. He deserved to get home safely through the fire. It was one of the most impressive things I have ever seen done."[32] Given would not have been so chivalrous if he had known what was about to follow.

Unfortunately, the Forty-second Division had little training in how to deal with gas. In a supply blunder of dire consequences, the Rainbows had not been issued gas masks, pistols, steel helmets, or machine guns until February, three months after they had landed in France. By the time they reached the trenches, only thirty percent of the men had been through a gas chamber. The division's top surgeon warned, "This if not corrected will eventually lead to disastrous results."[33]

That disaster hit Moynahan's Third Battalion. For three hours, more than four hundred mustard gas shells and seven thousand high-explosive and shrapnel shells landed squarely on K Company, commanded by Capt. John Patrick Hurley. Hogan called it a hideous inferno. "The earth around us boiled and churned and heaved and groaned and shivered," he recalled. "The air above us hissed and roared and snapped. The steady streaming rush of the messages of the guns withered our hearts as they smote and smote our trench." He remembered how the "gas flooded unaware over the trenches, chlorine, tear and mustard gases. The shrapnel pieces flew thick among us. And then the high explosives rained down and tore our trenches up in masses."[34]

Although the Germans had quit firing during the night, the following day they resumed their bombardment. Between fourteen hundred and four thousand shells—four-fifths of them mustard gas—walloped the 165th again. The gas rolled through the trenches, fearsome and lethal. Reports put the total number of casualties, American and French, at 542. Of that number, 417 had been doughboys.[35]

Fragments from one of the shells struck an old Seventh Regiment transfer, Harry McCoun of Brautford, Ontario, ripping off his left hand. He held up his stump, according to Duffy, and shouted, "Well, boys, there goes my left wing."[36]

McCoun was carried back to the first-aid station, where Lieutenant Patton worked feverishly on gas victims. His gas mask a hindrance, Patton yanked it off so he could work unimpeded and see clearly the wounds inflicted on the men. Howard Kelly, who had come over with McCoun from the Seventh, watched Patton tend to him and others in the midst of the barrage. "One of the old 7th Co. H boys [McCoun] had the wind pipe of his gas mask severed by a piece of shrapnel," he wrote, "and soon after was struck in the arm by another fragment of shell and his forearm was dangling, shattered, when the doctor came up and operated after taking off his own mask, with the gas shells plunking in the mud all around."[37]

Patton's efforts were in vain. McCoun died the next day.

Another casualty was First Lt. George Benz. He described how "mustard gas . . . burns the tender and wet parts of the skin. It usually affects damp portions of the back, under the armpits and even the feet. Also, it will burn out the lungs. It takes very little to do horrible damage."[38] Because of his gas wounds, Benz received a discharge and went home to become a reporter on the *Evening World*. Weakened by the gas, he was struck down by pneumonia a few days before Christmas 1918. Wanting to be with his parents, he made it to their home near Philadelphia and when his mother opened the door he fainted and fell to the floor. A few days later he died.[39]

Hogan went blind, one of over two hundred men whose sight was burned from their eyes. Tears started streaming from his eyes and then a "gray, impenetrable mist closed thickly round me and I fell upon my knees to steady myself."[40] He crawled through the muck of the trench, his hands and knees stinging from the gas until someone stumbled upon him and carried him to the dressing station, and there he was treated.

Patton also lost his sight. "By dawn," Father Duffy recorded, "the men were going blind one after another."[41] Hurley lost his sight. Moynahan and Captains Merle-Smith and Martin Meaney were also casualties. One of the luckier doughboys had been the Rouge Bouquet survivor Alf Helmer. When he had headed for the trenches, Helmer had taken his gas mask out of its haversack and replaced it with doughnuts from the YMCA canteen. Smelling gas, he held his breath and buried his face in the mud. He stayed face down in the mud for as long as he could, then took quick small gulps of air. He survived and was not listed as a casualty, although he suffered from a blistered groin and a serious cough for the next few weeks.[42]

Lawrence handled gas cases all night and all the next day. "Poor Lyttle & boys are all in. Fawcett got touch of gas working on men in dugouts. L Co. was relieved. Wish we were, as I'm afraid of tonight. I'm worked up & probably look it. Sure enough, about 7:30 over came a terrific bombardment of mustard gas. All over us & Bn Hqrs. During night, plenty of Shrapnel. Spent bad night, sleep about 2 AM."

On the third day of the gas attack Lawrence noticed there was "still lots of gas around." He went to the hospital in Lunéville to help with the hundreds of gas cases.[43]

Joe Jones noticed that almost all the boys in K Company had gone blind and were sent to the hospital, and that there was nobody left to protect their guns, many of them abandoned in the trenches. He was put on watch, and his eyes started to blur. "Germans sending over more gas. I am very tired." He was taken to the hospital and then sent by train to Base Hospital 18, an eleven-hour ride. In his diary he wrote, "Hair cut off all over my body and staying in agony."[44]

Another victim had been Capt. Richard Ryan. Not expected to live out the night, the tough, crusty, forty-one-year-old soldier fooled a doctor at the base hospital who was too anxious to visit Paris and therefore did not want to wait for the Watertown resident to die. Believing his patient was a goner, the doctor marked him down as "Expired—Died of Wounds," and left for Paris. Although the War Department telegrammed his wife that he was dead and Watertown held a solemn memorial service, Ryan left the hospital on his own and resumed command of his company.[45]

Meanwhile, in a letter to his wife, Given had written, "It does seem that quiet sectors are not necessarily very quiet."[46]

The day before Given wrote his letter, the relative quiet on the Western Front exploded. General Erich Ludendorff, the *de facto* commander-in-chief of the German Army, had launched an offensive meant to win the war. His objective was to push the British out of the Somme and the French out of the Aisne and hit Paris. Ludendorff was emboldened by the recently signed Treaty of Brest-Litovsk that had knocked Russia out of the war. Thousands of German troops from the Eastern Front now poured into France. The heavyset, prototypical Prussian officer, with short-cropped hair and a monocle screwed into his eye, wanted to deal a knockout blow to the Allies before the Americans became a factor, and he wanted to do it before the end of spring. And on the first few days of the offensive, his armies marched deeper into France as specially crafted Krupp guns pounded Paris from seventy miles away.

14

"From a Canny Scot to a Bold Irishman"

"War is a time of sudden changes and violent wrenches of the heart strings," Father Francis Duffy penned on 9 May 1918, "and we are getting a taste of it even before we enter into the period of battles."[1]

Two months had slipped by since the 165th Infantry had been pulled out of the "quiet" Lunéville Sector. It had been sent to the Baccarat Sector, where the Forty-second Division relieved three French divisions that had been redeployed in the wake of Germany's latest offensive. Because of its numerous gas casualties, the Irish regiment had at first been held in reserve. But as more and more of the wounded regained their health—specifically, in most cases, their eyesight—they returned from the hospitals about fifty miles southwest of Baccarat.

In Baccarat and in Deneuvre, where it had set up its headquarters, the regiment held the line and raided German trenches across no-man's-land. In one of these daring raids, a number of prisoners had been rounded up. In an astonishing coincidence, Cpl. Billy Munz from Hackensack, New Jersey, whose parents came from Germany, was interrogating the prisoners in their native tongue when a captured officer spoke up.

"Where are you men from?"

"New York," Munz replied.

"I have an aunt living there," the officer said. "Mrs. Bertha Bequest."

Munz's eyes widened. "Why, that's the name of my aunt, too!"

"I also have an aunt in Hackensack, New Jersey. Mrs. Anna Munz."

"She's my mother! You must be my cousin, Gustavo Wincklemann, of Bremen!"

"I am!"

For the next hour Munz and Wincklemann rattled on about their family, then the prisoner had to be taken away.[2]

For the most part, Baccarat proved to be the quiet sector that Lunéville was not. Soldiers discovered *estaminets*, small French cafés and restaurants. They supplemented their meals with omelets and French fried potatoes, wine and beer. They also discovered "maison number two," a "house of pleasure" where it seemed a "whole battalion lined up" until the military police had placed it out of bounds. There was a "lot of wailing from the boys as well as the inmates," lamented one soldier, "but it was explained to us that we were there to fight and not to frolic."[3]

Al Ettinger, now a motorcycle dispatch rider, discovered a bordello on the road to Deneuvre. The madam allowed him free rein among the ladies as long as he drummed up business by telling the boys about the place. "I'd never before seen women dressed, or rather undressed, that way, draped all over the room. But soon I became keen on a girl no older than I. She was absolutely lovely, and after a most pleasant sojourn, I took my leave."[4]

On the other hand, George Patrick McKeon worried again about his eldest sister, Daisy, taking care of their poor family back in Brooklyn. He wrote, "I am in the best of health and spirit, hoping at home all are the same." He let her know that he had signed over his allotment to her and she would start receiving it soon.[5]

What hit the 165th the hardest had been those sudden and wrenching changes that Duffy warned of in his diary. They started at the very top.

Col. John Barker, almost four months to the day he had taken over as regimental commander, was called to Washington to serve on the General Staff Corps. His replacement was a friend, confidant, and aide to former presidents Roosevelt and Taft and generals Leonard Wood and Pershing, on whose staff he now worked.

Forty-three-year-old Frank Ross McCoy had already led a fascinating life when he took the reins of the 165th—a command he coveted as a West Point graduate and career soldier. Before the colonelcy was offered to him, word spread through Pershing's headquarters at Chaumont that Barker was to be transferred. (William Haskell once again hoped to get the nod to replace him and asked McCoy to argue his case before Pershing. McCoy did so, although he himself also fought for a spot in the infantry.) McCoy had earlier sent a memorandum to Pershing's chief of staff, James Harbord, for whom he worked, requesting a transfer to the First Division. "I am not unmindful of the great honor and fine association and work here at GHQ, and it is with real personal pang that I officially request to be assigned to duty with troops." Harbord then explained that "while [he is] pleased at the spirit which prompts it, he is unable to spare Colonel McCoy from the important duties he is performing at this time,"[6] and his "high hopes" for a transfer were "dashed."[7] Thinking he would not be part of the First Division, then, McCoy was surprised when Pershing's plans for the 165th did not include Haskell.

"The General hit the table with his characteristic motion," McCoy related to his mother. "'I have selected you myself for that particular regiment'."[8] Pershing had said, "I have decided to give Harbord the Marine Brigade and you will get the 165th Infantry." He assured his mother that the 165th was in a quiet sector with a "gallant French regiment . . . on my left."[9]

Born on 29 October 1874, in Lewiston, Pennsylvania, McCoy was descended from a long line of Scotch-Irish warriors. His great grandfather had fought in the Revolutionary War; his grandfather had been in the militia in the War of 1812; and his father, Thomas, had campaigned with Gen. Winfield Scott in the war with Mexico, and during the Civil War was breveted a brigadier general of the 107th Pennsylvania Volunteers. It was natural that McCoy should enter West Point, where he graduated in 1897, and was soon in the African-American Tenth Cavalry—along with Pershing, then a young captain. In the Spanish-American War, the Tenth Cavalry was shipped to Cuba. It saw action at La Guasimas and inflicted heavy casualties on the Spanish forces there, then pushed on toward Santiago. On 30 June 1898, American forces were ordered to take a fortified ridge blocking the approach to Santiago. Two bluffs made up part of the ridge—San Juan Hill and Kettle Hill. Led by Roosevelt, the Rough Riders and the Ninth and Tenth Cavalries stormed Kettle Hill. During the charge, which drove most of the Spaniards off the ridge, half of McCoy's fellow officers were killed or wounded.

During the occupation of Kettle Hill a sniper's bullet struck McCoy in the left leg. The wounded officer was dragged down the hill and put under the shade of a tree at a place the soldiers nicknamed "Bloody Ford." McCoy watched the fight continue on the ridge above him. He later wrote that he could hear the curses of officers and men and the crack of whips as "Drivers lashed the mules and horses pulling the heavy guns and wagons." "The air was filled with gunpowder smoke and the crash of shells and the whine of bullets."[10]

As he lay there, unable to move, the blood from his wound still flowing, the Rough Rider's top officer spotted him and noticed the seeping blood. Leonard Wood, a Boston physician before joining with Roosevelt to organize the First Volunteer Cavalry, knelt next to the lieutenant. He applied a dressing to the wound, and as the two soldiers talked hurriedly under the tree, they forged a lasting friendship. McCoy served Wood as his aide-de-camp for two years in Cuba and was with him in the Philippines.[11]

McCoy also was senior aide to President Roosevelt in the early 1900s. Later, when war with Mexico loomed in 1915, Roosevelt wanted to raise a volunteer cavalry division with McCoy as chief of staff. Instead, McCoy wound up as Pershing's chief of staff during the Punitive Expedition against Pancho Villa. After the United States declared war on Germany, Roosevelt again sought to raise another division and again wanted McCoy as chief of staff. But when President Wilson nixed that division, McCoy ended up on the general staff at Chaumont as secretary to Harbord, Pershing's right hand man.

After McCoy's arrival in Baccarat, he wrote his mother, "I've changed [overnight] from a canny Scot to a bold . . . Irishman. There's nothing short of Cork so really amusingly Irish as this regiment, and of course it's a real handful. Colonels have had their heads cut off from failure to man handle. So its a sporting proposition. I won't fail you, by heck!"[12]

On a "charming spring morning," McCoy, filled with "gay and good humor," drove to his new headquarters in Deneuvre. Next to the driver, sitting atop McCoy's field kit, was Bert Williams, his pet terrier named after the Zeigfield's Follies' famous black comedian. That night he messed with the officers that he now commanded. During the dinner, Duffy intently watched his new colonel. Within five minutes he decided that McCoy had dignity, charm, and an "alert and wide-ranging intelligence that embraces men, books, art, nature. If he only thinks as well of us as we are going to think of him I prophesy that he will have this regiment in the hollow of his hand to do what he likes with it." He was also struck by the fact that in the army McCoy had never missed a fight. "A good omen for the 'Fighting Sixty-ninth'."[13]

Basil Elmer wrote his parents about the new colonel. "He is a real soldier. The interesting part and the thing that is quite a coincidence is that his brother, Jack, roomed with me for over a year at the Beta Club in New York. Everything seems to be breaking right for me. I can't complain about anything. . . . I have the best intelligence service in my regiment of any in the division. Now I want a division all to myself."[14]

Spring had come to the Western Front, and while the 165th awaited its next orders, Alf Helmer found peace in the rolling hills covered with forests. Recovered from his ordeal at Rouge Bouquet, he felt that he could live in that part of France for ten years, except that he would miss home, mother, and Coney Island. He wrote his father of the "grandest bunch of woods, hills and dales around this section that you ever did see. Once in a while I grab a companion and go on an exploring trip." He described lazy days, writing letters, and washing clothes or himself in "some beautiful little shady brook."[15]

Bill Donovan was also struck by the beauty of the place, despite many reminders that they were at war. "All the country through here to-day looked like the Genesee Valley as it begins to turn green, but the fields are studded with graves of French and German soldiers alike who fell here in the early days of the war."[16] His aide, Oliver Ames, wrote home that battalion headquarters was "now in the most beautiful place. Going out of the back door you come into this trench with apple trees and apple blossoms dropping over you, and lilac bushes also."[17]

Elmer and his Intelligence Section also enjoyed the warm spring weather and the surrounding beauty. They were in forested hills, keeping watch, reporting on what they saw. They lolled on the ground, sunned themselves, smoked pipes and mused about life, arguing theology.

By now Joyce Kilmer had been promoted to sergeant and transferred into Elmer's tight-knit group. He informed his friend, Robert Cortes Holliday, of his new rank, telling him that intelligence work was most fascinating—"more thrills in it than in any other branch except possibly aviation. And it's more varied than aviation. Wonderful life! But I don't know what I'll be able to do in civilian life—unless I become a fireman!"[18]

Although the men in the Intelligence Section had been aware of Kilmer's fame and impressed with his poem "Rouge Bouquet," they did not see their intelligence work as romantic the way Kilmer did. Emmett Watson, in the midst of illustrating "Rouge Bouquet" for *Scribner's* magazine, thought the poet took his work too seriously, unlike Elmer who, he said, "never stood on military formality." Watson felt Kilmer "at first thoroughly disapproved of the easy informality existing between us all, and on duty insisted upon the observance of promulgated regulations." Watson recalled how on a march with full packs they halted for a rest. When the "bucks" felt refreshed they jumped up and resumed their hike—without waiting for any orders from their new sergeant. Kilmer barked, "Detachment Halt!" He then bawled out his men for their lack of discipline. Taking his place in front of the detail he ordered them to continue their hike. In another episode, he described how Kilmer had come across a shell casing that he claimed was a "discovery of the greatest importance." The fragment, according to Watson, was "brittle and crumbled around its edges under normal thumb pressure." Kilmer was convinced it was evidence that Germany's mighty steel industry had hit hard times, and he wrote up a many-paged meticulous report "on that hypothesis." Watson, however, was convinced that the shell had been unearthed during a recent artillery attack and dated to 1914, to the opening salvo of the Great War.

Yet Kilmer impressed Watson and the others in some ways, especially in his daring. Kilmer could hardly wait for night to fall so he could accompany patrols outside the wire into no-man's-land. "We grew to like Joyce Kilmer greatly," he admitted.[19]

And Kilmer got to enjoy the lazy days the Intelligence Section spent. He described them to Aline.

This afternoon you would have been amazed at the material picture before you, had you seen me. Just outside the edge of the forest of firs and spruce in which we fourteen men live is a lovely meadow. There, among the knee-high buttercups, lay in the May sunshine all afternoon three warriors—myself being one. Whiles we smoked and gazed at the lovely valley miles below us—whiles we took turns reading aloud from—what do you suppose? The Oxford Book of English Verse! We read Gray's Elegy, the first chorus from Atalanta in Calydon, "They told me, Heraclitus," that witch poem of William Bell Scott, "Love in the Valley," "Lake Isle of Innisfree," "Keith of Ravelston," and half a dozen other poems, all of which brought you most poignantly and beautifully before me.[20]

Elmer also partook in those joyous afternoons. Painting a picture to his parents of lounging on a mountaintop amongst dense woods, he gushed "We are off all by ourselves having a wonderful time. Every minute the sun shines down through the boughs of the trees."[21] In another letter, he remarked on how truly lazy they all were in the mountains.

No cares, no worries and a clean conscience—what could be sweeter? Can you picture me in a white silk shirt and khaki breeches, lying at full length in the shade, my horse and my orderlies 25 ft. away also resting, an occasional aeroplane overhead, an occasional rumbling boom of the guns away off in the distance and otherwise, everything quiet and natural—so natural that even now the cuckoos are calling and the magpies fly close. And then as I turn over I look out over the beautiful plains with the red-roofed villages and then further on the Vosges. This cannot be war! The world is at peace. The war is but a dream.[22]

The Intelligence Section's lookout post was a basic wood platform built high in the pine trees. They kept their spying eyes on the Germans off in the distance through a long-range telescope. Beneath it the platform was a crude shack where they lived. Their mattresses were pine boughs. It sounds rustic, and was, but, noted Watson, the enterprising Americans "slept and ate in splendid seclusion, even being assigned a cook to prepare our meals, and for a time we luxuriously employed a young girl from the nearby village of Neufmaison to wash our messkits."[23]

About the time Kilmer joined the Intelligence Section, Lieutenant Ames went on patrol in no-man's-land and "had the most wonderful time imaginable." He told his "Ma" that there was not much difference between no-man's-land and North Easton at night, except there were no "Boche" in the Massachusetts city. He reminded her of his "scouting" expeditions with his sister, Olivia, when they would try to sneak up on their own brother and sister. "I used to be much more excited in those scouts than I was the other day."

Ames also went on a midnight patrol with Elmer. On the way back through the village to battalion headquarters, they were sure they saw a rifle leveled at them from a darkened doorway. "Both of us jumped a mile and put our hands on our revolvers." The rifle turned out to be a bag of wood and the two officers felt ashamed.[24]

Ames and Elmer were not the only soldiers who saw phantom enemies in the shadows. Such sightings got 2nd Lt. Thomas Stone of C Company arrested and Capt. William Kennelly in hot water with the commander of the Eighty-third Brigade.

Stone was put in charge of a squad of snipers ordered to slip into a cemetery at Ancervillers and capture or kill a German sniper there. The German had been harassing the First Battalion nightly, and Donovan wanted him out of action. On a foggy, rainy night, Stone and four men snuck through an abandoned trench that wound its way to the cemetery. When they reached the edge of the damp burial ground, the lieutenant spread out his men and there they waited for the sniper to show himself. For two hours the squad waited in the fog. Finally three shots rang out from the cemetery. Flares lit the sky. Stone and his men saw nothing—it was quiet again. Another hour passed. Then Stone heard a "screak" in the barbed wire out in front of him. Staring hard in the direction of the eerie noise he saw two platoons of Germans creeping in a long column toward him—at least eighty men.

"Keep heads low, lay quiet," Stone whispered. He raised his head above the parapet. Now the Germans were knelt shoulder to shoulder, inching through the wire. "There were so many of them," he said, "I realized that there was no possible escape for us and nothing to gain. I then told my men we must get back and notify Lieutenant Newton if possible."

The men with him also swore that at least two platoons of Germans were coming toward them—more than a hundred of them, according to two of Stone's men. The Americans worked their way back to their waiting platoon leader, 1st Lt. Raymond Newton, one of the heroes of the 165th's first raid into enemy territory. Stone warned him of an imminent attack and urged him to call down an artillery barrage. Newton asked Stone whether he had actually seen the enemy and ordered the barrage when Stone confirmed that indeed he had. Ill and shivering, Stone went back to his billets to lie down.

The American barrage hit the cemetery, the barbed wire in no-man's-land, and the abandoned trench. The Germans countered with their own fire. In the meantime, Kennelly had his men "stand to," ready to repulse the Germans. He ordered Stone to report to him. According to testimony, Stone did not report, even after Kennelly had called for him three times. First Lt. Joseph Damico tracked him down at his quarters. Stone was half-asleep, exhausted and "fogged out." First Lieutenant Damico arrested him.

Damico said, "It is my painful duty to inform you that you're under arrest and that I am to bring you to the Post of Command of Captain Kennelly."

"Why in hell?" snapped Stone. "I saved the whole damn outfit and run my legs off."

But no Germans attacked C Company, raising doubt whether any enemy had been out there at all. And the brigade commander questioned the judgment of the officers in firing its artillery and thus bringing down a German artillery barrage on the 165th's location, endangering hundreds of men. After a hearing, however, Stone was exonerated.[25]

As Duffy had written, changes kept coming. Alexander Anderson, also promoted, took over Second Battalion. With Maj. Tim Moynahan suffering from gas poisoning, Capt. Jim McKenna was promoted and took over Third Battalion. Capt. McKenna was the soldier that Martin Hogan swore the entire Shamrock Battalion would follow into the "worst muss on earth."

Hogan had been recovering from his own gas wounds when he heard of McKenna's promotion. To him, the new major was the most "fearless, gay-hearted and lovable officer [to ever break] lances with the Germans during the more than four years of war."[26] Hogan could not wait to get back to his company. His stay at the hospital had been a frightening ordeal. "The pain in my eyes and head had grown intolerable, and the burns about my knees added to my discomfort," he wrote. "The water flowed in such a stream down my cheeks that I began to fear that my eyes themselves were running out."[27]

The Shamrock Battalion also got another new officer, and he fit right in with Van S. Merle-Smith's L Company, where he had been assigned. Like Merle-Smith, 1st Lt. William Spencer was a Princeton man. A few years behind Merle-Smith and Lt. Charles Baker, Spencer, a Pennsylvanian and the son of the president of First National Bank of Erie, had graduated in 1915. While students there he and classmate F. Scott Fitzgerald had collaborated on a musical for the Triangle Club. Spencer was a fine piano and mandolin player and had written his own operetta. The new officer's downfall, however, was chocolate. He confessed that after joining Merle-Smith's outfit, he "lost no time . . . looking through all the shops for chocolate, my everlasting task as I almost lived on it the entire time I was in France. It became quite a joke with the boys because I was so constantly on the search for this life-saving delicacy, but I noted that they never laughed when I offered them some."[28]

While Spencer was engaged in his first hunts for French chocolate, Kate Merle-Smith, the wife of his company commander, received a letter from an old beau. George Patton, now a lieutenant colonel at headquarters of the First Tank Center, had been reeling from the recent death of his in-laws. Kate had written to him and he had replied immediately. After telling her everything about his tank experience, he changed his tone. "I have naver met your husband but envy him such a wife" he wrote. He noted that the 165th Infantry had been nearby, but was now elsewhere. "I m soo sorry I did not know your husband was in it at the time." He said that those he had met in France who knew Van had spoken highly of him. "If I were you I would not think too much about his coming home in a box. Up to last January only fourteen men per thousand in all the armies had been killed. One would have to be very unlucky to be of so select a groop. And your husband was bourn lucky or else he would not be your husband. Hence don't worry." He closed the letter, "Perhaps you would permit me to advise you to tell your husband to stay in the line. That is the place for real men, not the staff."[29]

Kate also received a letter from Gene Gannon, her husband's first sergeant from Whitestone, New York. Kate and the other wives and mothers of the old Sixty-ninth—the women's auxiliary to the 165th Infantry—had sent the boys gifts such as a cigarettes and scarves, along with "remembrances." Gannon thanked her on behalf of all the men of the company. "I had intended writing long 'ere this but my hands have been so filled with rifles, bombs, bayonets, etc., that I had no room for a pen. The whole Company wanted to autograph this letter but they couldn't be spared from the firing line; so (although I am not very big) I shall have to represent the company."

He gave her a report on the company's doings, telling her how the boys were trying to learn a little French so that they might meet some girls. "If one cannot speak French to the lady of his choice he might just as well be tongue-tied or else remain in camp." He related that because of a shortage of bread they had been given something else to eat. "What do you think the Fighting Irishmen of the 69th were presented with? I'll whisper it easy—Matzohs. What is the world coming to? If this is some more German propaganda it will prove a boomerange, for the fellows are out for blood. Probably the Quartermaster's Dept., thought we were the Jewish Ex. Forces-Palestine instead of the Am. Ex. Forces-France."

He assured Kate that "We shall bring home three very important items viz: The bacon, Wilhelm II and Captain Merle-Smith." At the bottom of the letter, Merle-Smith wrote, "Censored: Van S. Merle-Smith Capt. 69 165th Inf. – Very amusing."[30]

While Colonel McCoy got down to running the regiment he found himself drawn to Duffy. In almost every one of his early letters, he wrote about the chaplain and his work. He reported that when the priest visited the wounded in the nearby hospitals, he did not give them sympathy but rather got them laughing. He had been taken by the fact that Duffy knew every soldier by name. In one instance, he described how Duffy went up to a bedridden soldier, saying, "Patrick, you dead beat, you think ye and the King of Spain can afford to be sick in these times. Up with ye and show your Colonel the stuff ye is made of."

In the same letter he wrote that he dined with Duffy each evening and was more impressed with each meal. "Although the Chaplain is that par excellence and the beloved of the men, he is one of the most interesting of men to me . . . Very learned. And he has helped me to nick into my new regiment most thoroughly."[31]

On Memorial Day, McCoy and Duffy, accompanied by Maj. Gen. Charles Menoher and Col. Douglas MacArthur from division headquarters and Brig. Gen. Michael Lenihan from brigade headquarters, visited the freshly dug graves at the roadside cemetery at Croixmare, where some of the dead at Rouge Bouquet had been interred. McCoy noticed that the French villagers had erected a simple fence and planted a hedge with flowers and vines.

Duffy collected children from the village and they decorated each cross with flowers.

"The little children in snowy-white dresses sallied forth to pluck the lilies and poppies which tossed their pretty heads in the brilliant sunlight, and filled the air with exquisite fragrance," recalled Pvt. Peter Rogers of F Company. "Little did I know that their innocent hearts went out in sympathy and love to the fallen heroes who silently slept in the cozy cemetery by the edge of the wood a little way off." Rogers watched the children plant the poppies and lilies in little pots at each grave and, like all the soldiers who had come to pay their last respects to their comrades, was deeply touched.[32]

Duffy remarked that "Colonel McCoy saw to it that the grave of every one of our dead was properly honored on this day—in Southampton, in Langres, in Ancervillers and here in Baccarat." He mentioned how the villagers had kept up the graves in beautiful condition—"a tribute to our dead which warms our heart to the people of France."[33]

That day the chaplain sent letters to the mothers of the regiment whose sons lay buried in France.

> It was a source of great satisfaction and gratitude to us to find that the graves we have had to leave behind in our movements have been carefully tended by French soldiers and civilians. Day after day women and children from the villages have spent the twilight hours with soldiers trimming the grassy edges and cultivating flowers until our little cemeteries are more blooming and beautiful than most one finds at home. . . . Our Colonel wishes me to convey this information to you with renewed expression of the sympathy which he and all of us feel for you in the sacrifice you have been called upon to bear in the cause of our country.[34]

Perhaps the thing that had affected McCoy the most was Duffy's wonderful relationship with the men, especially on the Sabbath.

> These rollicking Irishmen are most sympathetic and as all the villagers are devout Catholics, the village church is crowded on Sundays. Father Duffy says mass with the Curé, and the band plays through the street to the church,

gathering soldiers, children, little girls in their communion frocks, often hand in hand with the soldiers from the Bowery. This morning, Sunday, the 27th, they stepped out to the tune of "Onward Christian Soldiers" and before the church was reached it looked as though the Pied Piper of Hamlin was leading. Father Duffy says "It's nothing less than scandalous the way Presbyterians, Episcopalians, Methodists, Romanists, Baptists, Y.M.C.A + Knights of Columbus are working together." This after he had asked me to backup his effort to get a Protestant chaplain in the regiment.[35]

Instead of a Protestant chaplain, the War Department sent to the 165th another Catholic. Father James Hanley, assistant pastor at Cleveland's St. Bridget's Church, had been one of Ohio's first chaplains to go off to war. He came back with the American Distinguished Service Cross and enough gas poisoning to kill him before he reached middle age.

The new chaplain turned out to be a good match for Duffy and the Irish regiment. Duffy had been relieved to get him as he made clear in one of his letters to the Knights of Columbus. "The 42nd. Division is lacking in priests. We are two—Father Harrington with the 151st Artillery and myself. There are about 6000 Catholics in the Division, of whom half are in this regiment. I can handle my regiment, though with some difficulty."[36]

Hanley was a first-generation Irishman—his father having been born in County Cork. He was tending his parishioners at St. Bridget's in 1917 when a letter arrived at the Cleveland Diocese from the New York Diocese. The author was Duffy's old friend and the rector of St. Patrick's Cathedral, Msgr. Michael Lavelle, who had been selected to head the chaplain's committee of the National Catholic War Council. He was recruiting more chaplains than the government was willing to commission, more than five hundred, as well as the funds to pay for them. "We must find the Chaplains in sufficient number;" he wrote, "and we must raise the money to support them in their mission, than which nothing more holy can be conceived." The chaplains Lavelle desired had to be "strong, young, zealous, resourceful, self-sacrificing Priests who, over and above the sanctity and devotion which characterize all our Clergy, have a clear vision of the needs of the imperiled souls and bodies."[37]

In Cleveland, Hanley met the monsignor's requirements and became the first priest from the city to earn a chaplain's cross and the first to land in France. Once he had finished his training, he wrote to his sister, "The old army game for me." At the time he was tenting at his camp in Hattiesburg, Mississippi and, looking up into the winter's sky, he continued:

> The same moon shines brightly over us all and I know the same God protects us, but the distance from home rises like a nightmare. But I am in this thing until the last shot is fired, then back I come to those I have loved and shall never forget. I surely would not have been true to my God or calling, to my friends and family, nor to my self had I remained at home when the best blood of American manhood was in danger of going before God with an unanswered cry for the Sacraments.

The new chaplain added that although he could not shoulder a gun, he would go to the front line where "I know there is not a German bullet made that will get a Hanley."[38] In France, he was attached to the Forty-second Division and sent east where he caught up with the 165th Infantry. The regiment had recently arrived in the Champagne region, taking up positions in the Espérance and Souain sectors as part of the French Fifth Army. A new and deadlier phase of the war was about to begin. In his last letter to his sister before reaching the 165th, Hanley assured her again that he would come back. "I wouldn't give up my experience for any thing in the world. I am seeing Europe as few have seen it. Time or travel shall not change me. I am just the same today as I ever was. Just as happy and the same smile is there. Ready to do whatever orders say."[39]

As new orders arrived, Duffy observed on 16 June, "The 42nd Division has finished its preliminary education and is to start off for some more active front two days from now."[40]

That active front would challenge not only the untested doughboys of the Forty-second Division, but also the toughest veterans of the war. From mid-July through the first week of August, the Germans made yet another offensive against the Allies. This time the Allies counterattacked. Commonly known as the Second Battle of the Marne, this engagement proved to be the turning

On a hillside in the Baccarat Sector, an old woman enjoys the view with her new friends from New York. *Signal Corps/National Archives*

In the quiet Baccarat Sector, soldiers receive a trim and then . . .

. . . dash for a bath and a rub down. *Signal Corps/National Archives*

point of the Great War. Ludendorff's daring gamble would fail, and on both sides the cost in casualties would be in the hundreds of thousands.

For the soldiers of the 165th, now basking in the springtime of a quiet sector, the coming weeks would make the last six months feel like a picnic—especially when they reached the banks of a winding little river known as the Ourcq.

15

"It Will Be a Happy Day"

Before embarking for France, Jim McKenna, now a major, had warned his father that the Sixty-ninth was going to be in the "thick of the scrimmage and court death over and over again for their country's flag" and that he counted on playing a big part in that bloody scrimmage. Now on the eve of the Second Battle of the Marne, the new leader of the Third Battalion was anxious to get into the fight. To Father Francis Duffy and other officers he seemed distressed that the regiment was losing its Irish heritage before it had a chance to uphold its Celtic warrior traditions.

"Bide your time," the chaplain cautioned. "Our boys will have their innings. Don't be impatient."

McKenna, who had a shamrock nailed over the door of his headquarters and ordered his runners to wear green armbands with shamrocks on them, was quiet for a time before answering his priest. "We must show the whole world where Irishmen stand, Father. We must show that we are in this fight for liberty—heart and soul."[1]

Yet the world knew—at least the people who kept tabs on the old regiment knew. When it had marched out of Baccarat on a moonlit June night a number of its men sported medals, the *Croix de Guerre* on most of them. The French award for bravery had been pinned on the Americans for their work at Rouge Bouquet, the first raiding party into no-man's-land, and for their valor during the frightful gas attack. When Maj. Bill Donovan had heard that he was to receive a medal, he shot off a letter to his wife. "Orders have gone through they tell me, citing me for the Division Croix de Guerre, which they say is to be presented at a big review in a city near here. I do not relish that part of it very much."[2] Among the other recipients had been Sergeants Danny O'Connell,

For gallantry at Rouge Bouquet and for their first raid into no-man's-land, men of the First Battalion as well as two French chasseurs, receive the *Croix de Guerre*. The Americans (from left to right): lieutenants Arthur Cunningham and Oscar Buck and sergeants William Moore, Danny O'Connell, Spencer Rossell, Carl Kahn, and Bill Bailey. Missing from the ceremony is Sgt. Abe Blaustein, who at first was snubbed because he was Jewish. Maj. Bill Donovan refused the *Croix de Guerre* unless Blaustein was also honored. *Signal Corps/National Archives*

Spencer Rossell, William Moore, Abe Blaustein, and Cpl. Alf Helmer for their action to free the entombed E Company soldiers. First Lt. John Norman had received the medal posthumously. At first, Blaustein, had been passed over for the medal because he was Jewish. Discovering the slight, Donovan said he would not accept his medal unless Abe got one. "They finally decided that Blaustein was as worthy of that cross as Dan and I, and he got it," he told a newspaper reporter.[3]

In mid-June the Forty-second Division slipped quietly out of the Lorraine sector, with the 165th Infantry departing Baccarat on the 18th, as Duffy put it, "on our hunt for new trouble."[4] Col. Frank McCoy explained to his mother that "War is movement. . . . And we do move."[5]

The first night out the Rainbows marched past replacement troops. These were the Seventy-seventh, a division of draftees known as "New York's Own," a moniker the Irish regiment resented. When these New Yorkers, almost all them from Manhattan, tramped by, McCoy felt struck by the "great" sight. A full moon cast an eerie glow upon the soldiers, those on foot and those riding in automobiles, motor transports, and mule-drawn wagons; there arose the grinding of gears, the crack of whips, the steady crunch of boots on a chalky white road that had once felt the marching feet of Julius Caesar, Attila the Hun, and Napoleon Bonaparte. McCoy sensed his own men tense up, now "feeling and marching like veterans passing and chaffing the green division hiking cheerfully too."[6] Insults were slung back and forth, most in Irish brogues.

Shouted one of the Seventy-seventh's drafted doughboys, "We're going up to finish the job that you fellows couldn't do!"

"Look out for the Heinies or you'll be eating sauerkraut in a prison camp before the month is out!" Duffy recalled the back-and-forth banter.

"The Germans will find out what American soldiers are like when we get a crack at them!"

Then big Mike Donaldson's voice roared out, "What are you givin' us? We was over here killin' Dutchmen before they pulled your names out of the hat!"

Shot back a draftee, "Well, thank God we didn't have to get drunk to join the army."[7]

Another Seventy-seventh man yelled, "Hell, I thought the Sixty-ninth had all been gassed!"

"D' Boche tried to, idiot, but we smelled em first. They'll get you sure!"

Other voices called out in the silvery night. "Anyone there from the Bowery?"

"Hey there, d'ya live on Eighty-third Street?"

More voices sought out brothers and cousins. McCoy saw that brothers "met by calling out for each other as they went along."[8]

"It was like a noisy game of blindman's bluff," a soldier wrote.[9]

From both sides of the road, the New Yorkers sang to each other.

East side, West side,
All around the town,
The tots sang ring-a-rosie

London Bridge is falling down.
Boys and girls together,
Me and Mamie O'Rourke,
We tripped the light fantastic
On the sidewalks of New York.

A few days later McCoy sent his terrier, Bert Williams, away and recommended 1st Lt. Elmer Basil for captain.

Hearing he had been recommended for a captaincy, Elmer felt "very happy indeed"—so that the war did not seem to bother him one whit. The early summer weather had been perfect, and he wrote to his parents, "I must say that I cannot complain of either temperature or climate, however, in as much as I neither hike nor ride horse-back when we move now. I ride in the colonel's automobile which to say the very least, makes this the best war I have ever fought in. They can keep up the conflict along these lines, if it takes all summer, as far as I am concerned."[10]

The newest officer in the regiment, chocolate-loving Lt. William Spencer, agreed. "This war isn't half bad after all," he wrote to Loi, a girl he had been dating while at Princeton. "I wish you could see me now—seated under a tree in a cool breeze, a 5# box of Reymers beside me, some excellent letters to read and Erie Dispatch at hand, and not much to worry about. What more could a man want to complete his happiness." Moments earlier, Spencer had climbed out of bed and seen the red morning sun rise "over a forest in a clear pink sky, and just above the sun were bunches of little white puffs of smoke from bursting shrapnel, fired at an enemy plane." He told Loi, perhaps trying to make her jealous, that in the home that served as his billets lived a handsome girl named Marie. One night he had tried to put the make on her. "The sad part was when she rebuffed me—I tried to kiss her good night but nothing doing and I went to bed kissless. Tough isn' it? Gosh, she was pretty." He tacked on that he always let Van S. Merle-Smith and Charles Baker read her letters. And "they read every single word in them. . . . [It was Charlie Baker's] sister who saw you in a canoe at the Millstream, and told me afterwards you were one of the most beautiful girls she had ever seen. Those were the days, were they not?"[11]

The war soon changed for Spencer and Elmer so that they would long for the bright, peaceful summer days in the French countryside, especially in the part of France where they now were—the

picturesque province of Champagne. Flowers filled the countryside. Elmer saw them in blues and poppy reds and picked some and
gently tucked them into a letter. "I enclose some of these flowers
not from the garden, but from a wild field along side a road where I
went on horse-back yesterday, out in the country."[12]

However, the more the regiment moved, the more the countryside transformed itself into a landscape that reminded the veterans of 1916 of their Mexican border days. It was as if they were
in the desert again. The heat rose. The flowers and trees disappeared. First Battalion Adjutant Oliver Ames reported to his wife
that on "the hottest day yet, they won't even let us take off our
blouses marching about, which almost makes me insubordinate."
He said he now knew how his men suffered and the "next time
will let them remove blouses."[13] The chalky earth choked the troops
as they kicked up dust on the trail. When it rained, the chalk turned
into a gooey white paste that sucked feet into the ground—sticky,
thick, and slippery. At night the air was still and breathless and the
men perspired freely while the cooties bit into their flesh.

"Wearily we trudged along and as the spires of a town hovered
in view we thought that possibly this was our destination," one
boy wrote. "But on we went."[14]

"Oh! What a hike!" complained F Company's Nathaniel "Nat"
Rouse.[15]

Because the regiment was always on the move, Chaplain Duffy
joked to his father, "When I get back I am going to look for a job
managing a circus."[16]

On the 24th, McCoy celebrated an anniversary, reminding his
mother that it had been twenty years ago that he had his first "fight"
in Las Guasimas, Cuba. "And we're on our way to the biggest
fight of all."[17]

The Forty-second arrived at Camp de Châlons, part of the
Marne salient. They were attached to the French Fifth Army Corps,
preparing for a push against the Germans on the symbolic date of
the Fourth of July, American Independence Day. But the French
high command soon realized that the Germans were not going to
wait—instead they were gearing up for another major assault, the
year's fifth crack at the Allies. Thus the division went on the move
again, although this time it did not travel far. Now part of the
French Fourth Army, it was commanded by one of the great heroes of the war, a one-armed general who knew how to fight and
backed down to no army.

At fifty-one, Henri Gouraud had seen enough blood shed to last a hundred lifetimes, much of it his own. For most of his military career he had served in the French Colonial Army. His exploits in the jungles and deserts had become legendary and had earned him the title "Lion of Africa." At the start of the Great War he had commanded the Tenth Infantry Division and taken a bullet in the shoulder in the Argonne Forest. In another battle he was struck by a shell that ripped apart his body: he lost an arm and nearly lost a leg. But those wounds had never slowed him down. In December 1915, he took command of the French Fourth Army.

Duffy thought Gouraud a remarkable military figure. One of the things that made him so in the chaplain's mind was the "touch of distinction from his empty hanging sleeve and stiff leg."[18] Douglas MacArthur, now a brigadier general, had been equally struck by Gouraud. Although he knew of the general's reputation, MacArthur wrote, "I was not prepared for the heroic figure to whom I reported. With one arm gone, and half a leg missing, with his red beard glittering in the sunlight, the jaunty rake of his cocked hat and the oratorical brilliance of his resonant voice, his impact was overwhelming. He seemed almost the reincarnation of that legendary figure of battle and romance, Henry of Navarre. And he was just as good as he looked."[19]

Under Gouraud, the Rainbow Division reported to the French XXI Corps and was ordered to take up positions along the front between Rheims and the Argonne. The crafty general believed the main thrust of the German attack would be aimed at the center of this front, in the sectors of Espérance and Souain. Here he placed the Eighty-third Brigade west of the strategic road to Châlons-sur-Marne and the Eighty-fourth Brigade east of it. Behind the Eighty-third he positioned the 150th Machine Gun Battalion from Wisconsin. If the Germans broke through here and captured Châlons, the way to Paris would be wide open. The 165th and 166th Regiments moved up to the Suippes River, which ran through the village of St. Hillaire-Le-Grand. Three to four miles southeast of St. Hillaire, Brig. Gen. Michael Lenihan set his brigade headquarters at a place called Suippes Farm, close to Gouraud's headquarters. Closer to the front, McCoy located his regimental command post at Camp Bois de la Lyre, deep underground. One to two miles northwest of St. Hillaire, holding down the division's left flank, the colonel deployed to the front line the Second Battalion of twenty-nine-year-old Maj.

Alexander Anderson. He kept in reserve Donovan's First Battalion and McKenna's Third. East of the regiment the Ohioans of the 166th Infantry dug in. Then came the Eighty-fourth Brigade's Alabamans of the 167th and further to the east the Iowans of the 168th.

Gouraud's plan was to have a token French force greet the German attack in the advance trenches, making them think his full army was there. When the enemy reached the near-empty trenches he would pull back his token force and, once the Germans were out in the open, counterattack with a tremendous artillery bombardment. And the rout would be on.

Gouraud knew the German offensive was set for about midnight on 14 July, the date of France's national holiday—Bastille Day. In his famous order of 7 July, which went to all men, the general warned of the imminent attack. He warned, too, of the horrible bombardment, of an assault so fierce the battlefield would be engulfed in clouds of smoke, dust, and gas. But he believed in his men, telling them:

"In your breasts beat the brave and strong hearts of free men.

"None shall look to the rear; none shall yield a step.

"Each shall have but one thought: to kill, to kill, until they have had their fill.

"Therefore, your General says to you: You will break this assault and it will be a happy day."[20]

McCoy sent a follow up order to his officers. After outlining the plan of resistance, he stressed the number one mission: "To defend position . . . in every event and at all costs."[21]

As the days passed and the words of Gouraud still rang in the ears of the Rainbow Division, Ames learned that 12 July was truly a happy day for him. He had received a cablegram from Boston. His wife had given birth to their first child, a daughter born on the 3rd. Now all he could think about was his baby and how happy she made him. "Swell-headed," he admitted to his wife. "My natural inclination is to go around boasting about my child, but so far I have contained myself pretty well, but how long I can do it I don't know. I can hardly wait for your next letter."[22] The first soldier he told was Elmer. He said that because he was a father he had new responsibilities to worry about. Elmer was happy for him. On the 14th the intelligence officer got around to writing his parents. Before he mentioned Ames he declared that all day there had been an "air of expectancy" about the coming night. "Why and what it is

I can't say, but there is a bit of thrill in the atmosphere." He closed, "By the way, Ames has a daughter, the lucky kid."[23]

On the afternoon Elmer wrote home, Gouraud dined at his headquarters with his French generals and colonels and their counterparts in the Forty-second Division. Red and white wine flowed and the dinner, although simple, was deliciously prepared by French chefs. It was only natural, Gouraud explained to his American guests, that on the eve of battle the commander and his officers sit down to a friendly meal.[24]

Duffy knew the natural place for him was up front, with Anderson's battalion. He told McCoy his spiritual duties demanded it. He left for the front lines right after reading Gouraud's orders. For five days he slept in Anderson's command post, a crude "elephant hut," a five-foot hole in the ground fortified with sandbags and a corrugated iron roof. He walked among the soldiers at all hours. "They will have need of all their courage," he wrote, "for if this general attack is made it's going to be a tremendous one."[25]

After a week, the chaplain needed to report back to the regimental command post. McCoy's motorcycle dispatch driver went to get him. Pvt. James Wadsworth, who had transferred into the Sixty-ninth with Donovan, roared up, excited to be at the front. Duffy climbed into the sidecar and away they went. After dining with McCoy and providing him with the latest news on Anderson's battalion, the chaplain walked back to the front.

At eleven o'clock on the night of the 14th, Duffy closed his diary by noting, "Everything that can be done for the men has been done. There remains the simplest task in the world, though often the hardest—waiting."[26]

While G Company, Second Battalion, awaited the upcoming battle, the colonel of the French 116th Infantry, who commanded that sector of the front lines, sent a message to Capt. John Prout. He ordered him to arm his most trusted noncommissioned officers with pistols and place them in back of his troops. If anyone tried to run away the noncommissioned officers were to shoot them on the spot. Prout tore up the order, flung it to the ground and stomped on it. To the chaplain of the 150th Machine Gun Battalion, he said, "That French colonel must think that my men are a pack of cowards!"[27]

The Stokes mortar company prepares to fire on 3 June. *Signal Corps/ National Archives*

Shortly after midnight the waiting ended.

Duffy marked the time at 12:04. "No crescendo business about it. Just one sudden crash like an avalanche, but an avalanche that was to keep crashing for five hours. The whole sky seemed to be torn apart with sound—the roaring B-o-o-o-m-p of the discharge and the gradual menacing W-h-e-e-E-E-Z of traveling projectiles and the nerve racking W-h-a-n-g-g of bursts. . . . They were all mingled in one deafening combination of screech and roar, and they all seemed to be bursting just outside."[28]

Sergeant Richard O'Neill of D Company recalled, "Shells dropping all around, gas and shrapnel and high explosive."[29]

Rouse wrote, "Oh God, what a night!"[30]

The French opened up first, firing artillery shells toward the German lines. Caught off guard, the Germans responded. Shells fell like a blizzard. The ground shook violently. In Paris, a hundred miles away, citizens felt and heard the shock of the great eye for an eye bombardment. "The world bucked like a mule," recollected Charlie MacArthur of the 149th Field Artillery.[31] Col. George Leach of the 151st Field Artillery observed from his dugout behind the lines how "the whole country lit up with bursting shells, flares and all kinds of German rockets, so that it was almost as light as day."[32]

To Bill Spencer it seemed as if every gun in the world had gone off at the same time. "It was a steady sound of terrific pounding— almost a hum, the shells so fast," he recounted to Loi. "They sent 150's at us, and they are wicked. But you can always hear them coming and have plenty of time to duck. Just before they land, when about 50 feet in the air, you can actually see them. It is fascinating—the terrific speed and then the explosion."[33]

Clinton Bushey of Yonkers, barely seventeen years old, had been caught out in no-man's-land stringing wire with sixty-six other boys from H Company when the shelling started. Those who were not struck down in the initial explosions ran for their lives. They streaked across the churned up earth with the "shells dropping a foot apart from each other." Even after they reached the trench, the concussion of the shells knocked Bushey flat twice. "I certainly did think I would never see dawn," he later wrote from a hospital. "The fragments of the shells and pieces of shrapnel would swish over the trench and spent and hot pieces would drop into the trench and smoulder there. Great luck (luck was the only thing that I could see) saved us from being wiped out."

Toward dawn, with no let-up in the artillery bombardment, Bushey poked his head above the parapet. "The trees were laid low, and charred stumps stuck up all over the ground. It looked as if some big giant had swept the whole woods with a big scythe." The surviving H Company boys huddled together, lit cigarettes, and waited out the barrage. Bushey heard the swish and roar of an incoming shell and then the sudden, horrible boom. Ten of his companions were killed instantly. He felt like he had been struck in the right side by a sledgehammer. "I don't see how I escaped. The man on my right and one on my left and the one directly across from me were killed, and I only got a piece in the side." The survivors dropped back to a French dressing station and were led to a field hospital which was shelled as they were being treated. "I certainly am the luckiest fellow on two feet. I don't want to come so close to death again as I did up there when the Germans began their drive."[34] Bushey's wounds were so serious that, unknown to any of his company officers, he was sent to Base Hospital Number 20. While he was recovering, his parents in Yonkers received a telegram from the War Department informing them that their son had been killed in action.

One of the shells smashed into Prout's command post, burying him, his first sergeant, Charles Grundy, and several others. The concussion blew off their helmets and gas masks and covered them from head to foot in white chalk. By the time they dug their way out and surfaced, "we looked more like ghosts than humans."[35]

The heaviest part of the bombardment roared until near dawn before seasoned veterans of six German divisions moved forward behind a rolling barrage, passing through three other divisions held in reserve. These soldiers knew the terrain well. They expected to push the Allies back and take the Suippes River by noon and to be sweeping through the streets of Châlons by four the following morning. As the German infantrymen advanced, dozens of airplanes buzzed along the American trenches like deadly birds of prey, raking the bewildered doughboys with machine-gun fire. General MacArthur reported, "Bombs were dropped on roads and towns and the enemy planes fired with machine guns on moving troops and convoys."[36] Duffy claimed the "German planes for two days had complete mastery" of the skies.[37] Tanks crawled forward, too, inching across the torn up ground. And far behind the Allies' lines, long-range shells hit Châlons, collapsing buildings and ripping up cobbled streets.

"The Dutchmen shelled far back of the line and those big Bobbies were landing all over the fields and screaming overhead," Herbert Gross of Headquarters Company grumbled. "Hundreds of planes were battling above us."[38]

Wounded in the head and foot, F Company's Hugh Haggerty was astonished at the airplanes. "When the dawn was breaking they sent up about fifty airplanes," he later wrote home. They shot machine guns at us and dropped bombs in our trenches. Well, Mother, I just prayed hard, saying an act of contrition and asked the Blessed Virgin to help me. My prayers were answered and I kept fighting and got away lucky."[39]

Another wounded soldier, Pvt. C. M. Taylor, described how "The German planes came over by the score and flew so low you could almost see the aviators. They would play their machine gun up and down and one of our infantry boys brought one down with an automatic rifle."[40]

The sharpshooter who brought the plane down, Pvt. Mike Foody, was cited in several dispatches. Foody, from Morningside Heights, had heard that a country boy from Alabama had plucked a German aviator from the sky the day before. Foody, a known crack shot at the Coney Island shooting galleries, asked Capt.

James Archer if he could try to duplicate the Alabamian's feat. Archer nodded and Foody jumped to the parapet. He took aim at a plane, snapped off a shot and brought it down. When Archer commended him for his marksmanship, Foody looked at him through bloodshot eyes. "Sir, there ain't nothing them country jakes can do that we can't do in the big town."[41]

Wadsworth, McCoy's motorcycle dispatch rider and cousin to U.S. Senator James Wadsworth, had a harrowing race against an airplane. Wadsworth's motorcycle had been giving him trouble and when he was not delivering messages he would tinker with his machine outside the regimental command post, trying to get it to run more smoothly. But when the colonel's phone conked out, Wadsworth leaped onto his motorcycle and sped toward Anderson's Second Battalion to get the latest report. He made it without incident, although artillery shells fell around him. Anderson gave him a message and young Wadsworth was off again, roaring over the pitted road, weaving around exploding gas shells and *minenwerfers*. Within moments, an enemy airplane bore down on him, chasing him back to McCoy. The daring motorcyclist at last eluded his pursuer and skidded into the dusty white ground that surrounded the command post, his machine sputtering. He reported to his colonel, who ordered him to get something to eat. The exhausted, chalk-spattered private grabbed a tin plate of food from the camouflaged mess tent and, chatting with Cpl. Lawrence Flynn, who stood nearby, strolled out into the open where he had left his motorcycle. Three shells crashed close by; hot shrapnel flew across the open ground and tore into Wadsworth. He fell as Flynn ran to catch him. Drifting into unconsciousness, the twenty-year-old former aide to Wild Bill Donovan worried about his motorcycle, then his parents, and then died.

Covered by their deadly airplanes, the attacking Germans passed over the sparsely held advance trenches and pressed on to meet the untested Americans.

To their surprise, two companies of frenzied Alabamians on the Eighty-third Brigade's right flank poured out of their trenches, hacking away at the enemy with Bowie knives. The Germans countered with stick grenades. When the melee was over, fifty Germans had been killed and twenty-five taken prisoner.

In Anderson's Second Battalion, holding down the left flank, the New Yorkers fought with a fury that stopped the enemy.

Chocolate-loving Lt. William Spencer attended to the wounds of Capt. Van S. Merle-Smith at the Ourcq River. *Courtesy of James Tierney*

"I must say, mother, it was a terrible day for the Germans," Private Haggerty described. "They attacked us about 6 o'clock and we just heaped up a dozen high. There were a number of our boys wounded and killed but the number did not compare with that of the Germans. Their dead were heaped up so high they could not advance."[42] Private Gross penned home, "Our orders were to stick to the guns and, believe me, we did it. A shell would finish one gun grew, but in a minute the dead were piled and another crew in place."[43]

In front of G Company, Prout looked on as the Germans came at his men with bayonets. His First Platoon commander, Lt. Kenneth Ogle, ordered everyone to fix bayonets and then led them out of the trenches, pell-mell into the onrushing Germans. Prout said that the bayonet charge had been their only chance and "Ogle took that chance." The charge drove the enemy back, he said, and his company held its position.[44] MacArthur cited this battle in his summary report that night, describing how a raiding party of twenty-one Germans had attacked a platoon of the 165th Infantry. "Our men went over the top to meet them and killed the entire party with the bayonet without loss to themselves."

A squad in E Company led by Alf Helmer fought off a pack of Germans with rifle grenades and small-arms fire; the enemy scattered through the underbrush. No sooner had they disappeared then Helmer heard a German crying, "Father, Father." The pitiful wailing lasted for hours. Finally, without a word to each other, he and Patrick McCarthy, also upset by the cries, went in search of the wounded soldier. Helmer called it a "sort of spiritual understanding we had both long enjoyed." They climbed the parapet, worked themselves through tangled wire and found the boy. "Near him lay killed an older German soldier, a handsome man with snow white hair and goatee. Pat and I could not determine then and never did whether the older man was the boy's father or whether the boy had been calling his spiritual 'Father'." They carried the boy back to their own lines and gave him to a stretcher bearer.[45]

Joe Jones, also, recorded the bayonet fight, as well as all of the events of the day in his swift, staccato style. "2nd Batt. Hold first line of attack against the Prussian Guard. 3rd Batt. Move up. German plane shot down. Shelter tent ripped by shrapnel. 1st Batt. Suffer losses. Germans take 3 kilos from French. Our 2nd Batt. Holds the line, killing with the bayonet. ATTACK."[46]

Over in the Third Battalion, Martin Hogan, a runner for McKenna, watched the fury of combat. "Clubbed rifles were splintered against skulls and shoulder; bayonets were plunged home, withdrawn and plunged home again; automatics spit here and there in the line; grenades exploded; while a man occasionally shot his dripping bayonet free from his enemy's body."[47]

To confuse the Americans, a number of Germans donned French helmets. A platoon leader with a French helmet atop his head approached an American machine-gun crew, yelling not to shoot, he and his men were French soldiers. When he neared the machine gunners he tossed a stick grenade into their midst. The explosion wounded the triggerman, but his teammate sprang to the unmanned gun and put the enemy to flight.[48] The ruse disgusted Vivian Commons. "Here is one of the dirty tricks the Huns tried to pull over on the boys," he related to his parents. "They came over in French uniforms, some with Red Cross bands on their arms and stretchers and on the stretchers they had machine guns. They received the same deal the rest of them get so they didn't get away with their trick."[49]

O'Neill described how four Germans with Red Cross armbands carried a stretcher up to the lines. "When they got close enough to us, they threw this blanket off of the stretcher and opened up with a machine gun."[50]

"The morning the Germans made the attack on us was the worst of all," wrote Pvt. C. Irving Levin of I Company. "The artillery on both sides hammered away and just as it was getting to us, we opened up and the noise was the worst you ever heard. We were hammering them with grenades, machine guns, auto rifles and infantry. The earth all around us was quaking just as in an earthquake."[51]

Pvt. Harry Rubin from the Lower East Side, whose comrades in the Irish regiment had changed his name to Mike O'Brien, remembered how "the Germans started from their trenches, six hundred yards away. They came on in mass formation, shoulder to shoulder. For miles, it seemed, their thick, gray lines were visible." The Germans had not gone far when the artillery hit them. "They just rained the iron on the Heinies and made those in the rear climb over heaps of dead as they advanced. The attacking party was practically annihilated after coming halfway across no man's land. A thin remnant crawled back to their trenches. Their dead fairly covered the ground they had traversed."[52]

Spencer wrote, "The Germans pulled off a local attack about 100 yards to our right against our second battalion, coming down through the bayous. Ten times they attacked, but ten times they were driven back by our counterattacks. Our men fought magnificently, and quite swept the Huns off their feet. Any number of them were killed, and naturally we suffered too, a little. Many prisoners were taken also, and nearly all of them were boys, 16 to 20 years old. They themselves didn't put up much of a fight, but their officers fought splendidly, quite contrary to what I thought of the German officer"[53]

In the endless bombardment, explosive powder, fine as early morning mist, hung over the raging fight and over the road leading to Châlons, and shrouded the leafless trees in black. Shelled ammunition dumps on both sides burned like pyres, black smoke swirling skyward. Farmhouses and stone barns and outbuildings, some used as barracks, were aflame. Maddened, shrieking farm animals raced wildly across the fields, going nowhere. Wounded and dying horses littered the roads. The bodies of soldiers blotted the plain of battle. And the chalky earth of the Champagne province rose in puffy white clouds.

As early as five in the morning, casualties were being hauled off to the ambulance station. By six-twenty, two men had been reported killed, three severely wounded. At nine there still had been no news from Anderson's Second Battalion. At the end of his desperate motorcycle run, Wadsworth had been carrying bad news: twenty-three of Anderson's men had lost their lives, one was missing, and 103 were wounded. The heights in front of Anderson swarmed with Germans. What was happening there was unknown for most of the afternoon, but as evening closed in, the fighting tapered off along the entire front, and it looked as if the Rainbows had held. At least Gouraud felt so. He wired congratulations. Brigadier General Lenihan, now that he could see the Germans withdrawing, passed on the congratulations to his colonels. But at ten forty-five he got a sobering report from Anderson. "Will make an earnest effort to get you a complete list of casualties before morning. . . . Request that 6 M. C. [Medical Corps] men be sent out as early as possible for dressing wounds. Many slight wounded have been returned to duty. Will use every effort to keep you posted as to changes in situation." He informed the general that his counterattack had succeeded, "killing all." Anderson was not sure of the number of enemy casualties.[54]

The major himself had almost been one of the casualties. In the earliest bombardment, a powerful crash outside his command post knocked him out of his chair. A soldier near him wailed to Duffy, "Oh, Father, the Major is killed." Anderson got up with a slight cut on his knee. The chaplain smiled and said he had "gotten a right to an easy wound stripe."[55]

Outside, however, two men had been killed and others wounded. One of the dead, Pvt. Homer Hunt, had tucked into his pocket a cablegram from his wife letting him know that she had given birth to their first child. The other dead soldier was Edwin Jelley. Later the priest heard that Joseph Dunnigan, at whose marriage back at Camp Mills he had assisted in, had also been killed.

Realizing his place was at the front line comforting his men, Duffy stayed throughout the worst of the shelling and the harrowing hand-to-hand combat. Maj. Tom Reilley saw the chaplain constantly exposed to enemy fire as he tended the wounded and carried them on stretchers to the nearest dressing stations. "His religion consisted of a cheery word, a smile and a slap on the back," Reilley recalled. "He made himself dear to many a doughboy by handing out cigarettes just at the right time."[56]

Maj. Alexander Anderson was twenty-nine years old when he led the Second Battalion during the German offensive in the Champagne sector. *Courtesy of James Tierney*

In the Third Battalion, held in reserve, Hogan observed, "One look into Father Duffy's face was good for jaded nerves; for his face radiated a cheerful calm which made the hell around us seem unreal. He might just as well have been walking down the silent aisle of some majestic cathedral for all his face told of heeding danger or of wrought-up nerves. He spoke little personal things to each of the men; it was as though his thoughts were not on the battle, as though no battle were going on."[57]

When the fight was at its worst, Anderson asked the chaplain if he wanted some grenades. The priest said no. "Every man to his trade. I stick to mine."

Anderson then took hold of his battalion flag, stroked it as if it was the most cherished thing on earth. "Well here, then, this is my battalion flag. If things break bad in the battle you will see that it don't fall into the hands of the enemy. Burn it up if it is the last thing you find time to do before you go."

"All right," replied Duffy, "I shall look out for your flag. That is a commission that suits my trade."[58]

When the first day of fighting had closed, Lt. Col. Harry Mitchell personally trekked to the Second Battalion and from Anderson's command post sent a note to McCoy. He informed him that Anderson's men were in excellent spirits and "there is no question about their fighting to the last." He said that the dead would be buried that evening under the chaplain's supervision. "Much to the joy of everyone concerned," he ended, "Father Duffy remains on the job."[59]

Although the Germans had withdrawn, they regrouped during the night. The next morning they stormed back, again mostly with artillery and airplanes. They had been cheered by the fact that even though the Allied line had held the day before, more than thirteen thousand prisoners had been rounded up. On the second day the Germans made sporadic infantry assaults. Each time they were repulsed.

Private Rubin, a.k.a O'Brien, later recollected, "We were to stand and meet them—no retreating or surrendering. . . . We just waited for the Fritzies. The artillery was dropping them, but new increments would come up quickly and fill in. Their advance men got within grenade-throwing distance of us, and it became a battle of infantry to infantry, with grenades as the chief weapons. For three hours the fighting continued, the Germans retreated. That is, a few of them did, because dead men do not walk."[60]

Jones entered in his diary, "Bavarian Guard attacks. Germans attack twelve times with tanks, but fail to break our line. 2nd Batt. Goes over the top at once."[61]

In F Company, Donnie King, a replacement soldier from Comanche County, Oklahoma, carried an American flag, folded and placed inside his uniform next to his heart. The flag had been a gift from a fellow Oklahoman King had met while on his way to New York to board the troop ship *Tuscania*. "Mail the flag back to me when you reach France," the Oklahoman had requested. A German U-boat torpedoed the *Tuscania* and two hundred soldiers had drowned. King and his flag survived. Now, on the 16th, a shell fragment tore open his chest. Evacuated to a base hospital, he stayed there for four months. Before he had gone down, he had killed a bunch of Germans—at least he said so in a letter from the hospital. "Papa, tell the boys if they want to know that I am getting my share of [Dutchmen]. It is like hunting rabbits in the snow." While recuperating, King mailed the flag back to Oklahoma—stained with his own blood as well as sea brine from the north Atlantic.[62]

Communications between Anderson's battalion and the regimental command post were cut off again, and at two in the afternoon McCoy sent Mitchell cross-country once more to find out what was going on. The lieutenant colonel was unable to use any of the roads because of heavy shrapnel fire. While he worked his way forward, McKenna met up with Anderson and reported back to the division, "All quiet on front now." Mitchell then surveyed the damage of two days' fighting and sent a runner back with a list of casualties, including the death of 1st Lt. Thomas Haldene Young of F Company. Witnesses said that Young, a graduate of the Plattsburgh Camp, was leading his men in turning back a violent attack when one of his soldiers suffered a wound. He scooped up his rifle, shot three Germans and yelled that he was satisfied with that. He was racing off to plug up another hole in the line when a grenade got him. His last words to Anderson were, "Our men have got them licked to a standstill, but they have got me."[63] Then he yelled at his men. "Get after them, boys!"[64] Mitchell warned McCoy that the number of casualties, now at more then a hundred, would go higher. He recommended that "an additional surgeon be sent here and could use litter bearers if you have any men available." McCoy played down the bad news to Lenihan. "All very satisfactory. . . . Men in line tired, resting, full of spirit and ready for the next fight."[65]

But he also sent several surgeons up front, Austin Lawrence among them. At dusk they started out on foot for Anderson's position. In the darkness, Lawrence got separated from the others.

He was soon lost. "Wandered up & down awhile & then turned back," he scrawled in his diary. "After fussing around an hour or so started again. I felt badly & stayed back with Wilson & the boys with cart. Some weird night way out in the open fields. Shells bursting on all sides & whistling over our head. Flares & signal rockets by the hundreds. Will never forget this night."[66]

Although rivers of blood soaked the white chalk along the trenches of the Second Battalion, the second day ended quietly. When Private Taylor, waiting for the next assault, looked out across the battlefield, he was sickened. "The bodies lay around in such numbers you could not go out in no man's land without stepping on them," he wrote to his brother. "The smell after two days was something fierce."[67]

"I was in hell for 6 hours," wrote Private Rouse. "I haven't had any sleep or anything to eat for 50 hours. I don't know how I stand it."[68]

Emmett Gordon of L Company (who had two brothers in C Company, one of whom was missing in action) made sure his parents in Long Island City knew that at least he was okay. "We came out all right, thanks to the prayers of those at home," he wrote, "for there wasn't anything else in God's world that helped outside of a little shelter of a truck which was about as good as the service on the Vernon avenue line."[69]

At ten-thirty that night, Donovan wrote to Ruth, filling sheet after sheet of paper meant for field messages. Reune Martin, one of his lieutenants, was off to the states to be a captain and Donovan wanted him to carry the letter home and mail it. "He leaves to-night so I have little time," he explained. He told her the last two days had been warm "in weather and in excitement." He described how he had gone up on a little knoll to watch the fireworks, a "tremendous spectacle." When it was over, "Dawn came and with it the dead and wounded." The destruction of the land was "like we know Buffalo after a heavy storm. Broken trees and unstrung wires and a general air of a terrific beating." He told of the "jumble of dead horses" and bodies that "once were human." Such death and destruction might have seemed remote to Ruth until he added, "Young Wadsworth was killed in front of the regimental P.C. He had been doing good work. He died without suffering. He was hit in the head with a piece of shell." Near the end of his letter he said that on the "16th I buried some of the men, acting as chaplain, and burying them in the little roadside French cemetery while Boche shrapnel broke around us."[70]

Donovan had almost lost his adjutant in another close encounter with a motorcycle. Ames had commandeered a motorcycle and driver from the 117th Engineers and, riding in the sidecar, barreled into the First Battalion's command post. He hopped out moments before a shell struck the motorcycle. The remains of the machine and driver were never found.

On the start of the third day, Elmer, his intelligence team keeping an eye on any German movement, noted that the enemy was not returning fire. As the day wore on, each regiment sent back news that all was quiet. McCoy hiked down to visit Anderson. "Men tired but able to continue," he wired back. "Morale splendid."

A report on casualties came next. "Killed—Off. 1; E.M.—36. Wounded: Off.—3; E.M. 175. Missing—Off. 0: E.M.—6. Total: Off.—4. E.M. 217."[71] Not part of any report was the number of dead horses in the division. More than a hundred had been gunned down or blown up.

McCoy felt that the men in his command post had been fortunate because the German artillery shells landed either far back of it or on the lower ground along the Suippes River. "Anderson and his noble battalion," he reported, "put up a great fight in the front lines. Time and time again the Germans got into his lines, but not one of them ever left, and at the end of the attack the 2nd Battalion, though battered and suffering from heavy losses, retained their spirit and morale."[72]

Sixty Irish soldiers had been killed in the three-day fight, almost twenty-five percent of the total killed in the division, and back in New York their families would soon mourn them. Anderson's battalion suffered forty-seven dead. His H Company, caught out in no-man's-land stringing wire, had been hit the hardest, with twenty-eight "gone west," as the doughboys said of those killed in action.

Cpl. Samuel Forman of the Machine Gun Company had written to his wife, Loretta, boasting that although he had been wounded earlier, no hospital was to keep him out of the fight. The ex-detective of the New York Central Railroad bullied the doctors at the base hospital and left before his wounds had properly healed. Shell fragments killed him on his first day back. In Brooklyn, his widow promised she would try not to go into mourning because her husband had told her not to. "If I did," she had said, "Sam would come back and haunt me."[73]

In his last boast to his folks, F Company's Pvt. Jimmy Kane, a Hell's Kitchen truck driver, vowed he would get ten Germans before they got him. He was killed on the 15th.[74]

Private First Class George Patrick McKeon never uttered a boastful word. He had rarely written to his eldest sister, Daisy, but left his death benefit to her and the family, and it kept them going through the 1920s. He had been hit by a shell while holding off the enemy with an automatic rifle. When being taken back to a dressing station he had seemed fine; he had even chatted with the litter bearers. But he had died there. In his pocket, Lt. John Connors, his platoon commander, found a small prayer book that Duffy had put together for the men. It was in French and English and enabled dying soldiers to make their confession to French padres if their own chaplain was elsewhere on the battlefield. It contained the "Act of Contrition," "The Our Father" and "The Hail Mary."[75]

"I am over here . . . doing my bit—a good, brave soldier and not afraid to die a martyr for a just and worthy cause," Cpl. Walter Reilly, one of the many H Company boys killed, had written his aunt in Brooklyn. "From the very beginning there has always been a struggle between right and wrong, and still the struggle goes on. I am lucky to be fighting for humanity and democracy, although war is cruel and we did not believe in it. It was forced upon us. Let us all be patient and persevere for a little while and in doing so we will conquer in the end."[76]

Another Brooklyn lad, B Company Sgt. Henry Kiernan, in his last letter home, had urged his brother "If you ever hear anybody praising or talking in favor of the Germans, don't hit him with your hand, but get the biggest baseball bat you can find and crack his skull, because the only fellow of that type who is any good is a dead one."[77]

The death of Kiernan's comrade in B Company, Pvt. Arthur Viens, had hit Duffy hard. Viens had been one of the first boys to show up when the priest opened Our Savior parish in the Bronx.

Two of the H Company boys to go down were first cousins, Sergeants Bill O'Neill and Bernard Finnerty. Bill had two brothers in the company as well as his cousin Bernard. They all lived at 212 East Ninetieth Street. The brothers were Danny, also a sergeant, and Jerome. Their family, which hailed from the Irish seacoast town of Bantry, was so close-knit that Jerome, who carried an Irish flag with him at all times, sought a reduction in rank from first sergeant to sergeant so that Danny could have a chance at being first sergeant. On the first day of fighting, Bill was wounded by a shell fragment. He was wounded again by machine-gun fire, but refused to quit. Finally, he was killed in a charge against a strong enemy position. Bernard single-handedly took on a squad of Germans, driving them back. Duffy later recalled how he had rushed the foe, hurling grenades until he was brought down. One account said he had been hit in the head by shrapnel; another claimed that a sniper had taken him out. Pvt. Bill Halpin from Astoria picked up his body and then "I laid him down again and his body was not removed until three days later. There was constant fighting, but we held the ground."[78] The chaplain buried Bernard close to his cousin Bill and close to Sam Forman, near where they had fallen, on the road to Châlons-sur-Marne.

16

"The Last Joy Ride Any of Us'll Ever Get"

The Germans were stopped cold by the Allies for the first time since shifting division after division from the Eastern Front. The Rainbows played a large part in this event. With Ludendorff's army now in retreat, Allied Commander-in-Chief Foch believed the time was ripe for a bold counterattack. Gen. Jean Degoutte of the French Sixth Army figured the back-pedaling Germans were in disarray and would put up little resistance if the Allies acted fast—and he wanted at them. Thus, Foch set 18 July as the date to strike back. In the end, with the Americans fighting alongside the French, the Germans would be routed in the Aisne-Marne sector, suffering a mortal blow that would be felt the entire length of the Western Front.

But in the meantime, there was one problem. The Germans were not making the full retreat Degoutte envisioned. They were regrouping, setting up strong defenses along the Ourcq River and other strategic points in the Aisne-Marne. Wherever the Allies showed up, the Germans would be ready.

Eager to go after the enemy, Gen. John Pershing had his I Army Corps, then an element of Degoutte's Sixth Army, poised along the front from Château-Thierry to Belleau Wood—six combat divisions, each twice the size of a French division. Four were regular army, two were National Guard.

On the day the Allies launched their counterattack, the Forty-second was in military limbo. It had been pulled out of Champagne, detached from Gouraud's forces, and placed "at the disposition of the Commander-in-Chief of the French Army." The soldiers had been given two days' travel and forage rations and sent westward by rail—the "definite destination . . . unknown."[1]

A week later they were fighting for Degoutte, rushing across wheat fields and through orchards and wooded hills to flush the Germans from the north bank of the Ourcq—a formidable task for a division yet to take the offensive.

But in the meantime, the division was entrenched along the Suippes River, awaiting orders. Maj. Jim McKenna, who, although he still suffered from the effects of mustard gas, nevertheless relished his regiment's stout defense, reminded his father, "I've told you we could lick the Germans in a square fight. Now we've done it. All is not velvet, but from now on the odds will turn more and more in our favor."[2]

McKenna also sent a letter to his Fordham University law professor, Michael Dee. "We have had lots of fun since last I saw you in New York," he updated him. "From the early days of last year, when the American was a rarity, until the present, when he is as common as vin rouge, we have had a personally conducted tour of France and we have learned many things beside the language. One of those things is that we can trim the German every day we meet him in a straight fight—no, he is not easy, and we must work, but we can and do hand him the K.O. when the punch comes. Of course he puts one over once in a while, but how can we beat nine men and the umpire?" McKenna added, "You will be pleased to know that my brother Billy has been promoted to Captain and I have been made a Major. We are pleased to have received the promotions in France and will try to be worthy of the wonderful men we are leading."[3]

Nearby, Col. Frank McCoy, worn out but happy commander of the 165th, sent a missive to his mother. "The Boche are being driven back all along the line and my regiment is going strong. And they know they can beat the Huns' best effort." He assured her there was no need to worry. "Colonels are safe most of the time, and for the moment I'm 35 feet under the chalk of a hill which the Boche have bombarded for three days without bothering us here at our work."[4]

Maybe the bombardment had not bothered McCoy. But the cratered landscape around his command post was strewn with the dead. The 117th Sanitary Train, an ambulance and field hospital unit of the Eighty-third Brigade, had administered to 2,205 soldiers. The worst of the wounded were then rushed by train to base hospitals. A medic in the field said that nothing in Dante's *Inferno* could compare to the scene at the Suippes River.

> Men piled in great heaps, the dying with dead—legs, arms, heads and torsos; gray and blue, and khaki cloth intermingled; blood, red or clotted black; torn, seared, crying flesh—all in a labyrinth of mutilated trenches as though old Mars himself had planned the scene that would shock the world for all eternity. There were searchers carrying odd ghastly sacks slung over the shoulder as one would carry grain. But of these bags, each one contained all the human remains of some comrade and whatever pieces of his clothing might be clinging to those fragments of flesh and bone.[5]

McCoy certainly was aware of the carnage, but unaware that during the monstrous artillery bombardment more than four hundred doughboys in the division had lost their minds. They had been carried to hospitals, hysterical and in shell shock.[6]

At Base Hospital No. 1 in Vichy, nurse Edith Bishop said she would never forget the night when casualties started to pour into the Hotel Ruhl, set up as a hospital with a capacity of two thousand. The walking wounded arrived first, then the blind and those suffering from head injuries. Bishop assigned four patients to a room, but she could not keep up with so many, and soon bewildered soldiers were wandering the halls. "I never saw so many boys, beds and rooms in my life," she later cried. "I was dizzy—my head went around in a whirl." The following day "ambulance after ambulance, truck after truck emptied their loads at the door of the Ruhl, all that day, and all that week."[7]

One of the few female doctors, Anne Tjomsland, found it "strange to handle men with the smoke of battle still hanging about them." Later, after the Meuse-Argonne, that battlefield stench would be worse. But now "It was all as new and shiny as death to us: strange to hear them say they had 'jumped off' the morning before, strange to hear the reverberation of the barrage, to feel the all-pervading insanity of strife wipe out our best convictions—to live, when all of us had gone mad!"[8]

Among the many soldiers who were carried in was K Company Pvt. Jeremiah Mulcahy. After a few days he wanted out. He called a nurse, Theresa Rutledge, to his side and said that since they were both from New York, she from Bellevue and he from the West Side, maybe she could do something for him.

"Sure there's nothing the matter with me but a little gas in the chist and I am as good as any man in the regiment," he argued. "I tell you, Miss, I can't stand it here. Sure I haven't slept in a bed in months and here I am, supposed to get into that bed and stay there for the night. Sure the nights are that long I think I will never see the sun rise in the mornin'. And what is there to do durin' the day? Walk around the park and them hussies wig-wagging you. Why up at the front you never mind the time goin' at'all. You're goin' over the top in the mornin; or there is someone gettin' kilt durin' the day. Somethin' to take a man's time every minute." Mulcahy begged every day to be returned to his outfit, Rutledge said. Soon enough he was on his way north, but he did not make it back to the 165th in time for the crossing of the Ourcq, and this was a lucky thing for him. He survived the war, and Rutledge later discovered that "Jerry never married, but in the section of New York where he lived he was a godfather to all soldiers' families. If anyone happened to be hard up, there would be milk bottles and food at the door in the morning. It was Mulcahy still standing by his outfit."[9]

While Mulcahy was begging to return to the 165th, the Forty-second got its orders. On the 24th, a confidential bulletin from General MacArthur informed commanders that the division had been reassigned to Pershing's I Corps, attached to Degoutte's Sixth Army. The bulletin described the German forces arrayed in front of the Allies. "The enemy is holding his line with greater firmness, and the orders to retreat have been countermanded." Further, the enemy's artillery had been reinforced. MacArthur reported that heavy fighting was under way and that "Soissons is still held by the enemy, but the heights West and South of the city have been taken and the French are still pushing the attack."[10]

The Rainbows were to relieve the 167th French Division and the Twenty-sixth United States Division—the New Englanders— that were then south of the Ourcq River engaged in a fierce battle.

McCoy assured his mother that everyone was ready. "I and my regiment our fit as fiddles after a hump of sleep and keen to move where the Boche are to be struck again."[11]

Nathaniel Rouse had been grateful for that "hump of sleep," and prayed it would not end. His F Company had camped in a patch of woods. There he found a little stream. He stripped down for a much-needed, soothing bath. But alas, afterwards he entered in his diary, "We move tonight for the front. No rest."[12]

The 165th was off, and Martin Hogan described the mood of the troops best: "Château-Thierry . . . signified plentiful and tough fighting, and the very name filled us with a certainty that, as the Champagne was the frying pan, so this would be the fire."[13]

The first leg to the front was by train. To the surprise of many of the soldiers, the route took them past the outskirts of Paris—for most of them their first sight of that fabled city's skyline. Father Francis Duffy described traveling through the night, "rolling through France"; and in the morning there was Paris in the distance. Using binoculars, he saw the Eiffel Tower. "Judging from our experience with the elusive furlough, that is as near to Paris as most of us will ever get."[14] Col. George Leach of the 151st Field Artillery, attached to the 165th for the upcoming battle, had been amazed at the extraordinary number of troop-jammed trains rattling out of Paris bound for Château-Thierry.

Along the route, the citizens of each village stood along the tracks and cheered the Americans. "Every station, every village, every farm window was hung with colors," Duffy wrote.[15]

Vivian Commons spotted American flags everywhere, as well as signs that read "Hurrah for Americans." "It made our hearts feel good, and cheering, you never heard anything like it."[16] Everywhere the division had passed, French citizens lined the way, hurrahing. Near a gravesite, a sign had been hung. It read, "Remember the Lusitania." As Commons pushed toward the front, his mother, in her Greenwich Village apartment, was responding to an old letter she had received. "My dear boy, I keep thinking of you all the time and hope you keep well and have a brave heart to do your part in this great work before you. All need to give the best that is in them, and I know you do. . . . I pray God will take care of you. All our love to you, and some to the boys."[17] She wrote again several days later, not knowing that he was about to fight his way across the Ourcq. "You must have seen some terrible doings. We are all on edge to hear that the Huns are really on the verge of being trapped between Rheins and Soissons, and hope we shall soon hear the news."[18]

The second leg to the front meant riding in a convoy of French trucks. When the men first got on board they had been surprised to see that they were driven by Asians. Hogan called them "Japanese chauffeurs."[19] Duffy said they were "little sun-burned, almond-eyed, square-cheeked Chink[s]."[20] A soldier in one of the other regiments thought they were Chinese. Actually, they were Vietnamese, from French Indochina.

As he awaited his ride, Oliver Ames "grabb[ed] a second" to write to his parents. "We're off this time for some real fun, as we hope to continue pushing the Germans back. . . . The men are fine, full of enthusiasm and keen for another scrap. . . . I'm the proudest father you've ever seen, and the happiest. . . . I've got to run now, as I hear the camions coming."[21] The lieutenant took a seat next to his boss, and Bill Donovan observed that his adjutant was a like youngster, "enjoying every minute."[22]

Two other officers wrote home, too, begging their parents to send them certain necessities right away. Charles Baker wanted a thousand cigarettes so he could pass them out to the men in E Company. William Spencer had a more pressing request. "Dear Father, How about some more chocolate. My supply has run out."[23]

Cpl. Harry Hardt of B Company, who had been wounded on 15 July, sat in the back of his truck, hungry for revenge. To his sister in the Gashouse District he vowed, "We are going to have Fritz crawling back into his hole."[24]

An artilleryman, Louis Collins, observed the highways clotted with traffic and soldiers.

> From the tops of the hills along the way, curving trails of dust clouds could be seen in the valleys and along the sides of the hills, marking the course of the roads, but the country itself was just as it must have been before the war, peaceful and smiling. And then, like stepping from sunlight into darkness, the regiment entered the zone of war and passed through country which had been the scene of a terrific struggle—buildings, trees and orchards blasted by shell fire; fields, disfigured by shell holes, trenches, and barbed-wire entanglements; and roads strewn with empty ammunition cases and discarded equipment with here and there the wreck of a gun or a caisson.[25]

It did not take a New Yorker long to utter a wisecrack as the division closed in on its destination. "This is the last joy ride any of us'll ever get. The next ride'll be in a Red Cross ambulance."[26]

On their march to the Ourcq River, the New Yorkers felt the destruction of Vaux was worse than its neighboring village of Château-Thierry. *Signal Corps/National Archives*

The village of Château-Thierry as it looked to the men of the Forty-second Division in late July. *Signal Corps/National Archives*

Soon afterward, the convoy rumbled through Vaux on its way toward Château-Thierry a few miles to the east.

Austin Lawrence entered in his diary that Vaux was a total wreck. "Dead still lying unburied. Such havoc the shells wrought along the road. Trees cut clean in half & immense big shell holes. Thru Château-Thierry a fine big city once. Signs of hasty evacuation & hand to hand fighting. Detrained on road & walk couple of K to woods. Most wonderful thing to me was the thousands of trucks & wagons on the road in broad day light."[27]

Much of the traffic was dead-tired American soldiers, pulling away from their battle with a supposedly retreating German army. Like Lawrence, Donovan was astonished at the sight. "The Germans were only 3 days ahead of us," he wrote to Ruth, explaining that his division was relieving the Twenty-sixth. "We passed thru fields and towns still filled with their and our dead. The roads were choked with supply wagons, artillery and machine guns. Artillerymen were asleep on their horses. Machine gun drivers were going along with their heads on their knees and their reins dragging in the dirt."[28]

Château-Thierry, for some reason, had been spared much of the destruction that had leveled Vaux. The retreating Germans had looted the city, though, and as the division marched through the streets and beyond to the village of Epieds five miles to the northeast, they came across women's clothing, sewing machines, bedding, curtains and quilts, silverware, plates, pots, and pans. In Château-Thierry, Donovan walked through old mansions. The senseless destruction inside appalled him. Beautiful books had been pulled from shelves, paintings ripped from walls and clothing and paper scattered everywhere, and for no reason. In the hallway of one mansion he ran into a French soldier. The soldier offered him a hunk of cheese, a crusty slice of bread and a couple of swigs of canteen water. It was his first meal of the day and he was grateful for it.

The worst the men faced was the dead littered about, and the farther the doughboys got from the center of Château-Thierry, the more bodies they came upon: gray-uniformed Germans and then Americans in khaki. At first, Basil Elmer did not want to mention the devastation to his parents. Then he broke down. "Strewn on both sides of the road were vast amounts of German equipment, helmets, rifles and bayonets and haversacks, as well as an enormous amount of unused artillery and ammunition. I wasn't going to mention the dead, but I will. They were mostly Germans and in a very bad state of decay. Together with the dead horses, they made a terrible stench, but enough of that. I just mention it to show the haste of the enemy retreat—too hurried to bury the dead."[29]

Charles Holt, the Brooklyn lad whom Al Ettinger had called a "pampered momma's boy," eyed the slaughter. "Here and there a dead German reared his ugly head—sometimes only a skull, sometimes buried with the exception of his feet. Dead horses made the air filthy and the small towns were unutterable masses of destruction. In one of the latter I saw an aged woman sitting amid the ruins of her home, weeping bitterly, and I marked just one more against Fritz's score."[30]

Like mustard gas, that smell of rotting flesh wafted across the land. Hogan called it the "nightmare smell of the battlefield." When it became too strong, the soldiers donned gas masks. Wrote the corporal: "The peculiarly penetrating and arresting odor of the battlefield's over-ripened fruits of men and animals is one of the hardest features of war to become accustomed to."[31]

One of the artillerymen stumbled over a slain American "whose legs had been blown fifty feet away. Beside him lay a German with half his face gone, black now, maggots pouring from the wounds."[32]

As the convoy ground into Epieds, Van S. Merle-Smith heard the driver of his truck say that it was as far as they were going, everyone out. Looking at the side of the road Merle-Smith saw an entire German machine-gun squad, all dead. Up ahead he heard the sporadic snap and pop of rifle fire. The road was blocked in that direction and he and his men were forced to hike northeast of Epieds, past the village of Courpoil. Here the entire 165th Infantry camped in a stretch of thick woods while the regimental staff found accommodations in what Duffy reported as the "outbuilding" of a château. "We threw ourselves down," Merle-Smith recalled. "About thirty minutes of sleep and a battery of long 155's went off over our heads. We had bivouacked almost under their camouflaged muzzles. I hope they scared the Germans as much as they scared us. Thereafter sleep was impossible. The guns bounced us off the ground about every thirty seconds."[33] Lawrence also slept in the woods. "It was cold," he said.[34] Hogan looked around the forest and thought, "We were in regular lone wolf country." The droning of artillery was constant and the corporal figured it an "augury . . . that heavy fighting lay just a break or two in the tangle ahead of us."[35]

On the eve of the Battle of the Ourcq River, Capt. Merle-Smith's troops line up for a final portrait. From left to right, first row: Richard Kelly, Eugene McCue, and Leroy McNeill. Standing: Samuel Birdsall, Alexander Jornest, Christian Bezold, Albert Schirmer, Maurice De Long, John Sullivan, and Tony Miller. Jornest and McNeill were killed on 28 July. *Courtesy of James Tierney*

The break in the tangle was the Ourcq River, a shallow tributary of the Marne. Here the Ourcq, fed by several smaller streams, was eighteen feet across and not much more than three or four feet deep at best. For the boys from New York it was not much when compared to the Hudson or East rivers. They laughingly called it the "O'Rourke." As he eyed it, Sgt. Richard O'Neill overhead a soldier remark, "If this is a river the Hudson must be an ocean."[36] Bill Fleming, a corporal in H Company, wise-cracked, "Oh, if you spit in it, it was an addition."[37]

The Ourcq ran on a southeasterly course through Fère-en-Tardenois, Villers-sur-Fère, and then Sergy, on the southeast. Tardenois and Sergy were on the northern bank. Villers-sur-Fère, the largest village (with more than one hundred buildings, including an umbrella factory and brickyard), lay on the southern bank. Two stone bridges crossed the Ourcq—at Sergy and Seringes-et-Nesles.

In more peaceful times, the little valley had been idyllic—open, rolling farmland and dense, sheltering woods. Several hills dominated the steep north bank. Large farms were plentiful on both sides of the river. Their thick stone homes, huge barns, and walled courtyards offered ideal ambuscades for machine gunners, and each farm had been transformed into a lethal stronghold. Among the strongest were Croix Rouge on the south bank and Meurcy on the north. The capture of Meurcy had been assigned to the Eighty-third Brigade. Crossing wheat fields, tangled under-brush, and the marshy ground sloping down to the Ourcq, cross-ing the Ourcq itself, scrambling up the banks and through the woods and into the clearing around Meurcy Farm, dislodging the enemy there and from Seringes-et-Nesles and the hills, forests, and villages beyond, and pushing them north in disorderly retreat—all of this steeled the officers of the 165th to the grim task ahead.

On the morning of 26 July, McKenna, who still felt the linger-ing effects of the mustard gas he had inhaled almost two weeks earlier and as a result had a hard time keeping down food, and Donovan were off on reconnoitering missions. They had been ordered to see what lay ahead for their battalions. While they were gone, Duffy passed through the ranks, including those of the 166th Infantry, hearing last-minute confessions.

The evening before, Donovan had shared with some of his men a fresh melon that had been brought from Paris by an officer. That night the weather turned cold and rainy, with artillery from both sides rocking the ground. The major and Ames crawled into an ambulance and slept on the floor. Early the next morning, the scouting party set out. It included four of Donovan's company commanders, one them 1st Lt. Oscar Buck. They crept close enough to witness, on their right flank, the Eighty-fourth Brigade's battle to take Croix Rouge farm. "It was very hot and bloody," the major reported.

Two of Donovan's commanders suffered wounds from the nearby fight and a gas shell exploded over his head. "The rain of rocks and dirt and tile fell about my head and I got a beautiful mouthful of gas. For the next 20 minutes it was very uncomfort-able." When his detachment staggered back to brigade headquar-ters a doctor had Donovan sniff some ammonia, poured boric acid on his inflamed eyes, and forced him to sleep on a billiards table.[38] Donovan planned to spend the night there, but around midnight he was awakened: his battalion had to move to the front immediately.

The Eighty-third had been instructed to complete its relief of French troops from the 170th Infantry Regiment of the 167th Division and take Villers-sur-Fère and the south bank of the Ourcq.

The battalions leading the way would be Donovan's First and McKenna's Third. Support for Donovan's troops would come from Colonel Leach's 151st Field Artillery while support for McKenna's would be elements of the 151st as well as Col. Henry Reilly's 149th Field Artillery. Backing the assault would be the Ohioans from the 166th Infantry and the Wisconsinites from the 150th Machine Battalion.

In the dark, intermittent rain pelting down, Donovan led his battalion through dense woods. His soldiers hiked in stretched-out columns of twos with fifty yards separating each platoon and a hundred yards between companies. To Donovan, the long line of shadowy figures moving through trees and underbrush looked more like an army than a battalion. Holt remembered how the "moon threw a ghostly light on us as it suddenly appeared from behind the clouds, showing the men strung out on single file as far as the eye could see."[39] Up front with Donovan was Grayson Murphy, an observer sent down by division headquarters.

Murphy had donned his uniform only a few months earlier after resigning from his post as the Red Cross's European commissioner. But he was no stranger to the military. A former West Point classmate of General MacArthur's, the thirty-nine-year-old Murphy, described by a friend as "mystical," left the army in 1907 and by 1915 had become vice president of the Guaranty Trust Company. When he decided to go back into the army, he was commissioned a major and assigned to the Forty-second as assistant chief of staff under MacArthur. Now, on his nine-kilometer march with Donovan and the rest of the First Battalion, dodging pot shots from German snipers, Murphy composed a poem that he later put down on paper. He called it, "The Army Moving Up to Fight." It reads, in part,

I

Boots and spurs and wind and rain,
The straining horses through the night,
The plodding columns pushing on,
   The Army moving up to fight!

II

Beyond the crests the sky ablaze
With flaming flares and cannon light,
The wounded creaking slowly back.
   The Army moving up to fight!

III

Gaunt forms athwart the midnight sky,
The poor calm dead to left and right,
The cursing teamsters in the mud,
    The Army moving up to fight!

IV

The column pushes grimly on,
Above it moves as unseen flight.
That tends to bless us as we go,
    The Army moving up to fight![40]

When the battalion reached its jumping off point, the worn-out doughboys threw themselves down for a little sleep. The ailing Donovan wrapped himself in a blanket and dozed for an hour.[41] When dawn broke, there was an eerie stillness. The enemy had pulled back in the night, heading for the heights across the Ourcq. Villers-sur-Fère was deserted.

Meanwhile, McKenna's Third Battalion traversed terrain littered with dead Germans and horses while shells exploded. Many of the Irish soldiers suffered headaches and some went stone deaf. Wrote K Company's Victor Van Yorx, from Mount Vernon, "We tore through dense woods, over fields that had been plowed up with the big shells, through towns that stunk something terrible from the dead horses and 'squareheads' [Germans]. We kept this up until we hit a town that bordered on the river. [Villers-sur-Fère] This was our objective for the night." Large trees had been cut down and crisscrossed the road leading in and out of the village. "It would take more than trees to hold us up, I'll tell you."[42]

McKenna's men found several Frenchmen in the village who swore that there were no Germans around, they had gone across the river. Capt. John Hurley, back in action after being temporarily blinded by gas in Lunéville, moved his K Company up toward the top of a hill outside of Villers-sur-Fère for better observation. He left one squad to search the village for any enemy that might be in hiding. Van Yorx's older brother, Ted, stayed with the squad, while Victor climbed the hill.

The previous day, McKenna, instead of reconnoitering himself as Donovan had done, had sent Merle-Smith and two of his L Company sergeants ahead to see if the Germans had cleared out of the woods. The trio had moved swiftly overland until they reached a field. On all fours, they crawled over open ground to a drainage ditch. From across the river, the Germans had their eyes on them the whole time and fired a few gas shells their way. Before the Americans had a chance to slip on their masks, gas engulfed them; in seconds their lungs were afire. They retreated, vomiting with almost every step. The sergeants were sent to a dressing station. Merle-Smith claimed that "rapid and continuous nausea cured me by evening. The episode was taken to mean the Germans had retired and it seemed a reasonable conclusion because no rifles or machine guns fired on us when we left the gassed ditch for the open field."[43]

These events convinced McKenna that it was safe to press on. By early evening, his battalion, advancing on Donovan's left flank, reached the crest of the hill around Villers-sur-Fère. On the crest of the hill stood a stone farmhouse, still intact. A sign hung over the front door. *Münchener Bier hier.*

"From the hill we could plainly see the fields over which a recent battle had swayed," wrote Hogan, "and we had a creepy sensation that the Germans would open fire on us as soon as we passed the house."[44]

McKenna lined up his men in battle formation and had them quick march into the protection of the forest. He next moved them downhill, through thick underbrush and gnarled trees, literally "a virgin wilderness," to a city-bred boy like Hogan.[45] Here the battalion gouged out holes in the damp ground and bedded down for the night.

With Villers-sur-Fère empty, McCoy brought his headquarters forward posthaste, placing it in a stone farmhouse in an orchard on the northern outskirts of the village, and very near the front line. Seeing this, Duffy remarked that although the colonel was "a bold as well as a careful commander and he felt that he could best handle the situation by being where he could see just what was going on."[46] Maj. George Lawrence and his medical staff also moved forward without delay, entering Villers-sur-Fère to set up a field hospital in the cellars of the stone houses there.

It was now near midnight, and the Forty-second Division had its four infantry regiments just about in a straight line at last, facing the northern heights of the Ourcq River. On the New Yorkers' right flank were the Alabamans and on the left, the Ohioans.

Donovan reported to brigade headquarters that his battalion was now "in contact by shoulder touch with the 167th Inf."[47] No one knew for certain what lay ahead. The Americans had rushed forward in "pell mell pursuit," like hounds after a fox, but with only the sketchiest of intelligence about the forces they were chasing.[48] Yet General Degoutte believed the Germans would turn tail and run at the first sign of an attack. He relished the thought and to make it a most glorious moment he ordered the Americans to charge with bayonets only.[49]

The latest orders from Lenihan to McCoy were clear even if German movement and troop strength were not.

> The enemy has continued his withdrawal on the whole front. Contact has not been established with his Infantry. It is thought that he may have taken up position on the North bank of the OURCQ approximately parallel to the river. This Brigade will attack at 3:45 A.M. Objective: SERINGES—NESLES—NESLES from SERINGES— NESLES, exclusive, to a point one kilometer east thereof. . . . The advance will be by infiltration with no artillery preparation. Greatest reliance will be placed on the bayonet. Your regiment will constitute the first line of the attack, covering the entire Brigade sector. The 166th Inf. will be in reserve.[50]

That order, which had come down from corps headquarters, troubled Duffy. "The assumption of a retreating enemy against whom infantry bayonets and charging cavalry could be effective was not justified by what the front line could detect," the chaplain skeptically put in his diary, adding that McCoy was of the same opinion.[51] The cavalry he had mentioned was French.

And so, a few hours before dawn on the morning of 28 July, the Irish doughboys, still not sure of what lurked on the heights across the Ourcq River, would assault an entrenched enemy in one of the first engagements of open warfare—versus trench warfare— since 1914. As the night wore on and zero hour neared, Elmer listened to the roar of the "heavies" and thought that in a few hours the world would be turned into a deadly inferno. "This at last [is] the real thing—that the other sectors had been mere training areas. This [is] war in the highest degree. And it [is] America's war."[52]

17

"All You Want Now Is Guts and Bayonets!"

Through no fault of the 165th Infantry, the Forty-second Division bungled its predawn assault, losing any chance of surprise. At three-forty-five the entire division was to attack along a two-mile front, cross the Ourcq and clear the Germans out of the villages, farms, and hills north of the river. Brig. Gen. Michael Lenihan first sensed something was amiss when he could not locate Col. Benson Hough of the 166th Infantry, which had been ordered to support the Irish regiment. Aggravating the situation was the fact that his telephone lines had been cut.

And it got worse. Brig. Gen. Robert Brown, of the Eighty-fourth Brigade, informed Lenihan less than a half-hour before the attack that his men could not advance without artillery preparation. A mounted messenger galloped up to Lenihan's command post with this disheartening news. "My latest reports show that my Brigade, which fought all last night, cannot do it," Brown admitted. In a way he was right. The 167th had been in a bloody battle to take Croix Rouge Farm and, although itself suffering heavy casualties, still left 283 Germans scattered about the farm, bayoneted to death. "I will try to advance at 4:00 A.M., and if possible will do so," Brown continued.[1]

Lenihan then tried to contact Col. William Screws of the battered 167th, sending an orderly to find the Alabama commander, whose men were on the 165th's right flank. Screws could not be found either. A report from First Army Corps that the French had captured Fère-en-Tardenois proved mistaken. The village had not fallen. The Germans were still in control of the entire north side of the river.

In spite of these setbacks Lenihan was not ready to call off the attack. At three-forty-five, the 165th honored its part of the

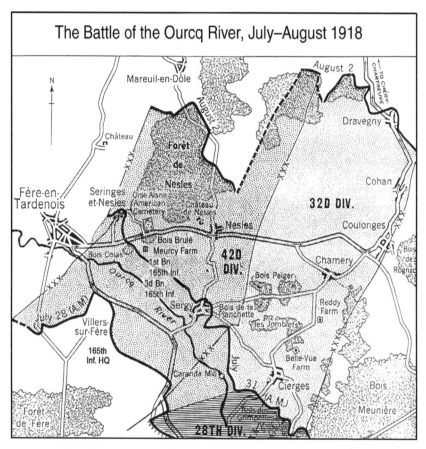

The Battle of the Ourcq River
Adapted from *American Armies and Battlefields in Europe: A History Guide and Reference Book*, American Battle Monument Commission (GPO: Washington, 1938).

responsibility, which was to take Meurcy Farm. Col. Frank McCoy's men moved toward the Ourcq while another horrendous German bombardment rumbled the earth and tore down whatever trees had survived the earlier artillery fire.

Leading the way for the regiment, Maj. Jim McKenna's Third Battalion came down from the hill where it had spent a few hours resting up. Out in front was K Company, commanded by Capt. John Hurley, a civil engineer who had been educated at Queen's University in Dublin and at Cornell University in the United States. Second in command was 1st Lt. Patrick Dowling, who when he was sixteen had sailed from Ireland as a stowaway. The company's other first lieutenant was not Irish. Howard Arnold, five feet five inches tall, was Jewish. Like Hurley, Arnold was an engineer and an Ivy Leaguer, having graduated from Yale in 1914.

The plan for Hurley's men was to push ahead of the other companies in the battalion and then for I Company, commanded by Boer War veteran Capt. Richard Ryan, and L Company, headed by Capt. Van S. Merle-Smith, to leapfrog them, crossing the Ourcq first. Capt. Martin Meaney's M Company was to march in reserve.

As K Company and the rest of the Shamrock soldiers advanced toward the river their line was "thin and jerky," recalled Martin Hogan. "It was a movement of each for himself, guided by the officers' general order to advance."[2] It did not take long for the German guns to mow down the woods behind the Americans where they had been encamped half the night. Victor Van Yorx wrote, "We got about 100 feet from the woods when hell let loose. Machine guns from both flanks and right square in front of us. Their guns were right in the woods on the bank of the river. The dirty greasers saw us coming and let us get right up to them. It was pitch dark and we couldn't see."[3] "The line of the Shamrock Battalion quickened its pace," according to Hogan, "covering the rough ground at a brisk double-quick in the direction of the enemy."[4]

In L Company, Merle-Smith's boys hadn't had a meal for the past twenty-four hours—just bacon and dry bread. Merle-Smith described them as "poor, tired fellows" who, during the night, had "[dug] small individual shelters. Many utterly exhausted, were lying asleep in small ditches along side the road. Machine gun bullets and shells whistled over us."[5] That night, Merle-Smith and Cpl. Lawrence Spencer, his personal aide from Tarrytown, New

York, realized that the attack would be "a most difficult and dangerous fight." They talked about the risks and, recalled Van, "how much more it meant to our wives than to us, and decided, however, that they would much rather have the fullest duty done, with the greater risk, than half, and the lesser risk."[6]

After a short, fitful sleep in the rain, L Company roused itself and headed toward the river. Merle-Smith later remembered the "early light" as his company went "down across the fields to the . . . Ourcq under scattering enemy fire." He remembered how eager K Company appeared as it reached the Ourcq, pushing his company to the sector assigned to the Eighty-fourth Brigade.[7] He noticed that no other troops had yet taken up position on his battalion's flanks "to make the attack with us." The rangy, six-foot-four-inch captain hurried back to McCoy's command post, and there the faces of his colonel and commander told him he and his men would be going it alone. "The Major and the Colonel looked white, but orders were orders, so we literally repeated the charge of the Light Brigade."[8] One of Merle-Smith's lieutenants, the chocolate-loving Bill Spencer, described how his platoon had gotten started late, with only half its men. "We formed a skirmish line—automatic rifles in front firing as they advanced—crossed a wheat field and into some woods, which was certainly lousy with machine guns, snipers, light machine guns, etc. I never hope to hear such a terrific fire."[9]

Bill Donovan's First Battalion was perched on another hill overlooking the river and Sergy. "The town was on the other side of the Ourcq and looked very suspicious to me." He held his battalion back from descending the hill and crossing the Ourcq so that they could first join up with some French units that he knew to be nearby. Sending out several patrols to find them, he waited. Soon a troop of French cavalry spurred by. The former officer of New York's First Cavalry watched enviously as the troops disappeared down a sunken road and galloped toward a narrow bridge spanning the Ourcq. "It made my heart ache to think I was no longer in the Cavalry," he later confessed. Sudden machine-gun fire ahead told him the French troops had ridden into an ambush. They galloped back, one horse bearing an empty saddle.

For the First Battalion, contact with the enemy had now been made, and the threatened Germans opened an artillery barrage on Donovan's tenuous hilltop position. "All of us lay on our stomachs while the shells began to burst all around," he wrote. "It was a perfect place for a fight."[10]

With the Eighty-fourth Brigade still in limbo and not knowing exactly what was happening, Lenihan felt it "too hazardous to push the attack." At five-fifteen he sent one of his staff officers to McCoy, ordering him to suspend his advance "pending the advance of our neighboring organizations." He ordered Colonel Hough to stop the 166th Infantry. He broke the news to Maj. Gen. Charles Menoher at division headquarters. "Attack not launched at 3:45. Brown unable to advance. McCoy holds VILLERS-sur-FERE with approximately two battalions; Hough in his rear. Recommend that attack be made only after artillery preparation. Medical assistance urgent. Casualties principally due to interdiction fire on approaches."

It was now five-thirty-five.

One half-hour later, Lenihan received unsettling news. The 165th had not stopped, as he had thought. Reports indicated that five of its companies were across the Ourcq—unaware that the attack had been suspended and were pressing toward Meurcy Farm. "One Company (K), was advancing in the sector of the 167th Inf. and had nearly reached the top of the hill from the river."

Lenihan acted swiftly. He ordered Hough to move his First Battalion across the river to support McCoy's left flank. He now knew he had to press the attack even if the Eighty-fourth Brigade was not in position. He let division headquarters know what was happening. "One battalion and one Co., 165th Inf., have crossed OURCQ and advancing towards objective. Remainder of Brigade advancing. 84th Brigade not advancing at last report. (5:10 A.M.)" What he did not know then was that the 167th had, in fact, moved into place on the 165th's right flank.

McCoy, meanwhile, informed Lenihan, "Am sending in 2nd Bn. to protect McKenna's left. Request that 166th be sent on our left and 167th on our right. Advance hampered by hostile machine guns. Request artillery preparation against M.G. nests on Southern edge of Forêt de Nesles."[11]

Maj. Alexander Anderson's Second Battalion—decimated on Bastille Day when it made its stand to check the all-out German attack—had left its support position at three-fifty-two. Working its way through the woods south of the Ourcq in the predawn darkness it, too, came under heavy fire. Before it crossed the river, a messenger roared up, ordering Anderson to halt the advance.

"Hell," Anderson growled, "I can't stop now!"[12]

When K Company went down the hill to approach the river's edge, Corporal Hogan reported, machine-gun fire made a continuous sheet of bullets "scything its way toward us now." It seemed there was a machine gun hidden behind every tree. "One felt a queer uneasy sensation as one ran to think of the myriads of steel needles streaming through the air around him, and one felt from minute to minute that the end could only be a matter of the next step or two. The air was alive with death and the mocking rat-a-tat and crackle of death."[13]

"I offered up a prayer that all the boys would come through safe," wrote Victor Van Yorx, who was already suffering from a wound to his ankle. "Out across that 500-yard open stretch we went, with the German machine guns in the woods on the other bank of the river. Some of the fellows were dropped stepping from the road on to the field. Such a banging I never heard in my life. . . . The bullets whistled around and threw the dirt right up into your face."[14]

K Company ran and dodged and dropped down, got up and charged again and again. Men fell, some fatally shot. But the company refused to stop, and it fought to the river's edge. The Germans hit it with a withering fire, and the Americans toppled all along the riverbank. To cross here would mean suicide; the soldiers faltered for a moment. But Hurley leaped in front of his men and in front of the roaring German machine guns.

"Come on, boys!" he yelled. "We're going to pull off a thing here that the Germans ain't tried yet! We're goin' to give 'em a bellyful of Uncle Sam's cold steel!"

Into the river jumped Dowling, his platoon sergeant Frank Doughney, Cpl. Jim McGovern, and Pvt. Tom Lyden. Hogan saw Dowling grin broadly, his pistol in his hand. Enemy bullets churned up the river and zinged past the four men as they pressed forward. One of the bullets struck Dowling in the left arm. Another hit Doughney, killing him. The wounded Dowling and the unscathed McGovern pulled the sergeant's body across the river to the far bank. Now the rest of the company plunged into the Ourcq, firing as it went. Watching his men cross, Hurley was gravely wounded. A bullet burrowed into his leg, another struck his chest. He complained about the leg wound, but never let on that he had been shot in the chest, and so no one knew.

When Van Yorx hit the river he thought it was only two feet deep. The water reached his chin. He crossed safely and scrambled up the bank. Crawling through woods that fringed the river, he spotted a German repositioning his machine gun in a shell hole. The Mount Vernon lad shot him through the head.

With Hurley out of action—wounded and in a shell hole—Dowling, as ranking officer, took charge of K Company. In front of him and his men, lined up along the north bank of the Ourcq, was a long, sloping hill and Meurcy Farm, or as a couple of Irish wags now called it, Murphy's Farm. Dowling knew his men had to take the fortified farm and the equally fortified stands of woods encircling it. Reaching the farm and overrunning the woods was going to test the courage of every soldier.[15]

Once K Company had made it over the Ourcq, other companies in McKenna's battalion forded the stream. Dead Americans and Germans littered the ground and bodies bobbed in the water that now had a pinkish hue from the blood spilled in the crossing. The Irish in all the soldiers had reached a boiling point: not a single German would be left alive.

McCoy, the Scot, wrote, "My 3d Battalion, Major McKenna, went over at daybreak and reached their objective without great loss, but their fighting Irish got the better of them, and they streamed up the open slopes to take the Boche machine guns with their hands and teeth."[16]

Merle-Smith remembered how the soldiers of the Shamrock attacked alone. "We crossed a small river raked by machine gun fire, after having traversed 500 yards of machine-gun-swept open field, then through woods—the mad wave of the attack breaking over the machine gun nests, which in our front fired until we were 100 feet from them. They stood up and shouted 'Kamerad.' We didn't give them mercy."[17]

Feeling like he could lick the world, Van Yorx silenced a machine nest in front of him. When he sensed that it had been knocked out, he charged up the hill. "I was running right toward the gun when a big 'fathead' climbed out with his hands over his head and started to yell, 'Kamerad.' All he got was 'Kam.' My bayonet went into his mouth and out the back of his head. I think he died of fright before I hit him. We were all yelling like a pack of Indians and nothing could stop us."[18]

But the German machine gunners were everywhere and their artillery had found its deadly range. Sgt. Peter Crotty, who had gone off to the Spanish-American War as a twelve-year-old water boy, was hit and mortally wounded. It took him five days to die. His last words, muttered to a nurse, had been for his wife and three children. He said, "Carry on, Dear."[19] A shell hit Dowling and blew his legs off at the hips. He was rushed down the slope and across the river. At the dressing station he was in such a state of shock that the medics could not lift him from the litter. He died ten hours later. His legs were later found in front of Meurcy Farm, identified by the wrapped leggings marked with his name. "The trail of the Shamrock Battalion up that hill was marked out clearly by its losses," Hogan wrote.[20]

The battalion ground to a stop. Messengers trying to get reports of the fight back to Hurley and then on to McKenna had been unable to make it through. A frustrated Lieutenant Arnold, now leading K Company, decided he had to try to reach Hurley on his own; he wanted his commander to know that enemy defenses had stiffened and losses were mounting. Turning command over to Sgt. Herbert McKenna, one of the orphans from Staten Island's Mission of the Immaculate Virgin, Arnold dodged back down the hill. Because he was short, he made a difficult target. He got to Hurley's shell hole, reported the dire situation and began his journey back to his men through the storm of gunfire. He hollered, "We got them now!" He had not gone far when bullets slammed into his head and heart, throwing him to the ground. Cpl. Frank Caracher remembered Arnold about to leap into a ditch when he moaned, "Oh God, I'm hit!" Pvt. Ralph Cuccioli from Brooklyn was near the officer when he was shot. Cuccioli heard Arnold's words of encouragement and then he, Cuccioli, took a bullet in the knee. Pvt. Christopher Byrne, a native of Tipperary, crawled over to Arnold. The dying lieutenant said, "I'm beyond relief. Carry on, you." Pvt. Kilner McLaughlin from the Bronx cried bitterly "Arnold, Kelly . . . killed. . . . We attacked and the ground was held. Arnold was my platoon commander; he was a Jew, but a white Jew. All were fine fellows."[21]

When Hurley heard that his lieutenant, just a week shy of his twenty-fourth birthday, was dead, he groaned, "Arnold is gone. Arnold is gone."[22]

Sergeant McKenna now had charge of K Company. Already suffering a bullet wound in the arm, he pushed the remnants of his platoon forward. The carnage around him must have hurt the young man, who when war had been declared, had convinced at least thirty of the orphans at the Mission of the Immaculate Virgin (M.I.V.), where he, too, had lived, to enlist in the Sixty-ninth. He himself had taken them from their remote corner of Staten Island to the armory, and there they had joined Hurley's company. Before the day ended, four of these orphans were killed and another was missing. McKenna's action earned him the Distinguished Service Cross.

One of the Mission boys, Cpl. Jim Rice, later wrote to the orphanage about the heroics of its alumni. "Herbie McKenna was ready at a minute's notice to go over the top with his platoon, among whom were thirteen M.I.V. boys. There was no need of their going, though, for I think that 'Fritz' didn't feel it a sure thing to come out of his hole. If he did, I tell you he would have got all he was looking for, because our boys were just like a herd of wolves, ready to eat up anything they saw."[23]

Throughout the struggle, Father James Hanley kept on the move, tending to the wounded, trying to comfort and cheer them up, and, for the dying, hearing their confessions and all too often giving them the last rites. At one point he heard that a soldier had made it to the top of the hill only to be cut off from the rest of the company and shot. Father Hanley decided to go after him, sending word back to Hurley telling him what he planned to do. When he learned of it, the captain quickly detailed two men to follow their chaplain and to make sure nothing happened to him. "[The] bullets would have clipped me had I raised my elbow," Hanley wrote. He then heard a rustling behind him and saw the two soldiers dispatched by Hurley. "They said the captain had sent them to carry me back if anything happened. . . . I sent them chasing back to their company and crawled ahead. Just as I got to the ridge the bullet got me. My wounded man was across an open space and I knew I couldn't get to him. I was afraid if I waited till dark I'd bleed to death, so I put a tourniquet on my leg and started back."

A day later, the chaplain found himself in a hospital in a cot next to Hurley. The medics dressed both leg wounds, Hanley's and Hurley's. When they cut away Hurley's shirt, he let out a howl. "The shirt was stuck to his chest with blood," Hanley observed. "He had a wound there that the doctors at the dressing station had never discovered. . . . All the time he'd been sending men out to take care of me he'd had that shirt frozen over his big heart with his own blood."

The chaplain scolded him and asked why he had not mentioned the wound.

"You know we had orders to hang onto that dinky hill," Hurley said. "And we're awful busy."[24]

The soldiers of L Company had broken into the German lines, driven the enemy momentarily from Meurcy Farm, and reached the top of the hill. On the way up, a bullet nicked Merle-Smith in the arm, but staying ahead of his men he kept struggling toward the summit. "On top of the hill, almost wholly surrounded and without cover, we lay under the machine guns and shell fire, grimly holding on to what we had gained," he wrote.[25]

Huddled close to Merle-Smith was Lieutenant Spencer. His platoon had spent most of the morning moving up the slope and onto the top of a plateau. Once on top they had no place to go. "So here we held, as it was certain death to advance further, in the open, and against a perfect field of fire." Their enemy grew in strength and, bringing up more guns, fired on the Americans from the flanks. "Pretty soon we were getting it on all sides. The machine gun fire was terrific—the Germans would just skim the earth and unless you watched yourself or kept in dead angles, there wasn't much chance. It is remarkable how closely I learned to hug the ground—bullets when they fly around you crack sharply, and the one thing to do is to face the direction from which they come, flop down and snuggle behind your helmet—the most comfortable friend you have."[26]

Trying to dislodge the Americans from the hilltop and retake Meurcy Farm, the Germans counterattacked with bayonets. Pvt. Karl Thum from Rockville Centre, looked up and saw a horde of "Fritzes" rushing toward L Company. "But when we charged up the hill it was funny to see them turn tail and run," he told his father afterward. "They can't stand the cold steel."[27]

"We continued right on to the top of the hill, which was our objective," wrote Van Yorx. "When we got there we only had about 30 men left out of the whole company. We were holding the top of the hill when I got a whack in the arm." The bullet slammed into his left forearm and exited just above the elbow. "One of the fellows threw me a tent rope and I tied my arm up as good as I could and waited for the reinforcements."[28]

An exploding shell burst over the head of Pvt. Myron Dixon of Brooklyn, knocking him out. He awoke in a field near Meurcy farm, his nose, lips, and throat caked with dried blood. Sprawled around him were dozens of dead doughboys. He heard a soldier groan and crawled to him. The soldier had just come to. Together they rushed into a stone barn, as Germans sprayed machine-gun bullets in their direction. They slammed the door and dropped to the floor in the dark. Then the door swung open, flooding the inside of the barn with sunlight, and seven Germans ran in, bits of shrubbery stuck on their helmets. Dixon "played possum" but the Germans were not fooled. Poking him with a bayonet, they shoved him outside. Dixon thought they were going to kill him and his new friend. Instead the two were marched behind the German line.

"A high staff officer examined us with great interest," Dixon remembered. "He spoke good English and cut our identification tags from the cord around our necks. We were given shovels and told to dig a trench. Then the most unbelievable thing happened. One of the soldiers handed me a mess kit of barley soup. He told me to share it with my buddy." The Germans prodded them further to the rear. They passed through a gas attack and, since they had no gas masks, covered their faces with their own woolen shirts. They saw troops marching toward the battlefield, singing patriotic tunes. After a ten-mile hike they came to a château. Here they were given tea, bread, and cigarettes. An officer explained that they were to be examined by Eitel Friedrich, the son of Kaiser Wilhelm II.

"A handsome uniformed gent approached us, surrounded by his staff of under officers. His highness wore a pleasant smile and proceeded to examine our clothing." He checked the soles of their shoes and "felt the quality of our clothes, and everything he noted was recorded by an assistant." When the examination was over, the prisoners were marched deeper into German territory. "We walked all night and, when daylight came, we were ushered into a yard enclosed with barbed wire and sat on the ground in the morning sunshine."[29]

Merle-Smith had an awful feeling that, with the Germans firing at them from all sides, the fight to take the hill was "all useless sacrifice, and what we took would probably accomplish nothing." When he got his company to the hilltop he looked out across a "great, flat plateau, fringed with woods and prepared positions—front, left and right, and from each a leaden stream of bullets." His men battled forward another fifty yards, but they were mowed down from the flanks. He watched as one of his men, in a crouching run, was shot in the legs. He fell to his knees, but was hit again in the legs and arms. He pitched onto his face. Another bullet cracked his skull open. "It was no use to go forward further—not a man could have gone [on], so I gave the order to dig in."[30]

Listening to the cries of the wounded all about him, Merle-Smith's heart broke. "Their calling on me to help them and I absolutely helpless." For an hour he held the hand of a dying boy because the boy had begged him to do it. Lawrence Spencer stayed close to him—his job now to protect his captain and look after the moaning wounded. Van tried to keep him from going out to them, but he himself was hit by another bullet and three more tore apart his gas mask. Bullets also rammed into Lawrence Spencer, and Merle-Smith saw that his aide was in excruciating pain. He ordered him back to a dressing station, but Spencer refused to leave. "He protested, but went when commanded." On the way down the hill he was killed.[31]

As Merle-Smith mourned the loss of his aide and friend, Lt. Bill Spencer slipped up to him. He studied his captain, observing that he had been shot in the arm and was thoroughly exhausted. He begged Van to leave the hilltop and let the rest of the company fight it out. As Spencer made his plea, a vivid picture of Van's wife, Kate, and their children flashed through his mind. "It seemed unfair to me that a married man of his type, with family depending on him, should perish while I should go on." Merle-Smith refused to leave his men, arguing that he did not want to be babied. Spencer begged him to at least dress his wound. He had a difficult time cutting the sleeve off while they both lay on the ground with bullets whistling over their heads. Somewhere close by they heard the whimpering of Pvt. Alexander Jornest, a native of Russia, who had been shot in the gut and kept calling for his mother. He was too far away and too exposed for help. When Spencer finished dressing Van's wound, he rose up on his knees. He fired at several Germans about a hundred yards away and ducked down as they fired back. Knowing that he would never get Merle-Smith to withdraw, he slid off to tend to his own men. The last words he heard came from Jornest. "My God, are you going to leave me? Are you going to leave me here?"[32]

On Merle-Smith's left the bellowing voice of I Company's Capt. Richard Ryan swept across the hillside. Van had been told

Capt. Richard Ryan, a Boer War veteran, was twice listed as killed in action. He urged his I Company men forward on the slopes of the Ourcq River with the cry, "Guts and bayonets!" *Courtesy of Ryan Family*

that Ryan had been shot twice. As far as he could tell, I Company was "getting it as badly as we are."[33]

Ryan had led his men across the Ourcq and up the hill toward Meurcy Farm. They had moved in short spurts. When machine-fire seemed heaviest, he stood before his men, daring the Germans to hit him. With a voice loud enough to carry down the hill, he yelled, "Drop your packs! If you come back you can have them again and if you don't you won't want them!" Then, louder still, "All you want now is guts and bayonets!"

His company rose up, screaming, "Guts and bayonets!"

First Lt. Herman Henry Smith was one of the first to jump up, urging his platoon on. "Keep forward!" he told them. Near him, 1st Sgt. Frank McMorrow was inspired, watching his officers as they stood in front of enemy fire. A sniper shot Smith in the forehead. He dropped, falling across one of his own men, and died. Second Lt. Clayton Beach, a big, rugged athlete from the Midwest, dashed ahead of his company but was shot down. He groaned and rolled over. Sgt. Frank Mulligan tried to reach him, but a shell exploded, and its impact bounced the hefty lieutenant down the hill—a boulder of blood and flailing limbs.

Sgt. Billy McLaughlin, also trying to inspire his men, ordered them to follow him as he raced forward. Sergeant Frank Mulligan saw McLaughlin throw up his hands. A bullet had punctured his throat.

"Over the top we went," recollected Pvt. John Murray from Brooklyn, "as the captain yelled. We had nothing but 'guts and bayonets.' The regiment with a mad yell tore on through the wheat fields. We took a dozen machine gun nests without the loss of a man, and then we charged up a hill. Then men began to drop down like apples from a shaken tree. The air was full of lead." Murray felt a sledgehammer-like hit to his helmet. Taking it off, he saw that it had "a hole in it as big as a man's fist."[34]

Pvt. Walter Bryan, a Rockaway Beach neighbor of Sgt. Danny O'Connell, wrote how I Company had the "Fritz buffaloed." He told how "our bunch of wild Irishmen" roared over the top. He made it sound like a lark, a picnic. "After him we went, like wildmen and sticking them like pigs. Talk of sport, oh boy! Well, I was having the time of my life until something knocked me down kind of sudden like and I knew I was hit." Bryan crawled back to a dressing station at Villers-sur-Fère. "This was in the center of a little town that was directly in range of the big German guns. They blew the first aid station down, but outside of having the ceiling and one of the walls fall on me, I escaped entirely. They finally got us away in ambulances over a road that looked like a sieve with monster shells threatening to put ambulance and all into kingdom come."[35]

Pfc. Benjamin Heineman from the West Side had bandaged up Pvt. John Bradley when a shell burst near them, blowing Bradley to bits. Heineman staggered to his feet, wiping blood and parts of his internal organs from Bradley off his face. Without rifle or bayonet, he moved forward with his surviving I Company companions until he came across Cpl. John O'Rourke, who had been shot in the leg. With no first-aid packet left, Heineman ripped off the bloody leggings of his uniform and tied a tourniquet above O'Rourke's knee to keep the corporal from Hell's Kitchen from bleeding to death. O'Rourke begged to be carried off the field, but Heineman said it would be certain death to move him. He left the corporal to work on two other wounded men, one who had been shot in the wrist, and another, Pvt. Benjamin Gunnell, who had been struck in both knees. Gunnell's wife of less than a year had recently died back in New Jersey. Heineman carried him down to a dressing station. He went back up for O'Rourke, slung him onto his back, and headed down again. A sniper shot O'Rourke in the spine, and there was nothing more Heineman could do for him. He placed the dead soldier on the ground.

Heineman's work was not finished. He took another wounded soldier to the dressing station and hiked up again to carry yet another of his comrades to safety. As he turned to go once more, Major McKenna stopped him, set him on the ground, and said that his work for the day was done, it was time for him to take care of his own wounds.[36]

Ryan had kept ahead of his men. For a moment he advanced unscathed; then a bullet pierced his arm. Ignoring the wound, he continued to lead I Company up the hill. He was hit again and knocked down. One of his officers ran to him, ready to lug him down the hill and out of the line of fire. Ryan roared at the officer, yelling that he would shoot him or any man trying to remove him from the fight. But Ryan's fight ended soon anyway. A lethal artillery shell landed a few feet away. It literally ripped apart the men nearest him, sending arms and legs and heads and gobs of stringy intestines flying in every direction. The exploding shell lifted Ryan's body twenty feet in the air, maybe fifty feet, according to several eyewitnesses. At least twenty-three shrapnel fragments punctured him from head to foot as he was thrown down the hill. Huge clumps of earth showered down on him, burying him on the spot. Later on, the medics found only body parts, and they were unable to tell which leg or arm belonged to which soldier. Because they failed to locate Ryan, or any part of him, they believed he had been killed in action.[37]

At eleven-twenty at the regimental command post in Villers-sur-Fère, McCoy sent Lenihan a message with the information

that the Third Battalion had reached the crest of the hill between
Meurcy Farm and the village of Sergy. Since it had suffered heavy
casualties Lenihan ordered that it be withdrawn and replaced by
Donovan's First Battalion. Because of incessant machine-gun fire
from the woods on the north side of the Ourcq, he had ordered the
First and Second Battalions to "dig in and wait for nightfall for
further advance."

Word also came to Lenihan that dressing stations in the cellar
and on the first floor of the château in Villers-sur-Fère had been
overwhelmed with casualties.

Maj. George Lawrence and his sanitary crew worked feverishly as "stretcher cases and walking wounded men were constantly
arriving and the vicinity of the château was crowded by an assem-
blage of wounded, stretcher bearers and members of the 166th
Inf. The château and vicinity were under direct enemy observation. The cellar in which the P.C. [post command] was established
was becoming more and more crowded with wounded officers
and men, and it was impossible to make an organized effort to
clear it."[38]

German planes raked the grounds around the château. "All
during the fight," wrote an officer, "our dressing stations at Villers-
sur-Fère were subjected to a heavy bombardment of gas and high
explosives. The Germans absolutely dominated the air. Their low
flying planes would chase individuals through the streets of the
town and machine gun the ambulances when they passed."[39]

Lawrence's brother, Austin, recorded, "Big rush of wounded
coming in all the time. Then Bosche started shelling us. Made three
direct hits, killing some of our wounded. Spencer Ely killed. Had
been wounded in arm & leg. Johnson and Metcalf both wounded
in arm. Had terrible time during shelling. Bill Helgers a wonder.
Kilcourse sent to rear. Lyttle and Martin up to help out. . . . Airplanes bombed us for hours too. Altogether the most miserable day
I ever put in."[40]

McKenna's battalion adjutant, Capt. H. K. Cassidy, watched
as the "wounded were passing in a constant stream to the rear.
Constant reports came to the P.C. of first one officer, then another
wounded or killed; then came the aeroplanes in droves, in pairs,
and single; flying overhead a hundred feet in the air they rained
machine gun bullets down on the defenseless men in the open,
dropping bombs by the score and soon clearing the far slope we
had taken of what few men remained alive there."[41]

One of the defenseless soldiers was the widower Private Gunnell. A German bomb landed almost on top of him, ripping his legs off and killing him.[42] Vivian Commons, shot in the right arm, was blown off his cot. "Our hospital was covered with flags," he observed, "and the Hun aviators knew what building it was well enough, but that did not stop them from trying to knock it to pieces."[43]

After some time of enemy planes buzzing around Villers-sur-Fère, harassing the medical staff, killing wounded soldiers, and wounding doctors (including Austin, who took a splinter in the back), Sgt. Frank Gardella of the Machine Gun Company had had enough of the butchery. The Manhattan resident waited down near the river until two planes buzzed into sight, one flying directly above the other. Gardella stepped out in the open and aimed his machine gun at the top plane. He riddled it badly enough that it burst into flames. Plummeting to earth, it collided atop the other plane. Both planes crashed and burned.

At noon, McKenna and Cassidy, a corporal, and the severely wounded Captain Hurley recrossed the Ourcq to give McCoy a first-hand account of how they had barely captured Meurcy Farm that morning, to receive further orders, and to get Hurley patched up so he could resume command of his company. They also needed food; in the last three days they had not eaten much and they were hungry. Hurley limped at the front of the weary group, slightly ahead of McKenna. Cassidy and the corporal carried a wounded soldier. As they came into view of the orchard where McCoy had his command post, a shell exploded close to them. Its powerful concussion knocked them all to the ground.

Cassidy staggered up. Hurley and the corporal also got to their feet. The adjutant checked on the wounded soldier he had been carrying: he was dead. Concerned, Cassidy turned toward McKenna. The major lay perfectly still. There was not a mark on him. "I ran to him. He was unconscious but his pulse beat very faintly. I asked Captain Hurley to run for a litter, and tried artificial respiration for a moment, but to no use; so we tried to carry him. He was dead outright."[44]

Capt. Tom Reilley, of the First Battalion, called McKenna the "whitest, squarest and gamest man in the world. [He] went out as he would have liked to, after a good fight in which he had whipped the other fellow, and showed the Germans that this outfit was there. His feeling for the Irish and the old Sixty-ninth amounted to almost a religion."[45]

When Father Duffy got word of McKenna's death, he eulogized him in his diary. "They bore him in sorrowing, as every man in the regiment sorrowed when the news went round at the loss of a brave and beloved leader whose talents fitted him for a high destiny if life were spared him, but to whom had fallen the highest destiny of all, and one which he had always expected would be his—that of dying for his country."[46]

18

"I Guess I Have Been Born to Be Hanged"

"Before we got going," Maj. William Donovan wrote to Ruth, "the first ten men crossing dropped, shot, and yet the next without a falter went over."[1]

It was late morning on the 28th, and Donovan's Third Battalion moved forward, splashing across the Ourcq, to relieve Maj. Jim McKenna's battered Third. The withdrawal of the Third had been orderly despite harassing enemy machine-gun fire and artillery bombardment. In the relative safety of the woods west of Château de la Forêt, what was left of the original one thousand Shamrock soldiers regrouped and marched back to Villers-sur-Fère—six officers and 414 men.

Donovan's fighters pressed on. Angered by the stalled battalions on his flanks—one from the 166th Infantry, the other from the 167th, both waiting for artillery support, the Irish major decided to keep advancing. He yelled at one of the officers, most likely from Alabama, that his men "would go forward in accordance with our orders whether we had assistance or not, or whether our flanks were protected or not!" It had nothing to do with courage, he explained; it was, rather, "simply a matter of duty. And if a Battalion Commander is lacking in the stomach to tackle a job that looks difficult, we can never win this war." He instructed his own officers to have their men attack in the style of open warfare—one or two or three at time, "moving fast, and when they had advanced a few yards to flop. This gives the machine gunners a small target to fire at. And the smaller the target and the less time we could present it, the better we would be."

He ordered his machine-gun squads to fire a steady stream of bullets to cover their fellows as they darted forward. Next to his machine gunners he placed snipers to pick off any exposed enemy. "With that system working we went up the valley," he wrote. "It was more difficult on the hill slopes because there we had to charge machine gun nests with resultant losses."[2]

Recounting the advance, Cpl. Dave Rittow of A Company described rushing forward fifty yards at a clip. "After the first rush when we dropped on the ground, I noticed the bullets dropping around me pretty thick and called the lieutenant's attention to it," he said. "Of course there was no going back once we started forward, but the lieutenant cautioned the men to keep low."[3]

Another corporal in A Company, Charles Hallberg Jr., never had a chance to keep low. He was hit crossing the Ourcq, and fell into the river. When he tried to pull himself up the bank, a German broke out of the underbrush. Hallberg dove back into the shallow stream and swam along the edge of the bank while the German chased him. He escaped, but the gunshot that had landed him in the river knocked him out of action.

D onovan's anger was brought to the boiling point by the charade played over and over by the German troops: taking the enemy off guard by sporting Red Cross armbands; opening fire on them; and then, if the encounter didn't go their way, playing for sympathy by yelling "Kamerad!" while throwing up their arms in surrender. These cowardly acts deserved no mercy. The "blood lust" this treatment stirred in Donovan's own soldiers led them to kill in most cases rather than take prisoners.

"I did not blame them," Wild Bill confessed.[4]

First Lt. George Patton, the decorated doctor, felt the same way. Without objection, he had witnessed 1st Sgt. John O'Leary as he hauled in a haughty prisoner who spoke perfect English. O'Leary warned him to stop strutting around, his body ramrod straight. Finally fed up, O'Leary asked him if he had any family or friends. The German said he had a wife and five children, and started to strut again.

"You're a liar!" O'Leary screamed. And then, as Patton later told the story, he jammed his bayonet into the prisoner's heart. "You've got a widow and five orphans!"[5]

C Company Sgt. Arthur Totten, from an old New York family, called the Germans the worst cowards living. "We showed no quarter to the machine gunners. We would attack a machine nest and the German gunners would kill as many of us as they possibly could.

When we got within 20 yards up would go their hands and they would yell 'Kamerad.' But we finished them. If they only had nerve enough to keep firing we could never reach them."[6]

Not all First Battalion men answered surrender with slaughter. Pfc. Sylvester "Sylvie" Moran and several C Company comrades captured fifteen Germans. They searched the prisoners for souvenirs and the Germans "didn't even have a box of matches, except one guy who had a watch," Moran wrote. "When I took it from him he cried like baby and begged me to give it back to him because his mother gave it to him when he was a boy. So I gave it back, although that's more than a 'square-head' would do for an American boy."[7]

Leading First Battalion's advance, B Company's Capt. Tom Reilley soaked in the panoramic vista that stretched ahead for miles. He saw everything in front him as the First Battalion marched in columns, squad after squad, beneath a canopy of enemy shells. It seemed surreal, a rehearsal, not the real thing. "It was the first time that the outfit had ever advanced against artillery fire in the open," Reilley told one of the division's artillery colonels. "Everything previously had been trench warfare."[8] To a newspaper reporter, he added, "Despite the fact that this was our first advance in open warfare and men fell all around, you could hear the low-spoken commands of the sergeants and corporals from the east and west sides of Manhattan, from the Bronx and Brooklyn, 'Keep moving!' 'Close up, there!' They were all cool and businesslike and hardly any different in their manner from their practice maneuvers."[9]

Following Donovan's order to attack in short bursts, Reilley's men rushed between two wooded groves, dodging both artillery and machine-gun fire. "You would think the men had been doing this all their lives," he thought. An exploding shell killed two men and bowled the big athlete over as searing shrapnel burned into his legs.[10]

Killed in the advance, twenty-two-year-old Pvt. Mike Tierney never got the chance to avenge the deaths of his brother and mother. His brother had fallen two years earlier fighting in the British army and the news of his death had broken his mother's heart and killed her. When his father had heard that Mike, living in Brooklyn since 1912, had enlisted in the Fourteenth Regiment, he pleaded, "Mike, I want you to avenge the death of John Joseph. Your mother was so shocked when his clothes arrived that she never recovered, and you must avenge her death also." A friend in B Company, Pvt. Jimmy Dwyer from the Gashouse District, crouched close to Mike when a bullet slammed into his head just behind the ear. "Mike called to me and I went over to him," Jimmy wrote to his sister. "Before I reached him he was hit again. I was just getting a grip on him so I could drag him back when I was hit. He then said, 'Save yourself, Jimmy, save yourself!' Then he became quiet. That is how Mike died."[11]

Nearby, Capt. Henry Bootz, the extremely tall German native who had won the Distinguished Service Cross in the Lunéville sector, staggered and fell. A bullet had punched through one side of his chest and popped out the other. According to Father Duffy, it would have killed another man, but Papa Bootz, he observed, "merely grinned, took his pipe which he used in action to signal to his men and threw it to Lieutenant Earl Betty, saying: 'Here, son, I won't need this for a while'."[12]

Bootz's men loaded him onto a litter and carried him to a dressing station near a small creek that trickled toward the Ourcq. Donovan ran to Bootz and knelt next to him, asking about the position of his troops. As he did so, he beheld 2nd Lt. Oliver Ames, now in charge of a detachment from Headquarters Company, bounding down a hill toward him "like a young football captain bringing his team on the field." Donovan had grown fond of his adjutant and had let the Ames family know that he regarded him "like a younger brother." But he did not want the new father close to him in the midst of battle because of the reckless chances Donovan himself took. He ordered Ames back, but the slight New Englander only smiled and said he needed to take care of his major.[13]

A hundred yards distant, in a field near a stone farmhouse, a dead horse made a perfect shield for a German sniper. The sniper sighted Donovan over the bloated corpse and took aim; he pulled off a round. Bullets "whizzed over our heads," Donovan later recollected. "I half turned, and as I did, a sniper's bullet crossed my shoulder and struck Ames in the ear." Donovan reached for his dying adjutant, and the sniper struck again, and a bullet whacked Donovan in the hand. He rolled into the creek.[14] Those around Donovan were stunned by Ames' death. Donovan never mentioned it to any one, but according to Pfc. Fred Thorne of A Company, "The Colonel cried like a baby when [Ames] was killed, thought so much of him. He simply could not get over his death, he felt it so keenly."[15]

Cpl. Pete Gillespie vowed to get the sniper. Staying on his belly, he wiggled out into the open field under blistering machine-gun fire. When he felt he had gotten close enough, he trained his rifle on the dead horse and waited. Wrote Duffy, "Suddenly he saw something had moved behind it. He cuddled his rifle, waited and fired. They could see the sniper behind the horse half rise, then drop. The beloved lieutenant was avenged."[16] Gillespie worked his way back and then kept up a steady protective fire against other snipers so that Donovan and the other officers could slip away safely.

When word got back to the Intelligence Section that Ames had been killed, Elmer Basil wept. He had just been ordered to take over command of I Company, replacing its missing captain, Richard Ryan.

"Ollie! Ollie!" Elmer cried. He thought of Ames's newborn child, his wife and mother, people Elmer had never met; then he thought of his own parents. "How dear you two are to me! Nothing else matters to me—only you. What a big thing life is, yet how small. After all, Ollie and his wife will be happier together sometime. There will be no war then and in the meantime, what a wonderful thing he has to pass on to his wife and daughter. . . . He was my best friend, and he died so bravely that I cannot forget."[17]

The death of Ames meant Donovan needed a new adjutant. Sgt. Joyce Kilmer volunteered, and Donovan agreed to take him on as acting adjutant. He also needed Kilmer to serve as his acting sergeant major, and so the poet left the Intelligence Section.

Donovan had little time to grieve over the death of Ames—there were other losses. The loss of even a private deeply hurt him, especially that of the tall and ungainly John Kayes from the Gashouse District. Kayes had followed Donovan everywhere, even after the major had admonished him once to stay back. "With his great height [he] was a shining mark," Donovan warned. Down by the creek where Ames had lost his life, Kayes stumbled and, as he hit the ground, a sniper's bullet winged him in the foot. Another shot ripped through his right thigh. A third bullet nailed his hand, and then a fourth tore through his cheek. Kayes slid into a sheltered spot so anyone tending to him would be out of danger. "I bound him up and he was taken away making everyone he saw promise to look out for his major." His wounds proved fatal, though, and he died on 7 October.

Another of Donovan's men to fall was Cpl. Robert Foster, who had carried the Irish flag over the top in the Lunéville raid. Like Kayes, he was struck in the cheek by a machine-gun bullet. It killed him instantly.

Later, after yet more soldiers of his battalion had been either killed or wounded, Donovan shivered, thinking of the "loyalty of these men and officers immediately about me who have given freely to me in spite of my strictness and sometimes irritability with them."[18]

As a replacement for Ames (and, in a psychological sense, for Kayes), Kilmer also "felt it his duty to look out for [Donovan]." To be at the major's side "suited" him, Father Duffy believed, because Donovan always planted himself in the thick of the fighting. "To be in a battle, a battle for a cause that had his full devotion, with the regiment he loved, under a leader he admired, that was living at the top of his being," the chaplain reckoned.[19]

For Kilmer, leaving the Intelligence Section had nevertheless been bittersweet. He liked his intellectual companions there, and they him. In one of his letters to Aline, he explained why they meant so much. "Dangers shared together and hardships mutually borne develops in us a sport of friendship I never knew in civilian life, a friendship clean of jealousy and gossip and envy and suspicion—a fine hearty roaring mirthful sort of thing, like an open fire of whole pine-trees in a giant's castle, or a truly timed bombardment with eight-inch guns. I don't know that this last figure will strike you as being particularly happy, but it would if you'd had the delight of going to war."[20] In another letter he said of all the men in the regiment, "We are peace-makers, we soldiers of the 69th, we are risking our lives to bring back peace to the simple, generous, gay, pious people of France."[21] The last poem he wrote was titled "The Peacemaker." Elmer was one of the first to read that poem. He then copied it out in a letter to his parents and sent it off, stating, "Kilmer, one of my sergeants, wrote this sonnet this morning."[22]

One of the intellectuals in the Intelligence Section, Emmett Watson, had been surprised when Kilmer volunteered to go with Donovan. "Certainly there was no reason or compulsion for [him] to serve with a front-line battalion," he had reasoned. "As a sergeant in the Intelligence Section, he was assigned to regimental headquarters, where he could have remained with complete honor in the same comparative safety as the rest of us."

From that place of comparative safety—an observation post on a ridge overlooking the Ourcq battlefield—Watson "saw the brave assault of the 69th without artillery preparation or support as they crossed the stream and moved up the open slopes opposite under withering fire, with men falling everywhere." At that moment, Watson did not know that Kilmer was down there—one of those soldiers fighting for their lives.[23]

On the First Battalion's left flank, Maj. Alexander Anderson's Second Battalion battled up the northern slope of the Ourcq. In the first line were E and F Companies, with E on the right. Anderson's men had forded the Ourcq after seven that morning and worked their way two hundred yards up Hill 156. Here, on the road leading to Fère-en-Tardenois, they came under tremendous fire that drove them back. They regrouped and pushed on up the hill where it reached the outskirts of Seringes-et-Nesles. For the rest of the day, Anderson's men attempted to flank the town on two sides. But the enemy held "very strongly," reported Capt. George McAdie, "with perfect observation and a clear field of fire, rendering it impossible for our troops to hold positions gained."[24]

Having been wounded in the attempt to flank Seringes, Louis Doan, the Jew who had changed his name to get into the Irish regiment, scoffed at misfortune. A sergeant in E Company, Doan had been wounded on 15 July. He had been dressed and piled into an ambulance, but when the "first aid man had his back turned I beat it as fast as I could back up to the lines." He was struck in the head by shrapnel and bits of a tree and knocked out. He awoke twenty-four hours later in the dressing station at Villers-sur-Fère. "For two days I was here and the Boche planes bombed us constantly," he wrote home. "I was pretty lucky, though, for I am only blinded slightly on my left eye and totally deaf on my left ear. Outside of this I am all right and I don't see how the surgeon had the nerve to mark me unfit for further combat duty."[25]

While the Second Battalion waited, stymied by the stiff German defense, the 166th Infantry moved up, reinforcing its rear and left flank. By ten o'clock the 167th Infantry had crossed the Ourcq to the right of Donovan's battalion, and closed in on Sergy. Further to the northwest, French troops advanced toward

Fère-en-Tardenois. Back of the Rainbows, Villers-sur-Fère was being pounded. Trees fell across roads leading into and out of the village and, together with huge bomb holes, made travel impossible. The 117th Engineers went in to clean up the mess. Reports received at Eighty-third Brigade headquarters "were all the effect that our line was advancing on the objective, overcoming strong resistance, especially from machine guns, which were difficult to locate."[26]

At noon, Lenihan heard from Frank McCoy. The news was not promising. "Several of our companies have been forced to withdraw by incessant M. G. [machine gun] fire from South edge of woods North of Ourcq, which artillery and special arms have been unable to keep down. Have ordered Bns. on other side to dig in and wait for nightfall for further advance. Request that reserve Bns. be put at my disposition to cover withdrawal."

Lenihan replied. "Dig in and hold where you are. Artillery officers now going forward to reconnoiter M.G. positions. The Artillery will dispose of all nests which you can locate for them and will render any other assistance you may desire to further infantry advance."

Douglas MacArthur radioed Lenihan not to advance beyond the original objective, Seringes-en-Nesles, not knowing that Lenihan's infantry had already ceased to advance. "Nothing positive had been accomplished," he reported, "though the fighting had been hard and at least one counter-attack on our left had been repulsed by the 2nd Bn. 165th Inf."

The hillside was littered with dead and wounded Americans. In his war diary entry for 28 July, Anderson wrote, "18 killed, 100 wounded, 60 missing";[27] twenty-six of his Second Battalion boys had been slain that Sunday. Donovan lost eighteen men. In McKenna's Shamrock Battalion, eighty-nine soldiers were killed, including McKenna. Van S. Merle-Smith's L Company had thirty-five dead. Richard Ryan's I Company suffered the greatest number of losses, with thirty-six. Ryan was not one of them, although he had been listed as killed in action. He had dug himself out from under the dirt and rocks and, though gravely injured, worked his way back to a safe place, only to be nearly shot by a sentry from E Company. He described the incident to his son:

Damn fools, those boys, but they could shoot, alright. Sonuvabitch put a slug in the mud three inches in front of my nose. Would've killed me if I hadn't remembered an old Irish curse, which translated meant your mother slept in a pigpen to conceive you. The sentry was dumb alright, but he was smart enough to know no German would know that much about his parents.[28]

Among the most seriously wounded was Charles Baker, the Princeton classmate of Merle-Smith and William Spencer. A bullet had struck him in the neck and burrowed down his back, tearing a large blood vessel and lodging close to his spine. When he was taken off the field, he was in good spirits. Merle-Smith saw him at the dressing station, and Baker told him the wound was not serious. In fact, the boys in E Company remarked how Baker took care of the other wounded before letting the medics tend to him.

The regiment's total dead reached 145. They included five from the Machine Gun Company, four from Headquarters, Kayes, who died three months later, and Baker, who died at Base Hospital 34 in Nantes. At first the doctors had thought they could save Baker. But after they had amputated his arm, the bullet wound became infected, the infection spread, and Baker grew delirious. During his ordeal, a Red Cross nurse, Alice Maxwell Appo, grew fond of the big, handsome captain. In a letter to his father, she later wrote, "He was always calm, master of himself, very considerate of others, strong and fine in his attitude towards his condition and the events which brought it about. He bore everything with extraordinary fortitude, and made such a fight to get well that he became the admiration of all who knew him here." She told his father that one day she asked Charles if he would like ice cream.

"Oh, would I!" he exclaimed.

She gave him a plateful, and right away he asked, "Have the others got some?"

She wrote, "Captain Baker is buried in the American military cemetery far from the battle front, and secure from even the disturbance of city life. One goes down a country lane bordered with hedges to reach it, and finds it on the top of a gentle slope of farm land. Plain white crosses mark the graves and an American flag waves over them. All is kept in good order. French women come often with their children, and put flowers on the graves."[29]

Charles MacArthur, the artilleryman, saw no glory on the north bank of the Ourcq where the New Yorkers had just fought and died.

> The roads were strewn with our doughboys, gray faces in the mud, blue hands frozen to their guns. Near the Ourcq, a sixteen-inch shell had blown a German from his grave for the third time. His face bore such real resentment that some doughboy wrote a sign and hung it on his chest:

> "For the love of God, leave me alone. I got appendicitis."

> More bundles of what once had held life sprawled on the river's edge. German, American and French—all gone and nobody gave a damn. In the poppy fields the living lay with the dead; it was hard to tell which was which.[30]

The carnage sickened 1st Lt. Frank McNamara, who had been in charge of a Stokes mortar outfit. "All about me, as far as I could see, were dead bodies. I buried fifty of them that afternoon—all that I could look after. The slaughter was terrible. And the grief of having to bury so many of our own men, many of whom were my friends, I shall never forget. I saw buried that afternoon ten and fifteen men in one trench. We used shell holes for graves. We found dead men in holes which they had dug themselves, hollowing them out with their hands as shelter from the galling fire of the Germans."[31]

The chaplain had been one comforting constant amid the death. A newspaper correspondent described Duffy as "coatless, covered with mud and grime." He reported how he had been "in the thick of the fighting, cheering on the living, administering the last rites of his Church to the dying, filling the place of a stretcher bearer who had been struck down by a bullet, assisting the wounded, darting hither and yon, a ministering angel truly affording the one human touch and supplying the last link between Christian civilization and the barbarism which is war. For 117 hours he was under fire without rest."

Undaunted, Duffy had been quoted afterwards as saying, "No Hun bullet can touch me." Another of his sayings, according to the correspondent, was "Give 'em hell!" But while the battle raged on, the priest had been seen weeping.[32]

As dawn broke on the 29th, the valley shrouded in low fog, the Americans were still not sure what they faced—if and when they resumed their advance across the Ourcq. At ten-fifty-five the night before, the Forty-second Division had received a field order from First Army Corps headquarters that, if true, was encouraging. It claimed the enemy had "given way before our pressure." Then it detailed the American's mission for the 29th.

> Tomorrow the Army will continue rigid pressure of the enemy, concentrating artillery fire on points of resistance and advancing by manouever around those points with mixed advance guards composed of Infantry and Cavalry. Contact will be maintained constantly tonight and tomorrow to prevent, at all cost, the enemy from stealing away. This duty is mandatory on all.[33]

The advance was to resume at eight in the morning. Lenihan placed Donovan's First Battalion in front with Anderson's Second Battalion in support and the Shamrocks in reserve. Donovans's men were to clear out Meurcy Farm once and for all and advance north of it to Bois Colas and Bois Brulé, small hillocks with little creeks that trickled down into the Ourcq. On the left, Lenihan brought up the 166th Infantry. General Brown's 167th Infantry was to go up on Donovan's right.

Although the advance had been scheduled for eight it did not get started until nine-thirty. Right away the 165th ran into trouble. The Alabama soldiers failed to advance alongside the Irish soldiers. "The liaison was soon lost and the flank of the 165th Infantry unsupported," Lenihan noted in his daily report.[34] He moved Anderson's Second Battalion up from its support position to protect Donovan's right flank. The gap that soon existed between the 165th and the 167th and the "failure of the troops on the right to keep abreast," according to McCoy, would later be partly responsible for the difficulty that Donovan's men would have in retaking Meurcy farm.[35]

The main objective, of course, was to secure the stone farm and then move on. But throughout the night, the Germans had regrouped. In the orchards and groves of trees they had reinforced their machine-gun squads. Donovan reported, "On the hill slopes to the east, which were covered with wheat and clover, they had light and heavy machine guns upon such emplacements which controlled the valley."[36] Grayson Murphy, still an observer and close to Donovan's side, wrote to his son, "The Bosch has done most of his fighting with machine guns, which are very effective and very deadly in open country, particularly when, as here, the Bosch has been able to hide them on the edges of patches of forest on the heights and fire on men as they come up the open hills from the tiny river."[37]

One of the men pushing up the open hill had made himself a hero at Rouge Bouquet by working furiously with Donovan to free soldiers who had been buried alive during the artillery bombardment. Sgt. Danny O'Connell, the former altar boy from St. Rose of Lima's Church in Rockaway Beach, dodged exploding shells and whining machine-gun bullets as he and the others in A Company closed in on Meurcy Farm. Further down the hill, dodging the same barrage, was O'Connell's friend from Rockaway Beach, Cpl. Charlie Carman of Headquarters Company. That morning he and Danny had gotten together for an hour, but had to separate because they were in different companies.

Later, Carman wrote to Catherine, his seventeen-year-old wife, "Gee, that was some battle." His letter was upbeat as he told her how the boys just walked over the Germans. "We encountered a lot of machine guns and snipers in the woods and wheat fields and I must say the most unpleasant thing in the world is the music of a lot of machine gun bullets whizzing past your ears."[38]

Carman and five others, including a lieutenant, dove into a shell hole. The young officer stood up and bullets crashed around him. He dropped down, a frightened look on his face. "One of the boys put his helmet on the end of his gun and raised it just bit over the edge of the top. Immediately little spats of dirt would be seen on one edge and the bullet would go singing over the other edge. A couple hit the helmet and put a hole in it."

While Carman was trapped in the shell hole, knowing that the "darned Boche machine gunner [had] made up his mind we weren't going to get out," O'Connell, according to witnesses, rose up and charged Meurcy Farm, yelling, "Heaven, Hell or Hoboken by Christmas!" The Germans shot him down. It would be a week before Carman heard the news. Danny was eighteen years old.

Also killed was Cpl. Harry Horgan, the muleskinner from Arizona. Horgan had reached a slice of woods when he saw a wounded soldier lying in the field in front of Meurcy Farm. He called to Pvt.

Thomas O'Connor to help him rescue the man. Both he and O'Connor were killed in the attempt, Horgan's head shattered by a machine gunner.

The taking of the farm was so slow because of Donovan's tactic of having a few men at a time rush forward and then drop to the ground. Now and then they flanked a German machine-gun position and rushed it. On a "poker hunch," as he called it, Donovan led a rush to a trench; when he and his men got there they found a German platoon about to charge them. The Americans killed all but two of the Germans. In the assault, Donovan was struck on the head by either a stone or a chunk of shrapnel, and whatever it was ripped off his gas mask. Shrapnel then ripped his left heel, throwing him off balance. A third chunk got him in the leg, but there was no damage. It was this incident that made him write to Ruth that he guessed he had been born to be hanged.

Anderson's Second Battalion, brought up from its support position to protect Donovan's right flank, recorded in its war diary for the day. "Another hard day of infantry fighting." But it also reported, "Our troops succeeded in taking Meurcy farm after a hand to hand fight. The enemy machine gunners in the grain fields along the ridges north of the Ourcq kept up a constant fire on our lines. Our casualties: 12 Killed; 90 Wounded; 130 Missing."

Donovan's battalion suffered thirty-seven men killed, nineteen from A Company and twelve from D. One of the casualties had been Lt. Edwin Daly, the son of a Massachusetts state representative. Leading his platoon up Hill 212, about a kilometer away from Meurcy Farm, he was hit three times, once in the forehead. Before he died, he clutched his crucifix and rosary beads and said to Pvt. Ed Lopez, "You lead a charmed life." In 1920, when Theodore Roosevelt's wife led a campaign, in which Secretary of War Newton Baker and Gen. John Pershing participated, to keep the bodies of American soldiers in France, Daly's father insisted that his son be brought home and laid to rest next to his mother. He told Mrs. Roosevelt that it was unfair of her and the others to keep the soldiers overseas. Speaking for the thousands of gold star mothers and fathers who wanted their sons returned, he wrote, "We that mourn . . . alone don't want monument or honors from anything human, but want all to stand aside and give us those we love. . . . I want my boy's body at once."[39] The body was disinterred and sent home.[40]

Although the Third Battalion had been held in reserve, it also suffered looses, including seventeen deaths. The worst hit was K Company, with eight killed. One of those was 2nd Lt. Gerald Stott from Oakland, Maine, who received his fatal wound at the dressing station. A bullet had shattered his knee and, on the way to Villers-sur-Fère, another punctured his stomach. But what killed him was a bomb that exploded near his cot, bringing the roof down on top of him. Pvt. Tom Feeley from Brooklyn, who had carried Stott back to the village, wrote to the lieutenant's mother, "Right after we came out of the first aid station a Boche aeroplane came over and dropped a bomb. He was killed instantly." Sgt. Ted Van Yorx recalled Stott's last words to Capt. John Hurley. "Well, I guess they got me this time."[41]

The casualties were fewer than on the previous day—sixty-six soldiers killed. It put the two-day total at 209. But the death that would shatter the Irish soldiers came the following day, when one of its sergeants would bring eternal glory to the old Fighting Sixty-ninth.

19

"We Sure Hated to See Him Get Killed"

Sergeant Richard O'Neill, leader of the Second Platoon, D Company, First Battalion, drew a deep breath. Tuesday, 30 July, had broken clear and beautiful. For the entire infantry of the Forty-second Division, the hard fight to clear the Germans from the north slope of the Ourcq River was about to enter its fourth day; for the 165th Infantry, its third day. O'Neill snapped his bayonet to the barrel of his rifle. He checked his pistol. The fighting so far had been brutal and bloody, and on this sunny day he expected nothing less. The Germans were still holed up on the hills, hidden in the forests and farms, behind the stone walls, and in every dark corner of the small villages on the road running east from Fère-en-Tardenois to north of Cierges. They were ready, he knew—their fingers wrapped around the triggers of hundreds of machine guns. It had been made obvious in the last forty-eight hours that no army knew how to use machine guns better than the German army. O'Neill thought of his Harlem sweetheart, Estelle Johnson, whose photograph he carried over his heart. He touched the cherished picture. He believed that in a tight spot a soldier always thought of his sweetheart and his mother, hoping that if something happened to him it wouldn't hurt them too much.[1] Then his steel-gray eyes looked out at the valley and he thought what a fine morning it would be for a stroll through the French countryside. And as he got ready to lead the Second Platoon toward its destiny, he said aloud, "Dick, this is a hell of a morning to pick to get killed."[2]

Again, the Forty-second Division had been ordered to press the attack. All that was known beforehand, according to intelligence reports, was that the Rainbows controlled Hills 138, 184, and 212, Sergy, the crossroad leading into Seringes-et Nesles

Sgt. Richard O'Neill, New York's most decorated hero of World War I, earned
the Medal of Honor during the Battle of the Ourcq River. He kept his girlfriend's
photograph next to his heart. *Courtesy of William Donovan O'Neill*

and, tenuously, Meurcy Farm. The German line, buttressed by the
Fourth Guard Division, Ninety-third Reserve Regiment and the
Fifth Grenadiers, ran in an easterly direction from the north slope
of Hill 184, north of Seringes, Bois Brulé, Hill 200, and the thick
groves of woods all the way to Cierges.[3] On the far right flank,

Estelle Johnson, Sergeant O'Neill's sweetheart, grew up next to him in Harlem. After the war, Father Francis Duffy married them. *Courtesy of William Donovan O'Neill*

near Cierges, the Thirty-second and Twenty-sixth U.S. Divisions were set to attack toward the north. And on the far left flank, the French were also in position to strike north.

Until zero hour, artillery would soften up the German defenses. At nine, the entire Eighty-fourth Brigade would push past Sergy, north to the Château Nesles, and take the small, fortified village there and the equally fortified Le Tuilerie Farm. The assignment for Brig. Gen. Michael Lenihan's Eighty-third Brigade was for the 166th Infantry to move into Seringes-et-Nesles and for Col. Frank McCoy's 165th Infantry to solidify its capture of Meurcy Farm and then push up the hill beyond to Bois Brulé, where the woods were crawling with Germans. Lenihan believed Meurcy Farm, being in the middle of the battlefield, "was really the key of the entire position" and that meant, he reported, that "Bois Brulé and strip of woods S. W. thereof were strongly held by enemy Machine Guns."[4]

With this knowledge in mind, O'Neill realized that his "stroll" across the French countryside would be bloody. Earlier that morning, Maj. Bill Donovan had pulled him aside and pointed toward machine-gun emplacements tucked among rows of trees. The machine gunners there blocked the way to Bois Brulé, one of Donovan's objectives.

"Dick, it would be a lot better if your boys could knock out those guns," Donovan had said. "We could move faster."

The ground ahead would not be easy to traverse: for two hundred yards it sloped upward, "rough and hummocky," and on the east it slanted toward a small stream that gurgled past Meurcy Farm.

At the time Donovan gave his order, O'Neill had charge of a tattered knot of fifteen men. D Company itself, once two hundred and fifty strong, was down to one officer and forty-two men. As O'Neill waited for the nine o'clock zero hour, two officers came up, looking for the commander. They were told there were no officers. Tom O'Malley, a tough veteran from the East Side, cracked, "Sure and there's no officers here. Oh, we'd see them all the time at the camp; Christ, you'd be tripping over 'em! But here, none atall." The officers, decked out in their Sam Browne belts that only officers wear, felt they had better commission O'Malley on the spot. Someone had to run the company. O'Malley turned the offer down. "No Sam Browne belt for me! Now take that nice young man Dick O'Neill—we'll make Dick the acting captain. I'll see the boys do what he says."

Now, instead of being in charge of a paltry platoon, O'Neill led a full company, or what was left of it after two days of fighting. He probably would have preferred to have O'Malley as boss, or his own brother-in-law, 1st Sgt. Ed Geaney. But the command had fallen on him, and his first order of business was to knock out several machine-gun emplacements for Major Donovan.[5]

Awaiting zero hour at his command post—a hole in the ground near Bois Colas—Donovan found he had to get used to his acting adjutant, Joyce Kilmer. He trusted O'Neill, a proven combat sergeant; Kilmer was another matter. Although he had made a name for himself in the Intelligence Section, by the time he showed up at Wild Bill's command post on the morning of the 29th, the chunky sergeant had an almost-established reputation for pomposity. He arrived soon after the body of Oliver Ames had been carried down to Donovan's dugout and buried close to it. All that day, the major, not sure how the poet would act under fire, watched his every move. He liked what he saw. "The battalion was obliged to march by the flank and pass a narrow draw, through which heavy German machine gun fire was penetrating." He noted how Kilmer kept order among the troops he led as he got them safely through. "During the remainder of the 29th and all through that night he worked unceasingly and efficiently."[6]

Father Francis Duffy believed it did not take Donovan long to place "great reliance on [Kilmer's] coolness and intelligence and kept him by his side."[7] Duffy had been right as Donovan himself discovered that not only did Kilmer "find soldierly joy in the conflict and actually seek danger, but he was a cool headed soldier."[8]

The Second Battalion, lying low in the strip of woods north of the Ourcq and, equally beat up as the Shamrocks, was placed in support of Donovan's First. Its role was to resist any German counterattacks. Maj. Alexander Anderson, whose battalion had been reduced to sixteen officers and three hundred men, did not have much to work with.

One of the more efficient of his noncommissioned officers still standing was not much to look at. Sgt. James Monroe Hyland Jr. from Brooklyn, twenty-two years old, stood all of five feet four inches tall. When he had tried for a commission at Camp Mills, the officers had scoffed because he was so short. But Jimmy, as his friends called him, was a born leader, so persuasive in his talk that he seemed a natural politician and was, despite his size, tough as a walnut. Before enlisting in the Sixty-ninth in May 1916, he worked as a clerk at the Wall Street law firm of Brooks & Brooks. He was seventeen when he showed up for the job interview, wearing short pants and

scuffed shoes. A partner in the firm said that when he interviewed
the boy he asked him why, if he was seventeen, he still wore
knickers.

"I never knew that the length of one's trousers made the man,"
Jimmy had replied. He got the job.

On the Mexican border as a sergeant in E Company, he had
been even shorter than in France: five-two. But he grew two inches
during the months he spent sweltering in the cactus and sagebrush.
He also became one of the Sixty-ninth's best rifle shots. When the
regiment left for France, Jimmy bid good-bye to the woman who
had taken care of him since his mother had died, Mrs. Mary Lee of
Fort Greene. "Mother, you may never see me again," he said to
her grandiloquently. "But you will always be proud of me, for I
have dedicated my life to liberty, and I am willing to die if need be
to realize President Wilson's ideal to make the world a better place
to live in."[9]

With boys like Hyland, Anderson, a tough, young man himself, felt his battalion could withstand anything the enemy threw
at it, although back at corps and division headquarters no one expected the Germans to mount any kind of attack. They had been
backpedaling ever since their failed offensive in the Champagne
sector and the consensus was that they probably planned to regroup north of Vesle River, ten miles away.

But the Germans, who had turned counterattacking into an
art, had a surprise in store for the Allies.

"It didn't take the Germans long to open up on us," O'Neill
said. "Christ, there were bullets flying all around. One of them
knocked the rifle out of my hand, but being a sergeant, I still had
my pistol. I didn't realize it at the time, but I was running so fast
that I was way out in front of the men I was leading."[10]

Beating the Americans to the punch, Germans poured down
from the hills between Seringes-et-Nesles and Meurcy Farm.
Donovan's men braced themselves for the onslaught.

In the hand-to-hand melee, O'Neill had, indeed, outdistanced
his company and was up near the ridge, alone, with just a pistol
and some grenades. The only protective chunk of real estate was a
camouflaged gravel pit. He dived in—and all around him were
twenty-five Germans, manning machine guns. The sight of all those
Germans shocked him; the Germans were also shocked to see an
American drop through the netting. Yelling as loudly as he could,

O'Neill flipped a grenade into their midst and then at point-blank range fired away, hitting three before the rest reacted. A few Germans scrambled out the far end of the pit while the others went after him. Lead tore into the sergeant. He was shot four, five, six, seven times. Bullets pierced his side, his left shin, and his left arm. Still he returned fire.[11]

And then, quite miraculously, the Germans surrendered. Their hands went up. They called out "Kamerad!"

"Here I am with twenty or so Heinie prisoners smack on top of the German lines," he said. "They're all jabbering away a mile a minute while I'm pointing a pistol at them that probably didn't have any rounds left in it. I was the one in a hell of a spot, but I guess these Krauts didn't know it."

O'Neill started to march them down the ridge when off to his left, German machine gunners opened up. They killed several of their own men; they also hit O'Neill, knocking the "jesus" out of him. His right leg was struck. "I couldn't walk," he later said, "couldn't crawl." So he rolled. Down he came like a human barrel, bouncing over the hummocky ground, blood flying from his dozen wounds. Even as he rolled away the Germans peppered him with bullets, hitting him several more times. At last he reached his own troops, dazed and dizzy. There, Pvt. Pat Crowley looked at his sergeant.

"Je-sus, Dick me boy, you're leaking all over the place! I should carry yuh back on me back."

O'Neill was wrapped in a blanket held like a sling and, on the way to the dressing station, he ordered the men carrying him to take him to Donovan: he had to tell the major what awaited the battalion at the top of the ridge and beyond. O'Neill saw Donovan, and then, "The lights went out while I was making my report and I awoke several weeks later in a hospital." The first thing he did was search for Estelle's photograph. It was gone. "I guess the picture was spoiled by that time," he said.

For his action, O'Neill earned the Medal of Honor. He was not the only hero from D Company that day. Another one was his brother-in-law, Ed Geaney. Geaney had toted a wounded officer off the field, although his own arm had been shattered by a bullet. Cpl. John Gribbon, after his patrol was nearly wiped out in a crossfire, went back up the hill to rescue a wounded soldier. Under extreme machine-gun fire sweeping the hillside, he half-carried, half-dragged the man to safety. The men earned Distinguished Service Crosses.

At ten-fifty that morning, McCoy sent a message to Lenihan. "Donovan has repulsed the counterattack. German infantry got as far as his line coming down from Bois Brulé. Three enemy were killed inside our lines and the rest driven off." Five minutes later another message arrived, this time from Donovan. He had earlier called for an artillery barrage, but now complained that he had not gotten it. It was vital to shell Bois Brulé, where there were at least forty machine-gun emplacements. He reported that his Stokes mortars had "smashed" Meurcy Farm and that A Company had been engaged in a firefight at the wire entanglements thrown up by the Germans in front of the stone farmhouse. The last words of his message were, "Can you give us special concentration of fire on Bois Brulé?"[12]

Men from Headquarters Company manned the Stokes mortars. They had dragged the small, heavy cannons across the river the day before, "scuttling along as low as possible to keep from drawing fire on ourselves," and up the hill in front of Meurcy Farm, according to Charles Holt, one of the mortar men. "We passed the bodies of three officers who had a few minutes before been killed by a shell. Then out we went on an open field. The battle was stretched out before us like some Civil War paintings I have seen, though the line of barrage fire made it far more terrible and two towns nearby were in flames."[13]

Scattered around Holt were dead men and horses, ammunition belts, helmets, weapons, implements of war. As they neared the farm, Anderson ordered them to train their mortars on the farmhouse. Holt saw that it had been fortified with German machine gunners. "Our boys had been trying to take it all that day, but had been mowed down by the murderous fire. We were to blow the house to pieces."

The house withstood all attacks, and both sides waited through night. Now the shelling began all over again, as Holt and his comrades lobbed mortars onto Meurcy Farm. Holt was hit by a shell that "felt like a ton of bricks. I didn't know that the skin had been broken until I suddenly put my hand to my back and found it bloody and the man next to me said that a piece was about two inches long, whereupon I decided to go to the rear."

Malcolm Troop Robertson was not as fortunate as Holt. He volunteered to move his Stokes mortar closer to Meurcy Farm. He and his six-man crew were out in the open when a German shell exploded and its shrapnel tore his head off. Cpl. Joseph Dugdale recalled how most of the Stokes mortar men had scattered when the German artillery zeroed in on them. They flattened themselves on the ground and started crawling away. Robertson remained standing, yelling, "Don't leave fellows. Stay and we will get them!"[14] Robertson was still on his feet when, said Dugdale, "A shell hit a rock nearby, killing him instantly."[15]

Donovan said the Stokes mortars struck "shell holes where the Germans were hidden, and then as they would start to get away we would shoot them up with our machine gun."[16] The heavier barrage he had called in to support the Stokes mortars had good results. As the shells hit the Germans, they at last fell back, up the hill. But down below, their artillery was striking the forward field hospitals, blowing up ambulances and men. One shell pierced the heart of Capt. William Hudson, a doctor who had just set up a temporary dressing station. Sgt. Danny McConlogue had been sitting at a table with Hudson. The tall, heavily built Hudson had been smoking a great big pipe when the shell came thundering through the roof. The explosion knocked the men to the ground, Hudson falling on top of the sergeant. McConlogue struggled up, yelling for help, and stretched the doctor out on the table.

"Never mind," Hudson groaned. "I'm gone."

McConlogue unbuttoned the captain's tunic and saw that a piece of shell had struck his heart.[17]

McCoy was livid watching the wounded pile up, awaiting evacuation. He called for medical help and reported that his men were charging up the hill after the enemy in small groups. At eleven-forty-six, he boasted, "It is only a question of minutes before crest assured. Germans are retreating."[18]

Across the Ourcq, artilleryman Elmer Sherwood watched the pitched battle and in his diary that night wrote, "This has been a day of savage attacks and counter-attacks." He saw one company from the 165th capture eight machine-gun nests and "turning the machine guns the other way gave the Germans a dose of their own medicine. The war cry is 'guts and bayonets,' and, believe me, they are using both."[19]

On the right flank, the Eighty-fourth Brigade punched up the hill north of Sergy. On the left, the French, according to reports, secured Hill 184. But McCoy worried about another counterattack, this time east of Meurcy Farm. He called for more artillery to pound the woods that formed a rectangle south of Bois Brulé and along the edge of the farm, and to keep pounding until he called it off. The shells landed short of the target, crashing into Donovan's troops at Bois Colas. McCoy screamed at the artillery to concentrate all its fire on the southwest edge of Bois Brulé.

Cpl. Louis Collins of the 151st Field Artillery counted 6,943 rounds fired on the 30th. "Much of the fire was on the northern part of Seringes and on Meurcy Ferme, where the Germans had succeeded in gaining another footing."[20] He did not mention that some shells fell short.

Donovan then rallied his troops, sending a message that left little doubt that he had taken the battle into his own hands.

"My intention is to proceed forward, guiding the 166th and maintaining that guide throughout. Lt. [Earl] Betty is hooked up with the right leading Company of the 166th. I connect with Lt. Betty by liaison patrol. Lt. Betty's right is only 300 yards from me. 11:30 time for start."

His battalion moved up into Bois Brulé, which Donovan now called "the vital point of the entire line." A special gas detachment fired phosphorous bombs on Bois Brulé. "The bombs made a very dense white smoke," recorded Col. George Leach, "which rose to a height of about one hundred meters."[21]

By one-ten in the afternoon, scouts from observation posts had spotted Germans fleeing Bois Brulé. From that distant vantage point the battle looked promising, but elsewhere, other enemy forces were counterattacking Col. Benson Hough's 166th, and, as one of Donovan's officers reported, "Looks like attack might succeed." More artillery fire was called in. On the right, elements of the Eighty-fourth Brigade had fallen back, according to McCoy, leaving his flank uncovered.[22]

Then, at three, McCoy lost contact with Donovan. The major, with Sergeant Kilmer by his side, had taken charge of a company whose captain had been wounded, and was leading it up past Bois Brulé over the hill. Exactly what followed may never be known for sure. There were many witnesses—or many soldiers who claimed to be witnesses. The first was Wild Bill himself.

"We [he and Kilmer] were lying together along the Bois Colas," he testified. "Machine gun fire was coming down the draw from the village of Seringes. A bullet hit him full in the head killing him instantly."

Cpl. Leslie Smith of M Company claimed that a shell fragment had hit Kilmer. An eyewitness from Headquarters Company, Pvt. George Dickson, said he was only a few hundred yards from Kilmer when a sniper killed the sergeant. "At the time he was at the river in the Intelligence Section, looking for snipers and a machine gun position," he said. "He was a fine man; the finest man we ever had."[23] The most fantastical account came from the great grandson of Cornelius Vanderbilt, Cpl. Vanderbilt Ward, a Seventh Regiment transfer. "When we attacked we moved so rapidly chasing the Huns that the artillery had no chance to catch up. . . . Poor Joyce Kilmer was one of the first to fall, with five machine gun bullets, one of which went through the heart."[24]

Perhaps the most compelling eyewitness was Sgt. Maj. Lemist Esler, a Harvard graduate. Esler recalled seeing Kilmer heading alone into no-man's-land ahead of Donovan's battalion to reconnoiter the rolling farmland and forest on the far side of the hills above the Ourcq. The Americans had shoved the Germans off the heights. After a bit, Kilmer returned "full of enthusiasm and eager to push back into the woods, where he and others had suddenly discovered enemy machine guns." Since the regiment's arrival in France Esler had seen first hand Kilmer's eagerness to court danger. A supply sergeant then, Esler had observed that Kilmer tried to find ways to get to the front. As soon as Kilmer had transferred to the Intelligence Section, "night after night he would lie out in no-man's land, crawling through barbed wires in an effort to locate enemy positions and enemy guns, and tearing his clothes to shreds. On the following day he would come to me for a new uniform." He was still courting danger on 29 July, when Donovan ordered a patrol to push over the hill to find the exact location of the machine guns. As the patrol crept into the woods, Esler noticed that, as usual, Kilmer had gone ahead by himself. The patrol was continuing its advance when Esler spotted "Kilmer lying on his stomach on a bit of sloping ground, his eyes just peering over the top of what appeared to be a natural trench. Several of us ran toward him, thinking he was alive and merely lying there with his attention fixed on the enemy."

Esler called to the sergeant. When there was no response, he hurried over to him. He rolled him onto his back and found that "he was dead with a bullet through his brain." Esler guessed that after Kilmer reached the crest of the hill, he had been unable to resist peering over the top to see where the enemy had placed its machine guns. "In that position the bullet found him."[25]

Pvt. Billy Biber, also from Headquarters Company, said that Kilmer's body had been "buried . . . pretty nearly where it was found. . . . The boys gave him a decent burial, and the bayonet, with identification tag, and the helmet were put above the grave." Private Dickson remembered the gravesite, stating that Kilmer was "buried between a grove of trees that ran along the bank [of the Ourcq River] and the wheat field." He said an unpainted white cross with his whole name written on it marked the spot. "We sure hated to see him get killed."[26]

Pvt. John Nugent, who had seen Kilmer that morning, came across his body on Hill 305. "I was going over to see if there were any wounded who had not received first aid. It was on this hill that I met a burying detail in charge of Chaplain Duffy who buried Kilmer along with men of my regiment who were killed in that vicinity." Pvt. Jim Hanley also came across Kilmer's grave. It was on a hillside, he said. "He is buried with a lieutenant of his outfit. The grave has a cross with the tags tacked upon it."

The lieutenant was Oliver Ames. "They were buried together, just the two graves near a small woods at the foot of a hill," said Sgt. John McAuliffe of C Company. "I know the place right well and looked after the graves the last time we were up there. The graves are marked all right and we made mounds about four inches high over them."

A third grave had been placed next to Ames and Kilmer: that of Malcolm Robertson. His commanding officer, Capt. Frank McNamara, buried him there and said a prayer over his body.

B asil Elmer had been too busy leading Ryan's I Company in support of the First Battalion to hear right away of Kilmer's death. The former commander of the Intelligence Section actually found he enjoyed taking troops into battle. He liked the rough and readiness of it all, telling his parents, "I spent nine days without washing, brushing my teeth or even taking off my raincoat or shoes, once. As you can imagine, I am now filthy." His "most wonderful experience" came when he and his undermanned company made contact with the enemy. "It was here that I fired my first shot of the war. We were going along through a wood. We went a couple of miles and as we came to the edge, we were fired on by a machine gun. I located him and fired. I like to think that I got him." As the fighting intensified, Elmer rolled into a shell hole under heavy shelling and machine-gun fire and there for the first time came face-to-face with a dead soldier, his body crawling "with innumerable rats and vermin."²⁷

While Elmer shared a shell hole with the dead, little Jimmy Hyland and a platoon of E Company boys were in the streets of Seringes-et-Nesles, slugging it out door-to-door, block-by-block, well into the afternoon and early evening. There was not much left of the buildings, knocked into rubble by constant bombardment. German snipers and machine gunners kept Hyland's men pinned down. A news reporter later told how they "kept picking off [the Americans] with pitiless regularity." An attack against one of the machine-gun nests failed. Then ammunition ran low. As it got dark, only Hyland and one other soldier were left unhurt. They remained steadfast at their post, holding off the Germans until reinforcements reached them at last and drove the enemy out of the village.²⁸

Late that afternoon, McCoy reported that fire from the Germans had slacked off, that another counterattack had been repulsed, and that Donovan and his men were moving forward again in step with elements of the 166th Infantry. An hour later the 167th resumed its advance. For the rest of the day and into the evening, the Rainbows pressed the attack.

Behind the infantry, support units, particularly dressing stations and field hospitals, continued to suffer under artillery fire and gas shelling. Many of the victims were doctors like Hudson. One of them was McCoy's chief medical officer, Maj. George Lawrence, joining his brother, Austin, in the ranks of the wounded. Austin, however, had been evacuated to the nearest base hospital, at Couleumers—four hours away by truck. There he was "put to bed & fed & given cigarettes & chocolate."²⁹

Driving the severely wounded off to distant hospitals placed an incredible strain on the drivers. As one medic of the 117th Sanitary Train noted, "Not only was this hard on the patients but it meant that every ambulance driver was obliged to stay at his wheel seventy-two continuous hours, without sleep and often without a bite of food. Reaching their limit of human endurance many of these men finally fell into a stupor at their steering wheels, and had to be removed and replaced by some less experienced driver, who was, in every case, a litter bearer nearly as tired as the man he relieved."³⁰

Colonel Hough reported that the 166th Infantry had gained no ground throughout the day and was right where it had started that morning. He sent some of his men as reinforcements for Donovan, as McCoy expected the Germans were mounting yet a third counterattack, driving a wedge between the two regiments.

"The fight kept up all night and no rest," Colonel Leach wrote in his dairy. "Losses are very heavy. The 84th brigade on our right is not keeping up. From midnight until morning, the heavy artillery fired a counter preparation which made a terrible roar as it passed overhead for hours. Each shell sounded like the rumble of an express train, but they are very welcome sounds, as they mean much discomfort for the enemy."[31]

The call for more artillery that continued through the night came from McCoy, whose regiment was under constant attack.

Donovan, in his warrior-like way, downplayed the danger. "We were not without our discomfort. They would pour fire into the edge of the wood that would make us hug the ground. A few youngsters near me we were potted, but on the whole we had a pretty successful night."[32]

Long before daylight on the 31st, the Germans greeted their foes with another murderous artillery barrage across the Ourcq valley, and attacked Seringes-et-Nesles, hitting the 166th hard. Donovan recalled that all through the day there was "constant heavy bombardment." Airplanes "swooped" down on his men.[33]

Leach recalled, "When daylight came, it was surprisingly calm for a little while and a great relief. At noon the fight became furious again."[34] Louis Collins called the ammunition expenditure on the 31st the 151st's "biggest day of the Battle of the Ourcq. . . . Three times on that day the regiment laid down protecting barrages in front of the advancing 165th Infantry and also concentrated its fire on machine-gun nests and on fleeing targets, firing a total of 8,452 rounds of ammunition. Many gas shells were used in an effort to clear the south edge of the Forêt de Nesles of machine guns and at one-fifteen in the afternoon a gas detachment from the 165th Infantry fired phosphorus bombs on Bois Brulé and machine gun nests to the eastward."[35]

Van S. Merle-Smith, acting commander of McKenna's Shamrock Battalion, had been snatched up by McCoy to direct artillery forces in where to drop their shells—from Leach's field unit to the big guns at corps. As an infantryman wounded on the heights above the Ourcq, Merle-Smith was physically unfit to lead men on the field. The wound he had suffered a few days earlier had left his arm sore, swollen, and utterly useless. Before being ordered to McCoy's command post, he had believed that his "life seemed to be charmed throughout however, though I was rather afraid to get wounded for fear the Battalion would go to pieces at seeing a second battalion C.O. wounded or killed. They were pretty nearly done out, because so tired and worn."[36]

The regiment's headquarters was in the cellar of the château at Villers-sur-Fère, and day and night it was under endless bombardment. Here the colonel and his staff toiled like trolls. "I wish you could have seen us," Merle-Smith wrote. "A dozen men working frantically on everything under the sun; three telephones going all at once all the time, and all being reported at once into my ears or the Colonel's, and all the while feverishly working our co-ordinates of targets for one battery here, another there, or 37 m.m. guns at this place, and big Army corps guns way in the rear on some wagon train just reported coming along a certain road—perhaps a mile behind these lines; working out the speed of the wagon train, for all these guns feed at points on the map." Three bombs hit the château, but the damage above failed to bother the men below. The whole time, Merle-Smith directed artillery fire, hoping that the coordinates he gave would not be where his own men were. He noticed with "astonishment" how quickly his arm healed even though the doctors made "dire prophecies." He wrote, "I fooled them."

The battle stretched into another day, with the Rainbows holding their positions, and the enemy, weakened and equally worn out, began to slack off. The change was noticeable.

"I had no more than 1-1/2 or 2 hours sleep all the night," Donovan wrote. "I had no one in command of the Companies, only 2d Lieutenants and it was a real test to keep these youngsters, who were game, but nervous, up to their jobs and make everyone feel that no matter how bad everything looked, we were going to hold on." Then at two-thirty in the morning of 2 August, the Third Battalion took over. "At 3 o'c I lay on the ground and slept a very refreshing sleep until 6 o'c when the Lieut-Colonel awakened me, and announced that the Germans had pulled out."[37]

20

"I Have Been Very Happy in Command of the Regiment"

The fight to take the northern heights of the Ourcq River was far from over. For the hungry, bone-weary, and blood-ied Forty-second Division there was more to do. One of the original orders had been not to let the enemy get away; the great chase was on.

The chase went on without Wild Bill Donovan's men of the First Battalion, their days and nights of fighting over. On the blood-soaked hillside, the doughboys searched for their own dead. "We found 5 Germans for everyone of us," Donovan observed. At each body they stuck a rifle into the ground, bayonet first, to let burial parties see that here was a dead American. When the task ended, Donovan's troops paused to look over the valley, each man won-dering how they had done it—fought so long, so hard, and with-out any thought of giving up. To Ruth, he wrote, "We marched back . . . thru the old farm we had taken, crossed the stream we had crossed some days before, and not a sound from the men."[1]

The morning was misted in a light, gray rain when they came down off the hills. Along the road leading into Villers-sur-Fère, Illi-nois soldiers from the 149th Field Artillery stood by, saying not a word to the New Yorkers. Charles MacArthur, from the 149th, never forgot what he saw. "They had flung all unnecessary equipment aside, preserving rifles, rations, and a single blanket apiece. They looked like wash-women, each with a blanket over his head, shawl style, with sodden poppies in their hats. Ordinarily we mixed with New York on sight and swapped experiences like monkeys, but it was no time for jabber now. The backs of our eyeballs were coated."

MacArthur recalled how, as they trooped by, an Irish sergeant said in "comforting confidence," "Stick wid us, Hunert an' Forty-nine!"[2]

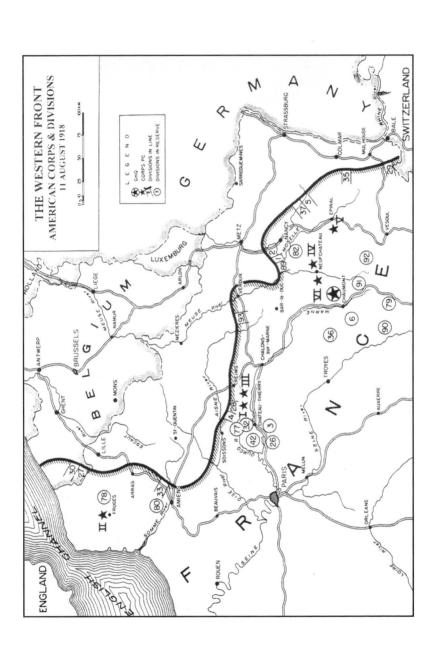

The Western Front

Adapted from *United States Army in the World War; 1917–1919: Military Operations; Vol. 9* (Center of Military History, U.S. Army: Washington, 1990).

Hobbling along with his men was Tom Reilley, the six-four, two-hundred-sixty-five-pound captain who had been hit in the legs by shrapnel. Overcome by the events of the last few days, he thought about what they had just been through and tried to express his emotions to his father by describing the situation.

The advance along miles of front with shrapnel cracking overhead; the boom of the big stuff blowing the mortal remains of those it hits to the four winds; the spiteful crackling of the machine guns from wooded slopes or wheat fields crowning the crests overlooking meandering streams called rivers in France—but where the rivers of blood flow more freely than the streams of water; the steady advance of men upstanding against the various engines of destruction; the smitten men, the closing up and steady press forward; the foolhardy, but brave doings of men who rose to their feet to fire from the shoulder at machine guns 100 yards away, because they could not see from a prone position; the taking up of quarters in a shell hole twenty-five yards above them on a hillside; the gazing down into the livid faces of a half platoon where the machine guns had cut them down, each and every one fallen forward with rifle and automatic rifle still held in the position of firing, with their death masks glaring in the lurid sunlight—bathing the side of the hill.[3]

With Father John Hanley, the only other Catholic chaplain in the regiment, in the hospital, Father Francis Duffy felt as if he would collapse. Fatigue crept into his bones. In his gaunt face his dark eyes seemed sunken. He still smiled, not a surface smile, as one reporter explained, "but a real sincere smile that spreads from the heart out. It lights up his smooth, rugged face like a spot on a dark stage."

"Never mind how Father Duffy looks," a doughboy told the reporter. "All we remember is how he came running down . . . during these last fateful minutes before zero hour, his hands and pockets full of cigarettes. The five minutes before zero seem to the fellows waiting there with their bayonets fixed for Jerry like five centuries. Some of the boys are gloomy, some are half hysterical, some tense, some fidgety. If you could only jump over and get it out of your system! That's where the Father gets in his wallop. Along he comes, shoves you a cigarette, grips your hand, gives you a slap on the shoulder and an earnest 'Go get 'em boys.' You never taste the smoke. Too nervous. A couple of drags and it is gone. But it helps; gee, how it does help! So does Father's 'Go get 'em,' because you know he is going over the top with you."[4]

It was the chore that came when the fighting ended that the weary chaplain dreaded—burying the dead. He called it a "heart-breaking task . . . hard for everybody, but particularly I think for myself, because I knew these men so well and loved them as if they were my younger brothers."[5]

McCoy kept an eye on his chaplain as he buried the dead, believing he was on the verge of a nervous breakdown. When the priest had finished, the colonel went to the wounded Maj. George Lawrence and ordered his chief surgeon to forcibly put Duffy into a car and send him away for a rest. Then he wrote to Dan Brady, the brother of Diamond Jim. Dan had charge of the Fund to Benefit the 165th Infantry. Duffy desperately needed rest, he informed him, "after weeks of constant strain and night and day work amongst the men, with all his wonderful self into it, whether in the hospital under heavy fire, or in the trenches. He has looked after the wounded and dying and buried all our dead. During the last day on the battle-field, he held a memorial service for our dead warriors, brought tears of remembrance to our eyes, and then preached a noble sermon which sent us off in such fighting spirit that our General, who reviewed us shortly after, allowed that the Regiment looked as though it was marching to a fight instead of coming out from one."[6]

It was a good thing that Duffy's ministering to the dead and wounded had kept him from the château at Villers-sur-Fère when the commanding general of the Fourth Division, George Cameron, arrived. Cameron's fresh division was leapfrogging the Rainbows to go after the Germans. It was "dark, wet and disagreeable," and, when Cameron saw a wagon train stopped in the yard behind the château, he jumped all over the men tending the animals, assuming a general's god-like impunity. Overhearing him berate those drained soldiers who had just come out of battle, B Company's Pfc. Jim Gilhooey blew his Irish top.

"This is a hell of note," he growled. "We go and capture this place, and you guys come and live in it."

Cameron turned on the New Yorker, rebuking him by saying there were enough damn flies in the yard without bringing in a lot animals.

"Flies is it?" Gilhooey shot back. "If it is flies you want, go up on the hillside and you'll will see thousands of them feasting on the blood of our men!"

Donovan, who had witnessed the heated exchange, was satisfied that afterward Cameron kept his mouth shut and the train stayed where it was.

That night, Pvt. Mike Ragniny, a "kind of scullery maid to John Kayes," left the darkness of the wagons and approached Donovan. He said he had heard rumors that Wild Bill had been killed. "I wouldn't believe it, Major," he said, "I wouldn't believe it. I took my rosary beads and went out behind a tree and prayed for you and then I heard you had only been wounded."

The thought of Ragniny praying for him touched Donovan. "All devotion has not gone out of the world," he wrote.[7]

The casualty figures for the 165th Infantry were staggering. Of the more than three thousand combat troops in the regiment, fourteen officers and more than two hundred fifty men had been killed, close to twelve hundred wounded and another one hundred fifty missing.[8] Total losses mounted to nearly sixteen hundred. When Duffy sat down to write his book he attempted to mention every soldier who had fallen in the crossing of the Ourcq. The Forty-second Division, from 25 July through 5 August, when the battle was officially over, suffered 763 men killed, 2,713 wounded, another 896 gassed, bringing the total to 4,372 casualties.[9] As for the New Yorkers, their dead and wounded accounted for more than one-third the total for the entire division, a strikingly high number when all four regiments are added in along with the other units, including artillery.

Charles Carman of Rockaway Beach learned of the death of his friend, Danny O'Connell, days after that sergeant had been shot. Carman wrote home, "After we were relieved I was out in charge of a burying detail and we buried both American and German dead. The bodies had been laying there for several days, and God! It was the hardest detail I ever had, or ever hope to get." He had been digging graves when he heard that Danny was dead. "The news sent me into the blues and made me long for the end of the cruel war. If I had been the one to have found him while I was on one of the burying details, I don't think I could have finished my work for the day. The poor kid is now, God grant, in heaven and at peace."[10]

In a letter to Danny's mother, Duffy tried to comfort her.

His death was sudden, but not unprepared for. He had faced it steadfastly since first he enlisted for this service; he prepared himself for it religiously by making his peace with God; and he met it with a high and gallant spirit.

I buried him on the field where he fell—his fittest resting place. The cross marks his grave, and the place is properly recorded. May God grant peace and rest to his dear and noble soul—and comfort and help to hearts that mourn his loss.[11]

Basil Elmer collected the personal belongings of Oliver Ames to send home to his widow. As he sorted through them, besides many photographs of her, he found the cablegram telling Ames of the birth of their daughter. "I miss Ollie Ames even more than I imagined I would," Elmer told his parents. "I have the things that he had in his pocket when he was killed." He wrote that Ollie had gotten up just as the bombardment had started and said, "Come on men! Keep cool! We aren't going to lose a man." "But we did," Elmer added. "He was a man, a soldier, and my best friend; and he has done the noblest thing that any man can do." He described Kilmer's grave. "He and Joyce Kilmer are buried side by side at the edge of a pretty wood near a brook." On his cross were the words, "A kindly gentleman and a true soldier."[12]

Hearing that his colleague from the *New York Times* had fallen in battle, Sgt. Alexander Woollcott—now a reporter for *The Stars & Stripes*—and Grantland Rice, the sportswriter, made a pilgrimage to Kilmer's grave. On a sloping meadow above the Ourcq, Woollcott, in the name of all Timesmen, placed a cypress sprig on the grave.

"He lies buried beside Lieutenant Oliver Ames at the edge of a little copse that is known as the Wood of the Burned Bridge, so close to the purling Ourcq that, standing by the graveside, you could throw a pebble into its waters. Straight to the north, perhaps ten minutes walk up the unforgettable hill, lies what is left of Seringes, the tragic, half-obliterated village that Yankee troops captured the night before Kilmer was killed."[13]

Like Charles MacArthur, Woollcott had stood near Villers-sur-Fère when many of the soldiers were recrossing the Ourcq after being relieved. "I was with them in the woods the day they came out of the line to catch their breaths, and the news of Kilmer's death greeted me at every turn. The Captain under whom he had been serving for several months, the Major at whose side he fell, stray cooks, doughboy runners—all shook their heads sorrowfully and talked among themselves of what a good soldier he had been and what an infinite pity it was that the bullet had to single him out."

There was little to remind Woollcott that the war was still going on, except, he wrote, for the "boom of the cannon heard faintly from the direction of the Vesle and there on the horizon the sentinel balloons swaying ever so slightly in the wind."

In Litchfield, Connecticut, in her utter grief, Joyce Kilmer's mother, Annie, took out a little service flag that Joyce had given her before sailing for France. In the center was a tiny blue star. She felt she ought to place the flag on a bow of black ribbon. As she did so, she swore, she saw the blue star turn to gold.[14]

The dead and the wounded continued to pile up as the division took after the Germans, now retreating to the Vesle. One of the battalions leading the chase was the Shamrocks, led by M Company, commanded by Capt. Martin Meaney, whose battalion cry now was "Remember McKenna!" According to Duffy, Douglas MacArthur had asked if the 165th Infantry was ready to pursue the enemy, because he had been informed that the other regiments claimed to be "too fatigued." The general had said, "It's up to you, McCoy!" The colonel had turned to Meaney. "My men are few and they are tired, sir," Meaney had said, "but they are willing to go anywhere they are ordered, and they will consider an order to advance as a compliment."

"By God," MacArthur snapped back, "it takes the Irish when you want a hard thing done!"[15]

Van S. Merle-Smith, taken off the front lines because of his wounds, thrilled at the way his old Third Battalion, after its brief and insufficient rest, chased the Germans—especially because, back at McCoy's command post, he was directing the regiment's advance.

Well, at last the Boche weakened and we swept over their positions and across country. We went after them pell mell, though almost in our sleep. It was some sight—the Boche ahead of us blowing up ammunition dumps, houses, supplies and everything. The whole sky lit by a thousand volcanoes; infantry filing after them as fast as they could go; artillery coming up from the rear along the roads at a gallop; ammunition and supply trains without end, with sweating mules and cursing drivers filling every gap which wasn't

At Billigny on 7 September, cook J. A. Miller of Headquarters Company prepares stew for his men. *Signal Corps/National Archives*

filled with something else; mounted messengers galloping on horses nearly dead; hither and thither, men on foot and in reel carts stringing wire which the next moment was broken by an enemy shell or a charging battery and everything lit up by the flashes of the guns, flares and the explosion of ammunition dumps.[16]

In one of his daily reports General MacArthur wrote how the Forty-second, in eight days of battle, had "forced the passage of the Ourcq, taken prisoners from six enemy divisions, met, routed, decimated a crack division of the Prussian Guard, a Bavarian Division and one other division, and driven back the enemy's line for 16 kilometers."[17]

Donovan was not as giddy as MacArthur. As far as he could tell, the Germans had not given up much territory. The crafty enemy had withdrawn to the Vesle and could easily withdraw further, to the Aisne, and there "be ready for another blow." If he felt good about one thing it was the fact that the Ourcq served as a "very severe blow to his [the enemy's] morale."

Donovan was proud that he had been part of "holding off the Dutchmen at Champagne and now drove them back." Then he confessed to Ruth of the pressure he had been under. "Lack of sleep and the strain has pulled me down, but I feel pretty good. I think the Colonel and others thought I would crack under the strain, but the regular life behind me, and the athletic training have certainly been worth while. No one should get into this fight who hasn't the physical endurance and stamina. Courage is the smallest part of it."[18]

By 6 August, McCoy had had another "hump of sleep," as he liked to call it, able to get such rest because the Forty-second, after "pushing on the heels of the Boche," had been ordered to halt "while a fresh division marched through us."

McCoy, Merle-Smith, Elmer, and other headquarters men were up front in a thick forest, directing artillery fire on the retreating Germans. The night was aglow with fire and flames, burning ammunition dumps, Very lights, and shells screeching overhead. The French, advancing toward Soissons, sent up flares, signaling a barrage. The 165th was attempting to hit a nearby machine-gun nest. At that instant the brigade adjutant walked in with relief orders. "All my men dropped down and slept like tired dogs," McCoy wrote. Then he and Elmer went to the northern edge of the forest and stood watching "the great war" until the relieving force had marched through.[19]

Their relief meant that the Rainbows were on the move again, headed from one town to another, resting here, rebuilding there, and training thousands of green replacements. They went to Le Ferte-sous-Jourre, then on to Bourmont Haute-Marne, which was part of the American Expeditionary Forces training areas around their old stamping grounds of Rolampont. Bourmont lay fifty miles south of St. Mihiel, a village of ten thousand that served as the center of a sixteen-mile deep salient that had been in German hands for almost four years and that, like a menacing fighter with his chin jutting out, dared all to hit it.

McCoy found billets in the home of a war widow, but after a few days struck out for Paris with Donovan. They visited the city's famous sights, dined, and shopped. In fact, when they first reached Paris they enjoyed the sights so much they never stopped at a hotel. "[We] drove right through along the Seine up the Champs Elysée and through the Bois returning on the Boulevards and enjoying the passing throng and meeting of many friends." One night, McCoy deserted Donovan to dine with friends. As a senior aide to the former president, he knew the entire Roosevelt family. Now in

Paris, he enjoyed dinner with the Colonel's son, Ted Jr., who was recovering from a nasty wound, and his wife, Eleanor. On the way to the city he had made sure to visit the grave of Ted's brother, Quentin. McCoy wrote that he had "enclosed and marked it properly, so that I was able to assure them of this and to tell them he was buried in a charming hillside beside the fallen avion."[20]

McCoy also took time to write to Col. John Barker in Washington, the commander he had replaced as head of the 165th. He wanted to tell him of the heroics of the men he had been in charge of, if for only a short time. "It will give you proper pride to know that the Regiment led the attack over the Ourcq and stayed in the lead throughout very fierce fighting until the Boche were back of the Vesle." He listed the killed, including Jim McKenna, and all the wounded officers. "Like you," he continued, "I have been very happy in command of the Regiment, and of course now have a very great pride in the whole lot. We have been well handled and well armed, equipped and supplied, and only suffered the punishment and hardships of some great battles. We are now near our old training area, building up and waiting for the wounded to return and replacements to come." He closed with the words, "I hope you will see some of the good officers, who have been rewarded by being sent home and promoted, such as McAdie, Martin, Pratt and McNamara, so that you can get first-hand information about your friends here, all of whom send their best wishes."[21]

In Bourmont, the Forty-second Division endured major changes.

The first was the news that Gen. John Pershing's First American Army had been organized at last. The Rainbows became part of Pershing's new army and were folded into the IV Corps, led by Lt. Gen. Joseph Dickman, along with the Eighty-ninth Division and the First Division, now under Maj. Gen. Charles Summerall, a former artillery brigade commander of the Forty-second soon to be detested by every New York soldier.

In a leadership change at the top, MacArthur took control of the Eighty-fourth Brigade, replacing Brig. Gen. Robert Brown, whose hesitancy on the banks of the Ourcq had likely cost him his post.

McCoy received a promotion to brigadier general and, in a heart-wrenching move, was sent off to direct the Army Transport Service. It was "bitter medicine" for him to "gulp"[22] because at the moment of great victory, he had to leave the regiment he had grown so fond of. His loss soon left a void. "He has been with us less than four months," Duffy wrote in his diary. "Yet I feel as if I had known him for forty years, and this war is going to be a different sort of thing for me lacking his presence."[23] For Duffy himself, there was a change, as well. He was promoted to major.

Donovan moved up to lieutenant colonel. The odds favored him to succeed McCoy as the regiment's sixth commander since 1916, when it had entrained for the Mexican border. But Donovan did not want the post, and said so to his chaplain, who in his heart had long wished for his friend to get the job. "Oh, Hell, Father," Wild Bill admitted, "I don't want to be Colonel. As Lieutenant Colonel I can get into the fight and that's what I'm here for."

With Donovan declining to take over the 165th, the other logical choice was Lt. Col. Harry Mitchell, who had been McCoy's second in command throughout the terrible fighting from Champagne to the Ourcq. With McCoy pushing for him, Mitchell, a gentle, modest soldier, got the job.[24]

Elmer was sent to division headquarters to work in Intelligence. It was a desk job away from the front lines, and it pained him. "My conscience hurts me," he wrote. "So many of my good friends who were in the line, buried! It doesn't seem right! And yet someone, I suppose, must do this mahogany desk work." He tried to reason with himself that the change was okay. "But I had the experience of commanding a Company in an attack, making sixteen kilometers in eight days, which is something." Although his new work was interesting, he added, "But I am not very proud of this bullet-proof stuff."[25]

Duffy was off for his rest. He freely admitted that McCoy, along with Major Lawrence and Donovan, had had "to lay down the law" and send him to the hospital in Vittel. Even Brig. Gen. Michael Lenihan had gotten into the act, providing his own car to carry the chaplain away. While resting, the chaplain wrote to McCoy. He told him that he was getting along so well that he had finally gotten up and put on his uniform and "celebrated the event piously by going to mass—and put one over on the doctors by taking a little stroll in the park afterwards. Not too brash, though. It takes a little while to persuade me I am not so top notch, but even a philosopher like myself can feel the force of an argument when it knocks him down."[26]

While Duffy was away he could not leave his men without an able substitute. He asked for, and got, Father George Carpentier

from the 117th Sanitary Train. He said to Carpentier, "Your name
is French but it has the advantage of being the one French name
that is best known and most admired by our bunch of pugilists."[27]
Duffy referred to the great French prizefighter, Georges Carpentier.
Like Hanley, Carpentier came from Ohio. And like Duffy, he had
been a teacher, teaching at Aquinas College High School in
Columbus. He had enlisted in February 1918 and been assigned
to the Eighty-third Brigade. On 26 July, for action in Château-
Thierry, he earned the Distinguished Service Cross. When Duffy
returned to his post, he used his new authority as a major and the
division's senior chaplain to reassign Carpentier to the 166th Infantry, a natural place for him since both he and the regiment
were from Ohio.

When Duffy returned from his rest he learned that he, too, had
been recommended for the Distinguished Service Cross. He knew
who had recommended him for both honors, and when the time
was right, he wrote to McCoy. "Major Duffy, proud wearer of the
D.S.C., writes to thank the source of his new rank and honors. And
you kept it a secret. . . . I never once thought of myself as a possible recipient. But I was delighted to receive it whether I deserve
it or not. And because you thought I earned it, I'll wear it with a
prideful right." Whimsically, he continued. "When we get back I
wish you would have me made archbishop and I'll be entitled to a
tomb in St. Patrick's Cathedral. The only drawback is that I shall
begin to feel I am too important a person to risk being shot." He
signed the letter, "Chaplain Major Francis P. Duffy, D.S.C., Chaplain, 165 Inf."[28]

A mong the replacements was 2nd Lt. J. Phelps Harding, assigned
to the Third Battalion as its liaison officer. A 1916 Cornell
University graduate, Harding had close ties to Burlington,
Vermont, where his parents lived. He had enlisted in the Marine
Corps in August 1917 but transferred out to attend the Army officers' training camp. After his commission he had been sent to
Paris and there had learned that he was going to Villers-sur-Fère
to join the 165th Infantry, then fighting on the Ourcq. When he
arrived, the battle was over and the soldiers were returning. The
new officer had been thrust into the heart of war on a battlefield
still smoldering like a fire that was almost out, but could flame
back to life at any second.

"My company came out of the fight with a 2nd. Lieutenant in
command; another company was led by a sergeant," he wrote to his

father. "It was a case of taking strong machine gun positions across open country, up hill, without cover, and under fire from not only machine guns, but artillery and aeroplanes as well. It is a wonder that any men came out alive—but they drove the Huns back."[29]

Harding's first duty had been to censor soldiers' letters. "The men were pretty tired, and of course they felt the loss of their comrades. I realized this latter point best when censoring their letters. It is mighty hard for a boy to write home to his mother and tell her that his brother has been killed. I read two such letters in the first batch I censored. Each writer tried to tell how painless the death was, and how bravely the brother met it—but in each case I imagine the mother will think only of her loss, and not of the fact that her boy died a true American."

When the regiment reached its first rest area, the lieutenant felt a "million miles from the war" and noticed that for the veterans of Champagne and the Ourcq "the camp is a virtual paradise." When the 165th settled into Bourmont he was told the training would last a month, until mid-September at least. The training involved "hard, intensive drilling," he wrote, "not only close order but in stack formations and it is no easy matter to be a father to sixty men."

As he trained alongside his men he saw them change as they began to recover from their last two confrontations with the Germans. "They are showing many more signs of life. . . . Yesterday my platoon sang on its way back from drill—it is the first singing I have heard in the battalion. I consider this a mighty cheerful sign."

On 24 August he wrote, "Naturally, we are all wondering what is planned for us after we leave here. All sorts of rumors are afloat."[30]

Duffy, since his return to Bourmont after a "nice lazy week of it in Vittel," had had an ear tuned to the rumor mill. And the biggest rumor was of another great Allied offensive planned for the St. Mihiel salient.

"If it is a secret," he put in his diary, "all the world seems to know it."[31]

21

"Not a Fight, But a Promenade"

T he real fight over the St. Mihiel salient took place behind the lines, in Bombon and Chaumont—in a battle of wills between the supreme commander of the Allied forces, Ferdinand Foch, and a general without an army, John Pershing. Since the day he had landed in Europe in June 1917, Pershing had taken on prime ministers, premiers, and a king in his fight to mold an all-American army. After three years of slaughter, France and England had been bled dry of most of their manpower. They did not want a U.S. army—just the strength of a million American doughboys. Pershing had brushed aside their demands. Staring down Foch, he said, "The time may come when the American Army will have to stand the brunt of this war, and it is not wise to fritter away our resources. . . . It would be a grave mistake to give up the idea of building an American army."[1]

Foch gave in, and as the Forty-second Division knocked the Germans off the northern heights of the Ourcq River, Pershing got his army—the largest American force since the Civil War. He had taken command on 10 August. Now he wanted to show the world it could fight—and the place to do so was St. Mihiel.

"It was certain," he explained, "that the psychological effect on the enemy of success in this first operation by the American Army, as well as on the Allies, our own troops, and our people at home, would be of signal importance."[2]

The St. Mihiel salient jutted out of the Hindenburg Line between the Meuse and the Moselle Rivers like a dagger aimed at the heart of Paris. The Germans had held it for four years. Twice the French had tried and failed to recapture it. Strategically, it protected the huge railroad center at Metz, a fortress city twenty-five miles to the northeast. It interrupted the great rail line that

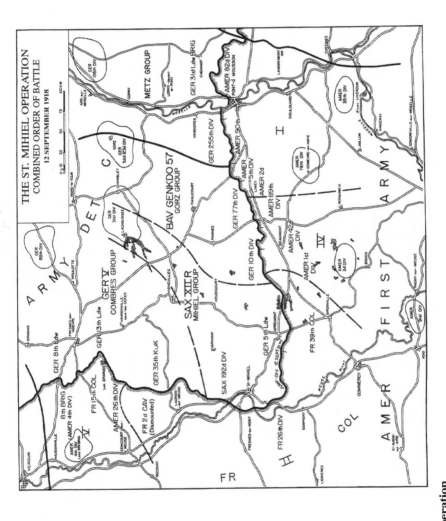

The St. Mihiel Operation

Adapted from *United States Army in the World War, 1917–1919: Military Operations; Vol. 8* (Center of Military History, U.S. Army: Washington, 1990).

connected Paris to the vital iron mines and coalfields in the industrial Saar region—sources of raw materials desperately needed by
France as well as Germany. For several years St. Mihiel had slipped
into being a quiet sector. The troops there, mostly Austrians,
Bavarians, Saxons, and Hungarians, had grown complacent. Not
among Germany's crack units, they had settled down and, after
herding away most of the Frenchmen of fighting age, lived with
their families, even marrying into them and starting their own
families. Still, the St. Mihiel salient remained strongly fortified,
with deep trenches and rock-solid artillery bunkers. At its
southwesternmost point, the two-hundred-fifty square-mile salient,
a triangle rather than a square, overlooked the Meuse River from
high, wooded bluffs. Further back, as the salient widened out, it
reached a flat section of land called the Woevre Plain. Covered
with more woods, as well as streams, lakes, and small villages, in
the rainy season it mushed into a swampy morass. The rainy season
usually started in mid-September. And when it got wet the roads
turned impassable.

It had been decided almost a year earlier that when an American
army finally became a reality, a punch at the St. Mihiel salient
would be its first offensive. Pershing drew up a plan for taking
St. Mihiel, and on 24 July he went over it with Foch and got his
blessing. It was simple: the French would demonstrate in front of
the salient while the Americans would attack its flanks. Hunter
Liggett's First Corps and Joseph Dickman's Fourth Corps would
launch the main attack, at the eastern flank.

It was all set: Pershing was ready. His army was ready. Troops
were rolling in from all over France—well over a half a million
enlisted men, five hundred officers, and a brigade full of tanks.
They would bust through the salient for old Black Jack, and he
would march them right up to the Hindenburg Line itself, take it,
and show off the fighting spirit of the American doughboy.

Then Foch had a change of heart. When the Allies had stopped
Germany's July offensive and counterattacked successfully, driving
the enemy north of the Vesle and then the Aisne, he had realized
that a grand assault along the entire Hindenburg Line by Belgium,
English, French, and American armies could bring Ludendorff
to his knees and end the war. And there was no time to lose. The
attack had to get under way before the end of September. He had
envisioned a combined Franco-American force moving into the

Meuse-Argonne valley, followed by the British First and Third
Armies, which would snatch Cambrai; the Belgians pushing eastward from the North Sea to Lys; and the British Fourth Army,
supported by the French First Army, storming the Hindenburg Line
between Cambrai and St. Quentin.

But a hold up at St. Mihiel might keep Pershing's forces from
joining the French in driving the Germans out of the Meuse-
Argonne. The supreme commander refused to take that risk. Foch
wanted a scaled back attack on St. Mihiel. Limiting it to just the
eastern flank would still give Pershing what he wanted—a chance
to show off America's might. Afterward, Foch would peel off several of Pershing's divisions and move them west so they would be
ready to fight alongside the French in the Argonne. The remain-
ing army would move into the Champagne sector to join Gen.
Henri Gouraud's Fourth Army. Foch threatened to abandon the
St. Mihiel operation altogether if Pershing balked at his plan.

But the obstinate American general was not about to let Foch
divide up his First Army. Pershing barked back, "Marshal Foch,
you may insist all you please, but I decline absolutely to agree with
your plan. While our army will fight wherever you may decide, it
will not fight except as an independent American army." He added
that his army "must be employed as a whole, either east of the
Argonne or west of the Argonne, and not four or five divisions here
and six or seven there."[3]

A "very pale" Foch acquiesced.[4] Pershing's army would not
be divided and the assault on St. Mihiel would go ahead, commencing 10 September (in actuality there was a forty-eight hour
delay until 12 September), before the rains came and the Woevre
Plain was awash in mud. However, it would be the limited offensive that Foch wanted. The generalissimo had set the dates of the
grand assault, and the start was the 25th, with the Americans leading the way. Thus, when Pershing had finished with St. Mihiel, he
was to move his army up the Meuse with great speed to where,
with the French Fourth Army in support, it would attack through
the Argonne Forest.[5]

The plans for the taking of St. Mihiel were meticulous; one
historian called them "beautifully done."[6] They still called for
the French to "exert a gentle pressure on the nose of the salient"[7]
while the Americans pinched off the two flanks. The battle would
then be over—this was all Foch desired, even though Metz would

stay under German control. The French force would include nearly one hundred thousand men while the Americans that Pershing was sending into battle would number more than two hundred thousand. On the eastern flank, one of the corps moving up for the assault would be Dickman's Fourth, which included the Forty-second Division.

Orders received at division headquarters spelled out what was ahead for the Rainbow soldiers. According to field order no. 17, "The 42nd Division will attack in the center and will deliver the main blow in the direction of the heights overlooking the Madine Creek, exerting its main effort east of Maizerais and Essey." The 42nd would not be working alone. The Ninetieth Aero Squadron had been placed at its disposal along with the First Tank Brigade, pieced together by Lt. Col. George Patton. His 327th Tank Battalion went to the Eighty-fourth Brigade while the Eighty-third Brigade received sixty-six French tanks. (Incidentally, Patton's arrival in the war zone brought him close to his old rival for the hand of the beautiful Kate Fowler, Van S. Merle-Smith, now regimental operations officer.)

The sector assigned to the Forty-second was in the center of the First Army—a narrow strip, two miles wide and nine miles long, running north from the village of Seicheprey to St. Benoit. The Rainbows were to capture St. Benoit on the first day of attack "without regard to the progress of neighboring division."[8] On the right flank would be the Eighty-ninth. Its first commander had been Maj. Gen. Leonard Wood, but it was now led by Maj. Gen. William Wright. On the left would be the First. Made up of regular army troops, it had been the first division to reach France in June 1917. Its commander, who had taken over on 15 July, was Rainbow veteran Maj. Gen. Charles Summerall—who at this point had yet to feel the ire of the 165th Infantry.

Two creeks cut across the long hunk of land the Rainbows were to traverse and, because the rainy season had started earlier than usual, these were swollen. The first was the Rupt de Mad, a narrow stream like the Ourcq that twisted and turned in a north-easterly direction and passed through St. Mihiel's sister villages of Maizerais and Essey, division targets. Just north of the Mad, the Madine paralleled the smaller stream on its way to the Moselle River. It flowed through Pannes, another target village. On the Madine's north bank, the land rose up through meadows, lakes, swamps, and thick woods dotted with farms, to St. Benoit.

Beyond St. Benoit stood Hassavant Farm, on the southern fringe of a deep forest. This was the designated goal of the division's push; it would secure the location and go no further.

As Pershing's First Army massed south of the St. Mihiel salient for its assault on the 12th of September, the enemy reduced its forces, not in a helter-skelter withdrawal but in a slow and methodical retreat. The German commanders had originally planned to employ the same strategy Gouraud had used in the Champagne, letting the Americans break through into the Woevre Plain, giving them a false sense of victory, and then striking back with one of Germany's patented counterattacks. The plan was scratched in favor of retreat when they realized the Americans would be coming at them from both sides of the salient.

It later became clear that the Germans' withdrawal had been too slow. They had rolled away the heavy guns first and, two days before Pershing launched his attack, men and supplies were moving north, where the Germans figured to regroup in strength at their rear defense line. But there were still plenty of forces ready to repel the Americans, and not a single officer in Pershing's headquarters expected a cakewalk through the St. Mihiel salient.

But that is what they got.

If the Germans had one ally, it had to be rain. As zero hour approached on the morning of the 12th, it had been raining steadily for several days. Nathaniel Rouse of F Company felt miserable in the march that brought the 165th up to the St. Mihiel salient. Beginning on 7 September his diary is filled with remarks about the horrible weather and conditions.

"We almost got lost, so dark."

"Rain. Walked all night. One of the darkest nights I ever seen. Wet to the skin. Then pitched tents in the mud."

"Walked all night. Rain, a terrible hike on our way to drive on Metz. I hope I get out of this."

"Stopped in woods getting ready for drive. Lots of rain. Great life."

"Rain. Didn't move, put tents up again last night. This is a mud hole."[9]

In the dark and muck and the persistent rain dripping off helmets, Bill Donovan, ready to lead his First Battalion into battle once again, was astonished at the fact that any of the many units assigned to the attack had found their way to the start line.[10]

He described the night thusly: "impenetrably dark—soul-seeking rain."[11]

Behind his battalion, stumbling through the dark forest, came the Machine Gun Company. Cpl. John Flint, along with the other machine gunners, stowed his pack in the woods. "The night was pitch black, good for our move, but hard for the machine gun outfit with mule-drawn gun carts. To get a mule to do anything generally requires a lot of cussing mixed with a club and more or less noise. We finally got our guns and ammunition out of the carts and formed up in the dark and wet for the next command."[12]

In the Shamrock Battalion, Martin Hogan, back from the hospital, felt the forest that closed in on him made the darkness thicker than ever. The spot he waited in was creepy, with "dark, rusty, soaked trees, ragged unkempt and harried by gun fire. No sane man would have claimed it. It was a jumping off place for jungle beasts, evil spirits and head hunters. It was a place to wish on one's worst enemy."[13]

Father Francis Duffy recalled that his men were "encamped in a forest of low trees, a most miserable spot. . . . We were living like paleozoic monsters, in a world of muck and slime." Before the attack he had noted how the rain fell in torrents and "the roads were like a swamp and the night was so dark that a man could not see the one in front of him." In this dispiriting mess he held a silent prayer meeting for the men. He told them how easily they could set themselves right with God, that in a time of danger there was always room for "an extra prayer for a serene mind and a stout heart."[14]

As Donovan waited in the pitch black, broken by artillery flashes, it startled him to see a soldier moving toward him, his patch of snow-white hair bobbing as he came. Donovan smiled when he recognized his old commander, Charles Hine, who had been escorted to his command post by Maj. George Lawrence. On his own, Hine had assigned himself to the 165th as an observer so he could go over the top with his old regiment.

"It was rather pathetic about Colonel Hine," Donovan wrote Frank McCoy. "He had heard of the advance and came up through all the mud and slime of the night, attached himself to my battalion, which was in the advance line, awaited beside me in No Man's Land until 'H' hour, and stuck with us the two days of the fight."[15] To a Rainbow officer he confessed, "I didn't have the heart to refuse so he tagged along."[16]

Several things worried Donovan. For one thing, after the Ourcq, sixty-five percent of his enlisted men were replacements. So were close to seventy-five percent of its officers, such as lieutenants Samuel Sedgwick Swift from Vergennes, Vermont, and Columbus Veach, a full-blooded Choctaw from Durant, Oklahoma. This was another concern—the ethnic composition of the regiment had changed; there were fifty Native Americans among the enlisted replacements. Donovan did not need to worry about Veach because several white soldiers later said they had preferred taking orders from the Indian than from an Irishman. And Wild Bill knew how tough his own job was going to be, and "frankly I never expected to come through." But during the night, as he lay on the ground with Colonel Hine close beside him and the First Army's artillery bombardment blasting German positions, he noticed that there was no return fire. He said to those around him, "The Germans are pulling out."[17]

J. Phelps Harding, one of the new lieutenants, had been troubled also. He had had a morbid premonition and had written to a friend that he had better not expect to hear from him for a while. "There is a good element of chance in the life I will be leading during the next few days—you haven't an extra rabbit foot, have you?" He asked him not to share the letter with anyone or to "hint of anything dangerous coming up, for such items have a way of getting to Mother and of causing her unnecessary worry." He warned his friend that by the time he got the letter he would probably have already read of the battle. "If anything should happen to me you can remember me as taking my share cheerfully and willingly."[18]

Bill Spencer, his wounds from the Ourcq fight pretty much healed and now on the regimental staff, had ordered his brother, in no uncertain terms, to let their mother know that "Not yet am I dead. No German has run a bayonet thru me as yet. . . . I'm coming back sometime—I'm not going to get killed or anything like it."[19]

On the night of the 11th, Rouse entered in his diary, "I wonder if I come through ok."[20]

The morning before the attack, intelligence reports brought into Forty-second Division headquarters showed little enemy activity. Bad weather had obscured troop movement and kept enemy airplanes out of the sky. Smoke from a train had been spotted, but because of poor visibility there was no way to know if it was carrying troops. But two men were seen riding horses near the village of Pannes and seven soldiers crossed a field southeast of Essey while several cars motored west toward the village. By afternoon it had become evident that the Germans were moving back toward Metz. At four in the afternoon a report issued by Charles Menoher's chief of staff stated, "The enemy is rapidly withdrawing and at the present writing is to be seen retreating east of the Bois de Thiaucourt."[21]

However, most of the German Tenth Division was still holed up, waiting for an attack, but not sure when it would come.

Pershing commenced his assault at one the next morning with a heavy bombardment. Four hours later hundreds of thousands of doughboys, supported by tanks and French allies, rushed forward—the first time that an American army had gone on the attack as a single unit since the Civil War.

Behind the 165th Infantry, the 149th Field Artillery had been hammering away since one, and so rapid was their work that Harding likened it to the "firing of six-shooters."[22] When zero

Crossing the Woevre Plain, an Irish-American patrol hunts for German machine-gunners. *Signal Corps/National Archives*

hour hit, one of those artillerymen, Charles MacArthur, thought "the view grand." He watched the long lines of tanks and soldiers push forward behind their rolling barrage, as exploding shells hit barbed wire and other obstacles. "The doughboys were scrambling out of trenches, clicking bayonets into place and yelling obscure things to each other," he wrote. "The lines filled up and trailed abreast of the tanks, which dipped and bobbed like cautious old ladies. They stopped at shell holes and seemed to hesitate. You felt they had left their rubbers home. Then a flash from the turret. A one-pounder into a patch just ahead, and two German machine gunners with their hands in the air."[23]

Tank commander Capt. Ranulf Compton—who had been with the Fifteenth New York, the state's first black National Guard regiment but had then transferred into Patton's outfit—jotted in his diary, "D-DAY." He noted the excellent spirit of the men and how, when the first tanks started out, it was a "scene never to be described with the din and the lights . . . shells and artillery and rifle fire. The tanks went slowly down the hill as it was quite dark, in columns." But soon the tanks hit trouble. "The shell holes were thick, the trenches 8-10-15 feet wide and the iron gabions and wire were continuous."[24]

To Harding, the strange tanks reminded him of "big bugs" as they plowed along "standing on their beam ends at times as they crossed the trenches or unusually bad ground."[25] It seemed to Duffy that the tanks advancing with "our infantry crawl[ed] like iron-clad hippopotomi over the wire in front to make a passage-way." The chaplain saw how many of them "came to grief" at the lip of a trench where, because of the soft ground, a tank would topple in with its "nose in the bottom."[26]

L eading the First Battalion, Donovan shivered in the cold, wind-driven morning as he moved up and down the line, smiling and urging the New Yorkers forward.

"There's nothing to it," he encouraged them. "It will be a regular walk-over. It will not be as bad as some of the cross-country runs I gave in your training period."[27]

Duffy was with Donovan and Hine, and he held his hands over the men, blessing them. And when the time was ready, he said, "Go to it, boys!"[28]

Hine also emboldened the troops, although his tagging along concerned Donovan. A West Point classmate recorded, "He went

The men of the 165th Infantry's B Company dug in near Hassavant Farm, their last objective during the Battle of St. Mihiel. *Signal Corps/National Archives*

over the top at St. Mihiel with the first wave of the men of his old Regiment, and well in advance of the lines." He added a romantic flourish: "The snow white head of their old commanding officer was the plume that beckoned them forward."[29]

Charles Carman of Rockaway Beach, still saddened over the death of Danny O'Connell, wrote how the regiment had "just slammed Fritz another kick in his rear." He continued, "Gee, dad, I sure had some excitement this time alright. I can duck machine gun bullets and shrapnel like an old timer now. . . . This last time it was some feeling to be lying in no man's land listening to a terrific barrage going over. With dawn just breaking, and then the machine guns in back of us as a further barrage, go over the top with nerves tingling and heart pounding, but not one of us thought of turning back and Fritz was on the run from the very start."[30]

Corporal Flint saw the same thing. "We went through that barbed wire, trenches, mud and anything those bologna benders put in our way as if it wasn't there. Once through the barriers we got them in the open and what we did to them was worth looking at." Flint soon became enraged at the "dirty work" of the Huns. They waved white flags while continuing to fire machine gun bullets at the New Yorkers. "I set up my guns and mopped those guys off the landscape after they had killed a couple of our boys. We licked them and kicked them, and played hell generally with them for three days and nights, doing in that time what we were given almost twice as much time to do."[31]

Tom Reilley, a major now at the front of the Third Battalion, was grateful after the fierce fighting at the Ourcq that St. Mihiel proved to be "the softest thing the American boys had in all open fighting in France. We had very well arranged artillery support, many tanks and the supremacy of the air." He called the "affair" a "romp."[32]

But it was not a romp for some boys. The number of killed on the first day reached twenty-four, with Donovan's battalion suffering the greatest number of deaths: eleven. After the battle was over the grim total hit forty-seven.

Rouse, who had wondered the night before if he would survive, had been moving up a grassy slope near a barn when the doors flew open and Germans dashed out, rifles ablaze. A bullet struck Rouse in the head. The bullet actually slammed into his helmet, which, in turn, tore open a vicious wound. Blood poured down his face and into his eyes. Stumbling back toward a dressing station he met another wounded soldier and together, leaning on each other, they made it there on their own. A day later, Rouse wrote in his diary, "Rain again. In the hospital, I never saw such fine people. Red Cross gave us cigarettes and tobacco."[33]

A noon report from the Forty-second's chief of staff revealed how easily the assault had gone. "The troops passed through the enemy's barrage without severe casualties and overcame the resistance of the enemy machine gunner in the forward positions. The advance was continued steadily, tanks accompanying the infantry. Our light batteries fired to the limit of their range to cover the attack and then commenced to advance by echelon. . . . The troops are reported to have advanced with splendid discipline and in fine spirits and our casualties have been comparatively light."[34] Harding took note of the wounded, agreeing that casualties had been light on the first day. "We passed dead men of both armies, but many more Boche than Americans." He had been surprised at the indifference he felt toward the dead, even the Americans. "They seemed a perfectly natural thing to come across, and I felt absolutely no

Waiting for the Battle of St. Mihiel to start, F Company's Nathaniel Rouse wrote in his diary: "I wonder if I come through okay." He took a bullet in the head, but survived. *Courtesy of Rouse Family*

shudder go down my back as I would have had I seen the same thing a year ago. Even the badly wounded seemed perfectly in place."[35]

The division report for the following day told of the continued German retreat, stating that "only small parties of the enemy have been encountered and on the front of this Division the enemy has evidently withdrawn to the so-called Hindenburg Line."[36]

The Germans that had stayed behind to fight surrendered in the thousands.

"For six hours we kept going over ground at a reckless clip before we saw the first group of prisoners dragging its way over a hill in front of us," Hogan remembered. "There were enough of these to constitute a standard American company. At this point the prisoners began dribbling in on all sides in knots, groups, platoons, battalions."[37]

Harding observed how fast they threw up their hands. "Before we had gone far prisoners began to come in, first by twos and threes, then by platoons and companies. We took 13,000 Boche that day."[38]

Donovan was surprised at how the Germans quit fighting. He and his men swam across the Rupt de Mad, about six feet deep, to get to the village of Maizerais. There he captured a lieutenant, forty men, one *minenwerfer*, and four machine guns. Then Germans came forward "in droves"; Donovan could not keep track of them. "[We] gave them a kick in the back and sent them on their way," he told an officer. "They went willingly and gladly."[39] Afterward he wrote McCoy. "We took so many prisoners that we lost account of them and let them drift back of their own accord, and no one seemed to mind that other units got the credit for them."[40]

Duffy felt that the prisoner roundup had taken on the atmosphere of a county fair. American soldiers drifted in from everywhere to see the prisoners, most of them Austrians from the Tenth Division. "Americans literally swarmed around the prisoners in idle curiosity while others rummaged through the German billets and headquarters looking for pistols, maps, German post-cards and letters—anything that would do for a souvenir."[41] MacArthur and men from the 149th Field Artillery climbed onto their guns and snapped wisecracks at the prisoners, "kidding the pants off them for being such mamma's boys. Whole regiments had surrendered at once and now they trooped by, waving sheets of American propaganda." In his memoir of the war, MacArthur explained that American aviators had dropped pamphlets on the salient. "In them the hungry Heinies were promised everything but the White House if they would quit clowning around and surrender." The artillerymen frisked a number of Germans, hoping to find a bottle or two of schnapps.[42]

The frisking of prisoners rankled Donovan, and he fumed because the fight had not been so difficult and discipline among the men from other units fell away after the attack. "I was the ranking officer of the entire Division on the front line and I went cursing up and down the line getting men into position. One tried to assert his rights as an American citizen, but I physically convinced him that his only right was to keep up forward."[43]

Spencer wrote to his brother about the "feeble resistance." Watching the attack through open country from a hilltop, he had literally trembled with excitement. Through field glasses he saw the artillery barrage move forward and troops and tanks move behind it. "We had taken the Boches unawares—they gave up in bunches and it was interesting to study them as they came by— young and old, but all happy."[44]

Spencer then came down off the hill and joined the assault. "I must confess I was shaky at first, having been out of things for two months almost, but it was all right after a time, and the shells and machine gun bullets didn't worry me much." To his mother he said the "scrap" had been an "excellent one—over in three

Private Sweeney (far left, first name unknown) and fellow doughboys demonstrate how he captured four Germans. *Signal Corps/National Archives*

days, and more of a picnic than anything." He boasted that "nothing could stop the boys."[45]

Donovan crowed, "Our little adventure was not a fight, but a promenade."[46]

As the New Yorkers moved into the villages that had been held for almost four years by the Germans, they were overcome by the outpouring of joy from the newly freed citizens. Regimental color sergeant, twenty-four-year-old Bill Sheahan, a native of County Limerick, was taken aback at the condition of the French women and children. To him they looked like they had "suffered considerably from torture and starvation." When they realized they were no longer held in captivity they broke down and wept. "They were so happy that when certain members of our regiment, one whose name is Patsy Flanagan, of the band, that they threw their arms around their necks and kissed them. It was the last place in the world to expect a kiss in 'No man's Land'."[47] One grateful family presented a bouquet of flowers to Colonel Hine.

Donovan took lodging in a house where the woman who lived there had had to endure four years as a slave to German officers. She had prepared their meals, cleaned their clothes, made their beds, and slept in the cellar. "This night after she fed us she put on her best waist and skirt and went out to visit her neighbors."[48]

Once the soldiers felt safe in the villages they went off in search of food and souvenirs. Sheahan fell in with some pals from the band, hoping to find sugar or "other sweet comestibles, as they like to partake of some sweet stuff to help the music sound sweet anyway. Instead of finding sweet stuff, we found barrels of sauerkraut."[49]

Spencer poked his head inside a dugout and his hungry eyes lighted on a loaf of brown bread, jam, crackers, corned beef, and the sugar that had eluded Sheahan and his pals. "Couldn't want much more. We had a most excellent breakfast." The bread was "heavy as lead."[50]

Harding and his friends located "some good Boche cigars, and some of the men enjoyed a smoke during the next advance."[51]

Donovan and Grayson Murphy, division operations officer, came across a bottle of champagne, cracked it open, and were drinking it when another officer barged in on them. "Wouldn't you know it," he said. "It'd take a couple of Irishmen to find a bottle of champagne in the middle of a battlefield."[52]

Col. Charles Hine, who tagged along with his old regiment during the attack on the St. Mihiel salient, is offered a bouquet of flowers from grateful French citizens just after the Rainbow Division freed their village. *Signal Corps/ National Archives*

The bottle of champagne had probably been found in St. Benoit, the goal of the 165th. When Donovan took his battalion inside the village walls, it was on the heels of a German corps commander. The officer had been on a looting spree and, Donovan admitted, "[although we] could not quite get him, he left a lot of beautiful paintings, porcelains and furniture in the court-yard of the chateau."[53]

In the meantime, a doughboy came across a horse grazing in a field. "So I says to myself here is where I get a fine ride and it was a pretty big field, so I mounted the horse and had the dandiest ride I ever had when on comes an American officer and he said to me, 'What the H____ are you doing?' I told him I wanted to know how it felt to be on a German horse. He said to me; 'When you get through give me a chance to find out.' I got off the horse after having a fine ride and on the officer leapt. No sooner did he do so than the horse started to kick and jump like H____. Well, Pa, I didn't stop laughing for a full hour."[54]

Sheahan and his musical cronies never found any sweets, but they found enough water to clean themselves off and a large house to bed down in. They located spotless linens and women's nightshirts and petticoats. That night they stripped off their filthy uniforms and put on the clean women's garments and then flopped into beds or on the floor. They had just dozed off when a shell landed in the courtyard, killing several mules. "None of us asked the others what we should do, but grabbed our clothes and took off for the dugout that was supposed to be shell proof. Crossing to the dugout the moon was shining on us, so we looked like September Morn as we were all fitted out with women's nightshirts and petticoats. I felt I was a baby once more with my garments on." The next morning they poked their heads out of the dugout, and "returned to what we thought was our happy home the evening before and found nothing left but the walls."[55]

On the 18th, Duffy sent a lengthy letter to McCoy about the battle. "Luckily, our last performance was comparatively a walk over. But it was a fine shipshape American job, done with neatness and dispatch. . . . We are ready for bigger things—but no need telling you that." He did tell him, however, that very few of the wounded officers who had fought with him crossing the Ourcq were back. "Only Father Hanley, in fact, limping when he heard the rumor of our new campaign. Buck, also, by the way. Bootz, Ryan, Hurley will be able for duty. But Jim Finn has lost part of his shinbone. His fighting and dancing days are over, poor fellow—and Charlie Baker lost his arm, and may not recover."[56]
Harding wrote his friend.

> We are trying to end the war by Christmas. But I am afraid that it can't be done. The regiment's battle cry at Château Thierry was 'Heaven, Hell or Hoboken Before Christmas!' A noble Irish idea, and one for which the regiment worked hard and fought hard. I am glad that I had a chance to join the 165th. It is a man's outfit, and it has done fine work over here. . . . I couldn't ask for any better soldiers than the Irish in the 69th. They are a hard hitting, dare-devil bunch, very religious, afraid of nothing, and sworn enemies of the Boche.[57]

On the first day of fighting, as this dare-devil bunch marched across the St. Mihiel salient, the sun slipped from behind a cloud and MacArthur, watching from a hill, looked down on the flashing bayonets that could be seen for twenty miles and wrote, "In the same moment a rainbow ran across the sky, and the division for which it was named let out a yell that rang high above the roaring barrage."[58]

The reduction of the German territory in the St. Mihiel salient, restoring two hundred square miles of territory to France, had indeed been a "promenade," as Donovan characterized it, although the dead would have felt otherwise. Pershing called it a "striking victory," declaring that it "completely demonstrated the wisdom of building up a distinct American army." He believed St. Mihiel "did more than any other single operation of the war to encourage the tired Allies. After years of doubt and despair, of suffering and loss, it brought them assurance of the final defeat of an enemy whose armies had seemed well-nigh invincible."[59]

Foch called the victory a "smashing success." In his memoirs he wrote, "For the American First Army would now be called upon to withdraw a considerable part of its forces and send them to the west of the Meuse. Here new tasks and new fortunes awaited them."[60]

At Hassavant Farm, Lt. Col. Bill Donovan greets a French officer. Donovan described the attack through the St. Mihiel salient as a "promenade." *Signal Corps/National Archives*

22

"Over the River a Thousand Yawning Dead"

Before the smoke and gas had cleared from the St. Mihiel salient, elements of Gen. John Pershing's First Army were on their way to the Meuse-Argonne. Roads west became clogged with an army on the move—428,000 men, 90,000 horses and mules, and 4,000 guns hurrying to keep their date for 26 September, when they would lead the Allied attack against the entire length of the so-called Hindenburg Line. Several battle-hardened divisions were left behind; Pershing felt the First, Second, Twenty-sixth, and Forty-second were spent and needed rest. "This prevented their transfer to the Meuse-Argonne in time to open the fight," the general explained. It also forced him to bring in several green divisions that had not yet finished training and were in many ways unprepared for the fight that lay ahead.[1]

Back at St. Mihiel, the Rainbows felt cheated. They knew something big was brewing and they wanted to be a part of it—not to spend their time mopping up. As the other outfits pulled out, they were assigned to harass the enemy in the Essey-Pannes sector and make them think the American army planned to continue its assault north to capture Metz. Charles MacArthur of the 149th Field Artillery summed up the feeling of most Rainbow soldiers. "There was talk of fighting in the North, and the toughest aggregation of star-spangled bums in the A.E.F. was spading up a lousy front that could have been held by any good football team—all because we had been suckers to take St. Mihiel in the first place."[2]

A frustrated 1st Sgt. Vincent Mulholland confided to Father Francis Duffy that he wished the war would end, "but not while the old regiment is back here in army corps reserve. I want to see this war end with the 69th right out in the front line, going strong."[3]

Bill Donovan and his commander, Harry Mitchell, also were miffed that the 165th Infantry had been held back. As each day passed and word of the great battle came from the west, they sensed the division would soon be back in combat. There was too much going on for Pershing to keep the Forty-second out of battle for long. "We don't know what we are to do or when we are to do it," Donovan wrote Ruth, "but by the time you receive this you will have had news of another scrap."[4]

While Donovan awaited new orders for the regiment he almost found himself transferred out. His reputation as a fighter and his keen mind had not gone unnoticed by the top brass from outside the division. The provost marshal general wanted Donovan behind a desk, where his skill as a lawyer and command of the French language would come in handy. But the division was not ready to lose him, if it could be helped. Maj. Gen. Charles Menoher and his two most trusted men, Douglas MacArthur, his old chief of staff, and Lt. Col. William Hughes, his new chief, fought to block any transfer that would take Donovan away.

As for Wild Bill, himself, a desk job would never suit his personality. He would rather fight beside the men of his battalion and his regiment. MacArthur, who, like Donovan, had to be up front where the real danger lurked, argued that if they must pluck the young lieutenant colonel from the division, his transfer should wait at least until after the Meuse-Argonne offensive.

Duffy also feared that Donovan's days as a Rainbow soldier were short. He recalled tramping along a muddy road one night when Donovan had "disburdened himself of a new worry." He told the chaplain that the provost marshal general believed that he would make a good assistant and that although the transfer had been thwarted it was only a matter of time before he was headed off to general headquarters.

"Donovan is disgusted and sore for the first time in my knowledge of him," Duffy wrote in his diary.[5]

As Donovan awaited his fate and that of his regiment in the Meuse-Argonne, Pershing's First Army slugged it out with desperate enemy forces determined to hold on to as much ground as possible. With the war grinding down at last, or seeming to, the German high command knew that when peace negotiations commenced in earnest, the more French and Belgian land Germany controlled, the stronger its bargaining power would be. If the

Germans stopped the Allies at the Hindenburg Line, which twisted from the Alps to the North Sea, then four years of the bloodiest war ever fought would not have been in vain.

The Hindenburg Line was a derisive name given by British soldiers in honor of German Field Marshal Paul von Hindenburg. Its official Teutonic name was *Siegfried Stellung*, or the Siegfried Line—a series of defensive strongholds, each one named after a hero of German folklore. The strongholds themselves—or most of them—were unlike anything yet devised in modern warfare. They comprised a series of heavily fortified strongholds protected by deadly coils of razor-sharp barbed wire and deep trenches and were dotted by thousands of concrete pillboxes manned by veteran machine-gun squads. One of the most daunting of these strongholds fronted the British Fourth Army at the St. Quentin Canal Tunnel, where the doughboys of the Twenty-seventh New York Division had been ordered to open the way so that the Australians could leapfrog them and drive the Germans out.

The stronghold in front of Pershing's First Army, crisscrossed by the Giselher Line, the Freya Line, and the Kriemhilde Line, was equally as deadly as the stronghold that faced the Twenty-seventh Division, but in a much different way. Especially the Kriemhilde Line. Instead of open land and a vast underground tunnel to be breached, like a series of dams it blocked the way through the steep, wooded highlands of the Meuse-Argonne. The key features of this chunk of rugged turf, bunched together over a twenty-four-mile-wide front, were the heights above the Meuse River in the east, the eleven-hundred-foot-high Montfaucon (Mount of the Falcon) in the center, and the Argonne Forest itself in the west. The Argonne was carpeted in clumps of wild thickets and briar patches. Swiftly flowing tributaries of the Aire and Aisne Rivers had gouged out deep ravines, and the going was a constant uphill-downhill struggle, slashing through the trees and underbrush. One writer described the forest as a "wild Hans Christian Anderson land of giant trees cunningly interwoven with the nests of machine guns."[6] Pershing himself stated, "These natural defenses were strengthened by every artificial means imaginable, such as fortified strongpoints, dugouts, successive lines of trenches, and an unlimited number of concrete machine-gun emplacements. A dense network of wire entanglements covered every position. With the advantage of commanding ground, the enemy was peculiarly well located to pour oblique and flanking artillery fire on any assailant attempting to advance between the Meuse and the Argonne."[7]

The coveted prize on the other side of the Hindenburg Line that would eventually cost more than 120,000 U.S. casualties was the Metz-Sedan-Mezieres railroad system, the vital transportation lifeline of the German army. Military strategists believed that if the Americans cut the line off or caused an interruption, then the Germans would not be able to withdraw safely from France, or even Belgium, and its army would collapse. To guarantee victory, Pershing planned to hit the enemy in a five-phase attack with the Forty-second taking part in the third phase. He felt that one attack after another would wear down his foe and push him out of the Meuse-Argonne.

Obviously, the stakes were high on both sides, all along the Hindenburg Line. While the Germans dug in, they looked for a way out of the war, talking of a peace with honor, which could be brokered by President Wilson. But the fact that they were putting up a stubborn, deadly defense that wreaked havoc on the Allies while they and the president spoke of peace angered Donovan. With the 165th still in reserve, but now closer to battle, he argued that after hearing so much peace talk Americans would be reluctant to fight.

> Germany has made her most effective counter-attack her peace drive. It could not have been delivered more opportunely, and I hope you are all set against it. It is important that Wilson should at once send an answer to tell them that we are not so easily beguiled. Frankly I am afraid of these peace overtures. I am afraid of their effect on public opinion, afraid of their effect on the fighting men. It is a most insidious weapon. It slips in under your armor. Men want peace and they are eager to get home. If the chance of peace seems near they are less eager to fight, they "stall," they hold off all in the hope that peace will be declared. I believe what we must all think of now is simply "Fight."[8]

While Donovan pondered the politics of peace and Pershing's army found itself stymied by the terrain and the enemy's overwhelming firepower, the Forty-second Division got the call to join the battle.

For nearly two weeks the battle had gone hard. The easy romp through the St. Mihiel salient had given the Americans a false sense of superiority. They had ripped through the German defense there with a nary a scratch. Here in the ridged forest of the Argonne and the Meuse highlands, beating back the enemy had proved no "promenade." Although the doughboys kept pushing forward, there were deep pools of blood for every inch of ground taken.

After a week of trying to reach the Kriemhilde Line—the fiercest of the three main lines of defense—in the first phase of Pershing's plan of attack, the Thirty-fifth and Ninety-first Divisions had been relieved by the First Division and the Thirty-second. For the next ten torturous days, these two units advanced to the front of the Kriemhilde (the second phase), while far on the left flank the British Fourth Army, supported by the New Yorkers of the Twenty-seventh, had not only broken through the Hindenburg Line, but were rapidly pushing the Germans back. The pace of Pershing's army had been too slow for Premier Georges Clemenceau, the snarling, impatient "Tiger" of the French government. He ordered Foch to fire the American commander on the spot, growling that the general had wanted his army and gotten it and now the Americans "can congratulate themselves for not getting one earlier."[9]

In his memoirs, however, Foch had written, "having a more comprehensive knowledge of the difficulties encountered by the American army, I could not acquiesce in the radical solution contemplated by Monsieur Clemenceau."[10]

On the night of 11–12 October, in the midst of this political firestorm, the Rainbows marched into Exermont, a village six thousand yards south of the Kriemhilde Line, and took over for the First Division, with orders to pick up where Charles Summerall's "Big Red One" had left off. The relief and ensuing attack made up the battle's third phase.

The First had fought courageously, suffering nine thousand casualties in eleven days, but had failed to crack through the defensive bulwark. It had taken the eight-hundred-foot-high Côte de Maldah and reached the edge of Sommerance, a key village in the sector now assigned to the Forty-second. Conceded Pershing, "The attacks during the preceding phase, although reaching the Hindenburg Line and even capturing portions of that position near Romagne and Cunel, left in the enemy's hands the strong defenses in the Bois de Romagne and Bois de Bantheville, both of which had to be reduced before further considerable progress could be made. To the west of Romagne heights, we faced the strongly fortified position which included Côte de Châtillon, Landres-et-St. Georges, St. Juvin, Bois de Loges, and Grandpré." According to the general, as a part of his third phase, "the III and V Corps, with fresh divisions (the 5th and 42d), were to drive the salients through the hostile position on both flanks of the Bois de Romagne and of the Bois de Bantheville."[11]

Thus, it was up to Michael Lenihan's Eighty-third Brigade to push north of the Kriemhilde Line and secure the road running between St. Georges and Landres-et-St. Georges, and then, after taking the road, mop up both villages. MacArthur's Eighty-fourth Brigade, on Lenihan's right flank, was ordered to capture Hill 288 and the heights at Côte de Châtillon, also north of the Kriemhilde Line, and southeast of St. Georges. The taking of Côte de Châtillon would be key to the Rainbow advance. Once taken it would protect Lenihan's flank, and his brigade would need all the protection it could muster since, unlike the Eighty-fourth, which would attack through forests, it had to cross mostly open land studded with rolling belts of barbed wire.

The Forty-second undertook most of its hike to Exermont at night. Martin Hogan started to feel that his Third Battalion ought to change its nickname from "Shamrock" to "Night-Owl." All the while he and several of his cronies figured their nighttime hours "would make even Old Broadway jealous." But as they got nearer to the Meuse-Argonne battlefield, the march switched to daylight and the Rainbows wished they were still cloaked in darkness so they would not have to see the carnage they were passing through. "The kiss of death had fallen on thousands upon thousands of agonized but determined defenders," Hogan recollected. "Two armies had fought like so many maniacs over every foot of this country, and the horror, the sublime horror, of that struggle was written plainly everywhere"[12]

Al Ettinger later recalled how the boys sang as they trooped along on the last leg of their march, even though singing had been prohibited. As they neared their staging areas, he was struck "to see the whole regiment under march singing away at the top of their lungs." In one of the ironic moments of the war, Ettinger looked to the top of a hill, and there stood Duffy, his arms upraised as he gave the benediction to his men. Down below, the soldiers' voices were plainly heard, belting out bawdy words. "We were 'banging away on Lulu' under full field back and full throat.

[Duffy] didn't care what we were singing, as long as we were alive and singing."[13]

In his diary, the chaplain failed to mention any bawdy songs. "As the companies marched up to take their place in line, I stood on a rising ground in the bleak and open plain to perform my duties in their regard, which for many of them would be the last time. The frequently recurring rows of rude crosses which marked the last resting places of many brave lads of the 1st Division were an eloquent sermon on death; so no words of warning from me were needed and I was able to do my holy business in a matter of fact way which soldiers like better than being preached at."[14]

Richard O'Neill had not yet rejoined D Company. He had to talk his way out of a base hospital. He told a skeptical doctor, "I could go ten rounds with Jess Willard. I want to get back with my outfit." The doctor then replied, "Oh for Christ's sake O'Neill, you looked like a pincushion when they brought you in. You've had your war!" O'Neill hammered at the doctor, who finally caved in. "If you want to kill yourself go ahead." O'Neill left the hospital and traveled alone back to the regiment as fast as he could. He rode on trains, hopped a truck, slept on bags of oats, and finally hitched a ride with a lieutenant. "I joined the boys sometime in October, right in the middle of that donnybrook called the Meuse-Argonne. I was shocked to find so few of the old-timers left."[15]

After a leave in Paris, William Spencer, the chocolate lover, had rejoined the regiment. But on first reaching Paris on the 25th, he had been in a "filthy condition, lousy all over." He washed up—taking "three consecutive hot baths before I was clean. It was one of the happiest days of my life as I am overjoyed to be out of that awfully dirty, flea-infested country we were in. No more sleeping on boards, scratching fleas for a while." But then it was over, too fast, and he was back with the regiment and on the way to Exermont. He also was miffed. Loi had sent him only one letter since St. Mihiel, whereas he had written her four times. "This ends it," he wrote, overlooking the fact that he had boasted of trying to kiss a French girl. "Farewell-forever. Four to one is too much."[16]

After shepherding his troops into Exermont and into their front-line positions from atop the hill, Duffy peered into the

Meuse-Argonne wilderness and got a sense of what lay ahead. He dashed off a letter to his sister, Agnes.

> I think there is enough of the Duffy in you to make you find real enjoyment in this place, although it is about the rottenest place I ever got into. We are encamped in a big forest with trees all gashed and smashed after years of war and almost every yard of ground pitted with shell holes, some of which are made yesterday. It has been wet and gloomy and cold, and the man who can find a hole in the ground to crawl into at night is the lucky one, but tough as it is, it is always interesting. There are air battles going on between the clouds, and while I write I can see little white and black puffs as our big guns are trying to keep the German planes away from our observation balloons, and up front the big guns are rolling, although further and further away. A battle has been going on and the Germans are retreating to new lines; to-day or to-morrow it will be our turn to take up the chase and we will be in the thick of it.[17]

Donovan, never one to wait around for something to happen, always looking to grab the initiative when he could, had gone in search of the First Division's top officer, Brig. Gen. Frank Parker. Parker had just replaced Summerall, who had been given the reins to V Corps. When Donovan's men marched into combat he wanted to know what was in store for them and how best to deal with any problems. When he reached Parker's command post he was informed that the general was up ahead, reconnoitering near Landres-et-St. George. A lieutenant volunteered to guide him. To Donovan, the devastation he now walked through was worse than his trip through Château-Thierry. He came across the scattered dead of the First and Thirty-fifth Divisions, as well as dead Germans.

"There were many more Americans dead than Germans," he related to Col. Henry Reilly, "showing the determination of the Americans to go forward regardless of cost."

Donovan found Parker at Côte de Maldah. Standing with him on the riddled heights that the First Division had recently, but tenuously, captured, Donovan looked off to the north at what his troops would now have to fight over. He asked if there were any American troops out there. "I was told that no one was out there and that it was a hell of place to be."[18]

Wild Bill returned to his command post to prepare his men and himself for the coming battle. He met with Maj. Tom Reilley, commander of the Third Battalion, which on the 14th was to lead the way when the 165th went "over the top." They selected as their jumping off spot a sunken road in the gully of a stream that ran in front of Côte de Maldah, about thirty-five hundred yards north of their target, the fortress village of Landres-et-St. Georges. Although the sunken road offered protection for the men during their night of waiting, both officers worried about their right flank once they got going—especially as they fought past Côte de Châtillon. Like Hill 288, Côte de Châtillon was the key stronghold of the Kriemhilde. Barbed-wire entanglements, deep trenches, and machine-gun nests lay thick on the ground in front of the 165th. Attacking alongside the New Yorkers were the men from Alabama, and Donovan was not keen on their chances of taking Côte de Châtillon and thus protecting his right flank.

Earlier, because he was now running the regiment in the field, Donovan had turned over his battalion to Capt. Mike Kelly. He next tabbed Ettinger to be one of his runners, counting on the cocky soldier to keep lines of communication open between his staff and the mortar platoon. When Ettinger reported to Donovan he found the lieutenant colonel in a shell hole with his striker, who was in the process of shaving him while artillery shells burst around them. Donovan wanted to look his best leading his men forward into battle. Not only was his face to be clean-shaven; his uniform had to be spotless and adorned with his ribbons and medals and rank. He had his boots and Sam Browne belt polished. Wild Bill wiped the lather from his face and ordered his new runner to follow him to the top of a ridge. They had to step over dead men and Ettinger figured there must have been at least a thousand bodies strewn over the ground.

"Oh my God! What a waste of lives," Donovan said. "What a waste! What a waste!"

Ettinger stared at a dead German. He had red hair and freckles, his "eyes staring at the sky—and he looked just like me."[19]

That night, unknown to Donovan, a game of one-upmanship took place between two swellheaded soldiers: Summerall, nicknamed by the Irish lads, who hated him, the "Old Prussian, Gen. Von Summeralz,"[20] and Douglas MacArthur. New in his role of leading a corps, Summerall had banged into MacArthur's brigade headquarters, weary and frustrated because the American advance

"Dynamite Mike" Kelly led the First Battalion during the Meuse-Argonne offensive. After the war, he accidentally killed himself while cleaning a pistol in his New York City apartment. *From* My Political Trial and Experiences

had been too slow and that sluggishness had shown up under his watch as commander of the First Division. MacArthur poured his new superior a tin cup of black, "throat blistering" coffee.

"Give me Châtillon, MacArthur," directed Summerall, whose anger would later get the best of him. "Give me Châtillon, or a list of five thousand casualties!" Not to be upstaged, MacArthur had replied, "All right General, we'll take it, or my name will head the list."[21]

T
he day before the attack, ammunition for the batteries of the Sixty-seventh Field Artillery Brigade had been hauled up for its 75-caliber and 155-caliber guns. The 75s were to fire eighty rounds per gun every hour while the 155s were to fire a half-round per gun every minute. Smoke bombs would be lobbed onto enemy positions as well. The barrage was to be a rolling one, behind which Lenihan's Eighty-third Brigade would attack. The shells were to land one hundred yards in front of the men as they advanced. The brigade had not yet moved to the jump-off line for fear that it might get hit by errant shelling from its own batteries when the opening barrage began.

At three-thirty in the morning of the 14th, shelling commenced. "Fired all night," George Leach of the151st Field Artillery logged in his diary, "and just before daylight finished our preparation for the advance."[22] Elmer Sherwood of the 150th Field Artillery recorded, "Our entire brigade has been firing since midnight. We are backing up our infantry again and we are giving them every ounce of punch we have."[23]

As far as Duffy felt, the barrage hardly amounted to much and was as much a danger to his own men as it was to the enemy. "Our artillery was firing with sparse ammunition on points on a map— which wasn't always where the map said."[24] Third Battalion liaison officer, Lt. J. Phelps Harding, however, called the barrage heavier than that of St. Mihiel, "and all the more terrible because we were very near its first landing place, for it fell fairly close to our trench. . . . As I sat in the trench with both our shells and those of the German counter barrage passing over me or breaking near— sometimes too near for comfort—it seemed as if all the cannons and machine guns in France had been turned loose on our particular front."[25]

Throughout the night tense soldiers had waited for the coming dawn. Weighing on Hogan's mind was the forest they would need to traverse before they broke into the clear. As a city lad, he feared the woods. Now the wilderness was dark and foreboding and he knew that enemy machine gunners, their resistance far from broken, were certainly hidden behind every bush and thicket and fallen tree. He knew how thoroughly the Germans had transformed the Meuse-Argonne into a fortress stronghold and he knew, also, that "they thought they could hold the forest until the crack of doom."[26]

Ettinger later recalled, "We spent a sleepless night in foxholes waiting for our attack."[27]

When morning came at last, with artillery blasting the ground three hundred yards in front of the division, the 165th pushed forward from the sunken road. The designated start time was seven-thirty, but the attack did not get going until nearly nine. Duffy watched with a heavy heart when the men finally left the encampment. As he wrote, the first wave ran into an enemy that it could not see but that had been expecting them. "From the beginning our men went forward through steady shell fire which increased as their purpose became more clearly manifested." He saw planes roar above the troops, strafing them with machine-gun bullets and "no doubt keeping their own artillery posted on the results of their fire."[28]

As Donovan had feared, his men were struck by enfilading fire from Côte de Châtillon. "As soon as we had passed a line abreast of the northern edge of the Bois de Romagne, the jumping off position of the Alabama regiment, on our right," he reported, "we began to get fire from the Côte de Châtillon as well as from the Germans to our front." He recounted how on his right his men "commenced to drop, some because killed and wounded, and the other because the fire was so heavy from Côte de Châtillon."[29]

In Reilley's Shamrock Battalion, which led the advance, the terrain itself was almost as much of an obstacle as the German's fire. "The way of our attack" wrote Hogan, "led up and down hill, over bowlders, through heavy patches of brambles and young saplings, between heavy trees, gullies, hollows and knolls, wooded into dark, uncanny recesses, with here and there barbed wire worked in with devilish ingenuity." The companies taking the lead were I and M, and when the Germans saw them coming they ran out to meet them in hand-to-hand combat. "Many a beautiful individual fight developed," Hogan said.[30]

Watching from a ridge, Charles MacArthur felt grateful that he was not in the infantry. Men were dying, and their bodies clung to bushes or fell into streams, and he thought, "Over the river a thousand yawning dead—a great pity, everything considered. Yet there, but for the grace of God, would lie all of us. The grace of God and New York's rusty bayonets, dead ahead."[31]

Victor Van Yorx, who had distinguished himself at the Ourcq before suffering a wound and was now back in action, led a platoon through the woods and into the open. As they dashed across the field, a shell burst twenty feet away. Fragments flew in all directions, a chunk slicing through the side of Van Yorx's head, just above the right ear. The impact nearly knocked him out, leaving him momentarily dizzy. Shaking his head, he saw only six of his men standing; the rest, although not all killed, were severely injured and unable to continue.

"That was the first shock. We lined up again, out of the woods this time, and began a promenade through Fritz' barrage. Fritz put on some barrage, too, I'm telling you. The shells were dropping all over, and the shrapnel whizzing all around. We kept right on through."[32]

Keeping pace with Hogan and Van Yorx, Harding felt clods of earth pounding against him, kicked up by exploding shells. The shells screamed overhead or punched the ground in front of him and his eight runners, and each time he heard the awful roar he feared he would be hit "squarely" by a shell. "Before we had been in action more than a couple of hours, I lost four of the runners. . . . All one can do is jump in a shell hole if he is lucky enough to be within jumping distance of one, or lie flat on the ground and cross one's fingers for good luck."

That the ground Harding's men traversed had turned soft by the endless rain was a lucky thing for many of them, because some shells burrowed deep into the mud before exploding. "The fragments didn't spread so wide laterally, saved a good many lives," he reported. He also described how the "bullets cut the grass at our feet, sailed over us, and some of them stopped, having done their little deeds. My pack stopped a couple—but better the pack than I!"[33]

As he sped across the open field, Alf Helmer, who had been buried alive at Rouge Bouquet, had the distinct feeling he was running on air, above the bullets, and when he looked down he swore that he was two feet above the ground, skimming along. For the next hundred yards or so, Helmer believed, he did not touch the ground at all.[34]

Van Yorx and four others loped forward, took cover, and then were "up and at 'em again." When a bomb burst close by they piled into the same shell hole. "While we were in this hole another shell plopped right on the edge of it and buried three of us," he wrote. "The worst of it was, it was a gas shell. You should have seen us unbury ourselves and get our masks on. We left that hole pretty 'toot sweet'."[35]

The German artillery hit behind the Shamrocks, severing them from any support that the other battalions might offer. And snipers picked off the New Yorkers from the trees. "There was every available German in this forest," Hogan believed.[36]

One of the boys hit by a sniper was Van Yorx himself. His thinned-out squad had taken refuge in a sunken road with banks about ten feet high. It looked safe enough, but a German bullet nailed Van Yorx above the left knee. When his squad moved on, he tried to follow, using his rifle as a crutch. He did not get far and had to sit down and wait until dark before he was carried back to a dressing station in a blanket. On the way back, he saw his brother Ted, who wrote to their parents.

> About Brother Vic, as I know you're worried. He's O.K. . . . Lieutenant Guigon told me he never saw any one like him. Let me tell you, folks, the boys hit hell, if there ever was one. Even worse than the Battle of the Ourcq. First Vic was hit by a piece of shell behind the ear, I think; next he was buried by the explosion of a gas shell. Lord knows how he escaped as one or two were killed and three others gassed pretty badly, and then he got it at last, and as he said, "I hadn't fired my rifle yet." God, he's some boy. They got him to the rear. He was happy and cheerful as usual. That's his fourth wound, and I think he's had enough.[37]

Harding had taken cover because an enemy machine gunner kept pounding away at him. "Any movement at all on my part drew a stream of bullets—they clipped the raised rim of my hole, so I just stayed there." He then raced to another shell hole, and kept advancing shell hole to shell hole. He felt that the Germans had singled him out, because the bullets followed him everywhere he went.[38]

All day and into the evening the regiment battled out from Côte de Maldah, pushing toward the wire along Landres-et-St. Georges road. During a firefight outside a stone farmhouse that blocked the way, Reilley and several men found a homemade bomb—grenades linked together by a single fuse. They peered down a cellar stairway and spied eight German grenadiers hidden in the dank, dark room below. Reilley lit the fuse and hurled the bomb down the stairs and into the cellar.

According to Lincoln Eyre of the *New York Evening World*, the "explosion tore the house to tatters and wounded one of the Americans, but 'ruined' eight Boches." Eyre observed that Reilley, as battalion commander, ought to have been behind his troops and not leading them. But now the officers were "obliged to stay with the forward waves if they want to personally direct the operations of their command."[39]

Later, Eyre observed the leader of Donovan's First Battalion, Capt. Mike Kelly (known as "Dynamite Mike") and some of his men as they "cleaned out a dozen cellars in two hours." When it was over they had left "their trail through the village filled with German dead."[40]

Another Mike, Donaldson, the pugilist from Haverstraw, who packed a pair of dynamite fists, had been pinned down in a sunken road. The big sergeant, along with his entire company, had been stopped by intense machine-gun fire that poured down from the crest of a hill. As he regrouped his men, he saw on the field that sloped up in front of him a number of wounded New Yorkers: one of them was Bill Carroll. Donaldson left the protection of the sunken road and moved as fast as his big frame could go, up the hill. The German guns roared and bullets buzzed around him. He lifted up Carroll and carried him back to the sunken road, stepping over the other wounded scattered about the hillside.

"There I was, lying out in no-man's-land with me face half shot away," Carroll said. "And I'd be there still but Mike crawled out there with all that shelling and picked me up in his arms and carried me back."

Big Mike was not finished. He braved enemy fire five more times to bring back the wounded.

"Why that man had no fear," Carroll said.[41]

For his action on the 14th, Donaldson received the Medal of Honor.

Despite the early success, the attack was not going well. According to Hogan, "The fighting reached its highest possible point at eleven that morning, and hung at this point all day."[42] To Donovan, "It was a pretty difficult place." Men were dropping all over. "Those who got to the wire were killed or wounded." When night came, the lieutenant colonel ordered Reilley to gather up his wounded and get back to the start line. Reilley lost twenty-three men, more than half the regiment's dead. He reported to the *New York Globe*, "In the advance we were badly cut up. The Third Battalion lost half its strength; only six officers survived."[43]

One of that day's casualties had been Hogan. The corporal, convinced that he was "bullet-proof," that the "Germans hadn't cast any bullet yet which could find me," spotted a sniper in a tree and hid. He knew he was exposed and actually felt the sniper taking deliberate aim at him. He fired away at the tree and the sniper blasted back. When there was a lull in their exchange, Hogan wondered if he had hit the other soldier. As he reloaded, Hogan heard the sniper's rifle ring out "and instantly I felt a sharp stab in my left hand, extended and holding my barrel. He had scored, hitting me on the knuckle of my left hand, tearing this knuckle away and ripping up the bones and flesh." It was dark by the time he ran and crawled away from the enemy line, with shells bursting about him. His trip back sickened him. "I saw men being carried with legs shattered, with blood-drenched clothes from the flow of ghastly body wounds, and I passed one man sitting against a tree with half his head torn away, probably one who had tried to make his way back to the dressing station when caught by a German shell. He must have seated himself here after the first shock to rest and have died moments later."[44]

Harding described the attack in a missive to his mother, "As long as I live I will remember that day. I know it must have been your prayers that brought me out of it alive, for from the jumping-off hour until late in the afternoon we were in a regular inferno of artillery and machine gun fire. We were up against a tough proposition, with the Huns fighting like madmen and only giving in when absolutely forced to do so. . . . Our casualties were heavy and our advance slight."[45]

Donovan had decided to stay put with Kelly's battalion for the night, thinking it might be able to sneak forward in the darkness. He talked the idea over with "Dynamite Mike" and Henry Bootz, twice cited for valor, once at Lunéville and again on the Ourcq River. Papa Bootz reasoned that a single company might get through. Donovan agreed. Bootz led his B Company, now packed with green replacements, toward the German defenses. Rockets exploded and the sky lit up like Forty-second Street. A number of his men were captured. When Bootz returned after unsuccessfully trying to make it through, he said, "I think we better wait until morning, as you can see all we have done so far is so thoroughly wake up the Germans. Look at the rockets going up along the whole line."[46]

One bit of intelligence that had been gathered during Bootz's foray into no-man's-land was that Germans were in front of and behind the jungle of wire that protected the village of Landres-et-St. Georges. To Ettinger, the fortification four hundred yards ahead, and up a slope, looked invincible. "In front of us were acres and acres of barbed wire, laced with pill boxes and machine gun nests, which barred us from taking the village."[47]

There also was confusion resulting from the fact that Donovan had assumed other units were near his battalion while it was right in front of the enemy defenses. He telephoned Van S. Merle-Smith, at headquarters, to find out where the 167th Alabama and the 166th Ohio had gone, saying he had had no contact with either regiment, "with the consequence that it looks as if we were in a forward salient by ourselves."[48]

After ordering trench mortars to be brought up, Donovan called it quits for the night, five hundred yards short of the wire. "I was so damned tired," he said, "I had reached the point where I didn't give a damn if [the Germans] did counter-attack."[49]

23

"You Expected to Have the Pleasure of Burying Me"

Field order no. 18, issued thirty minutes after midnight on 15 October by the adjutant of the Eighty-third Brigade, was blunt. "The attack will continue today." The start time had been designated as seven-fifteen with an artillery barrage aimed at destroying the wire five hundred yards in front of Lt. Col. Bill Donovan's troops. The barrage was to lift at seven-thirty and then resume twenty minutes later in front of the entire brigade's front, rolling ahead of the doughboys at a rate of one hundred meters every six minutes until it had reached the enemy wire. "The infantry will move forward close to the barrage line and at 7:30 will commence the passage of the hostile wire, following the barrage closely until the 3rd Objective is reached." That objective: break through the wire, mop up the trenches, and capture Landres-et-St. Georges.[1]

In his diary, Donovan was equally blunt. "New attack at 7:30. I was hit at 7:40. Remained in field until noon. Men blown up about me. Heavy shelling. Carried off field. One of the men hit."[2]

From the time the attack started and until he left the field in a blanket, Donovan and his boys fought as if possessed by demons against an enemy that refused to give an inch. The Rainbow's chief of staff recorded, "The enemy has continued his resistance with undiminished fury and has at no time showed any tendency to withdraw or surrender."[3]

Before the attack, Donovan had approached all the old veterans of his battalion, now under the command of Mike Kelly, to encourage them, "telling them that we had to go through and that they were the fellows to do it. When they started forward I went with them."[4]

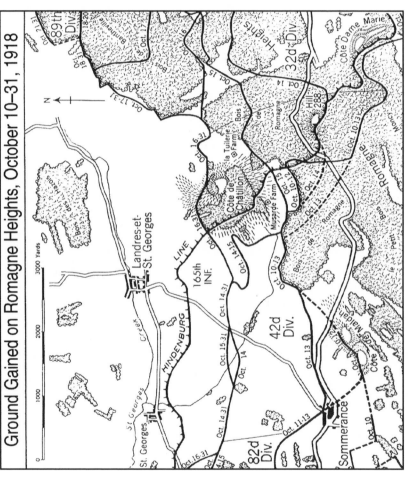

Ground Gained on Romagne Heights

Adapted from *American Armies and Battlefields in Europe: A History Guide and Reference Book*, American Battle Monument Commission (GPO: Washington 1938).

Father Francis Duffy, down among the men, hardly took his eyes off Donovan. It was now obvious that Wild Bill enjoyed a battle. "He goes into it in exactly the frame of mind that he held as a college man when he marched out on the gridiron before a football game, and his one thought throughout is to push his way through. 'Cool' is the word the men use of him and 'Cool' is their highest epithet of praise for a man of daring, resolution and indifference to danger." Duffy remembered Donovan yelling to his men as they bucked up the slope toward the wire. "Come on, fellows, it's better ahead than it is here. Come on, we'll have them on the run before long."

For two days, Donovan, dressed smartly, with the strap of his Sam Browne belt crossing his chest so that the enemy knew exactly who he was, had stood gallantly at the front, convincing his troops that no one in the old Sixty-ninth was "ever afraid." Turning toward them with a smile, he had yelled again and again, "Come on now, men, they can't hit me and they won't hit you!"[5]

But on the morning of the 15th, Wild Bill had hardly taken a step forward when a bullet crashed into his leg. He pitched to the ground. The bullet shattered his shinbone. As he struggled to sit up, the Germans came pouring out of the wire in a counterattack.

Although the pain must have been unbearable, Donovan refused to give up command now that his front was threatened. He called in artillery support and ordered his Stokes mortars, which he had brought up the night before, to pound the enemy. The artillery fire again proved weak, and the Germans kept coming. It would be up to the mortars to stop them. But from their poor position, the mortar men did not know where to lob their shells.

Knowing the need was desperate, Tom Fitzsimmons, from South Orange, New Jersey, a sergeant in one of the mortar platoons, bolted up the slope for about one hundred yards, exposing himself to machine-gun fire. At the crest of the hill he found a spot that gave him an excellent view of the approaching Germans. It also gave the Germans an excellent view of him. Father Duffy said the sergeant made "himself an easy cockshot for the German gunners while he signalled to his own men his corrections on their aim."[6]

Ettinger watched nervously for the signal from Fitzsimmons, who had come over with him to the Sixty-ninth from the old Seventh. He saw the Germans break from the corner of the woods, and yet Fitzsimmons held his hand and "we waited . . . and waited . . . and waited."[7] When Fitzsimmons figured the Germans were in range, he signaled for the mortars to let loose. The first bombs landed on top of the enemy; then Fitzsimmons called for rapid fire. The hits were direct, and the foe faltered.

Wrote Duffy, "[Tom] escaped himself by a miracle and had the satisfaction of seeing the shells dropping right amongst the Germans who were gathering for the attack, and doing dreadful execution."[8] Fitzsimmons—who Ettinger said had the "map of Ireland all over his face" and, along with Donovan, was one of the coolest man under fire[9]—received the Distinguished Service Cross.

Hearing that his lieutenant colonel had been shot, Alexander Anderson, the young warhorse whose Second Battalion now supported Kelly's First, made a trip to Donovan's command post. "It was broad daylight by the time we got to where we could see him," he said later. "He was lying in a fox hole on the reverse slope

The 165th Color Guard, from left to right: John Curtin, Bill Schmidt, Bill Sheahan, and Herbert Schwartz. Sheahan, from County Limerick, was killed in the Meuse-Argonne offensive. *Signal Corps/National Archives*

of the hill just in front of the German position. His position was not only isolated, but an extremely dangerous one."[10]

With the shelling thick and furious, Donovan suggested that the major and his aide, Capt. John Fecheimer, drop into a foxhole before they got blown to bits. Anderson squeezed in beside Donovan while Fecheimer found shelter next to Regimental Color Sergeant Bill Sheahan and Pfc. Patrick Connors.[11] Moments later a shell hit Sheahan's foxhole. The twenty-four-year-old native of Limerick was obliterated. Ettinger later located a web belt with the initials "W.S." on it and a hunk of what he said looked like roast beef. "Those were the mortal remains of Bill Sheahan," he confided.[12] Connors lost both legs. Before Connors died, Cpl. John Patrick Furey from Sligo, Ireland, leaped into the foxhole, picked him up, and, as he lugged him to the dressing station, kissed the mortally wounded soldier, saying over and over, "Me poor fellow, me poor fellow."[13]

When they had a chance, Anderson and Fecheimer scrambled back to their battalion.

Meanwhile, Duffy was among his boys in the muck while they stopped the counterattack and pressed their attack against the wire. C Company Cpl. Bill Gordon, from Long Island City, who had lost his brother Ed at the Ourcq River, described to his father the priest's heroics. "I suppose you have heard of our chaplain, Rev. Father Duffy. Well, he today is our father. If we are in trouble, we look for him. . . . When we are going into battle he will come around to everybody and tell them to say a little prayer and God will take care of us, and when the battle is over he is at the first aid waiting to say a good word to the wounded."[14]

As the battle raged, Pvt. Tim Nolan of the Bronx felt it was Duffy's courage that inspired the troops to hang on. "Wherever things were the hottest there was Father Duffy, crawling around from shell hole to shell hole, telling us it was not as bad as it seemed, to stick it out a while longer." The private could not believe Duffy's disregard for enemy snipers, machine gunners, and exploding shells. "Why I saw him with red eyes burying our dead right out in the open with Jerry looking down at him from machine gun nests a couple of hundred yards away. He was digging away with a pick by himself, just as a cool as though planting potatoes in his back-yard. How he got away with it, God knows."[15]

The German counterattack and the failure of the American ar-tillery to knock out machine-gun nests or even open the wire were the last straw for the wounded Donovan. Long-range gas and shrapnel shells, as well as enfilading fire from Côte de Châtillon, continued to rip up Kelly's First Battalion. Donovan believed that his men were alone, without any flanking support, and were about to be cut off. He thought it best to pause to regroup and then resume fighting afterward. Kelly and his men must retire. Donovan ordered his troops to pull back from the wire—a decision that brought down the ire of his superior officers.

Donovan's order came just when Brig. Gen. Michael Lenihan, aware that the advance in front of the wire had stalled, was calling for the attack to be renewed. At ten-thirty Lenihan telephoned his new order to Col. Harry Mitchell at his regimental command post. Relaying the order quickly from Mitchell to Donovan would be more difficult, because the phone line between them had been cut by shellfire. The only way to get word to Donovan in a hurry was by horseback. Mitchell dispatched two riders to tell Wild Bill that he was not to let up, but to press the attack. He sent the same orders to Anderson and Kelly. To the riders, he said, "Don't spare your horses!"[16]

As it turned out, it was already too late when the orders reached Donovan, according to the wounded lieutenant colonel. He had already made up his mind and sent word for Kelly to retire. After making the decision, Donovan was carried back behind the lines. On the way, he ran into Duffy.

"Father, you're a disappointed man," he said. "You expected to have the pleasure of burying me over here."

Replied the chaplain, "I certainly did, Bill, and you're a lucky dog to get off with nothing more than you've got."[17]

In front of the wire, Kelly, although weakened by a high fever, had not called it quits. Dynamite Mike's "fighting blood was up," Duffy said.[18] His battalion had closed to within two hundred yards of the wire, and was moving forward. Some of his troops had worked their way close enough that they could reach out and touch it. Others had gotten inside the entanglements and mixed it up in hand-to-hand combat with the enemy. Kelly believed his men still had the strength to push through. If Sgt. John Henry Dennelley of Great Neck was forced to withdraw his A Company platoon he would not leave the wire while any of his men were still in danger. He planned to stay and fight. His captain, Oscar Buck, badly wounded, also refused to go to the rear and hung on until felled by utter exhaustion. In B Company, after his lieutenant and sergeant had been knocked out of action, Matthew Brennan from Hoboken led his platoon close to the wire under a blistering machine-gun and artillery attack before withdrawing. A private in Brennan's company, Peter Hunt from the Bronx, recalled how the men "would creep forward a way, getting our clothes all torn and our skins torn on the barbs, then stand up and jump into the nearest shell hole. It took an hour to go a hundred yards."[19]

Charles Cain, from Waltham, Massachusetts, scoured the battlefield for ammunition for his brethren in D Company who were slugging it out with the Germans. Exposing himself to gunfire, he ran from body to body, stripping off cartridges and grenades from each dead soldier so he could resupply his men.

Because Kelly's men continued to fight, Donovan dispatched a runner with yet another order to retire.

Have sent you several messages relative to withdrawal. A Co. & B Co. in ridge covering your left. Anderson is moving forward to hold hill. You withdraw thru him. Start upon receipt of this. Go back to reserve position and reorganize. Bring back to hill top your dead and wounded. Donovan.[20]

In compliance with Mitchell's latest order, Major Anderson's Second Battalion was advancing to provide support when Donovan arrived on a stretcher. According to Anderson, Donovan continued to command in spite of his wound. And it was clear he wanted Kelly's battalion withdrawn.

"Have you received the attack order?" Anderson asked him.

Donovan answered yes, but it had reached him too late. The division's artillery had failed to clear the way. Tanks assigned to the brigade had not shown up. For the most part the tanks had been rendered useless. He worried that the regiment had no flanking support, that his men were too exhausted and sick to be effective—and the grim news reaching him was that the dead were piling up in front of the wire.

"But orders are orders!" Anderson said, although he agreed with Donovan the order had arrived late and the artillery barrage was no help. "I'm going to move out to the attack!"

"No, you cannot," countered Donovan. "I will assume responsibility for your not going."

Anderson's battalion, meanwhile, continued forward. Donovan said to him that Kelly's men were to retire through his battalion. Then he scribbled a message to Colonel Mitchell.

> Co. A & C against enemy, liaison men report entire companys lie dead in front of wire, 166 and 167 have not come up with us, we are receiving flanking M.G. fire, not only accross front but rear companys as well as support Batt. Artillery fire is firing, infilating fire from left. Your message for new attack received at 12:05 P.M. Major Anderson is now moving up to relieve Kelly. Send on orders for attack impossible to comply with present orders time has passed. Artillery is not putting out M.G. nests, the assaulting troops followed very closely up to enemy wire but there met with long range infillade fire from both flanks. Donovan.[21]

When Mitchell got the message he felt Donovan had erred. He later explained to division higher-ups.

> No matter what the cost apparently might be in carrying out such orders it sometimes became necessary for certain elements to advance when the prospect might not be of the best in succeeding in reaching the objective as it might be necessary to make sacrifices some places along the line in order to carry out or reach the main objective at some other part of the line, with which we were not familiar. I tried to impress upon them the gravity and risk an officer must assume in disregarding an order under these conditions.[22]

Mitchell felt he had no choice but to relieve Donovan of command, placing Anderson in charge. Wild Bill, with a tag on his right big toe, was then removed to a dressing station and brought to a base hospital. His wound, which he likened to what would result from being hit in the back of the leg by a spiked club, had crushed nerves and tendons below the knee, and opened a hole that extended two-and-a-half inches down the tibia.

The New Yorkers, in respect for their commander, named the slope in front of the wire entanglement, "Donovan's Ridge."

On the battlefield that day, B Company Sgt. Bill Thornton, of the Bronx, said, "Well, we got through a whole battalion of us.

William Donovan himself up there giving orders. Then we were too far ahead to go any further, so we dug in and that's about all, I guess."[23]

A running account from division headquarters, commencing at twelve-forty (soon after Donovan had been taken off the field), tells a desperate tale.

> Our elements against wire. Our flanking units have not come up. We are receiving flanking M.G. fire not only along the front but on the rear companies as well as support battalion. 2nd Bn. is now moving up to relieve Kelly.
>
> 2:40—1st Bn. retiring thru 2nd Bn. and getting badly shot up. 2nd Bn. given instructions to dig in and be prepared to stop any counter attack which may follow the retirement. They are under very heavy enfilading fire.
>
> 3:00—Heavy shelling of 77s and M.G. fire sweeping our left flank. Kelly with 1st Bn. ordered to withdraw and Anderson to hold hill on which his P.C. is now located. Cos. A and B will extend east from road junction. Co. B is holding the first slope of Hill W of Sommerance Landres road. D Co. will extend B's left. M.G. are on our right and left flanking us from a distance as well as from M.G. nests which we have coordinated are still firing upon us. Enemy artillery is very active and is thoroughly combing hill.
>
> 4:50—Our men moved into shell holes. Are receiving fire from right and left.
>
> 6:50—Visit from Maj. Gen. Summerall, C.G., 5th Army Corps to talk over situation.[24]

On the 14th, the 165th suffered fifty deaths. But on the 15th, the day "Von Summeralz" had stormed into Mitchell's headquarters, the First Battalion alone lost seventy-four men killed while the total for the regiment reached 111.

One of the wounded turned out to be Sgt. Richard O'Neill. He had made it back in time to take part in the last days of the fight only, to get hit by shrapnel. He later shrugged off the wound, saying that it was nothing compared to what had happened at the Ourcq. "I always figured [those shrapnel wounds] didn't count."[25] The total strength of Kelly's First had been pared down to six officers and 186 men. Anderson's Second was down to 480 men and Maj. Tom Reilley's Third, held in reserve, counted 496 men. As one historian has put it, "This regiment had a little over 40 percent of its combat troops left with which to fight."[26]

Summerall was beside himself with anger at the entire regiment, and over the next day or so he would clean house. And the fighting was far from over. Summerall wanted Landres taken on the next day—or else.

Charles MacArthur's disdain for Summerall was evident afterward, when he described how the doughboys had been "sleeping in the rain for weeks, a single soaking blanket between them and the cold October slop. They were less than 60 per cent effective on the morning of Saint-Georges: full of dysentery, pneumonia, and fight." MacArthur continued, telling how, when this information was presented to Summerall, "His Nibs took another chew of tobacco and ordered the doughboys to take the town or come back 100 per cent. dead."[27]

Again, on the 16th, the Eighty-third Brigade attacked the wire at Landres-et-St. Georges. Again, it was pinned down and again it was unable to crack the German line there. It was relieved, brought back to rest and regroup, and then, in a few days, to continue on. Meanwhile, the Eighty-fourth Brigade pressed the attack, and drove the Germans out of Côte de Châtillon.

As far as Duffy was concerned, the "situation" in front of the wire was a "stalemate." He lamented, "We had made an advance of three kilometers under desperate conditions but in spite of our losses and sacrifices we had failed to take our final objective. Well, success is not always the reward of courage." He added, "The most glorious day in the history of our regiment in the Civil War was Fredericksburg, where the Old 69th in the Irish Brigade failed to capture the impregnable position on Marye's Heights, though their dead with the green sprigs in their caps lay in rows before it. Landres et St. Georges is our Fredericksburg and the Kriemhilde Stellung our Marye's Heights."[28]

Summerall felt otherwise: there was no glory for the 165th Infantry or for the Eighty-third Brigade. He sacked Lenihan; Mitchell; Van S. Merle-Smith, the regiment's operations officer; and Lt. Earl Betty, the regiment's assistant adjutant. He brought in Henry Reilly, the artillery commander, and put him in charge of the Brigade. He moved the division's machine-gun commander, Lt. Col. Charles Dravo, into Mitchell's spot. Donovan, now in

Paris recovering from his wounds, escaped Summerall's wrath. He received the Medal of Honor instead.

The dismissal of two of the top officers in the division and the threatened firing of Col. Benson Hough of the 166th sank the morale of the Rainbow men. Raymond Cheseldine, a captain in Hough's regiment, believed the entire brigade had been given a bum rap. Referring to insufficient artillery support, he said that to "execute a considerable advance, any attack made without artillery would be sheer suicide."[29] Even Reilly, whose artillery units had not provided the cover the infantry needed, admitted, "In the Landres-St. Georges Battle the 165th Infantry not only repeated its Fredericksburg history in making repeated assaults but stayed there in the open receiving fire not only from the front but also from the right flank and in some cases even the right rear until the capture of the Côte de Châtillon by the 84th Brigade entirely changed the whole situation."[30]

Duffy called Summerall's decision wrong. In his diary, he wrote diplomatically, "I do not wish to adopt too critical a tone with regard to the action of the Corps Commander. He is the military superior, and his judgment must be accepted even if it is wrong."[31] But in a Thanksgiving Day letter to Gen. Frank McCoy, the chaplain took a different tone. It was in this letter that he had told McCoy that behind Summerall's back the soldiers called him "Von Summeralz" and that he, Duffy, "may get hanged" for telling him. He said after the general had met with the officers he returned to his headquarters and "off went their heads." He said Mitchell, Merle-Smith, and Betty were "mortally" and "mentally" defeated. He said Mitchell had been "too decent to defend himself" and that Merle-Smith was "too honest to be a diplomat and got into a controversy with the General about what can be expected of troops." Betty, he claimed, "who had come from the front was dazzled by the four stars as if they were four suns. And the General went away mad."[32]

Years later, a bunch of veterans were at the Sixty-ninth Armory on Lexington Avenue reminiscing about the Meuse-Argonne. One of them was Cpl. Bill Fleming of H Company, who believed that the wire that had stopped the 165th had afterward been broken by artillery fire.

"Oh God, everyone caught it there," Fleming said. "We were supposed to take this area, but we had no artillery. And they had acres and acres of that goddamned barbed wire."

"Jeez, I'll say so," another veteran piped up. "We left a lot of good men hanging on that wire.

"And that clown Summerall, he's sitting back in corps head-quarters on his fat ass wondering why we can't move. Why, we couldn't move because we'd had the hell shot out of us. Then he moves all these big guns up. Why, they had them lined up hub to hub. We'll, they pulverized that barbed wire. Then Summerall calls in the 2nd Division to take the place. Oh, they had not trouble atall. But why should they? There was no goddamn wire."[33]

It took the First American Army a month to punch through the defenses of the Meuse-Argonne and drive the Germans out of the steep ridges and narrow gorges. Once through, Pershing looked north to one last prize, a prize the French knew belonged to them and were not about to cede to the Americans—the city of Sedan.

24

"We Looked Down from the Last Crest Above Sedan"

"I do sleep and eat and enjoy myself except when some of my lads are killed," Chaplain Francis Duffy wrote to his father. "That's the hardest part and that is why I am praying the war will be over before any more go the unreturnable road."[1] When Duffy penned this letter on 28 October, many of the dead of the Eighty-third Brigade were still stuck on the wire in front of Landres-et-St. Georges. He had gone back to bury them, a job he loathed. Once, in the Champagne sector, after a burial detail, he had said to Frank McCoy, who then commanded the 165th, "Some people get the rotten end of your damned old war."[2] Now, again, he worked the "rotten end," going up to the wire with Sgt. Tom Fitzsimmons whose gallantry at the same spot two weeks earlier had put down a German counterattack. Duffy called it "my own sad quest."

At one point, a German shell hit four Americans and five German prisoners who had been walking toward them. The doughboys were from the Second Division, which, after relieving the Forty-second, fought through the wire and got credit for capturing Landres-et-St. Georges. Almost all in the group were killed instantly except one American and one German officer. This American's legs had been blown off. He did not know it, but sensed something terribly wrong. He tried to sit up, but Duffy put his hand on his chest and held him down. The priest gave him absolution and he died soon after, while next to him the German officer cursed his bad luck at being hit by his own men. Duffy stayed with the dead and wounded until an ambulance came up and then he and Fitzsimmons moved to the wire.

"On both sides of the Sommerance road as it neared the wire," he wrote, "we saw the bodies scattered, still well preserved and recognizable by reason of the cool weather. Right around the wire and in the sunken road that ran into it the Germans had buried them."[3]

When Duffy returned to headquarters and gave his report to Charles Dravo, new orders had been posted. The Rainbows were on the march again. Now attached to Lt. Gen. Joseph Dickman's I Corps, the Forty-second Division was to be part of a massive push made by Pershing's First Army toward the Meuse River south of Sedan.

It was a different regiment that headed off once again to battle the enemy. Since the Meuse-Argonne more replacements had poured in, new officers, new men. Many of the original soldiers were gone—killed, wounded, or transferred. Duffy took note of the change, especially at the top. He had gone through so many colonels that it was hard for him to remember them all. To McCoy, his favorite, he complained that since 1916 he had had seven commanding officers. But had acknowledged that, where it counted most, the 165th was still led by seasoned veterans (although he missed Wild Bill Donovan, now a celebrity recuperating at a Paris hospital). Maj. Alexander Anderson served under Dravo as second in command. Van S. Merle-Smith, who had been purged from the regiment by Summerall, had been reassigned to it because Lt. Gen. Hunter Liggett of the First Army found he had done nothing wrong. He was placed in charge of the First Battalion when Mike Kelly had to step down because of illness. Healed of his wounds, Maj. Henry Bootz returned to command Anderson's Second Battalion. Maj. Tom Reilley still led the Third. It was a comfort to Duffy that these men were still in charge.

On 5 November, the 165th passed through the Seventy-eighth Division, about fifteen miles from Sedan. Marching on its right flank was the Seventy-seventh Division, the New York draftees that the Irish soldiers had not crossed trails with since that magical night in the Lorraine sector.

First Lt. J. Phelps Harding, Maj. Tom Reilley's liaison officer, wrote to his mother, "We started chasing the Hun again, taking over a definite sector. It was this drive that pushed the Boche back to the Meuse and that gave us Sedan. . . . We marched and fought day and night for over thirty kilometers, up and down hill, meeting long range machine guns and harrassing artillery fire practically all the way."[4]

At the time, the Eighty-third Brigade had no idea it was in a race to reach Sedan: following close behind were the Fortieth French Division, as well as the First Division, which had orders to outleg the Rainbows to the Meuse. Charles Summerall who, as commander of V Corps, had misread an order from Pershing (perhaps purposely) so that his beloved First—in France longer than any other division—would enter Sedan before the other units. The order, which reached both the I and V Corps on the 5th, read that Pershing "desires that the honor of entering Sedan should fall to the 1st American Army." The next sentence assigns that honor specifically to Dickman's corps. "He [Pershing] has every confidence that the troops of the 1st Corps, assisted on their right by the 5th Corps, will enable him to realize that desire." But Summerall's eyes lit up when he read, further down in the order, "Boundaries [between units] will not be considered as binding."[5] To him this meant that the taking of Sedan was a wide-open race. He rushed to First Division headquarters "like a bat out of hell with his usual recklessness under fire"[6] and commanded that its top officer, Frank Parker, take the city "regardless of the tactical and operational situation in the field."[7] Few commanders knew of Pershing's order and none of them were aware that Summerall was off on a mad dash for glory. His order for the Big Red One to capture Sedan was almost one of the great blunders of the war.

For the French, Sedan was a symbolic city. Capturing it meant more to the nation in the closing days of the war than any other event. In 1870, during the Franco-Prussian War, the loss of Sedan had been one of France's worst military debacles. Now, driving the Germans out was paramount—and an honor the French demanded as a right.

Pershing felt otherwise. "It was the ambition of the First Army and mine," he wrote, "that our troops capture Sedan." He had proposed to Gen. Paul Maistre, who commanded the French Army Group on the American right flank, that boundaries be ignored "in case we should outrun the French." According to Pershing, Maistre "warmly approved." The American general then issued his order, and as he recorded in his memoirs, "I Corps was directed to bend its energies to capture Sedan . . . The 42d and the 1st then began a race for the honor of capturing Sedan."[8]

As they took up their march to the Meuse, the Rainbows were ignorant of their rivals in the First Division coming after them, crossing into their territory. They were too distracted by the retreating Germans' pestering rearguard action to be aware of any incursion by friendly soldiers. Soon elements of the Sixteenth Infantry ran into outposts of the 168th Infantry. Getting word that strange troops were in the area of his Eighty-fourth Brigade, Douglas MacArthur went to investigate. He was astonished to learn that they were from the First Division and he feared his own men might fire on them. Because MacArthur wore his hat floppy, not stiff on the sides, and had a woolen muffler around his neck, a young lieutenant in the Sixteenth mistook him for a German officer and took him prisoner at gunpoint. Moments later, with the lieutenant apologizing profusely, he was released.

In the Eighty-third Brigade, Col. Henry Reilly also ran into elements of the First Division. A signal corps major showed up, saying he was there to set up his division's command post. Reilly told him that he must be mistaken, that he had stumbled into the sector assigned to the Forty-second. The major replied that five columns from the First were already ahead of them, marching parallel to the Meuse. He informed Reilly that Parker was poised to cross the Meuse and advance on Sedan. Reilly learned, too, that the Fortieth French Division was moving toward Sedan with new orders from the French Sixth Army, under Maistre, to enter first, as this honor rightfully belonged to the French.

Reilly hurriedly fired off a memorandum to Menoher about the confusion—one division cutting into another's sector and the French demanding the right to enter Sedan. Menoher summoned him to his command post. When he arrived, the general was on the phone with an enraged General Dickman, who had just learned that First Division troops had "mingled with his on the firing line, and that their trains and personnel were complicating his operations in such a way as to make the situation impossible." Dickman also had learned from the Seventy-seventh Division that it had "encountered detachments from the 1st Division of various sizes, going in every direction." His orders to Menoher were straightforward "Take command of all troops in [your] sector."[9]

Although the receiver was pressed to Menoher's ear, Reilly plainly heard Dickman's sharp, angry voice. The corps commander then wanted to speak to Reilly. He gave him specific orders: find Parker and order him to withdraw his division without hesitation.

"Do you understand that message?"

"Yes Sir!" Reilly replied.[10]

While Reilly searched for Parker, the 165th Infantry slogged ahead, reaching Les Petites Armoises and Tannay. Duffy noticed how difficult it was to move forward because "every outfit had lost half of its animals and those that were left were in miserable condition."[11] The villages they passed through had white flags flying on church steeples, a sign to the allies that Germans did not occupy them.

Marching through the freed villages, where people poured out to greet them, the regiment was overwhelmed. "The people . . . treated us like their deliverers," Harding remembered. And what made it touching, he wrote, was that even though the Germans had taken away most of their food, "Still, when our troops passed through, muddy, tired and hungry, but still going strong, these people gave all they had. Old women stood in their doorways handing out German bread, coffee and raw vegetables. Coffee seemed plentiful, and people gave without end."

Because he was liaison officer, Harding usually reached villages before the rest of the troops. In one town, he rested in a café, sipping coffee. A French officer from the Fortieth Division appeared on the main street, the first French soldier in the village in almost four years. When he was spotted, doors were flung open. "The old women and men ran out crying 'Vive la France' and waving their hands; the children ran toward the officer and all tried to kiss him at the same time. The old people crowded around and shook his hand; then the old women hugged and kissed each other. Some of them crying in their joy. Then someone found a small tricolor, which caused another demonstration. It is probably hard for you over in the States to realize what it means to these people to be free again."[12]

The liberation of Sedan was near. For the 165th Infantry, all that stood in the way were two measly hills.

Hill 346 and Hill 252 held panoramic views of the Meuse Valley, and from the tops of them the skyline of Sedan was a mile away. The city's nearest suburb was Wadelincourt, which extended down the slopes of both hills along the south bank of the Meuse. Each hill offered strong defenses for the protection of Sedan. Germans were burrowed in and ready for one of the last, needless fights of the war. The Second Battalion of the 165th Infantry, under command of Papa Bootz, the tall, lanky German-American, had been ordered to take Hill 346 on the morning of 7 November.

In support was Reilley's Third Battalion and in reserve, Merle-Smith's First. After Hill 346 was swept clear of the enemy, Reilley's men would advance on Hill 252 and clean it up, and the way into Sedan would be open for the Eighty-third Brigade.

One of the foul-ups that resulted from Summerall's careless crossover into the Forty-second Division's sector was that all roads leading into Sedan were clogged, the traffic just inching along. Edwin James of the *New York Times,* on the day the 165th was to take Hill 346, tried to get into Sedan, but in vain. The roads, he reported, were "torn and so filled with traffic that it was impossible to get to the city." He had been able to look across the river. There he saw civilians "in the streets cheering to the Americans."[13] Because of the traffic, Menoher's artillery was unable to keep pace with its infantry; and rifle ammunition was running low.

Going up Hill 346 with no artillery support, inadequate rifle rounds, and a desperate enemy waiting on top with machine-gun emplacements did not thrill the Irish regiment. And if they had known their predicament was Von Summeralz's fault, each soldier would have wanted the chance to take a whack at him with the old shillelagh that had been given them by Maj. Gen. John O'Ryan when the Sixty-ninth departed New York a year ago.

Bill Fleming of H Company, who despised Summerall with all his Irish heart, later recalled the intense German fire that fell on the Second Battalion as it waited in the valley in front of Hill 346. "It was evident that [the enemy] intended making a more determined stand."[14]

Bootz ordered G Company, led by Capt. Louis Stout from Kansas City, and a platoon from Fleming's H Company to charge the hill.

Before the assault, one of Stout's replacement men, yet to taste battle, yelled, "Gimme some ammunition!"

"Haven't got any for myself," came a hollered reply.

"Only one clip left," shouted another replacement soldier.

"No ammunition. What're we gonna do?"

"Ah, whaddye want with ammunition?" snarled an old-timer. "When ye git oop on that hill show thim Heinies yer bay-nit and they'll run away!"[15]

Duffy, always close to his boys, remembered how Stout's thirty-eight men, "kept crawling in on the Germans."[16]

Fleming reported how the men "advanced in squad rushes." But their approach proved too slow. They tried platoon rushes, and that also was too slow. Then 1st Sgt. Pat Neary sprinted to the lead and shouted, "H Company follow me!"[17]

Duffy saw Stout call on his followers to fix their bayonets and "with a great cheer our fellows swarmed up the crest."[18] Reported Thomas Johnson of the *New York Evening World*, Stout "ran up to the head of the company and 'Fix Bayonets' he shouted. Then placing himself at the head of his men he took them forward and upward to the crest."

It was a brief fight. The Germans knew the war was over. Most of them threw down their weapons and threw up their hands. Those who stood and fought were bayoneted on the hilltop as the Irish doughboys went at them with "howls of anger." Johnson described how the Americans in "torn, faded khaki sprang upon the men in gray and the fighting was short—but very sharp."[19] The fight was indeed short and sharp. Five men in the battalion died on the crest of Hill 346, and a day later two more succumbed to their wounds.

Amid the dead, the victorious Second Battalion rounded up twenty-five prisoners and collected twelve enemy machine guns and other weapons. As Bootz came up the hill, Reilley, who's next stop was Hill 252, joined him. The officers were then surprised to see a strange captain struggling up behind them. It turned out he was from the Sixteenth Infantry, First Division.

The captain said to Bootz, "Well, Major, we have taken the hill."

"We?" said an incredulous Bootz. Then, according to Johnson, the "blood of Bootz's ancestors [came] to the fore as it has a way of doing when men are angry." Duffy, Reilley, and other officers from the 165th were just as angry, and they each recalled Bootz's reaction.

"Vell, if you took de hill vere's the booty?" Bootz said, his German accent thick among the dead and living enemy scattered atop Hill 346.

The First Division captain admitted he had no booty.

"Vell, I don't know what you found, but ve found quite a lot of Chermens. Some of 'em ve killed, some ve kept. You better get t'ell off our hill now because ve need it ourselves!" Duffy remembered Bootz adding, "This is my hill and my line of advance."

The captain slunk down the hill and soon the Sixteenth Infantry melted away from the heights overlooking Sedan, as Reilley's men in the Third Battalion came up.[20]

Now, with the artillery inside Sedan dumping shells on the Irish regiment, it was time for the Third Battalion to capture Hill 252—the 165th's last engagement of the war.

Meanwhile, Merle-Smith's First Battalion, followed by a unit from the Fortieth French Division, arrived on Hill 346. He had had the foresight to commandeer a 75-caliber gun and its crew from the French. Because it looked like the Americans were going to reach Sedan first, the crew was glad to help out. The gun was a godsend. After blasting Hill 252 and the woods surrounding it, a platoon led by Sgt. Bill Lyons from the Gashouse District advanced into the smoldering woods and captured or killed several machine gunners. One of Lyons's boys was shot and the sergeant carried him out of harm's way.

During the skirmish in the woods, Merle-Smith spotted what he figured were elements of the Sixteenth Infantry blending in with his own men in the rear of his battalion and taking part in the firefight. Several companies from the Second Battalion also were fighting and Fleming's company actually moved toward the Meuse. "It was necessary to scramble down a very steep hill to reach the marshy ground over which we had to travel to reach the stream," Fleming said. "As we hit the marsh the Germans brought their artillery into action for the first time in that sector and you can be sure we were glad on reaching the stream to get the order to return to our fox holes."

With the woods cleared, Reilley's battalion advanced on Hill 252. The major described it. "The advance was made down Hill 346 and up Hill 252 opposite in the face of comparatively severe machine gun fire. The battalion reached the crest of Hill 252 drawing off killing and wounding the German machine gunners. Some they bayoneted. From its top the Meuse River was in plain sight nearby." The way up Hill 252 was slippery and as the men ran ahead, ducked down, and lunged forward again, many of them lost their footing. Even Reilley took a tumble. "My feet went out from under me and I did a typical Charlie Chaplin fall. A machine gun bullet creased my tin hat. The fall was the only thing that saved me."[21]

Correspondent Johnson reported, "It was only through great courage amid bursting shells that the hilltop was reached, but little or nothing was found in the way of Germans." The machine gunners, he wrote, had taken off down the hill "to the river bank and disappeared in the undergrowth."[22]

Harding told his mother how the Third Battalion "dug in on the reverse slope of the hill from the Boche, and he promptly let loose with all his artillery, giving us the heaviest strafing we have had for a week or so. He threw everything at us—high explosives, gas and shrapnel—but we lost only a few men, thanks to luck and the fairly steep slope."[23]

With Hill 252 captured, Reilley waited until dark and then sent a reconnaissance patrol from M Company to the banks of the Meuse to locate bridges that the regiment could use to cross the river and enter Sedan. If the men discovered that Wadelincourt was unoccupied, they were "to penetrate it," Reilley said, "and hold it as long as they could." Before the patrol reached the river it came under heavy fire. Eighteen men were wounded, including its leader, Sgt. John Barrow from Hell's Kitchen, and two were killed, Pfc. Horace Baker and Pvt. James Smith. Cpl. John McLoughlin from Wards Island and two others went on by themselves. They snaked up to the Meuse although the Germans kept up a machine-gun barrage on them and then crept along the edge of the muddy banks, taking note of their surroundings. McLoughlin marked four machine-gun nests and which bridges were suitable to cross. He returned with excellent information, and, said Reilley, "As Wadelincourt was held in some strength the job of taking it was left until morning."[24]

The division reported,

At 15 hours the 165th Infantry had driven the enemy from Hill 252 and sent a patrol forward to Wadelincourt. The patrol was unable to enter the town on account of heavy machine gun fire from across the river and returned after receiving several casualties. The line of its advance marked the point farthest north reached by the American forces driving between the Argonne and the Meuse. At dark we held the line of the river with outposts along the whole of our sector front.[25]

The next morning the regiment was ordered to withdraw. For the Irish doughboys the war, basically, was over. Fleming said, "We pulled out for the last time. The French troops moved in."[26] Wrote Duffy to McCoy, "They sent us in again on the advance and we went at it with oldtime vigor, ending our career as we looked down from the last crest above Sedan."[27]

For political reasons, the French had been given the right to enter Sedan first. The Fortieth Division marched in, with a token company from the 166th Infantry, the Ohioans. A token company from the 165th was to go in as well, but a planning error kept the New Yorkers out. No token company from the First Division, however, had been invited to go along

The taking of Hills 346 and 252 resulted in 125 wounded and 17 killed. The high casualty rate might have been due to Summerall's crossing over into the Forty-second Division sector. However, no charges were brought against him, because the war ended a few days later, or perhaps because Pershing liked him—or at least because the general reasoned, "the splendid record of that unit . . . suggested leniency."[28] On the morning the 165th had made its assault on the hills overlooking Sedan, Summerall ran into Menoher; the Rainbow commander drove straight past him. Once again misreading events, Summerall recollected, "He did not stop though he could have and reported to me any complaint that he had to make of the First Division." It never occurred to the self-centered Von Summeralz that maybe Menoher had purposely snubbed him.[29]

Four days later, on 11 November, the war was over.

"I had always believed that the news of victory and peace would fill me with surging feelings of delight," Duffy mused. "But it was just the contrary; no doubt because the constraint I had put upon my natural feelings during the year were taken off by the announcement. I knew that in New York and in every city at home and throughout the world men were jubilant. . . . But I could think of nothing except the fine lads who had come out with us to this war and who are not alive to enjoy the triumph. All day I had a lonely and an aching heart. It would be a lesser thing to have been killed myself than to go back to the mothers of the dead who would never more return."[30]

Harding, who had fought his way up the last hill with Reilley, wrote to his mother. "The day after we left the line the guns stopped firing, and armistice started. May peace come—I've seen all the war I want!"[31]

In Base Hospital 27 in Nantes, Cpl. Martin Hogan, recovering from wounds he had gotten in the Meuse-Argonne scrap, recalled how the boys in the cots in his ward took the news of the armistice without emotion. The staff served up a special meal for the occasion. "We enjoyed the dinner," he recalled, "and let the armistice go at that."[32]

Pvt. Nathaniel Rouse, who had taken a bullet in the head at St. Mihiel, had moved from hospital to hospital. He found a job working for the YMCA to pass the time. In his diary on the 11th he wrote, "This is a RED letter day. They say the war is finis. I hope so. The bunch went wild at Red Cross."[33]

Sgt. Richard O'Neill, wounded again in the Meuse-Argonne, had been shuffled off to another hospital on the morning of the 11th. He wrote, "War over 11th month, 11th day, 11th hour. Arrive hospital 7:30 on 11th. A lot of celebrating galore."[34]

After being wounded, Lt. Austin Lawrence had been assigned to a hospital and then reassigned to the Seventh Aviation Instruction Center. He was on the road when the war ended. "La guerre fini," he entered in his diary.[35]

Jim McKenna was dead, not a scratch on him. Joyce Kilmer was dead, and so was Oliver Ames Jr., one shot through the forehead and the other through the ear. They were buried together, next to Malcolm Robertson, near where they had fallen on the banks of the Ourcq. Patrick Dowling was dead, his legs found on the north slope of the Ourcq. Charles Baker was dead, his arm amputated at the shoulder. John Kayes was dead. William Hudson was dead. Oscar Ammon had been killed by friendly fire. A platoon from E Company had been buried alive at Rouge Bouquet. The Four Musketeers and their leader Peter Crotty were all dead. Two of the three O'Neill brothers were dead, along with cousin Bernard Finnerty. Young Danny O'Connell, the altar boy, ("Heaven, Hell or Hoboken by Christmas") had died charging up the hill at Meurcy Farm. The quiet George Patrick McKeon was dead. Howard Arnold, the Jewish officer, was dead. Tom Minogue was dead, but never forgotten by his fellow soldiers at their neighborhood church in Hell's Kitchen. Bob Foster, who had carried the Irish flag over the top was dead. Color Sergeant Bill Sheahan was gone, too, blown to smithereens. The list seems endless. Duffy knew nearly everyone of them personally, and with the war over, he felt it his duty to travel to all the battlefields "to pay as far as I could my last duties to the dead, to record and in a rough way to beautify their lonely graves, for I knew that soon we would leave this place that their presence hallows, and never look upon it again."[36]

EPILOGUE

"We Want Him. We Need Him. He Has Earned It."

The war was over, yet it would be another half-year before the 165th Infantry boarded any troop ships to return home to New York. The Forty-second Division was ordered into Germany as part of the occupation forces. "Watch on the Rhine," the troops called it—another duty for the Rainbows. Since its border days in 1916, the old Sixty-ninth had been away from Manhattan Island, off and on, for twenty-nine of the past thirty-four months. With another six months soon to be tacked on, this would amount to an absence of nearly three years—one of the longest stretches of any National Guard regiment in the country.

Serving in the Rhine as part of the Forty-second, the 165th had spent 164 days in combat. The division itself lost almost three thousand men, killed in action or dead of wounds. Almost twelve thousand more had been wounded. Its casualty total of close to fifteen thousand was more than fifty percent of the division's force.

The 165th took the most casualties. Of those who died in action, or later of wounds and disease, the number of deaths reached 844. Wild Bill Donovan's First Battalion had the most, with 299. His A Company suffered ninety-four dead. The Second Battalion had 213 men who lost their lives, while the Third Battalion counted 255 "gone west."[1] The total figure for the regiment was actually higher than the official one— a figure impossible to count because no one will ever know how many unfortunate souls, after returning to the United States, later died of complications from the gas they had inhaled on the battlefield.

First Lt. George Benz from Conshocken, Pennsylvania, who had been sent home after his gas wounds and then worked for the *New York World* for a few months, died in December 1918. He is not listed as a casualty. Chaplain Father James Hanley, another unlisted mustard gas casualty, died of pneumonia on 25 May 1920, his thirty-third birthday, a year after returning home from the Western Front. All the religious relics Cpl. Leo Throop's parents had received from Pope Leo XIII failed to save him; gas got him a year after he returned home to Brooklyn. One more unlisted casualty, Throop was twenty-two when he died.

And neither is Capt. Samuel Sedgwick Swift of Vergennes, Vermont, on any casualty list. Swift had sucked in gas in the Meuse-Argonne. The Plattsburgh officer wrote to his Uncle Charley and Aunt Jessica from the base hospital in Vichy on 30 November. "My wounds are practically healed up now. I have begun to hobble around the room for a few minutes at a time now, clutching at the various beds and drawing down curses whenever I jiggle a compound fracture or some other sufferer. I am awfully weak after being in bed for so long—nearly seven weeks."[2]

Swift returned to Vermont and lived for almost ten years. But the gas that had burned his lungs finally took him on 20 August 1928. The cause of death as listed on his death certificate is Hodgkin's disease. The local newspaper recounted his last struggle for life.

He gave his all as an American soldier fighting courageously and desperately on the battlefields of France. Since that fatal wound he has fought with the same cheerful courage and the same pugnacious desperation to save his life. At times he was the victor. At times he lay prostrate as on that tragic day in France—October 11, 1918. Thus for this hero became not one war, but many, not one sacrifice, but a perpetual offering [sic]. He gave his all, only to give again and again for ten long years. Now the long conflict is ended. The captain is dead. Nature has triumphed, cruel, harsh, relentless nature.[3]

Swift's agonizing death was played out across the country countless times. Yet it was not always gas that got the veteran in the end.

Capt. Jim Finn, the powerful football star from Maine, endured a medical odyssey that would have killed lesser men a lot more quickly. He lost a sizeable chunk of his right leg on the north bank of the Ourcq River. At one time the doctors came close to amputating it. Finn stayed in hospitals for more than five years and it was not until 1 December 1923 that he was finally released and able to go back to work in New York. When he hobbled out of Walter Reed Hospital wearing a brace of steel and leather that ran from the sole of his right foot up to his hip, he was believed to be the last officer in the war to be discharged from a hospital.

Although never complaining, Finn lived in discomfort until 1957. When he died, the *Rainbow Barrage* wrote, "The good Lord reached down and took unto himself our beloved Captain Finn.[4]

Many other soldiers turned to drink to soothe their wartime nightmares. Pvt. Richard Leahy from East Harlem returned home and hit the bottle, trying to forget. One of his memories was that of his best friend, who had used to wear his helmet tipped forward over his eyes. A shell had hit the back of his head and blown it off. How could Leahy tell his friend's mother, when she asked how her boy had died, that his head just exploded away? In France Leahy had given up his good-luck necklace, a gift from his sister, Ann, trading it for a meal when there was not enough food. Ann had died while he was overseas. When he finally got home, his mother cried, "Ritchie went to the war sane, but came back crazy." Then in 1934, he made a pledge to his parish priest that he would drink no more. Leahy stayed sober for the rest of his life, and died at seventy-three.[5]

"Dynamite Mike" Kelly, who commanded Wild Bill Donovan's First Battalion in the Meuse-Argonne, accidentally shot himself in 1930. He was cleaning his service revolver when it went off and a bullet tore through his abdomen. His wife of twenty-one years heard the shot and ran into the living room of their apartment to find him slumped over a desk.[6]

On its march to the Rhine, the 165th Infantry received a new commander. While Lt. Col. Bill Donovan toiled unhappily for the provost marshal general, Col. Charles Roscoe Howland took control of his beloved regiment. A West Pointer, class of 1895, Howland had been an aide to Gen. Arthur MacArthur in the Philippines. He was the commander of the military prison at Alcatraz when the United States entered the war. Although he had received three Silver Stars for bravery and had been recommended for the Medal of Honor, his appointment did not sit well with Father Francis Duffy—or with Donovan. And it certainly did not sit well with the rank and file of the 165th.

Duffy led a quiet, behind-the-scenes mutiny to get Howland ousted and Donovan brought in as commander, to lead the regiment home. Duffy had once written to John Cardinal Farley that he was actively seeking some young major of Irish blood and Catholic faith to be colonel of the regiment. That search had taken more than year, but he had found his man on the battlefield, and he wanted him. Writing in his diary, he said of Donovan,

He is always physically fit, always alert, ready to do without food, sleep, rest, in the most matter of fact way, thinking of

Col. Charles Howland (third from left) took command of the 165th in
Germany. Lt. Col. Bill Donovan thought him a "stupid bore." Father Francis
Duffy (far left) plotted to have Howland replaced by Donovan. The man with
the Red Cross armband is Maj. George Lawrence. The others are
unidentified. *Signal Corps/National Archives*

nothing but the work at hand. He has mind and manners and
varied experience of life and resoluteness of purpose. He has
kept himself clean and sane and whole for whatever adventure
life might bring him, and he has come through this surpassing
adventure with honor and fame. I like him for his alert mind
and just views and ready wit, for his generous enthusiasms and
his whole engaging personality. The richest gain I have gotten
out of the war is the friendship of William J. Donovan.[7]

The feeling was mutual. Almost twenty years later, when the City
of New York erected a statue in Times Square to honor Duffy, Donovan
said,

It was [Duffy's] human quality that made him so real a chaplain.
He had great power of intellect and a wisdom that was more
than earthly. No priest held himself to a higher standard of duty.

After two years of trying to get the ideal commander for the old Sixty-ninth, Father Francis Duffy (right) finally got his man, Col. William Donovan. Remagen, Germany, 24 March 1919. *Signal Corps/National Archives*

All these elements of greatness were unified in a vivid, well-balanced sense of life. So it was that in his war service it was not the chaplain's insignia upon his shoulder, but the humanity in his heart that gave him the influence for good with the soldier of the A.E.F.[8]

Duffy drew Brigadier Generals Douglas MacArthur and Frank McCoy into his plot to get Donovan. As early as 14 November he had gotten MacArthur to act on Donovan's behalf and, in a letter to Wild

Women from the Knights of Columbus welcome home the old Sixty-ninth with flowers as the soldiers troop up New York's Fifth Avenue. *Signal Corps/National Archives*

Bill, Duffy wrote, "[MacArthur] says he is going to get you back at once to the Division."[9]

A few weeks later, on Thanksgiving Day, Duffy penned a plea to McCoy. "He [Donovan] has still hopes of getting back to us. Strong expectations, in fact. If you can give it a boost, I know you will. We want him. We need him. He has earned it. All potent reasons with Frank R. McCoy."[10]

A few months later, H. H. Bandholtz released Donovan from his job at the provost marshal general's office, and on Christmas Eve he rejoined his regiment in Remagen, Germany. Donovan did not take to Howland. In a letter to Ruth, without naming Howland, Donovan nevertheless made a clear reference to him; he called him "terrible" and a "stupid bore." "I don't see how he can last." He remarked on how the regiment was "united on me. It is very embarrassing for me—the men are very outspoken." He described a parade during which the troops yelled, "We want Donovan!" He wrote, "Perhaps a change will come. McCoy says so."[11]

The change did come. On 7 March 1919, Wild Bill was promoted to colonel and named commander of the 165th Infantry—the old Fighting Sixty-ninth. And on 21 April, with the mutinous chaplain by his side, he led it home to Gotham.

Father Duffy had his man at last.

Notes

Prologue

1. Alexander Woollcott, *While Rome Burns* (New York: The Viking Press, 1935), 50.
2. *New York Evening Post*, 27 June 1932, 8.
3. Ella M. E. Flick, *Chaplain Duffy of the Sixty-ninth Regiment, New York* (Philadelphia: The Dolphin Press, 1935), 106.
4. Woollcott, *While Rome Burns*, 46–50.
5. Father Francis Duffy, Archdiocese of New York archives, Yonkers, NY.
6. Woollcott, *While Rome Burns*, 48.
7. Martin Green, "Father Duffy Heroic in War," *New York Sun*, 27 June 1932, 15.
8. Green, "Father Duffy's Funeral Great City Tribute," *New York Sun*, 29 June 1932, 1 and 15.
9. *New York Times*, 29 June 1932, 21.
10. *New York Times*, 28 June 1932, 19.
11. Duffy, Archdiocese of New York archives, Yonkers, NY.
12. Green, "Father Duffy's Funeral Great City Tribute," 15.
13. William Donovan O'Neill, interview by author, 7 November 2003.
14. *New York Times*, 30 June 1932, 17.
15. Woollcott, *While Rome Burns*, 47.
16. Green, "Father Duffy Heroic in War," 15.
17. *New York Sun*, 29 June 1932, 15, and *New York Times*, 30 June 1932, 17. Accounts of Msgr. Michael J. Lavelle's eulogy vary, so I've combined reports from several newspapers.
18. *New York Times*, 30 June 1932, 17.
19. Francis P. Duffy, *Father Duffy's Story: A Tale Of Humor and Heroism, Of Life and Death With the Fighting Sixty-ninth* (New York: George H. Doran Company, 1919), 114–115.
20. Father Francis Duffy, Archdiocese of New York archives, Yonkers, NY.

Chapter 1

1. Very Rev. John F. Fenlon, "Father Duffy," *The Journal of the American Irish Historical Society*, 31, 1937, 139.
2. Thomas J. Shelley, "John Cardinal Farley and Modernism in New York," (Church History, 61: 3), 360.
3. Cardinal Farley to the Most. Rev. P. P. Stagni, Archbishop of Aquila, 4 March 1913. Archdiocese of New York archives, Yonkers, NY, Cardinal Farley, I 16, 1913.

4. Ella M. E. Flick, *Chaplain Duffy of the Sixty-ninth Regiment, New York.* (Philadelphia: The Dolphin Press, 1935), 18–19.
5. Observation by Thomas J. Conaty, rector of the Catholic University of America, 1 March 1897. Archdiocese of New York archives, Yonkers, NY.
6. Flick, *Chaplain Duffy*, 19.
7. Theodore Roosevelt, *The Rough Riders* (New York: Da Capo Press, Inc., 1990), 220.
8. Flick, *Chaplain Duffy*, 41.
9. Flick, *Chaplain Duffy*, 66.
10. Flick, *Chaplain Duffy*, 67.
11. Father Duffy to Cardinal Farley, 12 January 1916. New York Archdiocese archives, Yonkers, NY.
12. *New York Times*, 12 July 1916, 1.
13. *New York Sun*, 12 July 1916, 1 and 3.
14. *New York Sun*, 13 July 1916, 14. The *Post*'s editorial ran almost verbatim on the *Sun*'s editorial page.
15. *New York Times*, 12 July 1916.
16. Jeremiah A. O'Leary, *My Political Trial and Experiences* (New York: Jefferson Publishing Co., 1919), 3 and 5. Capt. Michael A. Kelly wrote a biographical sketch of O'Leary that was included in the book.
17. *New York Times*, 20 July 1916, 1.
18. Duffy, *Father Duffy's Story*, 26.
19. Duffy, *Father Duffy's Story*, 30.
20. Father Francis Duffy to John Cardinal Farley, 15 December 1916, Archdiocese of New York archives, Yonkers, NY.
21. *The Advocate*, 14 April 1917, 4.
22. Major General John F. O'Ryan, *The Story of the 27th Division*, vol. 1 (New York: Wynkoop, Hallenbeck, Crawford Co., 1921), 26–27.
23. *Brooklyn Daily Eagle*, 12 August 1916, 1.
24. *The Irish World and American Industrial Liberator*, 14 October 1916, 1.
25. *Brooklyn Daily Standard Union*, 14 August 1916, Section 2, 10.
26. *The Irish World and American Industrial Liberator*, 14 October 1916, 1I.
27. Father Duffy, letter to Cardinal Farley, 15 December 1916. Archdiocese of New York archives, Yonkers, NY.
28. *New York Sun*, 7 March 1917, 5.
29. Duffy, *Father Duffy's Story*, 331.

Chapter 2

1. *The Irish World and American Industrial Liberator*, 8 March 1917, 21.
2. From the papers of John T. Prout, copies of which are held by the estate of the late Col. Kenneth Powers, former historian of the Sixty-ninth Regiment, Westport, Conn.
3. Duffy, *Father Duffy's Story*, 28.
4. O'Leary, *My Political Trial*, 4.
5. Rupert Hughes, *Long Ever Ago.* (New York: Harper & Brothers Publisher, 1918), 86–87.
6. *New York Times*, 12 October 1860, 1.
7. Joseph F. Hourigan, "Brigadier General Michael Corcoran, 1927–1963," from History of the Fighting 69th, at Mr. Hourigan's website: www.69thny.com.

8. Interview with Phyllis Lane, 16 December 2004. Ms. Lane is one of the foremost authorities on Michael Corcoran.
9. O'Leary, *My Political Trial*, 9.
10. O'Leary, *My Political Trial*, 4.
11. *New York Times*, 6 October 1916, 3.
12. *The Gaelic American*, 7 October 1916, 1.
13. *New York Times*, 15 October 1917, 4.
14. O'Leary, *My Political Trial*, 47.
15. *Irish World*, 30 September 1916, 3.
16. *The Gaelic American*, 31 March 1917, 4.
17. Duffy, *Fathers Duffy's Story*, 13.

Chapter 3

1. Henry J. Reilly, *Americans All: The Rainbow At War*, 2nd ed. (Columbus, Ohio: F. J. Heer Printing Co., 1936), 26–27. In his book, Reilly, an officer in the Rainbow Division and a writer, collected personal remembrances from dozens of soldiers, including Gen. Douglas MacArthur and Secretary of War Newton Baker.
2. *New York Herald*, 3 June 1917, first section, part 2, 3.
3. Martin J. Hogan, *The Shamrock Battalion of the Rainbow Division: A Story of the "Fighting Sixty-ninth"* (New York: D. Appleton and Company, 1919), 5–6.
4. *New York Herald*, 3 June 1917.
5. *New York Herald*, 22 June 1917, 14.
6. *New York Herald*, 30 July 1917, 12.
7. Hogan, *The Shamrock Battalion*, 4–5.
8. Henry Berry, *Make the Kaiser Dance* (New York: Doubleday, 1978), 309.
9. Duffy, *Father Duffy's Story*, 332.
10. *Brooklyn Eagle*, 3 March 1918, 4.
11. O'Leary, *My Political Trial*, 125.
12. Duffy, *Father Duffy's Story*, 13–14.
13. *The Advocate*, 28 April 1917, 4.
14. Latham R. Reed, letter to Mrs. Van Santvoord Merle-Smith, 12 November 1918, Merle-Smith family papers, held by Grosvenor Merle-Smith.
15. Albert M. and A. Churchill Ettinger, *A Doughboy With the Fighting Sixty-ninth: A Remembrance of World War I*, (New York: Pocket Books, 1993, published by arrangement with White Mane Publishing Co., Inc.), 19.
16. *New York Herald*, 12 August 1917, first section, part 2, 4.
17. Duffy, *Father Duffy's Story*, 24–25.
18. Duffy, *Father Duffy's Story*, 26.
19. *Buffalo Courier*, 21 July 1916, 5.
20. *New York Herald*, 12 August 1917.
21. Maj. William Donovan to Ruth Donovan, undated, William Donovan papers, Military History Institute, Carlisle, Penn.
22. Rupert Hughes, "Jim Finn: Disabled Emergency Officer," *The American Legion Monthly*, January 1928, 14.
23. Duffy, *Father Duffy's Story*, 29.
24. Hughes, "Jim Finn," 14.
25. M.A. DeWolfe Howe and Others, *Memoirs of the Harvard War Dead in the War Against Germany*, vol. 4 (Cambridge, Mass.: Harvard University Press, 1923), 583.

26. Duffy, *Father Duffy's Story*, 27.
27. Hogan, *The Shamrock Battalion*, 106.
28. Duffy, *Father Duffy's Story*, 30.
29. Wilton Merle-Smith, *The Story Of A Life*, monograph about his son Van Santvoord, written circa 1911–12, Merle-Smith family papers.
30. *New York Times* article, undated, in scrapbook, Merle-Smith family papers. The scrapbooks are filled with newspaper clippings. The clippings are undated and the newspapers are mostly unknown.
31. George S. Patton to Kate Merle-Smith, 28 August 1916, Merle-Smith family papers.
32. Kate Merle-Smith letters to her mother, 16 September and 28 November 1916, Merle-Smith family papers.
33. Kate Merle-Smith, letters to her mother, 16 September and 21 September 1916, Merle-Smith family papers.
34. Kate Merle-Smith, letter to her mother, 16 September 1916.
35. Kate Merle-Smith, letter to her mother, 10 November 1916.
36. Mary M. (Fuller) Lawrence diary, mother of Maj. George and Lt. Austin Lawrence, from family papers of Stephen P. Lawrence.
37. Duffy, *Father Duffy's Story*, 25–26.
38. Reilly, *Americans All*, 29.
39. Duffy, *Father Duffy's Story*, 17.

Chapter 4

1. Hughes, *Long Ever Ago*, 17.
2. Duffy, *Father Duffy's Story*, 17.
3. Duffy, *Father Duffy's Story*, 17.
4. Kenton Kilmer, *Memories of My Father, Joyce Kilmer* (New Brunswick, N.J.: Joyce Kilmer Centennial Commission, Inc., 1993), 104.
5. Duffy, *Father Duffy's Story*, 16–17.
6. Annie Kilburn Kilmer, *Memories of My Son, Sergeant Joyce Kilmer* (New York: Frye Publishing, 1921), 1.
7. Christopher Morley, *Pipefuls* (New York: Doubleday, Page & Company, 1920), 106–107.
8. Peter P. McLoughlin, "Joyce Kilmer, Catholic Poet-Hero," *The Columbiad*, August 1920, 4.
9. Kilmer, *Memories of My Son*, 3–4.
10. Kilmer, *Memories of My Father*, 97.
11. Joyce Kilmer, letter to Father James J. Daly, 9 January 1914, Kilmer papers, box 1, folder 50, special collections, Lauinger Library, Georgetown University.
12. Kilmer, *Memories of My Son*, 4–5.
13. McLoughlin, *The Columbiad*, August 1920, 7.
14. Joyce Kilmer, *Joyce Kilmer, Volume One: Memoir and Poems*, ed. Robert Cortes Holliday (New York: George H. Doran Company, 1918), 180.
15. Kilmer, *Memories of My Son*, 112.
16. Joyce Kilmer, *Joyce Kilmer, Volume Two: Prose Works*, ed. Robert Cortes Holliday (New York: George H. Doran Company, 1918), 106.
17. Kilmer, *Memories of My Son*, 117–123.
18. Duffy, *Father Duffy's Story*, 18.

19. Martin Green, *New York Evening World*, 14 November 1918, 3.
20. Ettinger, *Doughboy*, 4–5.
21. Ettinger, *Doughboy*, 12–13.
22. Mary C. Heager, daughter of Vivian K. Commons, in a letter to the author, 27 October 2003.
23. Poem is among the Van Yorx family papers, held by Victor Patrick Van Yorx, Ann Arbor, Michigan.
24. Duffy to Mrs. Theodore Van Yorx, 21 March 1919, Van Yorx family papers.
25. *The Seventh Regiment Gazette*, 31: 11, 243.
26. *The Seventh Regiment Gazette*, 31: 11, 244, 246, 248.
27. *The Seventh Regiment Gazette*, 31: 11, 235.
28. *The Seventh Regiment Gazette*, 31: 11.
29. *New York Times*, 17 August 1917.
30. Ettinger, *Doughboy*, 6.
31. Duffy, *Father Duffy's Story*, 18.

Chapter 5

1. Ettinger, *Doughboy*, 7.
2. Frank Zarnowski, *The Decathlon*, (Champagne, Ill.: Leisure Press, 1989), 38.
3. *The Irish Advocate*, 21 July 1917, 1.
4. Donovan to his wife, 26 July 1917, William Donovan papers, Military History Institute, Carlisle, Penn.
5. *New York Sun*, 19 August 1917, 4.
6. Duffy, *Father Duffy's Story*, 22–23.
7. Duffy to Cardinal Farley, 16 September 1917, Archdiocese of New York archives, Yonkers, NY.
8. *New York Sun*, 20 August 1917, 5.
9. *New York Tribune*, 20 August 1917, 4.
10. *New York Tribune*, 20 August 1917.
11. Duffy, *Father Duffy's Story*, 15–16. (In his book, Duffy had the benefit game taking place on 25 July when in fact it took place almost a month later.)
12. Donovan to his wife, 21 August 1917, William Donovan papers, Military History Institute, Carlisle, Penn.
13. *New York Herald*, 19 August 1917, first section, part 2, 3.
14. Donovan to his wife, 21 August 1917, William Donovan papers, Military History Institute, Carlisle, Penn.
15. *New York Herald*, 17 August 1917, 3.
16. *New York Herald*, 21 August 1917, 11.
17. Joyce Kilmer, "Historical Appendix," in Duffy, *Father Duffy's Story*, 335.
18. Hogan, *The Shamrock Battalion*, 10.
19. *New York Sun*, 21 August 1917, 1.
20. *New York Herald*, 21 August 1917, 11.
21. *New York Sun*, 21 August 1917, 3.
22. *New York Tribune*, 25 August 1917, 10.

Chapter 6

1. Ettinger, *Doughboy*, 7.
2. Duffy, *Father Duffy's Story*, 18.

3. Robert Stewart Sutcliffe, *The Seventy-first New York in the World War* (New York, 1922), xi.
4. Sutcliffe, *The Seventy-first New York*, 21.
5. *Brooklyn Daily Standard*, 25 August 1917, 2.
6. *Brooklyn Daily Eagle*, 8 August 1917, 1.
7. *Brooklyn Daily Eagle*, 25 August 1917, 20.
8. Duffy, *Father Duffy's Story*, 18–19.
9. *Brooklyn Daily Eagle*, 30 August 1917, 1.
10. *New York Tribune*, 1 September 1917, 6.
11. *Brooklyn Standard Union*, 17 July 1917, 1.
12. *The Wave of Long Island*, 22 March 1918, 1.
13. *New York Times*, 20 September 1895, 9.
14. *Brooklyn Daily Eagle*, 28 August 1917, 10.
15. *New York Tribune*, 26 August 1917, 5.
16. *New York Tribune*, 27 August 1917, 5.
17. *Brooklyn Daily Eagle*, 29 August 1917, 1. The *Eagle* ran daily articles that captured the life at Camp Mills in anecdotes and quotations from the soldiers, many well worth repeating.
18. *Brooklyn Daily Eagle*, 29 August 1917.
19. *Brooklyn Daily Eagle*, 29 August 1917.
20. *Brooklyn Daily Eagle*, 9 September 1917, 5.
21. Ettinger, *Doughboy*, 54–55.
22. Henry Berry, *Make the Kaiser Dance* (Garden City, N.Y.: Doubleday & Company, 1978), 310–311.
23. *Brooklyn Daily Eagle*, 31 August 1917, 2.
24. *Brooklyn Daily Eagle*, 30 August 1917, 1.
25. *Brooklyn Daily Eagle*, 30 August 1917, 1, 17.
26. *Brooklyn Daily Eagle*, 9 September 1917, 5, 22.
27. Maj. Emmet P. Smith, interviewed by Dr. Thomas A. Belser, archivist, Auburn (Ala.) University, 3 July 1964. Auburn University Libraries.
28. *New York Age*, 6 September 1917, 1.
29. *New York Herald*, first section, part 2, 2 September 1917, 1.
30. William Heiss, letter to Thomas "Tim" Heiss, 28 January 1917, From the Heiss family papers, Appleton, Wisc.
31. William H. Amerine, *Alabama's Own in France* (New York: Eaton & Gettiner, 1919), 55–56.
32. Ettinger, *Doughboy*, 8–9.
33. James W. Frey Papers, memoir written in 1921. Forty-second Division AEF Collection, U.S. Military History Institute archives, Carlisle, Penn.
34. Accounts of Pvt. George Neff's suicide appear in numerous New York newspapers, including the *Herald* and *Tribune*, 18 September 1917.
35. *New York Herald*, 17 September 1917, 11.
36. Duffy, *Father Duffy's Story*, 21.
37. *New York Herald*, 17 September 1917.
38. *Brooklyn Eagle*, 12 October 1917, 3.
39. *New York Herald*, 17 September 1917, 11.
40. Donovan, letter to his wife, 30 August 1917, Donovan papers, Military History Institute, Carlisle, Penn.
41. Donovan to his mother, undated, Donovan papers, Military History Institute.

Chapter 7

1. M. A. De Wolfe Howe, *Oliver Ames, Jr.: 1895–1918* (Boston: Privately printed, 1922), 13–14.
2. Howe, *Oliver Ames, Jr.*, 12.
3. Van Santvoord Merle-Smith, undated paper titled "The Plattsburgh Camps," from the Merle-Smith family papers.
4. Basil Elmer to his parents, 1 November 1917, Elmer family papers, held by Stephen Elmer, Basil's son.
5. Livingston Parsons, letter to his father, H. De Berkeley Parsons, 1 November 1917. Parsons family papers, held by Sally Parsons Oriel, New York, New York.
6. Duffy to Cardinal Farley, 16 September 1917. Archdiocese of New York archives, Yonkers, NY.
7. *New York Tribune*, 10 September 1917, 4.
8. R. M. Cheseldine, *Ohio in The Rainbow: Official Story of the 166th Infantry* (Columbus: State of Ohio, 1924), 57.
9. William Heiss to Thomas Heiss, 30 September 1917, Heiss family papers, Appleton, Wisc.
10. William O. Semans diary, 6 October 1917, Semans family papers, held by William M. Semans.
11. Duffy, *Father Duffy's Story*, 25.
12. *New York Tribune*, 25 August 1917, 10.
13. *New York Tribune*, 29 August 1917, 5.
14. *New York Times*, 1 April 1970, 31.
15. *New York Herald*, 9 September 1917, 6.
16. Duffy, *Father Duffy's Story*, 27.
17. *New York Tribune*, 25 August 1917.
18. *New York Tribune*, 25 August 1917.
19. Donovan to his wife, 30 August 1917, Donovan papers, Military History Institute, Carlisle, Penn.
20. *New York World Magazine*, 7 August 1923, 1.
21. William D. O'Neill, son of Richard W. O'Neill, interview with the author 3 November 2003.
22. Berry, *Make the Kaiser Dance*, 327–328.
23. Richard W. O'Neill war notes, O'Neill family papers, held by William D. O'Neill.
24. Berry, *Make the Kaiser Dance*, 330.
25. *Irish Advocate*, 18 August 1917, 3.
26. Duffy, *Father Duffy's Story*, 26.
27. Elting E. Morison, ed., *The Letters of Theodore Roosevelt* (Cambridge, Mass.: Harvard University Press, 1954), 8:1, 236.
28. *New York Herald*, 7 September 1917, 12.
29. Donovan to his mother, undated, Donovan papers, Military History Institute, Carlisle, Penn.
30. Hogan, *The Shamrock Battalion*, 12–13.
31. Duffy, *Father Duffy's Story*, 21.
32. Kilmer, *Joyce Kilmer, Volume Two*, 136–137.
33. Annie Kilburn Kilmer, *Leaves From My Life* (New York: Frye Publishing Co., 1925), 120.

34. Kilmer, *Joyce Kilmer, Volume Two,* 136–137.
35. Kilmer, *Joyce Kilmer, Volume Two,* 138–139.
36. Tom O'Kelly, quoted in *New York Evening Sun,* 30 August 1917. From the family papers of Merle-Smith.
37. Donovan to unknown person, 12 September 1917, Donovan papers, Military History Institute, Carlisle, Penn.

Chapter 8

1. Duffy, *Father Duffy's Story,* 34.
2. Hogan, *The Shamrock Battalion,* 15–16.
3. Ettinger, *Doughboy,* 23.
4. William O. Semans diary, 18 October 1917, Semans family papers, held by William M. Semans.
5. Douglas MacArthur, *Reminisences* (New York: McGraw-Hill Book Company, 1964), 52.
6. Duffy, *Father Duffy's Story,* 34–35.
7. *New York Herald,* 1 December 1917, part two, 1.
8. Gertrude Silliman to her husband, no exact date, but written in November 1917. Also, from an autobiographical sketch by Gertrude Silliman, no date, in Charles A. Silliman, ed., *Selected Family Letters, 1881–1945,* (Wilmington, Del.: Privately printed, 1984), 208–210.
9. Kilmer, *Leaves,* 121.
10. Kilmer, *Memories of My Father,* 118.
11. Basil Elmer to his parents, 14 and 27 October 1917, Elmer family papers, held by Stephen Elmer.
12. Austin Lawrence diary, from the Lawrence family papers, held by Stephen Lawrence.
13. Joseph Jones diary and interview with James Jones, Joseph's son, 24 September 2002, Jones family papers, held by Joseph Jones III.
14. Richard W. O'Neill combat diary, from the O'Neill family papers, held by William D. O'Neill.
15. Donovan to his mother, undated, Donovan papers, Military History Institute.
16. George Patrick McKeon to his sister, 26 October 1917, from the family papers, held by Michael J. Fitz, grand nephew.
17. Duffy, *Father Duffy's Story,* 23–24.
18. Ettinger, *A Doughboy With the Fighting Sixty-ninth,* 13–14.
19. Hogan, *The Shamrock Battalion,* 16–18.
20. Van Santvoord Merle-Smith to his son, 2 November 1917, Merle-Smith family papers.
21. Hogan, *The Shamrock Battalion,* 16–18.
22. Austin Lawrence diary, 31 October 1917.
23. Donovan to his wife, Ruth. 28 October 1917, Donovan papers, Military History Institute, Carlisle, Penn.
24. Elmer, letters to his parents, 27 October through 8 November 1917, Elmer family papers.
25. The Journal of the American Irish Historical Society, volume XVII, 1918, 232.
26. Elmer, letters to his parents, 27 October through 8 November 1917, Elmer family papers.

27. Howe, *Oliver Ames, Jr.*, 19.
28. *Brooklyn Eagle*, 27 December 1917, 4.
29. Hogan, *The Shamrock Battalion*, 19.
30. Austin Lawrence diary, 31 November 1917.
31. Duffy, *Father Duffy's Story*, 36.
32. Ettinger, *Doughboy*, 24.

Chapter 9

1. *Brooklyn Eagle*, 27 December 1917, 4.
2. Vivian Commons, letter to his mother, 13 November 1917, Commons family papers held by his daughter and grandson, Mary Commons Haeger and Michael Haeger.
3. Ted Van Yorx letter, 12 November 1917, Van Yorx family papers.
4. Harper Silliman to his wife, 15 November 1917, in Silliman, *Family Letters*, 211.
5. Hogan, *The Shamrock Battalion*, 26.
6. Duffy, *Father Duffy's Story*, 37–39.
7. Kilmer, *Memories of My Son*, 124.
8. Hogan, *The Shamrock Battalion*, 28–29.
9. Ettinger, *Doughboy*, 26.
10. *Brooklyn Eagle*, 20 January 1918, 5.
11. Duffy, *Father Duffy's Story*, 341.
12. *Brooklyn Eagle*, 20 January 1918.
13. Elmer to his father, undated, Elmer family papers.
14. *Brooklyn Eagle*, 30 December 1917, 8.
15. *Brooklyn Eagle*, 13 January 1918, 7.
16. *Brooklyn Eagle*, 20 January 1918.
17. Ettinger, *Doughboy*, 27.
18. Donovan to his wife, 17 November 1917, Donovan papers, Military History Institute, Carlisle, Penn.
19. *Brooklyn Eagle*, 20 January 1918.
20. *Brooklyn Eagle*, 13 January 1918, 3.
21. *New York Sun*, 30 December 1917, 9.
22. Commons, letter to his mother, 13 November 1917, Commons family papers.
23. Kilmer, *Joyce Kilmer, Volume Two*, 171 and 173.
24. Elmer to his parents, undated, Elmer family papers.
25. Howe, *Oliver Ames, Jr.*, 23.
26. Donovan to his wife, 27 November 1917, Donovan papers, Military History Institute, Carlisle, Penn.
27. Kilmer, *Joyce Kilmer, Volume Two*, 167–168.
28. Duffy, *Father Duffy's Story*, 40–41.
29. Duffy, *Father Duffy's Story*, 341.
30. *Brooklyn Daily Star*, undated article.
31. *Brooklyn Eagle*, 1 January 1918, 3.
32. *Brooklyn Eagle*, 20 January 1918.
33. Howe and Others, *Memoirs*, 587.
34. Howe, *Oliver Ames Jr.*, 20–21.
35. Elmer to his parents, undated letter, Elmer family papers.

36. Howe, *Oliver Ames Jr.*, 25.
37. Elmer to his parents, undated, Elmer family papers.
38. *Brooklyn Daily Star*, 16 February 1918.
39. *New York Sun*, 30 December 1917.
40. Hogan, *The Shamrock Battalion*, 32.
41. Duffy, *Father Duffy's Story*, 342.
42. Kilmer, *Joyce Kilmer, Volume Two*, 171.
43. Austin Lawrence diary, 14–16 December 1917,
44. Col. Charles Hine to Commanding General, Eighty-third Brigade, Forty-second Division, 18 December 1918, National Archives and Record Administration, College Park, Maryland.
45. Duffy, *Father Duffy's Story*, 49.

Chapter 10

1. Duffy, *Father Duffy's Story*, 46–47.
2. Duffy to John Cardinal Farley, 21 December 1917, Archdiocese of New York archives, Yonkers, NY.
3. Duffy, *Father Duffy's Story*, 45–47.
4. Hogan, *The Shamrock Battalion*, 34.
5. Elmer to his parents, Christmas Eve, 1917, Elmer family papers.
6. Howe, *Oliver Ames, Jr.*, 29–30.
7. *New York Evening World Daily Magazine*, 25 May 1918, 1.
8. Ettinger, *Doughboy*, 34.
9. Hogan, *The Shamrock Battalion*, 35.
10. Duffy, *Father Duffy's Story*, 342.
11. Duffy, *Father Duffy's Story*, 47.
12. Austin Lawrence diary, 24 December 1917.
13. *The Rainbow Barrage Newsletter*, December 1947, no page number.
14. Elmer to his parents, 25 December 1917, Elmer family papers.
15. Berry, *Make the Kaiser Dance*, 331.
16. Ettinger, *Doughboy*, 38.
17. Hogan, *The Shamrock Battalion*, 34.
18. *New York Evening World Daily Magazine*, 25 May 1918, 1.
19. Hogan, *The Shamrock Battalion*, 34.
20. *New York Evening World Daily Magazine*, 25 May 1918.
21. From an undated newspaper article in the scrapbook of Van Santvoord Merle-Smith, Merle-Smith family papers.
22. Duffy, *Father Duffy's Story*, 48–50.
23. Col. Charles Hine to Commanding General, Forty-second Division, 2 January 1918. National Archives and Records Administration, College Park, Md.
24. Duffy, *Father Duffy's Story*, 48–50.
25. Undated newspaper article in the scrapbook of Van Santvoord Merle-Smith, Merle-Smith family papers.
26. Hogan, *The Shamrock Battalion*, 37–38.
27. Ettinger, *Doughboy*, 39.
28. *New York Evening World Daily Magazine*, 25 May 1918, 1.
29. Austin Lawrence diary, 26 December 1917.
30. Duffy, *Father Duffy's Story*, 343.

31. Capt. George McAdie to Col. Charles Hine, 1 January 1918, National Archives and Records Administration, College Park, Md.
32. Capt. James McKenna report to Headquarters, 165th Infantry, 30 December 1917, National Archives and Records Administration, College Park, Md.
33. Lt. Horace Stokes report to Colonel Hine, 2 January 1918, National Archives and Records Administration, College Park, Md.
34. Capt. Thomas Reilly report to Colonel Hine, 1 January 1918, National Archives and Records Administration, College Park, Md.
35. Ettinger, *Doughboy*, 42.
36. Duffy, *Father Duffy's Story*, 51.
37. *New York Evening World Daily Magazine*, 27 May 1918, 1.
38. Ettinger, *Doughboy*, 41.
39. Austin Lawrence diary, 28 December 1917, Lawrence family papers.
40. *Hempstead Sentinel*, 14 March 1918, 2.
41. Hogan, *The Shamrock Battalion*, 38.
42. *New York Times*, 20 April 1919, section 4, 1.
43. *New York Evening World Daily Magazine*, 27 May 1918.
44. Hogan, *The Shamrock Battalion*, 39.
45. From an undated newspaper clipping in the Merle-Smith family papers.
46. Duffy, *Father Duffy's Story*, 343–344.
47. Report March Detach. by Capt. Walter E. Powers, Captain, 165th Infantry, 31 December 1918, National Archives and Records Administration, College Park, Md.
48. *Brooklyn Eagle*, 10 March 1918, 7.
49. Report by Capt. Thomas Burcham to Lt. Col. D.S. Fairchild, Office of Sanitary Inspector, Forty-second Division, 17 January 1918, National Archives and Records Administration, College Park, Md.
50. Duffy, *Father Duffy's Story*, 51.
51. Fifty-eighth annual report of the Association of Graduates of the United States Military Academy, 13 June 1927, 135.
52. William Donovan to Ruth, various letters, 24 November through 18 December 1917, Donovan papers, Military History Institute, Carlisle, Penn.
53. William Donovan to Ruth, 24 January 1918, William Donovan papers, Military History Institute, Carlisle, Penn.
54. Duffy, *Father Duffy's Story*, 59.
55. Duffy to Cardinal Farley, 24 February 1918, Archdiocese of New York archives, Yonkers, NY.

Chapter 11

1. Report of Major Lawrence to Lt. Col. Joseph Grissinger, Forty-second Division surgeon, 16 January 1918. National Archives and Records Administration, College Park, Md.
2. Report of Major Stacom to Brig. Gen. Michael Lenihan, commander of the Eighty-third Brigade, 17 January 1918, National Archives and Records Administration, College Park, Md.
3. *New York Times*, 20 April 1919, section 4, 1.
4. Report of Colonel Barker to Maj. Gen. Charles Menoher, commander, Forty-second Division, 18 January 1918, National Archives and Records Administration, College Park, Md.

5. Berry, *Make the Kaiser Dance*, 331.
6. *New York Evening World Daily Magazine*, 27 May 1918, 1.
7. Ettinger, *Doughboy*, 58.
8. Duffy, *Father Duffy's Story*, 54–55.
9. Ettinger, *Doughboy*, 58.
10. The description of First Lieutenant Baker's crossing of the Atlantic is based on an account published in the *New York Times*, 8 May 1918.
11. *New York Times*, 12 October 1918.
12. Elmer, letters to his parents, 31 January through 7 February 1918, Elmer family papers.
13. Howe, *Oliver Ames, Jr.*, 37–38.
14. Howe, *Oliver Ames, Jr.*, 41–42.
15. Donovan to his wife, 3 February 1918, William Donovan Papers, Military History Institute, Carlisle, Penn.
16. Elmer, letters to his parents, 7 February 1918, Elmer family papers.
17. Elmer to his parents, 5 March 1918, Elmer family papers.
18. "Joyce Kilmer—Soldier," by Emmett Watson, *The American Legion Monthly*, September 1936, 26, 60.
19. Kilmer, *Joyce Kilmer, Volume Two*, 202.
20. Kilmer, *Joyce Kilmer, Volume Two*, 158.
21. Kilmer, *Joyce Kilmer, Volume Two*, 162–163.
22. Elmer, letters to his parents, 15 and 20 February 1918, Elmer family papers.
23. Howe, *Oliver Ames, Jr.*, 38–40.
24. Howe, *Oliver Ames, Jr.*, 43.
25. Duffy to Father Vincent Donovan, undated, Donovan papers, Military History Institute, Carlisle, Penn.
26. Duffy, *Father Duffy's Story*, 60.
27. Ettinger, *Doughboy*, 156.
28. Thomas J. Shannon burial file, National Archives and Records Administration, College Park, Md.
29. Duffy, *Father Duffy's Story*, 218.

Chapter 12

1. Hogan, *The Shamrock Battalion*, 55.
2. Duffy, *Father Duffy's Story*, 60.
3. Ettinger, *A Fighting Doughboy*, 71.
4. *New York Evening World Daily Magazine*, 28 May 1918, 1.
5. Elmer letters, 20 and 22 February 1918, Elmer family papers.
6. Kilmer, *Joyce Kilmer, Volume Two*, 183.
7. Duffy, *Father Duffy's Story*, 60.
8. Hogan, *The Shamrock Battalion*, 64.
9. *New York Evening World Daily Magazine*, 25 May 1918, 1.
10. Major Donovan Memorandum to First Battalion company commanders, 26 February 1918, National Archives and Records Administration, College Park, Md.
11. Donovan, memorandum to First Battalion platoon commanders, 4 March 1918. National Archives and Records Administration, College Park, Md.
12. *New York Evening World*, 18 April 1918.
13. Hogan, *The Shamrock Battalion*, 57.

14. *New York Evening World*, 18 April 1918.
15. Duffy, *Father Duffy's Story*, 60.
16. Occupation order no. 1, Company "D" 165th Infantry, 26 February 1918, National Archives and Records Administration, College Park, Md.
17. *Brooklyn Daily Eagle*, April 14, 1918, 7.
18. *Brooklyn Daily Eagle*, April 14, 1918.
19. *The Leader-Observer* (Brooklyn newspaper), 9 May 1918, 1.
20. Howe, *Memoirs*, 590.
21. Intelligence information memorandum, from Major Donovan to company commanders, First Battalion, 5 March 1918, National Archives and Records Administration, College Park, Maryland.
22. Memorandum from commander, Company B, to commanding officer, First Battalion, 4 March 1918, National Archives and Records Administration, College Park, Md.
23. *The Irish Advocate*, 18 May 1918, 7.
24. *New York Evening World*, 18 April 1918.
25. *Brooklyn Eagle*, 3 March 1918, 8.
26. A. S. Helmer, "The Real Story of Rouge Bouquet," an unpublished memoir, no date, 6, family papers of A. S. Helmer, held by his son, Jan Helmer.
27. Berry, *Make the Kaiser Dance*, 332.
28. This account is based on unpublished records to be found under "Reports & Correspondence, RE: Caving in of Dugout in 165 Inf. N.A.," National Archives and Records Administration, College Park, Md.
29. *New York Times*, 23 March 1918.
30. *New York Sun Magazine*, 30 March 1918, 7.
31. Helmer, "The Real Story," 2.
32. Diary of Pfc. Joseph J. Jones, 7 March 1918, Jones family papers.
33. Helmer, "The Real Story," 3.
34. "RE: Caving in" National Archives and Records Administration, College Park, Md.
35. Helmer, "The Real Story," 4–7.
36. "RE: Caving in."
37. Helmer, "The Real Story," 4–7.
38. "RE: Caving in."
39. Jan Helmer (Alf Helmer's son), interview with the author, 12 January 2005.
40. *Brooklyn Daily Eagle*, 29 December 1918, 6.
41. Ettinger, *Doughboy*, 79.
42. Helmer, "The Real Story," 11.
43. *New York Sun Magazine*, 6 October, 1918, 5.
44. Helmer, "The Real Story," 11–14.
45. Jan Helmer, interview by author.
46. Helmer, "The Real Story," 13–14.
47. "RE: Caving in."
48. *New York Sun Magazine*, 6 October 1918.
49. Helmer, "The Real Story," 14–15.
50. "RE: Caving in."
51. Helmer, "The Real Story," 15.
52. *Irish Advocate*, 5 May 1918, 7.
53. *New York Sun Magazine*, 3 March 1918, 7.

54. Duffy, *Father Duffy's Story*, 61–65.
55. *New York Sun Magazine*, 6 October 1918.
56. Kilmer, *Joyce Kilmer, Volume One*, 105–107.

Chapter 13

1. Proceedings, investigation into the death of Private Oscar Ammon, Board of Officers, U.S. Army, 13 March 1918. National Archives and Records Administration, College Park, Md.
2. Proceedings.
3. Duffy, *Father Duffy's Story*, 67–68.
4. Austin Lawrence diary, 12 March 1918. Lawrence family papers.
5. Hogan, *The Shamrock Battalion*, 75–80.
6. Duffy, *Father Duffy's Story*, 68.
7. *Irish Advocate*, 11 May 1918, 1.
8. *New York Evening Sun*, 27 June 1932, 15.
9. Duffy, *Father Duffy's Story*, 68.
10. *Irish Advocate*, 11 May 1918.
11. Ettinger, *Doughboy*, 81–82.
12. Duffy, *Father Duffy's Story*, 69.
13. Austin Lawrence diary, 17 March 1918.
14. *Brooklyn Daily Eagle*, 26 April 1918, 1.
15. *New York Evening Telegram*, 23 April 1919, 3.
16. *New York Times*, 2 July 1919, 6.
17. Ettinger, *Doughboy*, 90–91.
18. Duffy, *Father Duffy's Story*, 71.
19. First Lt. Henry A. Bootz, "Report of procedure and operations of Coup de Main," 21 March 1918. National Archives and Records Administration, College Park, Md.
20. *Brooklyn Daily Eagle*, 26 April 1918.
21. Lincoln Eyre, newspaper article syndicated by the Press Publishing Company, quoted in the *New York Evening World*.
22. *New York Evening Telegram*, 30 April 1919, 10.
23. *New York Evening World*, 17 September 1918, 1.
24. *Brooklyn Daily Eagle*, 26 April 1918.
25. *Brooklyn Daily Eagle*, 30 April 1918, 1.
26. Bootz, Report National Archives and Records Administration.
27. *Brooklyn Daily Eagle*, 30 April 1918.
28. *New York Times*, 20 April 1919, Section 4, 1.
29. Minogue's death recounted in undated newspaper article from the scrapbook of Van Santvoord Merle-Smith, Merle-Smith family papers.
30. *Brooklyn Daily Eagle*, 26 April 1918.
31. Duffy, *Father Duffy's Story*, 74.
32. 1st Lt. William Given to his parents, 19 March 1918, family papers of Van Santvoord Merle-Smith.
33. Rexmond C. Cochrane, "Gas Warfare in World War I, the 42nd Division Before Landres-et-St. Georges, October 1918," U.S. Army Chemical Corps historical study number 17, (Md: Army Chemical Center, 1959), 7.
34. Hogan, *The Shamrock Battalion*, 85.

35. Cochrane, "Gas Warfare in World War I," 9.

36. Duffy, *Father Duffy's Story*, 74.

37. From the scrapbook of Merle-Smith, Merle-Smith family papers.

38. *New York Evening World Daily Magazine*, 3 June 1918, 1.

39. *New York Evening World Daily Magazine*, 31 December 1918.

40. Hogan, *The Shamrock Battalion*, 87.

41. Duffy, *Father Duffy's Story*, 76.

42. Jan Helmer (son of Alf Helmer), interview by author, 10 December 2002.

43. Austin Lawrence diary, 21 March 1918. Lawrence family papers.

44. Diary of Pfc. Joseph J. Jones, 21 and 22 March 1918, family papers held by Joseph Jones III.

45. Carolyn (Atkinson) Hotchkiss (granddaughter of Richard Ryan), interview by author, 5 August 2003.

46. 1st Lt. William Given to his parents, 22 March 1918, family papers of Van Santvoord Merle-Smith.

Chapter 14

1. Duffy, *Father Duffy's Story*, 91.

2. *New York Evening World*, 1 July 1918, 1.

3. *The Rainbow Barrage Newsletter*, April 1958, 2.

4. Ettinger, *Doughboy*, 105–106.

5. Pvt. George Patrick McKeon to sister, 28 April 1918, family papers held by Michael J. Fitz.

6. Frank McCoy, memorandum to chief of staff, American Expeditionary Forces, 1 April 1918, collections of the Manuscript Division, Library of Congress, Washington, D.C.

7. Frank McCoy to his mother, 10 April 1918, letter no. 32, collections of the Manuscript Division, Library of Congress, Washington, D.C.

8. Reilly, *Americans All*, 208.

9. McCoy to his mother, 6 May 1918, letter no. 32, collections of the Manuscript Division, Library of Congress, Washington, D.C.

10. A. J. Bacevich, *Diplomat in Khaki: Major General Frank Ross McCoy and American Foreign Policy, 1898–1949*, (Lawrence, Kansas: University of Kansas Press, 1989), 6–10.

11. Hermann Hagedorn, *Leonard Wood: A Biography* (New York: Harper & Brothers, 1931), 275–276.

12. McCoy, to his mother, 21 May 1918, letter no. 38, collections of the Manuscript Division, Library of Congress, Washington, D.C.

13. Duffy, *Father Duffy's Story*, 92–93.

14. Elmer to his parents, 7 May 1918, Elmer family papers.

15. Alf Helmer letter to his father, 2 June 1918, Helmer family papers, held by Helmer's son, Jan Helmer.

16. *New York Sun Magazine*, 13 October 1918.

17. Howe, *Oliver Ames Jr.*, 64.

18. Kilmer, *Joyce Kilmer, Volume Two*, 116.

19. *The American Legion Monthly*, September 1936, 60.

20. Kilmer, *Joyce Kilmer, Volume Two*, 211.

21. Elmer to his parents, 15 May 1918, Elmer family papers.

22. Elmer to his parents, 21 May 1918, Elmer family papers.
23. *The American Legion Monthly*, September 1936.
24. Howe, *Oliver Ames, Jr.*, 59–63.
25. Daily activity report, Headquarters 83rd Infantry Brigade, 42nd Division, 29 April 1918. National Archives and Records Administration, College Park, Md.
26. Hogan, *The Shamrock Battalion*, 106.
27. Hogan, *The Shamrock Battalion*, 88.
28. Lt. William Spencer to his girlfriend, Loi, undated letter. The family papers of William M. Spencer, held by his son, Ed Spencer.
29. Lt. Col. George Patton to Kate Merle-Smith, 19 April 1918, Merle-Smith family papers.
30. First Sgt. Eugene Gannon to Kate Merle-Smith, 20 April 1918, Merle-Smith family papers.
31. McCoy to his mother, 4 June 1918, letter no. 43, collections of the Manuscript Division, Library of Congress, Washington, D.C.
32. *Irish Advocate*, 29 June 1918, 4.
33. Duffy, *Father Duffy's Story*, 103.
34. Francis Duffy, letter to mothers whose sons had died and were buried in France, Memorial Day 1918, papers of Frank McCoy, collections of the Manuscript Division, Library of Congress, Washington, D.C.
35. McCoy to his mother, 25 May 1918, letter no. 39, collections of the Manuscript Division, Library of Congress, Washington, D.C.
36. Francis Duffy to Mrs. Kiernan, 7 April 1918, Collection of Knights of Columbus, Supreme Council Archives, New Haven, Conn.
37. Michael Lavelle to W. A. Sullen, no date, Archives, Diocese of Cleveland.
38. James Hanley to Florence Hanley, 5 December 1917, Archives, Diocese of Cleveland.
39. James Hanley to Florence Hanley, 11 June 1918, Archives, Diocese of Cleveland.
40. Duffy, *Father Duffy's Story*, 114.

Chapter 15

1. Howe, *Memoirs*, 594.
2. *New York Sun Magazine*, 13 October 1918, 11.
3. *New York Evening Telegram*, 23 April 1919, 3.
4. Duffy, *Father Duffy's Story*, 114.
5. McCoy to his mother, 25 June 1918, letter no. 2, collections of the Manuscript Division, Library of Congress, Washington D.C.
6. McCoy to his mother, 23 June 1918, letter no. 1, collections of the Manuscript Division, Library of Congress, Washington D.C.
7. Duffy, *Father Duffy's Story*, 114.
8. McCoy to his mother, 23 June 1918.
9. *Rainbow Barrage Newsletter*, June 1958, 2.
10. Elmer to his parents, 19 June 1918, Elmer family papers.
11. William Spencer to Loi, 29 June 1918, Spencer family papers, held by Edson Spencer.
12. Elmer to his parents, 27 June 1918, Elmer family papers, held by Stephen Elmer.

13. Howe, *Oliver Ames, Jr.*, 67.

14. *The Rainbow Barrage*, June 1958, 2.

15. Diary of Nathaniel Rouse, Rouse family papers, held by Nathan Rouse. Diary is posted on the Internet at e.wa.home.mindspring.com/wwidiary.

16. Flick, *Chaplain Duffy*, 93.

17. McCoy to his mother, 23 June 1918.

18. Duffy, *Father Duffy's Story*, 123.

19. MacArthur, *Reminiscences*, 57.

20. Reilly, *Americans All*, 242–251.

21. Preliminary Plan of Defense, Headquarters, 165th Infantry, 7 July 1918. National Archives and Records Administration, College Park, Md.

22. Howe, *Oliver Ames, Jr., 1895–1918*, 71.

23. Elmer to his parents, 12 July and 14 July 1918, Elmer family papers.

24. Reilly, *Americans All*, 242–251.

25. Duffy, *Father Duffy's Story*, 125.

26. Duffy, *Father Duffy's Story*, 128.

27. Reilly, *Americans All*, 274.

28. Duffy, *Father Duffy's Story*, 129–131.

29. Richard W. O'Neill diary, 27 June to 15 July, O'Neill family papers.

30. Nathaniel Rouse diary, 15 July 1918, Rouse family papers.

31. Charles MacArthur, *War Bugs* (Doubleday, Doran & Company, Garden City, N.Y.: 1929), 85.

32. George E. Leach, *War Diary*, (Minneapolis Pioneer Printing, Minn. 1923), 79.

33. Spencer, undated letter to Loi, Spencer family papers.

34. *The Yonkers Statesman*, 20 August 1918, 5.

35. Reilly, *Americans All*, 276.

36. Summary events, 16 July 1918, midnight. Headquarters, 42d Division. National Archives and Records Administration, College Park, Md.

37. Duffy, *Father Duffy's Story*, 135.

38. *Brooklyn Eagle*, 8 August 1918.

39. *Brooklyn Eagle*, 5 August 1918.

40. *New York Evening World*, 22 August 1918, 3.

41. Martin Green in the *New York Evening World*, 8 August 1918, 3.

42. *Brooklyn Eagle*, 5 August 1918.

43. *Brooklyn Eagle*, 8 August 1918.

44. Reilly, *Americans All*, 275.

45. Alf Helmer, "My Part in Winning Friends for Freedom," from an unpublished article written by the soldier and held by his son Jan Helmer.

46. Joseph Jones diary, 15 July 1918, Jones family papers, held by Joseph Jones III.

47. Hogan, *The Shamrock Battalion*, 127–128.

48. *Brooklyn Eagle*, 21 July 1918.

49. Commons to his mother, 22 July 1918, Commons family papers.

50. Berry, *Make the Kaiser Dance*, 333.

51. *New York Tribune*, 23 April 1919, 4.

52. *New York Tribune*, 23 April 1919.

53. Spencer, undated letter to Loi, Spencer family papers.

54. Record of events sent to message center, headquarters, 83d Infantry Brigade, 14 July 1918. National Archives and Records Administration, College Park, Md.

55. Duffy, *Father Duffy's Story*, 131.
56. *The Irish World*, 1 February 1918, 6.
57. Hogan, *The Shamrock Battalion*, 125.
58. Duffy, *Father Duffy's Story*, 136.
59. Lieutenant Col. Mitchell, memorandum to commanding officer, 165th Infantry, 15 July 1918. National Archives and Records Administration, College Park, Md.
60. *New York Tribune*, 23 April 1919, 4.
61. Joseph Jones diary, 16 July 1918, Jones family papers.
62. Donnie King to his father, 21 July 1918, papers of Rosie Camp, granddaughter of Donnie King.
63. *Brooklyn Eagle*, 5 January 1919.
64. Pvt. Ralph Gassese, burial file, 14 January 1919, National Archives and Records Administration, College Park, Md.
65. Lt. Col. Mitchell, memorandum to commanding officer, 165th Infantry, 16 July 1918. National Archives and Records Administration, College Park, Md.
66. Austin Lawrence diary, 15 July 1918, Lawrence family papers.
67. *New York Evening World*, 22 August 1918, 3.
68. Nathaniel Rouse diary, 18 July 1918.
69. *Brooklyn Daily Star*, 21 August 1918, 1.
70. Donovan to Ruth, Rainbow Division Veterans Association records, Archives and Special Collections, University of Nebraska-Lincoln Libraries.
71. Record of events sent to message center headquarters 83d Infantry Brigade, 14–18 July 1918. National Archives and Records Administration, College Park, Md.
72. Reilly, *Americans All*, 273.
73. *New York Sun*, 3 August 1918, 4.
74. *New York Sun*, 3 August 1918, 4.
75. Letter to Daisy McKeon, family papers of George Patrick McKeon, held by Michael J. Fitz.
76. *New York Times*, 6 August 1918, 1.
77. *New York Times*, 3 August 1918, 4.
78. Account of Pvt. William Halpin, burial file, 17 February 1919, National Archives and Records Administration, College Park, Md.

Chapter 16

1. General orders no. 48, headquarters, 42nd Division, American Expeditionary Force, 20 July 1918. In Louis L. Collins' *Minnesota in the World War*, (Saint Paul: Minnesota War Records Commission, 1924), 1:239.
2. Howe, *Memoirs of the Harvard War Dead*, 593.
3. *New York Sun*, 11 August 1918, 8.
4. McCoy to his mother, 17 July 1918, collections of the Manuscript Division, Library of Congress, Washington, D.C.
5. Associated Staff, *Iodine and Gasoline: A History of the 117th Sanitary Train*, 84. Publisher and date of publication unknown. However, it is known that the history was written in 1919 in Bad Neuenahr, Germany.
6. Rexmond C. Cochrane, "Gas Warfare in World War I, the 42nd Division Before Landres-et-St. Georges, October 1918," U.S. Army Chemical Corps

historical study no. 1 (Washington, D.C.: U.S. Army Chemical Corps Historical Office, 1960), 24.

7. Edith Bishop, quoted in Anne Tjomsland, MD, *Bellevue in France: Anecdotal History of Base Hospital No. 1* (New York: Froben Press, 1941), 84–88.
8. Tjomsland, *Bellevue in France*, 75.
9. Tjomsland, *Bellevue in France*, 95.
10. General orders no. 48, headquarters, 42nd Division, American Expeditionary Force, 20 July 1918. In Collins' *Minnesota in the World War*, (Saint Paul: Minnesota War Records Commission, 1924), 1:240.
11. McCoy to his mother, 21 July 1918, collections of the Manuscript Division, Library of Congress, Washington, D.C.
12. Nathaniel Rouse diary, 21 July 1918, Rouse family papers.
13. Hogan, *The Shamrock Battalion*, 139.
14. Duffy, *Father Duffy's Story*, 152.
15. Duffy, *Father Duffy's Story*, 153.
16. Commons to his mother, 22 July 1918, Mary C. Haeger family papers.
17. Florence Commons to her son Vivian, 20 July 1918, Commons family papers.
18. Florence Commons to her son Vivian, 26 July 1918.
19. Hogan, *The Shamrock Battalion*, 141.
20. Duffy, *Father Duffy's Story*, 154.
21. Howe, *Oliver Ames Jr.*, 72–73.
22. Howe, *Oliver Ames Jr.*, 75.
23. William Spencer to his father, 23 July 1918, Spencer family papers.
24. *New York Evening World*, 6 August 1918, 3.
25. Collins, *Minnesota in the World War*, 1:86.
26. Hogan, *The Shamrock Battalion*, 141.
27. Lawrence diary, 25 July 1918, Lawrence family papers.
28. Donovan to his wife, 7 August 1918, William Donovan papers, Military History Institute, Carlisle, Penn.
29. Elmer to his parents, 5 August 1918, Elmer family papers.
30. *Brooklyn Daily Eagle*, 22 September 1918, 16.
31. Hogan, *The Shamrock Battalion*, 142–143.
32. Elmer Sherwood, *Diary of a Rainbow Man: Written at the Front* (Terre Haute, Ind.: Moore-Langen Company, 1929), 40.
33. Reilly, *Americans All*, 384.
34. Austin Lawrence diary, 25 July 1918, Lawrence family papers.
35. Hogan, *The Shamrock Battalion*, 144–145.
36. Berry, *Make the Kaiser Dance*, 334.
37. Berry, *Make the Kaiser Dance*, 311.
38. Donovan to his wife, 7 August 1918, William Donovan papers, Military History Institute, Carlisle, Penn.
39. *Brooklyn Daily Eagle*, 22 September 1918, 16.
40. Grayson Murphy to see his eldest son, 4 August 1918, Murphy family papers, held by Grayson Murphy III.
41. Donovan to his wife, 7 August 1918, William Donovan papers, Military History Institute, Carlisle, Penn.
42. Victor Van Yorx to his family, 5 August 1918, held by W. T. Van Yorx. This letter was published in several contemporary newspapers.
43. Reilly, *Americans All*, 384.

44. Hogan, *The Shamrock Battalion*, 151.
45. Hogan, *The Shamrock Battalion*, 152.
46. Duffy, *Father Duffy's Story*, 162.
47. Eighty-third Brigade message board for 27 July 1918, National Archives and Records Administration, College Park, Md.
48. Reilly, *Americans All*, 319.
49. General orders no. 51, headquarters, 42nd Division, American Expeditionary Force [A.E.F.], 27 July 1918, 9:30 a.m., National Archives and Records Administration, College Park, Md.
50. Eighty-third Brigade message board for 28 July 1918, National Archives and Records Administration, College Park, Md.
51. Duffy, *Father Duffy's Story*, 163.
52. Elmer to his parents, 5 August 1918, Elmer family papers.

Chapter 17

1. Quotations in this paragraph are taken from Eighty-third Brigade message board for 28 July 1918, National Archives and Records Administration, College Park, Md. The number of bayoneted Germans is cited on page 25 of Cochrane, U.S. Army Chemical Corps historical study no. 1.
2. Hogan, *The Shamrock Battalion*, 153.
3. Victor Van Yorx to his family, 5 August 1918, held by W. T. Van Yorx, and published in several newspapers.
4. Hogan, *The Shamrock Battalion*, 154–155.
5. Van Merle-Smith to his wife, undated, Merle-Smith family papers.
6. Merle-Smith to Mrs. Lawrence Spencer, 13 November 1918, Merle-Smith family papers.
7. Reilly, *Americans All*, 386.
8. Merle-Smith to his wife, undated first draft. The second draft of this letter deleted reference to the charge of the Light Brigade, Merle-Smith family papers.
9. Spencer to his brother, Jay, 18 August 1918, Spencer family papers.
10. Donovan to his wife, 7 August 1918, William Donovan papers, Military History Institute, Carlisle, Penn.
11. Eighty-third Brigade message board for 28 July 1918. National Archives and Records Administration.
12. Reilly, *Americans All*, 389.
13. Hogan, *The Shamrock Battalion*, 156.
14. Victor Van Yorx to his family, 5 August 1918, held by W. T. Van Yorx.
15. The account of how K Company reached and crossed the Ourcq was taken from Victor Van Yorx letter cited in note 14 and Hogan's *The Shamrock Battalion*.
16. Howe, *Memoirs*, 599.
17. Merle-Smith to his wife, undated, Merle-Smith family papers.
18. Victor Van Yorx to his family, 5 August 1918, held by W. T. Van Yorx.
19. *New York Telegram*, 23 September 1918, 1–3.
20. Hogan, *The Shamrock Battalion*, 164.
21. Eyewitness accounts of Lieutenant Howard Arnold's death are from Arnold's burial file, National Archives and Records Administration, College Park, Md.

22. Hogan, *The Shamrock Battalion*, 165.
23. *New York Sunday Herald*, third section, 22 September 1918, 6.
24. *The Gaelic American*, 6 November 1918, 7.
25. Undated Merle-Smith letter, Merle-Smith family papers.
26. William Spencer to his brother, Jay, 18 August 1918, Spencer family papers.
27. *Brooklyn Daily Eagle*, 22 August 1918, 4.
28. Victor Van Yorx to his family, held by W. T. Van Yorx.
29. "An Account of Private Dixon," Sixty-ninth Regiment archives, held by the estate of the late Regimental Historian Col. Kenneth Powers, Westport, Conn.
30. Undated Merle-Smith letter, Merle-Smith family papers.
31. Merle-Smith to Mrs. Lawrence Spencer, 13 November 1918, Merle-Smith family papers.
32. Spencer to his brother, 18 August 1918, Spencer family papers.
33. Reilly, *Americans All*, 387.
34. *Brooklyn Daily Eagle*, 27 October 1918.
35. *The Wave of Long Island*, 30 August 1918.
36. Reilly, *Americans All*, 401–402.
37. The account of Richard Ryan's charge and death comes from various newspaper accounts and an interview by the author with Carolyn (Atkinson) Hotchkiss, Ryan's granddaughter, 4 August 2003.
38. Eighty-third Brigade message board for 28 July 1918. National Archives and Records Administration, College Park, Md.
39. *New York Sunday Herald*, 27 April 1919, 8.
40. Austin Lawrence diary, 28 July 1918, Lawrence family papers.
41. Howe, *Memoirs*, 597.
42. From Pvt. Benjamin Gunnell's burial file, National Archives and Records Administration, College Park, Md.
43. *New York Times*, 10 December 1918, 5.
44. Howe, *Memoirs*, 598.
45. *Gaelic American*, 30 November 1918, 3.
46. Duffy, *Father Duffy's Story*, 175.

Chapter 18

1. Donovan to his wife, 7 August 1918, William Donovan papers, Military History Institute, Carlisle, Penn.
2. Donovan to his wife, 7 August 1918.
3. *Brooklyn Daily Star*, 12 November 1918, 8.
4. Donovan to his wife, 7 August 1918, William Donovan papers, Military History Institute, Carlisle, Penn.
5. From a newspaper article pasted into the scrapbook of Van S. Merle-Smith. No identifying information.
6. *Brooklyn Daily Eagle*, 6 October 1918.
7. *Brooklyn Daily Star*, 2 November 1918, 8.
8. Reilly, *Americans All*, 396–397.
9. *Gaelic American*, 1 May 1919, 8.
10. *Gaelic American*, 30 November 1918, 3.
11. *Brooklyn Daily Eagle*, 22 September 1918.
12. Duffy, *Father Duffy's Story*, 187.

13. Howe, *Oliver Ames Jr.*, 74–76.
14. Donovan to his wife, 7 August 1918, William Donovan papers, Military History Institute, Carlisle, Penn.
15. Oliver Ames Jr.'s burial file, National Archives and Records Administration, College Park, Md.
16. Duffy, *Father Duffy's Story*, 188.
17. Elmer to his parents, 5 August 1918, Elmer family papers.
18. Donovan to his wife, 7 August 1918, William Donovan papers, Military History Institute, Carlisle, Penn.
19. Duffy, *Father Duffy's Story*, 192–193.
20. Kilmer, *Joyce Kilmer*, 212.
21. Kilmer, *Joyce Kilmer*, 216.
22. Elmer to his parents, 14 June 1918, Elmer family papers.
23. Quotes are from Emmett Watson, "Joyce Kilmer Soldier," *The American Legion Monthly*, September 1936, 61.
24. War Diaries, Second Battalion, 165th Infantry for 28 July 1918 and a memorandum, headquarters, Second Battalion, 165th Infantry for 25 August 1918. National Archives and Records Administration, College Park, Md.
25. *Brooklyn Daily Eagle*, 10 November 1918, 13.
26. Eighty-third Brigade message board for 28 July 1918. National Archives and Records Administration, College Park, Md.
27. War diaries of 165th Infantry, Second Battalion, 28 July 1918. National Archives and Records Administration, College Park, Md.
28. Carolyn Atkinson Hotchkiss, granddaughter of Richard Ryan, interview by author, 4 August 2003.
29. Alice Maxwell Appo to Mr. Stephen Baker, 16 September 1918. Seeley G. Mudd Manuscript Library, Princeton University.
30. MacArthur, *War Bugs*, 107–108.
31. *New York Tribune Sunday Magazine*, 20 April 1919, 2.
32. *New York Tribune Sunday Magazine*, 20 April 1919.
33. Field orders no. 29, 28 July 1918, headquarters, 1st Army Corps, National Archives and Records Administration, College Park, Md.
34. Eighty-third Brigade message board, 29 July 1918, National Archives and Records Administration, College Park, Md.
35. Operations of the 165th Infantry from midnight 24–25 July to midnight 2 August 1918, 4. National Archives and Records Administration, College Park, Md.
36. Testimony of Maj. William Donovan before the Inspector general, 15 August 1918, National Archives and Records Administration, College Park, Md.
37. Grayson Murphy to his son, 2 August 1918, family papers, held by Grayson Murphy III.
38. Charlie Carman quotes come from *The Wave of Long Island*, 7 November 1918.
39. Lt. Edwin A. Daly's burial file, National Archives and Records Administration, College Park, Md.
40. Lt. Gerald R. Stott's burial file, National Archives and Records Administration, College Park, Md.

Chapter 19

1. *New York World Magazine and Story Section*, 7 August 1921, 1.
2. Berry, *Make the Kaiser Dance*, 335.
3. Forty-second Division summary of intelligence, 29 July to 30 July 1918, National Archives and Records Administration, College Park, Md.
4. Record of events at message center, headquarters 83d Infantry Brigade, 30 July 1918, National Archives and Records Administration, College Park, Md.
5. Berry, *Make the Kaiser Dance*, 335–336. Berry's account rings true and is supported by Sergeant O'Neill's son, William Donovan O'Neill, in an interview with the author.
6. Sergeant Joyce Kilmer's burial file, National Archives and Records Administration, College Park, Md.
7. Duffy, *Father Duffy's Story*, 192.
8. Sergeant Joyce Kilmer's burial file.
9. *Brooklyn Daily Eagle*, 31 July 1918, and *The New York Herald*, 1 August 1918. There is confusion as to when Hyland made his stand. Newspapers reported that it was on 28 July. However, war diaries and other official documents put E Company in Seringes-et-Nesles on the 30th. That's the day I decided to go with.
10. Berry, *Make the Kaiser Dance*, 336.
11. Account of O'Neill's Medal of Honor action comes from Berry's *Make the Kaiser Dance*, 336–337, *New York World Magazine*, 1 August 1921, 1, and a telephone interview between the author and O'Neill's son, William Donovan O'Neill on 3 November 2003.
12. Eighty-third Brigade message board, 30 July 1918. The message board has a running timeline of the entire day. Rainbow Division Veterans Association records, Archives and Special Collections, University of Nebraska-Lincoln Libraries.
13. Holt's story was printed in the *Brooklyn Daily Eagle*, 22 September 1918, 16.
14. Malcolm Robertson's burial file, National Archives and Records Administration, College Park, Md.
15. Joseph Dugdale's statement, given 8 May 1920, is among the papers of Malcolm Robertson, held by Princeton University's Seeley G. Mudd Manuscript Library.
16. Donovan to his wife, 7 August 1918, William Donovan papers, Military History Institute, Carlisle, Penn.
17. Captain William Hudson's burial file, National Archives and Records Administration, College Park, Md.
18. Eighty-third Brigade message board, 30 July 1918, Rainbow Division Veterans Association records, Archives and Special Collections, University of Nebraska-Lincoln Libraries.
19. Sherwood, *Dairy*, 48–49. In his diary, Sherwood had not used the word "bayonets," although it had in fact been a part of the Second Battalion's battle cry.
20. Louis L. Collins, *History of the 151st Field Artillery Rainbow Division in the World War, Vol. 1* (Saint Paul: Minnesota War Records Commission, 1924), 97.

21. Leach, *War Diary*, 105.
22. Eighty-third Brigade message board, 30 July 1918, Rainbow Division Veterans Association records, Archives and Special Collections, University of Nebraska-Lincoln Libraries.
23. Sergeant Joyce Kilmer's burial file.
24. *New York Times*, 15 September 1919, 8.
25. *The Home News*, 22 August 1918.
26. Words of Biber, Nugent, and McAuliffe are from Kilmer's burial file.
27. Basil to his parents, 6 August 1918, Elmer family papers, held by Stephen Elmer.
28. *Brooklyn Daily Eagle*, 31 July 1918, 1. The reporter said the date was 28 July, but E Company did not get into the streets of Seringes-et-Nesles until the 30th. The reporter also said one of the officers was killed. No E Company officer died either on the 28th or the 30th. Capt. Charles Baker was wounded, but did not die until several months later.
29. Austin Lawrence diary, 1 August 1918. Lawrence family papers.
30. Associated Staff, *Iodine and Gasoline*, 93.
31. Leach, *War Diary*, 104.
32. Donovan to his wife, 7 August 1918, William Donovan papers, Military History Institute, Carlisle, Penn.
33. Donovan to his wife, 7 August 1918.
34. Leach, *War Diary*, 106.
35. Collins, *History*, 97.
36. Words of Capt. Van S. Merle-Smith in this and the following paragraph are from a letter to the Knights of Columbus, 21 August 1918, Merle-Smith family papers.
37. Donovan to his wife, 7 August 1918, William Donovan papers, Military History Institute, Carlisle, Penn.

Chapter 20

1. Donovan to his wife, 7 August 1918, William Donovan papers, Military History Institute, Carlisle, Penn.
2. MacArthur, *War Bugs*, 111–112.
3. *The Gaelic American*, 30 November 1918, 3.
4. *The Advocate*, 18 January 1919, 1.
5. Duffy, *Father Duffy's Story*, 208.
6. Col. Frank McCoy to Daniel M. Brady, 21 August 1918, collections of the Manuscript Division, Library of Congress, Washington, D.C.
7. Donovan to his wife, 7 August 1918, William Donovan papers, Military History Institute, Carlisle, Penn.
8. There is no definitive reckoning of the 165th Infantry's casualties in the battle of the Ourcq River. Duffy's figures, which appear in his book, are lower than those compiled by Peter J. Linder, recognized as one of the leading authorities on World War I casualties. Linder lists 241 killed, but he missed two men, Capt. Charles Baker and Pfc. John Kayes, both of whom were wounded in the battle and died months later. He also lists sixty men, not mentioned by Duffy, who died of wounds from 25 July through 6 August; however, it is not known when these men were wounded.

9. Cochrane, U.S. Army Chemical Corps historical study no. 17. Cochrane cites official medical records (page 32 in his study) for his casualty counts for the Forty-second Division.

10. *The Wave of Long Island*, 7 November 1918, 4.

11. *The Wave of Long Island*, 7 November 1918.

12. Elmer to his parents, 10 August and 18 August 1918. Elmer family papers.

13. Woollcott's words on visiting Kilmer's gravesite are from the *New York Times*, section IV, 25 August 1918, 4.

14. Kilmer, *Leaves*, 122.

15. Duffy, *Father Duffy's Story*, 205–206.

16. Van S. Merle-Smith to the Knights of Columbus, 21 August 1918, Merle-Smith family papers.

17. Summary of Intelligence, headquarters 42d Division, 1 August to 2 August 1918, Rainbow Division Veterans Association records, Archives and Special Collections, University of Nebraska-Lincoln Libraries.

18. Donovan to his wife, 7 August 1918, William Donovan papers, Military History Institute, Carlisle, Penn.

19. McCoy to his mother, 6 August 1918, collections of the Manuscript Division, Library of Congress, Washington, D.C.

20. McCoy to his mother, 20 August 1918, collections of the Manuscript Division, Library of Congress, Washington, D.C.

21. McCoy to Col. John Barker, 21 August 1918, collections of the Manuscript Division, Library of Congress, Washington, D.C.

22. Bacevich, *Diplomat in Khaki*, 79.

23. Duffy, *Father Duffy's Story*, 229.

24. Duffy, *Father Duffy's Story*, 228–229.

25. Elmer to his parents, 18 August 1918, Elmer family papers.

26. Duffy to McCoy, undated, collections of the Manuscript Division, Library of Congress, Washington, D.C.

27. Duffy, *Father Duffy's Story*, 228.

28. Duffy to McCoy, 18 September 1918, collections of the Manuscript Division, Library of Congress, Washington, D.C.

29. Lt. J. Phelps Harding to his father, 16 August 1918. MacArthur Memorial Archives, Norfolk, Virginia.

30. Harding to his mother, 20 and 24 August 1918. MacArthur Memorial Archives, Norfolk, Virginia.

31. Duffy, *Father Duffy's Story*, 228.

Chapter 21

1. General John J. Pershing, *My Experiences in the First World War* (New York: De Capo Press 1931) 2:28.

2. Pershing, *My Experiences*, 2:225.

3. Pershing, *My Experiences*, 2:247.

4. Pershing, *My Experiences*, 2:247.

5. Marshal Ferdinand Foch, *The Memoirs of Marshal Foch*, trans. Col. T. Bentley Mott, (Garden City, N.Y.: Doubleday, Doran and Company, 1931), 399–401.

6. S.L.A. Marshall, *World War I* (Boston: Houghton Mifflin Company, 1987 Edition), 425.

7. Capt. B. H. Liddell Hart, *The Real War, 1914–1918* (Boston: Little, Brown and Company, 1964 re-issue), 456.
8. Field orders no. 17, headquarters, 42nd Division, A.E.F., 9 September 1918. From Collins's *Minnesota in the World War,* 1:255.
9. Rouse diary, 7 September through 11 September 1918, Rouse family papers.
10. Lt. Col. William Donovan to Brig. Gen. Frank McCoy, 21 September 1918, collections of the Manuscript Division, Library of Congress, Washington, D.C.
11. Reilly, *Americans All,* 562.
12. *Brooklyn Daily Eagle,* 3 November 1918, 9.
13. Hogan, *The Shamrock Battalion,* 204.
14. Duffy, *Father Duffy's Story,* 233–234.
15. Donovan to McCoy, 21 September 1918, collections of the Manuscript Division, Library of Congress, Washington, D.C.
16. Reilly, *Americans All,* 562.
17. Reilly, *Americans All,* 563.
18. Lt. J. Phelps Harding to "C———," 2 September 1918, MacArthur Memorial Archives, Norfolk, Virginia.
19. William Spencer to Jay Spencer, undated, Spencer family papers.
20. Rouse diary, 11 September 1918, Rouse family papers.
21. Forty-second Division summary of intelligence, daylight, 11 September to noon, 11 September 1918. Rainbow Division Veterans Association records, Archives and Special Collections, University of Nebraska-Lincoln Libraries.
22. Harding to "C———," 22 September 1918.
23. MacArthur, *War Bugs,* 142.
24. Ranulf Compton diary, 12 September 1918, property of his granddaughter, Nathalie Compton Logan.
25. Harding to "C———," 22 September 1918. MacArthur Memorial Archives, Norfolk, Virginia.
26. Duffy, *Father Duffy's Story,* 236.
27. Duffy, *Father Duffy's Story,* 235.
28. *Brooklyn Daily Eagle,* 3 November 1918.
29. "Charles Delano Hine," in the *Fifty-eighth Annual Report of the Association of Graduates of the United States Military Academy,* 13 June 1927, 135.
30. *The Wave of Long Island,* 24 October 1918, 4.
31. *Brooklyn Daily Eagle,* 3 November 1918, 9.
32. *The Gaelic American,* 1 March 1919, 8.
33. Rouse diary, 13 September 1918, Rouse family papers.
34. Forty-second Division Summary of Intelligence, noon, 11 September to noon, 12 September 1918.
35. Harding to "C———," 22 September 1918.
36. Forty-second Division Summary of Intelligence, noon, 12 September to noon, 13 September 1918. Rainbow Division Veterans Association records, Archives and Special Collections, University of Nebraska-Lincoln Libraries.
37. Hogan, *The Shamrock Battalion,* 212.
38. Harding to "C———," 22 September 1918.
39. Reilly, *Americans All,* 563.
40. Donovan to McCoy, 21 September 1918, collections of the Manuscript Division, Library of Congress, Washington, D.C.
41. Duffy, *Father Duffy's Story,* 238.

42. MacArthur, *War Bugs*, 144–145.
43. Reilly, *Americans All*, 564.
44. Spencer to Jay Spencer, undated, Spencer family papers.
45. Spencer to his mother, undated, Spencer family papers.
46. Donovan to McCoy, 21 September 1918, collections of the Manuscript Division, Library of Congress.
47. *The Advocate*, 26 October 1918, 4.
48. Reilly, *Americans All*, 564.
49. *The Advocate*, 26 October 1918.
50. Spencer to his mother, undated, Spencer family papers.
51. Harding to "C——," 22 September 1918.
52. Grayson Murphy III, interview by the author, April 2005. From an anecdote told by Grayson Murphy to his family.
53. Donovan to McCoy, 21 September 1918, collections of the Manuscript Division, Library of Congress, Washington, D.C.
54. *The Advocate*, 26 October 1918.
55. *The Advocate*, 26 October 1918.
56. Duffy to McCoy, 18 September 1918, collections of the Manuscript Division, Library of Congress, Washington, D.C.
57. Harding to "C——," 22 September 1918.
58. MacArthur, *War Bugs*, 143.
59. Pershing, *My Experiences*, 2:272.
60. Foch, *Memoirs*, 402.

Chapter 22

1. Pershing, *My Experiences*, 2:286–287.
2. MacArthur, *War Bugs*, 157–158.
3. Duffy, *Father Duffy's Story*, 254–255.
4. Donovan to his wife, undated letter. William Donovan papers, Military History Institute, Carlisle, Penn.
5. Duffy, *Father Duffy's Story*, 255–256.
6. William Manchester, *American Caesar*, (Boston: Little, Brown and Company, 1978), 104.
7. Pershing, *My Experiences*, 2:282–283.
8. Donovan to his wife, 8 October 1918, William Donovan papers, Military History Institute, Carlisle, Penn.
9. Gregor Dallas, *At the Heart of a Tiger: Clemenceau and His World 1841–1929* (New York: Carroll & Graf Publishers, 1993), 544.
10. Foch, *Memoirs*, 436.
11. Pershing, *My Experiences*, 2:338.
12. Hogan, *The Shamrock Battalion*, 228–231.
13. Ettinger, *Doughboy*, 169.
14. Duffy, *Father Duffy's Story*, 263.
15. Berry, *Make the Kaiser Dance*, 337–338.
16. William Spencer diary, 25 September 1918; and letter from Spencer to Loi, 3 October 1918, Spencer family papers.
17. Flick, *Chaplain Duffy*, 94–95.
18. Reilly, *Americans All*, 688–689.

19. Ettinger, *Doughboy*, 175.
20. Duffy to McCoy, Thanksgiving Day, 1918, collections of the Manuscript Division, Library of Congress, Washington, D.C.
21. MacArthur, *Reminiscencs*, 66.
22. Leach, *War Diary*, 140.
23. Sherwood, *Dairy*, 177.
24. Duffy to McCoy, Thanksgiving Day, 1918.
25. Harding to his mother, 14 November 1918, MacArthur Memorial Archives, Norfolk, Virginia.
26. Hogan, *The Shamrock Battalion*, 233.
27. Ettinger, *Doughboy*, 175.
28. Duffy, *Father Duffy's Story*, 268–269.
29. Reilly, *Americans All*, 691–692.
30. Hogan, *Shamrock Battalion*, 237.
31. MacArthur, *War Bugs*, 180.
32. *Mount Vernon Daily Argus*, 27 November 1918, 4.
33. Harding to his mother, 25 October 1918.
34. Jan Helmer, interview by author, 7 December 2002.
35. *Mount Vernon Daily Argus*, 27 November 1918, 4.
36. Hogan, *The Shamrock Battalion*, 238–239.
37. *Mount Vernon Daily Argus*, 26 December 1918, 1.
38. Harding to his mother, 25 October 1918.
39. *New York Evening World*, 18 October 1918, 3.
40. *New York Evening World*, 18 October 1918.
41. Berry, *Make the Kaiser Dance*, 315.
42. Hogan, *The Shamrock Battalion*, 239.
43. *The Gaelic American*, 1 March 1919, 8.
44. Hogan, *The Shamrock Battalion*, 242–249.
45. Harding to his mother, 14 November 1918, MacArthur Memorial Archives, Norfolk, Virginia.
46. Reilly, *Americans All*, 691–694.
47. Ettinger, *Doughboy*, 181.
48. Reilly, *Americans All*, 691–694.
49. Reilly, *Americans All*, 691–694, 694.

Chapter 23
1. Field order no. 18, 15 October 1918, headquarters 83rd Infantry Brigade, National Archives and Records Administration, College Park, Md.
2. Georgetown University Library, Special Collections Division, Joyce Kilmer papers, box and folder 3:31.
3. Summary of intelligence, 42d Division, A.E.F., noon, 14 October to noon, 15 October 1918, Rainbow Division Veterans Association records, Archives and Special Collections, University of Nebraska-Lincoln Libraries.
4. Reilly, *Americans All*, 695.
5. Duffy, *Father Duffy's Story*, 270–271.
6. Duffy, *Father Duffy's Story*, 281.
7. Ettinger, *Doughboy*, 185.
8. Duffy, *Father Duffy's Story*, 281–282.

9. Ettinger, *Doughboy*, 165 and 186.
10. Reilly, *Americans All*, 696.
11. Reilly, *Americans All*, 696.
12. Ettinger, *Doughboy*, 183.
13. Duffy, *Father Duffy's Story*, 274 and 283.
14. *Brooklyn Daily Star*, 7 December 1918.
15. Unidentified newspaper clipping from the scrapbook of Van S. Merle-Smith, Merle-Smith family papers.
16. Testimony of Col. H. T. Mitchell, report of investigation to determine responsibility for countermanding order for 165th Infantry to attack at noon, 15 October 1918, conducted at headquarters 42nd Division, 25 October 1918. National Archives and Records Administration, College Park, Md.
17. Duffy, *Father Duffy's Story*, 284–285.
18. Duffy, *Father Duffy's Story*, 275.
19. Unidentified newspaper clipping from the scrapbook of Van S. Merle-Smith, Merle-Smith family papers.
20. Donovan field message, 15 October 1918. Cited in report of investigation to determine responsibility for countermanding order for 165th Infantry to attack at noon, 15 October 1918, conducted at headquarters 42nd Division, 25 October 1918. National Archives and Records Administration, College Park, Md.
21. Donovan field message, 15 October 1918.
22. Mitchell testimony, report of investigation to determine responsibility for countermanding order for 165th Infantry to attack at noon, 15 October 1918, conducted at headquarters 42nd Division, 25 October 1918. National Archives and Records Administration, College Park, Md.
23. Unidentified newspaper clipping from the scrapbook of Van S. Merle-Smith, Merle-Smith family papers.
24. Summary of operations, 15 October 1918, 165th Infantry, National Archives and Records Administration, College Park, Md.
25. Berry, *Make the Kaiser Dance*, 338.
26. Casualty rates for the 165th Infantry are listed by Peter J. Linder, one of the leading authorities on World War I casualties. The historian quoted is James J. Cooke from his book *The Rainbow Division in the Great War, 1917–1919*. (Westport, Conn.: Praeger, 1994), 178.
27. MacArthur, *War Bugs*, 183–184.
28. Duffy, *Father Duffy's Story*, 275–276.
29. Cheseldine, *Ohio In The Rainbow*, 256.
30. Reilly, *Americans All*, 739.
31. Duffy, *Father Duffy's Story*, 277.
32. Duffy to Brig. Gen. Frank McCoy, Thanksgiving Day, 1918, collections of the Manuscript Division, Library of Congress, Washington, D.C.
33. Berry, *Make the Kaiser Dance*, 318.

Chapter 24

1. Flick, *Chaplain Duffy*, 96.
2. Duffy letter to McCoy, Thanksgiving Day, 1918, collections of the Manuscript Division, Library of Congress.

3. Duffy, *Father Duffy's Story*, 296.

4. Harding to his mother, 14 November 1918. MacArthur Memorial Archives, Norfolk, Virginia.

5. Joseph T. Dickman, *The Great Crusade: A Narrative of the World War* (New York: D. Appleton and Company, 1927), 175–176.

6. Reilly, *Americans All*, 807.

7. Byron Farwell, *Over There: The United States in the Great War, 1917–1918*, (New York: W. W. Norton & Company, 1999), 242.

8. Pershing, *My Experiences*, 2:381.

9. Dickman, *The Great Crusade*, 186.

10. Reilly, *Americans All*, 806.

11. Duffy, *Father Duffy's Story*, 297.

12. Harding to his mother, 14 November 1918.

13. *New York Times*, 8 November 1918, 1.

14. Reilly, *Americans All*, 826.

15. Thomas M. Johnson, *New York Evening Sun*, 15 December 1918.

16. Duffy, *Father Duffy's Story*, 301.

17. Reilly, *Americans All*, 826.

18. Duffy, *Father Duffy's Story*, 301.

19. Johnson, *New York Evening Sun*, 15 December 1918.

20. There are numerous accounts of this incident. I relied on Johnson's version in the *New York Sun*, as it parallels Duffy's in his book, *Father Duffy's Story* (302) and Reilley's account in *Americans All* (827–828), except for the German accent, written by Johnson.

21. Reilly, *Americans All*, 827–829.

22. Johnson, *New York Evening Sun*, 15 December 1918.

23. Harding to his mother, 25 November 1918, MacArthur Memorial Archives, Norfolk, Virginia.

24. Reilly, *Americans All*, 825–830.

25. Forty-second Division summary of intelligence, noon, November 7 to noon, November 8, 1918, National Archives and Records Administration, College Park, Md.

26. Reilly, *Americans All*, 810–827.

27. Duffy letter to McCoy, Thanksgiving Day, 1918, collections of the Manuscript Division, Library of Congress, Washington, D.C.

28. Pershing, *My Experiences*, 2:381.

29. Reilly, *Americans All*, 810–827.

30. Duffy, *Father Duffy's Story*, 304.

31. Harding to his mother, 14 November 1918.

32. Hogan, *The Shamrock Battalion*, 260.

33. Rouse diary, 11 November 1918, Rouse family papers.

34. Combat diary of Richard O'Neill, 11 November 1918, O'Neill family papers.

35. Austin Lawrence diary, 11 November 1918, Lawrence family papers.

36. Duffy, *Father Duffy's Story*, 305.

Epilogue

1. Peter Linder, an authority on World War I casualties, has compiled a list of every soldier from the 165th Infantry of the 844 who died, including their name rank, serial number, cause of death, and even where they are buried.

2. The Swift family papers, Sheldon Museum, Middlebury, Vermont.

3. *The Enterprise and Vermonter*, 24 August 1928, 1.

4. *Rainbow Barrage Newsletter*, October 1957.

5. Letter from Gerard Doyle, grandson of Richard Leahy, to author, 7 June 2005.

6. *New York Times*, 23 July 1930, 23.

7. Duffy, *Father Duffy's Story*, 326.

8. Address by Col. William Donovan at the unveiling of Father Duffy's statue at Times Square, New York, 2 May 1938, Donovan papers, Military History Institute, Carlisle, Penn.

9. Anthony Cave Brown, *The Last Hero: Wild Bill Donovan* (New York: Times Books, 1982), 68.

10. Duffy to McCoy, Thanksgiving Day 1918, Collections of the Manuscript Division, Library of Congress, Washington, D.C.

11. Donovan to Ruth Donovan, 15 January 1919, Donovan papers, Military History Institute, Carlisle, Penn.

Selected Bibliography

Adams, Samuel Hopkins. *A. Woollcott: His Life and His World.* New York: Reynal & Hitchcock, 1945.

Alexander, Robert. *Memories of the World War, 1917–1918.* New York: The Macmillan Company, 1931.

Allen, Irving Lewis. *The City in Slang: New York Life and Popular Speech.* New York: Oxford University Press, 1993.

American Armies and Battlefields in Europe: History, Guide and Reference Book. Washington: Government Printing Office, 1928.

Amerine, William H. *Alabama's Own in France.* New York: Eaton & Gettinger, 1919.

Anbinder, Tyer. *Five Points.* New York: The Free Press, 2001.

Anders, Leslie. *Gentle Knight: The Life and Times of Major General Edwin Forrest Harding.* Kent, OH: The Kent State University Press, 1985.

Appleby, R. Scott. *"Church and Age Unite!": The Modernist Impulse in American Catholicism.* Notre Dame, IN: University of Notre Dame Press, 1992.

Associated Staff, Lt. Col. Wilbur S. Conkling, commanding officer. *Iodine and Gasoline: A History of the 117th Sanitary Train.* No publishing location or date listed. Written in 1919 in Bad Neueunahr, Germany.

Ayres, Leonard P. *The War With Germany: A Statistical Summary.* Washington: Government Printing Office, 1919.

Bacevich, A. J. *Diplomat in Khaki: Major General Frank Ross McCoy and American Foreign Policy, 1898–1949.* Lawrence, KS: University Press of Kansas, 1989.

Bayor, Ronald H., and Timothy J. Meagher, eds. *The New York Irish.* Baltimore, MD: The Johns Hopkins University Press, 1996.

Bernstein, Iver. *The New York City Draft Riots: Their Significance for American Society and Politics in the Age of the Civil War.* New York: Oxford University Press, 1990.

Berry, Henry. *Make the Kaiser Dance.* Garden City, NY: Doubleday & Company, 1978.

Bishop, Jim, and Lee Virginia. *Fighting Father Duffy*. New York: Farrar, Straus and Cudahy, Inc., 1956.

Bittle, Capt. Celestine N. *Soldiering for Cross and Flag: Impressions of a War Chaplain*. Milwaukee, WI: The Bruce Publishing Company, 1929.

Blumenson, Martin. *The Patton Papers, 1885–1940*. Boston: Houghton Mifflin Company, 1972.

Braim, Paul. F. *The Test of Battle: The American Expeditionary Forces in the Meuse-Argonne Campaign*, 2nd rev. ed. Shippensburg, Pa.: White Mane Books, 1998.

Buckley, John Patrick. *The New York Irish: Their View of American Foreign Policy, 1914–1921*. New York: Arno Press, 1976.

Burrows, Edwin G. and Mike Wallace. *Gotham: A History of New York City To 1898*. New York: Oxford University Press, 1999.

Clifford, John Garry. *The Citizen Soldiers: The Plattsburg Training Camp Movement, 1913–1920*. Lexington, Ky.: University of Kentucky Press, 1972.

Cochrane, Rexmond C. *Gas Warfare in World War I: The 42nd Division Before Landres-et-St. George*. Study Number 17: Army Chemical Center, MD: U.S. Army Chemical Corps Historical Office, 1959.

Coffman, Edward M. *The War to End All Wars: The American Military Experience in World War I*. New York: Oxford University Press, 1968.

Collins, Louis L., and Wayne E. Stevens, eds. *History of the 151st Field Artillery, Rainbow Division. Minnesota in the World War*, vol. 1. Saint Paul, MN: Minnesota War Records Commission, 1924.

Commandini, Adele. *I Saw Them Die: Diary and Recollections of Shirley Millard*. New York: Harcourt, Brace and Company, 1936.

Cooke, James J. *The Rainbow Division in the Great War, 1917–1919*. Westport, Conn.: Praeger, 1994.

Corby, William, and Lawrence Kohl, eds. *Memoirs of Chaplain Life: Three Years with the Irish Brigade in the Army of the Potomac*. New York: Fordham University Press, 1992.

Covell, John E. *Joyce Kilmer: A Literary Biography*. Brunswick, Ga.: Write-Fit Communications, 2000.

Cuddy, Joseph Edward. *Irish-America and National Isolationism, 1914–1920*. New York: Arno Press, 1976.

Dallas, Gregor. *At the Heart of a Tiger: Clemenceau and His World 1841–1929*. New York: Carroll & Graf Publishers, 1993.

Demeter, Richard. *The Fighting 69th: A History*. Pasadena, Calif.: Cranford Press, 2002.

D'Este, Carlo. *Patton: A Genius for War.* New York: HarperCollins Publishers Inc., 1995.

Dickman, Joseph T. *The Great Crusade: A Narrative of the World War.* New York: D. Appleton and Company, 1927.

Dreiser, Theodore. *The Color of A Great City.* New York: Boni and Liveright, 1923.

Duffy, Francis P. *Father Duffy's Story.* New York: George H. Doran Co., 1919.

English, T. J. *The Westies: Inside the Hell's Kitchen Irish Mob.* New York: G. P. Putnam's Sons, 1990.

Ettinger, Albert M., and A. Churchill. *Doughboy with the Fighting 69th.* New York: Pocket Books, 1993. First published by White Mane Publishing, Shippensburg, Penn., 1992.

Evans, Martin Marix, ed. *American Voices of World War I.* London and Chicago: Fitzroy Dearborn Publishers, 2001.

Flanagan, Thomas. *The Tenants of Time.* New York: E. P. Dutton, 1988.

Flick, Ella M. *Chaplain Duffy of the Sixty-ninth Regiment, New York.* Philadelphia: The Dolphin Press, 1935.

Gibbons, Floyd. *And They Thought We Wouldn't Fight.* New York: George H. Doran Co., 1918.

Graham, Milton P. *History of Ambulance Company No. 161.* Aberdeen, Wash.: Welsh-Richards Co., Inc., 1919.

Hagedorn, Hermann. *Leonard Wood: A Biography,* Vols. 1 and 2. New York: Harper & Brothers, 1931.

Harris, Stephen L. *Duty, Honor, Privilege: New York's Silk Stocking Regiment and the Breaking of the Hindenburg Line.* Dulles, Va.: Potomac Books, Inc., 2001.

———. *Harlem's Hell Fighters: The African-American 369th Infantry in World War I.* Dulles, Va.: Potomac Books, Inc., 2003.

Hecht, Ben. *A Child of the Century.* New York: Simon and Schuster, 1954.

Hofmann, Arnold. *Old New York Neighborhoods and How They Grew.* New York: The National City Bank of New York, no date.

Hogan, Martin J. *The Shamrock Battalion of the Rainbow: A Story of the 'Fighting Sixty-ninth'.* New York: D. Appleton and Company, 1919.

Honeywell, Roy. J. *Chaplains of the United States Army.* Washington, D.C.: Department of the Army, 1958.

Hopper, James. *Medals of Honor.* New York: The John Day Company, 1929.

Howe, M. A. De Wolfe. *Oliver Ames Jr., 1895–1918.* Boston: Privately printed, 1922.

Howe, M. A. DeWolf, and others. *Memoirs of the Harvard War Dead in the War Against Germany.* Cambridge, Mass.: Harvard University Press, 1923.

Huber, Richard M. *Big All the Way Through: The Life of Van Santvoord Merle-Smith.* Princeton, N.J.: Class of 1911, Princeton University, Princeton University Press, 1952.

Hughes, Rupert. *Long Ever Ago.* New York: Harper & Brothers, 1918.

Hutchinson, William T. *Cyrus Hall McCormick: Seed-Time, 1809–1856.* New York: The Century Co., 1930.

———. *Cyrus Hall McCormick: Harvest, 1856–1884.* New York: D. Appleton-Century Co., 1935.

Jackson, Kenneth T., ed. *The Encyclopedia of New York City.* New Haven, Conn.: Yale University Press, 1995.

Jacobson, Gerald F. *History of the 107th Infantry, U.S.A.* New York: Seventh Regiment Armory, 1920.

Johnson, Lt. Harold Stanley, compiler. *Roster of the Rainbow Division: Major-General Wm. A. Mann, Commanding.* New York: Eaton & Gettinger, Inc., 1917.

Johnson, J. H. *1918: The Unexpected Victory.* London: Cassell Military Paperbacks, 1997.

Kilmer, Annie Kilburn. *Leaves from My Life.* New York: Frye Publishing, 1925.

———. *Memories of My Son, Sergeant Joyce Kilmer.* New York: Frye Publishing, 1921.

Kilmer, Joyce. *Joyce Kilmer, Volume One: Memoir and Poems.* New York: George H. Doran Co., 1918.

———. *Joyce Kilmer, Volume Two: Prose Works.* New York: George H. Doran Co., 1918.

Kilmer, Kenton. *Memories of My Father, Joyce Kilmer.* New Brunswick, N.J.: Centennial Commission, Inc., 1993.

Klein, Milton M., ed. *The Empire State: A History of New York.* Ithaca, N.Y.: Cornell University Press, 2001.

Knightley, Phillip. *The First Casualty.* New York: A Harvest Book, Harcourt Brace Jovanovich, 1975.

Lang, Louis J., compiler and editor. *The Autobiography of Thomas Collier Platt.* New York: Arno Press repr., 1974.

Langille, Leslie. *Men of the Rainbow.* Chicago: The O'Sullivan Publishing House, 1933.

Leach, George E. *War Diary: George E. Leach, Colonel 151st Field Artillery*. Minneapolis: Pioneer Printers, 1923.

Levinger, Rabbi Lee J. *A Jewish Chaplain in France*. New York: The Macmillan Company, 1920.

Liggett, Huner. *Commanding An American Army: Recollections of the World War*. Boston and New York: Houghton Mifflin Company, 1925.

MacArthur, Charles. *War Bugs*. Garden City, N.Y.: Doubleday, Doran & Company, 1929.

MacArthur, Douglas. *Reminiscences*. New York: McGraw-Hill Book Company, 1964.

Manchester, William. *American Caesar: Douglas MacArthur, 1880–1964*. Boston: Little, Brown and Company, 1978.

Marthlaer, Berard, ed. *New Catholic Encyclopedia,* 2nd ed., vols. 9 and 10. Farmington Hills, Mich.: Thomson-Gale, 2003.

McEntee, Girard Lindsley. *Military History of the World War*. New York: Charles Scribner's Sons, 1937.

Morison, Elting E., ed. *The Letters of Theodore Roosevelt,* vol. 8. Cambridge, Mass.: Harvard University Press, 1954.

Morley, Christopher. *Pipefuls*. Garden City, N.Y.: Doubleday, Page & Company, 1920.

Morris, Edmund. *The Rise of Theodore Roosevelt*. New York: Coward, McCann & Geoghegan, Inc., 1979.

Mott, Col. T. Bentley, translator. *The Memoirs of Marshal Foch*. Garden City, N.Y.: Doubleday, Doran and Company, 1931.

Nettleton, George Henry. *Yale in the World War,* vol. 1. New Haven, Conn.: Yale University Press, 1925.

New York City Guide, Federal Writers' Project. New York: Octagon Books, 1970 (Copyright 1939, Guilds' Committee for Federal Writers' Publications, Inc.)

O'Connor, Richard. *Hell's Kitchen: The Roaring Days of New York's Wild West Side*. New York: Old Town Books, 1993.

O'Leary, Jeremiah A. *My Political Trial and Experiences*. New York: Jefferson Publishing Co., Inc., 1919.

Order of Battle of the United States Land Forces in the World War, vols. 1, 2, 3, Part 1, 2, 3. Washington, D.C.: Center of Military History, United States Army, facsimile reprint, originally published 1931–49.

O'Ryan, Maj. Gen. John F. *The Story of the 27th Division.* New York: Wynkoop Hallenbeck Crawford Co., 1921.

Paschall, Col. Rod. *The Defeat of Imperial Germany, 1917–1918.* New York: Da Capo Press, 1994.

Pershing, Gen. John J. *My Experience in the First World War.* New York: Da Capo Press, Inc., 1995. Originally published as *My Experiences in the World War,* HarperCollins Publishers, 1931.

———. *Final Report of Gen. John J. Pershing: Commander-In Chief, American Expeditionary Forces.* Washington, D.C.: Government Printing Office, 1920.

Pershing, Gen. John J., Lt. Gen. Hunter Liggett, *Report of the First Army American Expeditionary Forces.* Fort Leavenworth, Kan.: The General Service Schools Press, 1923.

Persico, Joseph E. *11th Month, 11th Day, 11th Hour: Armistice Day, 1918.* New York: Random House, 2004.

Philadelphia Episcopal Hospital. *A Century of Care: A History of Episcopal Hospital.* Philadelphia: Philadelphia Episcopal Hospital, 1953.

Pringle, Henry F. *Alfred E. Smith: A Critical Study.* New York: Macy-Masius, 1927.

Reilly, Henry J. *Americans All: The Rainbow At War.* Columbus, Ohio: The F. J. Heer Co., 1936.

Robb, Wilfred E. *The Price of Our Heritage: In Memory of the Heroic Dead of the 168th Infantry.* Des Moines, Iowa: American Lithographing and Printing Co., 1919.

Roosevelt, Theodore. *The Rough Riders.* New York: Da Capo Press, Inc., 1990.

Schneider, Dorothy and Carl J. *Into the Breach: American Women Overseas in World War I.* New York: Viking, 1991.

Seldes, George. *Witness to a Century: Encounters With the Noted, the Notorious, and the Three SOBs.* New York: Ballantine Books, 1987.

Shannon, William V. *The American Irish.* New York: The Macmillan Company, 1963.

Sherwood, Elmer W. *Diary of a Rainbow Veteran: Written at the Front.* Terre Haute, Ind.: Moore-Langen Company, 1929.

Sibley, Frank P. *With The Yankee Division in France.* Boston: Little, Brown, and Company, 1919.

Silliman, George A. *Selected Family Letters, 1881–1945.* Wilmington, Del.: Wm. N. McCann, Inc., 1984.

Smith, Alfred E. *Up To Now: An Autobiography.* Garden City, N.Y.: Garden City Publishing Company, Inc., 1929.

Strouse, Jean. *Morgan: American Financier.* New York: Random House, 1999.

Sutcliffe, Robert Stewart, compiler. *Seventy-first New York in the World War.* Publisher not named, 1922.

Swetland, Maurice J. and Lilli. *These Men.* Harrisburg, Pa.: Military Service Publishing Company, 1940.

Taber, John H. *The Story of the 168th Infantry in Two Volumes.* Iowa City: The State Historical Society of Iowa, 1925.

Tevis, C. V. and D. R. Marquis. *History of the Fighting Fourteenth, 1861–1911.* Brooklyn, N.Y.: The Brooklyn Eagle Publishing Co., 1911.

Thompson, Hugh S., and Robert H. Ferrell, ed. *Trench Knives and Mustard Gas.* College Station, Tex.: Texas A&M University Press, 2004.

Tjomsland, Dr. Anne. *Bellevue in France: Anecdotal History of Base Hospital No. 1.* New York: Froben Press, 1941.

University of Pennsylvania. *History of United States Army Base Hospital No. 20.* Philadelphia: University of Pennsylvania, 1920.

White, Norval, and Elliot Willensky. *AIA Guide to New York City, Fourth Edition.* New York: Three Rivers Press, 2000.

Williams, Michael. *American Catholics in the War: National Catholic War Council, 1917–1921.* New York: The Macmillan Company, 1921.

Wolf, Walter B. *A Brief History of the Rainbow Division.* New York: Rand, McNally & Co., 1919.

Wolfe, Gerard R. *New York: A Guide to the Metropolis.* New York: New York University Press, 1975.

Woollcott, Alexander. *The Command Is Forward: Tales of the A.E.F. Battlefields as They Appeared in The Stars and Stripes.* New York: The Century Co., 1919.

———. *While Rome Burns.* New York: The Viking Press, 1935.

Yates, Stanley. *History of the 163rd Field Hospital.* Seattle: Moulton Printing Company, 1936.

Zabriske, Alexander C. *Bishop Brent: Crusader for Christian Unity.* Philadelphia: The Westminster Press, 1948.

Zarnowski, Frank. *The Decathlon.* Champagne, Ill.: Leisure Press, 1989.

Articles, Oral Histories, Speeches

Baillie, Hugh. "Camp Mills Is Like Magic City." *New York Tribune,* 21 August 1917.

Benz, George H. "Four Months in France With the 165th Infantry (The Old 'Sixty Ninth')." *New York Evening World Magazine,* eight installments, 25 May 1918 through 3 June 1918.

"City's Leaders Pay Last Honor to Father Duffy." *New York Herald-Tribune,* 30 June 1932.

Duffy, Francis P. "President Eliot Among the Prophets." *The Catholic World,* September 1909.

———. "The Life of Cardinal Newman." *The Catholic World,* April 1912.

———. "What Do the Methodists Intend?" *The Catholic World,* August 1912.

———. "A Catholic Word For Masons." Quoted in *The Literary Digest,* 1 December 1923.

Duranty, Walter. "Foe's Fight Stiffens In Narrowed Salient." *New York Times,* 31 July 1918.

Eyre, Lincoln. Three dispatches from France, *New York Evening World,* 29 July 1918 through 15 September 1918.

Finn, J. Michael. "The Chaplain Who Went Over-the-Top: Father George Raphael Carpentier, O.P.," Barquilla de la Santa Maria, Bulletin of the Catholic Record Society, Diocese of Columbus, Ohio. Volume XXX, Nos. 11 and 12, Nov. and Dec. 2005.

Forde, Frank, "The Sixty-ninth Regiment of New York," *The Irish Sword: The Journal of the Militia,* no. 68 (1989).

Fuhrman, Joseph H. "Mineola Is Way Station for New York's Fighting 165th to the Front." *New York Tribune,* 26 August 1917.

Gouraud, Gen. Henri J. E., as told to Bernhard Ragner. "My Memories of the Rainbow Division." *The American Legion Monthly,* November 1933.

Green, Martin. "Father Duffy's Funeral Great City Tribute." *New York Sun,* 29 June 1932.

Hourigan, Joseph F. History of the Fighting 69th, website *www.69thny.com.* Copyright 1997. Website under construction, as of August 2006.

Hughes, Rupert. "Jim Finn: Disabled Emergency Officer," *The American Legion Monthly,* January 1928.

Johnson, Thomas M. "69th Liked the Bayonet; Won Praise for Brave Fight." *New York Evening World,* no date. From the alumni file of Van Santvoord Merle-Smith, Princeton University.

McLoughlin, Peter P. "Joyce Kilmer, Catholic Poet-Hero." *The Columbiad*, April 1920.

Marshall, Marguerite Mooers. "What the War Looks Like as Viewed from the Seat of an American Ambulance." *New York Evening World*, 17 July 1918.

Martin, Don. Ten dispatches from France, *New York Herald*, 1 August 1918 through 26 September 1918.

Menoher, Maj. Gen. Charles T. "Story of the Famous 42d Division Told by Its Commander." *New York Times Magazine*, section 7, 27 April 1919.

"Military Funeral for Father Duffy." *New York Times*, 30 June 1932.

O'Brien, Pvt. Eugene J. "First Greyjackets Leave for France." *The Seventh Regiment Gazette*, September 1917.

O'Neill, Richard W. "A Veteran Speaks His Mind." *American Magazine*, November, 1932.

Powers, Lt. Col. Kenneth. Speech before the Central Intelligence Agency, during a ceremony honoring Col. William Donovan, 2 June 1986.

Russell, Francis. "When Gentlemen Prepared for War." *American Heritage*, April 1964.

Shelley, Thomas J. "John Cardinal Farley and Modernism in New York." *Church History*, 61, no. 3 (September 1992).

Index

About the Author

STEPHEN L. HARRIS is the author of two other books about New York City's National Guard regiments in the Great War. They are *Duty, Honor, Privilege: New York's Silk Stocking Regiment and the Breaking of the Hindenburg Line* and *Harlem's Hell Fighters: The African-American 369th Infantry in World War I*. A native New Yorker, he lives with his wife Sue in Weybridge, Vermont.